H. L. Mencken

on American Literature

H. L.

Ohio University Press

Athens

Mencken
on American
Literature

Edited by S.T. Joshi

Ohio University Press, Athens, Ohio 45701
© 2002 by S. T. Joshi
Printed in the United States of America

Ohio University Press books are printed on acid-free paper ♾™

10 09 08 07 06 05 04 03 02   5 4 3 2 1

Permission to publish H. L. Mencken's review columns is granted by the Enoch Pratt
Free Library of Baltimore, in accordance with the terms of the will of H. L. Mencken.

Jacket photograph of H. L. Mencken by Edward Steichen reprinted with permission of
Joanna T. Steichen.

Library of Congress Cataloging-in-Publication Data

Mencken, H. L. (Henry Louis), 1880–1956.
    H. L. Mencken on American literature / edited by S. T. Joshi.
        p. cm.
    Includes bibliographical references and index.
    ISBN 0-8214-1429-1 (alk. paper)
    1. American literature—History and criticism. I. Joshi, S. T., 1958–II. Title.

PS121 .M434 2002
810.9—dc21   2002017086

✒ Contents

Introduction
vii

A Note on
This Edition
xix

1: The Travails of a   *Eight Years of Reviewing*   1
Book Reviewer   *Books I Have Not Read*   7
1   *On Reviewing*   8
                          Fifteen Years of Book Reviewing   11

2: Establishing   *Mark Twain*   22
the Canon   *Edgar Allan Poe*   33
22   *Ralph Waldo Emerson*   35
                          Henry James   37
                          Theodore Dreiser   39
                          Willa Cather   73
                          Sherwood Anderson   83
                          James Branch Cabell   95
                          F. Scott Fitzgerald   109
                          Sinclair Lewis   115
                          John Dos Passos   136
                          Ernest Hemingway   139

3: Some Worthy   *Ambrose Bierce*   143
Second-Raters   *Edith Wharton*   147
143   *William Dean Howells*   150
                        Jack London   157
                        Abraham Cahan   159
                        Ring Lardner   162
                        Ellen Glasgow   169

4: Trade Goods   *O. Henry*   175
175   *Will Levington Comfort*   176
                        Marjorie Benton Cooke   180
                        Winston Churchill   183
                        Mary MacLane   190
                        E. M. Hull   194
                        Gertrude Atherton   198
                        Thomas Dixon, Jr.   204

5: Some Thoughts on   *Percival Pollard*   212
Literary Criticism   *Leon Kellner*   214
209   *Wilson and Helen Follett*   219
                        Paul Elmer More   222
                        Stuart P. Sherman   225
                        T. S. Eliot   227
                        Margaret Anderson   229

Notes
235

Glossary of Names
245

Index
277

⚒ Introduction

It is one of the many ironies in the literary career of Henry Louis Mencken (1880–1956) that he became perhaps the most respected, and feared, book reviewer of the early twentieth century almost by accident. In his last review column in the *Smart Set* (December 1923), Mencken himself admitted that he was unsure why he had been appointed the magazine's book reviewer in 1908. Up to that time, Mencken had worked chiefly as a reporter and editorial writer for the *Baltimore Herald* and *Baltimore Evening Sun*, although he had also served briefly as drama critic on both these papers prior to 1908. Whatever the case, the *Smart Set* assignment proved a boon: allotted an average of 4,500 words every month, Mencken's review column almost single-handedly elevated the *Smart Set* to a position of prominence among American magazines, and his thunderous pronouncements must have been greeted with both awe and trepidation by readers, writers, and publishers alike. After fifteen years in which he never missed writing a column, Mencken transferred his services to his new magazine, the *American Mercury*, and for another ten years he continued to offer magisterial judgments on a bewildering variety of books, from novels by Fitzgerald, Cather, and Hemingway to Hitler's *Mein Kampf*. For a quarter of a century, Mencken was judge, jury, and frequently executioner of American literature.

During this entire period, Mencken was voluminously producing the treatises that would secure him an unassailable place in American criticism. Even if we exclude his early works, *George Bernard Shaw: His Plays* (1905) and *The Philosophy of Friedrich Nietzsche* (1908), we must take note of such things as *A Book of Prefaces* (1917), with its penetrating discussions of Conrad and Dreiser; the landmark six-volume series, *Prejudices* (1919–27), which, probably more than any other of his works, established him as a trenchant critic of American culture; his provocative monographs, *In Defense of Women* (1918; revised 1922), *Notes on Democracy* (1926), and *Treatise on the Gods* (1930); and, of course, *The American Language* (1919), which instantly gave him status as a linguist and inspired two enormous supplements in later years (1945, 1948). How he managed to read the thousands of books that, over a quarter-century, served as the focal point of his monthly review columns while also writing these and other works, to say nothing of his thousands of articles for the *Baltimore Evening Sun* (1906–48) and other newspapers and magazines, almost defies comprehension.

In his posthumously published literary autobiography, *My Life as Author and Editor* (1993), Mencken offers some further clues as to the reasons for his *Smart Set* appointment. Although still maintaining that the offer came "as a bolt from the blue,"[1] he reports a conversation he had had in 1939 with Fred Splint, editor of the *Smart Set* in 1908. Splint informed Mencken that his assistant, Norman Boyer—with whom Mencken had worked briefly in Baltimore several years earlier—was chiefly responsible for bringing Mencken to his attention. It was, apparently, his early treatises on Shaw and Nietzsche that impressed Boyer with a sense of Mencken's competence as a reviewer, perhaps more than the occasional theater reviews he had written during his stints with the *Herald* (1899–1906) and the *Evening Sun*. The *Smart Set* had been founded in 1900, but in its array of fiction, articles, poetry, and epigrams it had never featured a book review column, although it did have occasional theater reviews (later taken over, famously, by Mencken's colleague George Jean Nathan). That changed with the November 1908 issue, when the first of Mencken's 182 columns appeared. He quickly fashioned this column into a penetrating dissection of contemporary letters, frequently using a single volume as the springboard for a wide-ranging analysis of literary, political, social, and religious questions. It is not surprising that a significant proportion of the essays in *Prejudices* derive from his *Smart Set* review columns. But, perhaps because he did not regard himself chiefly as a literary critic, Mencken rarely reprinted his reviews of American fiction, poetry, and essays, and the great majority of the material contained in this volume has not seen the light since its first publication more than three-quarters of a century ago.

Almost from the beginning, Mencken laid down the principles upon which his judgments would be based. Although not primarily a literary theoretician, he nonetheless evolved, at a surprisingly early date, a clear notion of the criteria he would utilize in his assessments of the literary, pseudo-literary, or sub-literary products that passed over his desk. In his third column in the *Smart Set* (January 1909), he opened with the query "What is a novel?" and answered it in a somewhat long-winded manner:

> A novel is an imaginative, artistic and undialectic composition in prose, not less than 20,000 nor more than 500,000 words in length, and divided into chapters, sections, books or other symmetrical parts, in which certain interesting, significant and probable (though fictitious) human transactions are described both in cause and effect, with particular reference to the influence exerted upon the ideals, opinions, morals, temperament and overt acts of some specified person or persons by the laws, institutions, superstitions, traditions and customs of such portions of the human race and the natural phenomena of such portions of the earth as may come under his, her or their observation or cognizance, and by the ideals, opinions, morals, temperament and overt acts of such person or persons as may come into contact, either momentarily or for longer periods, with him, her or them, either by actual, social or business intercourse, or through the medium of books, newspapers, the church, the theater or some other person or persons.[2]

In 1933, virtually at the end of his book-reviewing career, Mencken assessed the "hallmarks of a competent writer of fiction" in much the same terms:

> The first, it seems to me, is that he should be immensely interested in human beings, and have an eye sharp enough to see into them, and a hand clever enough to draw them as they are. The second is that he should be able to set them in imaginary situations which

display the contents of their psyches effectively, and so carry his reader swiftly and pleasantly from point to point of what is called a good story. And the third is that he should say something about the people he deals with, either explicitly or implicitly, that is apposite and revelatory—in brief, that he should play upon them with the hose of a plausible and sufficiently novel and amusing metaphysic. All of these kinds of skill you will find in every really first-rate novelist. They are what make him what he is.

For Mencken, the portrayal of human character is essential to the business of the novel. But mere verisimilitude is not enough: although his highest praise for Dreiser's *Sister Carrie* is that "Carrie Meeber is far more real than nine-tenths of the women you actually know," he goes on to observe that Dreiser is gifted with "that higher sympathy which grows out of a thorough understanding of motives and processes of mind."

It is in this context that Mencken utters another of his "articles of faith" for novelistic composition: "That faith may be put briefly into two articles: (*a*) that it is the business of a novelist to describe human beings as they actually are, unemotionally, objectively and relentlessly, and not as they might be, or would like to be, or ought to be; and (*b*) that his business is completed when he has so described them, and he is under no obligation to read copybook morals into their lives, or to estimate their virtue (or their lack of it) in terms of an ideal goodness." It is that second article that concerns us here, for it gets to the heart of Mencken's entire political, social, and literary theory: the scorn of didacticism or "uplift." In his own writing, and in his praise and blame of the writing of others, he most emphatically embodies that definition of "cynic" that Ambrose Bierce devised for *The Devil's Dictionary*: "A blackguard whose faulty vision sees things as they are, not as they ought to be."

If there is any source for Mencken's literary theory, it may be the work of two earlier critics whom he regarded as his mentors: Percival Pollard and James Gibbons Huneker. Neither of these critics was a theoretician, and probably all that Mencken derived from them was a penchant for iconoclasm and a vigorous, forthright, at times flamboyant manner of expression. Mencken's cordial relationship with Huneker in the decade preceding the latter's death in 1921 is poignantly etched in *My Life as Author and Editor* and elsewhere. Otherwise, it must be admitted that Mencken was largely a self-taught critic, and all he sought in literature was sincerity, vitality, penetrating insight into human character and society, and, above all, an avoidance of obvious moralism.

There may be a certain inconsistency, even a paradox, in Mencken's anti-didacticism. It is certainly not the case that the writers Mencken favored—Dreiser, Sinclair Lewis, James Branch Cabell, Willa Cather— are amoral, or that their works are morally empty. When he identifies the fundamental message in Dreiser's novels as the realization that "the riddle of life . . . is essentially insoluble," or states that Cabell's central theme is "simply the pathetic hollowness of all 'ideas'—the sheer fortuitousness and meaninglessness of the comedy, the eternal helplessness and donkeyish- ness of man," there is perhaps no direct contradiction to his proscription against reading "copybook morals" into the lives of literary characters; but it is evident that he approves of the moral thrust of Dreiser's and Cabell's work because he agrees with it—that he himself acknowledges the "don- keyishness of man" and relishes its relatively rare exposition in fiction. Per- haps his comment on Cather's *My Antonia* gets more to the point: "There is no hortatory purpose, no show of theory, no visible aim to improve the world." Mencken was, of course, combating a long-standing naïve moral- ism in American literary criticism—an embodiment, he believed, of the Puritanism that Americans had never relinquished since colonial times. All too often he encountered critics who assessed a literary work on other than literary grounds: Dreiser's works, for example, contained sordid sex- ual scenes, and therefore they were inferior as works of art and ought to be banished from polite society. Mencken never tired of tackling such Puritan-Victorian holdovers as Hamilton Wright Mabie, William Lyon Phelps, and even Paul Elmer More, whose criticism, he maintained, was intended to shield American readers from the harsh truths that Dreiser, Lewis, Cather, and others were revealing.

In 1922, Mencken asserted that "my literary theory, like my politics, is based chiefly upon one main idea, to wit, the idea of freedom." He elabo- rated: "My business, considering the state of the society in which I find myself, has been principally to clear the ground of mouldering rubbish, to chase away old ghosts, to help set the artist free." It is on this principle that Mencken justified his censorious reviews: "I can't remember a time when

I ever printed a slating that was excessive or unjust. The quacks and dolts who have been mauled in these pages all deserved it; more, they all deserved far worse than they got. If I lost them customers by my performances I am glad of it. If I annoyed and humiliated them I am glad of it again. If I shamed any of them into abandoning their quackery—but here I begin to pass beyond the borders of probability, and become a quack myself."

But there is more at stake here than merely causing momentary irritation to bad writers. It becomes evident that, in the twenty-five years of his career as a reviewer, Mencken was intent on establishing a canon of American literature—a ranking of authors, good, bad, and middling. He even managed to find occasions to pass judgment on many nineteenth-century authors, as when—in a review of Helen and Wilson Follett's *Some Modern Novelists* (1918)—he stated: "The United States, since 1776, has produced three artists of the first consideration in the department of letters: Edgar Allan Poe, Walt Whitman and Samuel L. Clemens." This triumvirate—from which such hallowed names as Emerson, Thoreau, Hawthorne, Longfellow, Whittier, Fenimore Cooper, Henry James, and others are pointedly excluded—remained high in Mencken's esteem for much of his career. (He was writing well before Melville's posthumous rise in critical esteem, beginning in the late 1920s.) His devotion to Mark Twain was unstinting: *Huckleberry Finn* is "one of the great masterpieces of the world" and Twain "was and is the one authentic giant of our national literature." Biographies of older writers allowed Mencken the opportunity to expatiate on their literary work, and in several instances—as in the case of Carey McWilliams's 1929 biography of Bierce—these works caused him to revise substantially his opinions of the authors in question.

Mencken began his reviewing career in 1908 at a time when American literature was at a relatively low ebb. Henry James and William Dean Howells—two authors whose work Mencken in any event found arid and artificial—had written their best work years or decades before, and Mencken managed to review only a few novels of their feeble old age. Dreiser had published *Sister Carrie* in 1900 and then maintained a literary silence until 1911. It was the heyday of such popular best-sellers as Robert W. Chambers, James Lane Allen, and Harold Bell Wright. In 1911 Mencken actually proclaimed the now-forgotten David Graham Phillips as the "leading American novelist"; unfortunately, Phillips was murdered shortly thereafter. Just at this time, however, Dreiser began producing an array of substantial novels that, in Mencken's mind, established him as a fitting successor to Twain.

As early as 1917, therefore, Mencken was able to report: "Sound literature, indeed, is being produced in this, our age. The rate of emission of good books is more rapid than ever before." His optimism continued unabated, although always with reservations, so that by 1920, when Lewis's *Main Street* appeared, he could report guardedly: "there is yet hope." In 1923 he wrote that the American writer "is free, but he is not, as yet, perhaps, worthy of his freedom." By this Mencken meant that authors were now at liberty to write in any manner and on any subject they chose without fear of censorship from the government or condemnation by stodgy critics: the attempts (chiefly by the New York Society for the Suppression of Vice, led by Anthony Comstock and his successor, John S. Sumner) to suppress Dreiser's *The "Genius"* and Cabell's *Jurgen* had only made those works notorious and popular. But the lure of easy money offered by magazines such as the *Saturday Evening Post* and Hearst's *Cosmopolitan* was a danger that not many could avoid: even Mencken's friend Joseph Hergesheimer succumbed, and Mencken on occasion sensed the same decline even in Willa Cather.

It is, indeed, in his reviews of the best-selling novels of the day that Mencken achieves his greatest heights of pungent cynicism. Once again, his censoriousness was not primarily vindictive, or vindictive at all: he was, in his judgment, performing an important function in exposing the insincerity, hollowness, and plain badness of the novels that the uneducated masses were lapping up. What, after all, is the aim of the best-seller? "The essence of this literature," Mencken wrote in his review of Marjorie Benton Cooke's *Bambi* (1914), "is sentiment, and the essence of that sentiment is hope. Its aim is to fill the breast with soothing and optimistic emotions— to make the fat woman forget that she is fat, to purge the tired business man of his bile, to convince the flapper that Douglas Fairbanks may yet learn to love her, to prove that this dreary old world, as botched and bad as it is, might yet be a darn sight worse." It can be seen that this definition places the best-seller at the exact opposite pole from the ideal novel as earlier defined by Mencken.

There were, however, two different types of popular writers. There were those who, like Gertrude Atherton and the American novelist Winston Churchill, actually tried but failed to write serious literature; and there were those who, like Marjorie Benton Cooke, E. M. Hull,[3] and Thomas Dixon, Jr., cold-bloodedly catered to inferior tastes, deliberately designing their work for the consumption of large masses of morons and semi-illiterates. It was the latter who invariably earned Mencken's greatest scorn. We can see the same dichotomy today with, on the one hand, John Grisham (who treats serious subjects but does so in a naïve, superficial, and sentimental way), and, on the other hand, Stephen King, Danielle Steel, and Sidney Sheldon, whose work is hokum pure and simple.

Mencken's reviews of potboilers certainly rank high among his most piquant works; he could almost be said to have invented a new genre, that of the satirical review. But humor, mockery, sarcasm, and persiflage are found from the beginning to the end of his review columns, as they are throughout his work as a whole. In a sense, this relentless wisecracking creates a kind of flippancy that undercuts his message, but Mencken was too much the satirist and wit to care whether that message was properly grasped by sober-minded academicians or overly serious readers. He wrote to entertain—not to entertain the same audience that devoured the bestsellers, but to entertain that now nearly vanished class of sophisticated general readers who purchased the *Smart Set* and the *American Mercury* precisely for the urbane, and at times outrageous, humor they featured. And outrageous indeed Mencken could be: when, in the course of reviewing Hemingway's *Death in the Afternoon*, he blandly recommends the inauguration of bullfighting in the American South so as to "offer stiff and perhaps ruinous competition to the frying of poor blackamoors," he becomes the true descendant of Swift and Bierce.

Important as was the removal of the "mouldering rubbish" represented by the best-seller, Mencken manifestly found greater intellectual stimulation in the discovery of writers who could elevate American literature to new levels. He had, indeed, an uncanny knack of identifying authors who both revealed promise and delivered upon it. He was justifiably proud in having singled out the merits of James Branch Cabell from so early a period as 1909; he saw, amid numerous flaws, a "very promising piece of writing" in Willa Cather's first novel, *Alexander's Bridge* (1912); Sherwood

Anderson's *Windy McPherson's Son* (1916) showed "unmistakable promise"; Fitzgerald's *This Side of Paradise* "offers a truly amazing first novel."
Probably the most surprising case was Sinclair Lewis, whose literary career
had begun in the first decade of the twentieth century and showed little
likelihood of ever advancing beyond the *Saturday Evening Post* stage—
until *Main Street* (1920) caught everyone by surprise. In *My Life as Author
and Editor* Mencken tells the story of his discovery even more engagingly
than in his *Smart Set* review:

> . . . before leaving the *Smart Set* office [I] gathered up an armful
> of review books to examine on the train. Among them was a set of
> proofs from Harcourt, Brace & Company. Ordinarily, I refused to
> read books in proof, for handling the loose sheets was an unpleas-
> ant chore, but this time, on a sudden and aberrant impulse, I took
> up the sheaf as soon as the train plunged into the Pennsylvania tun-
> nel. By the time it got to Newark I was interested, and by the time
> it got to Trenton I was fascinated. At Philadelphia I called a West-
> ern Union boy and sent a telegram to [George Jean] Nathan. I for-
> get the exact text, but it read substantially: "That idiot has written a
> masterpiece." The book was *Main Street*.4

And yet, for all his preference for the social realism of Dreiser, Lewis,
Cather, and Fitzgerald, there was another side to Mencken—a side that
sought pure beauty, chiefly beauty of style. James Branch Cabell was, pre-
eminently, the author who satisfied this yearning, although a number of
others—ranging from the Irish fantasist Lord Dunsany to his good friend
Joseph Hergesheimer—were worthy exemplars. But, at least as far as Cabell was concerned, there was more to his art than just a pretty phrase:
"What stands revealed is an artist, as artists go among us, of the first consideration—a man of novel and ingenious ideas, a penetrating ironist, a
shrewd and infectious laugher, a delicate virtuoso of situation, an
anatomist of character, one who sees into the eternal tragi-comedy of hope
and striving, above all, a highly accomplished doctor of words." It was, perhaps, the very modern irony in Cabell's best work that, in Mencken's eyes,
redeemed the fantasy element in so many of his novels—an element that
might otherwise render his works mere escapism and thereby banish them

from the realm of serious literature. It was this same irony that Mencken clearly appreciated in the work of Dunsany, whose unjustly forgotten work he published voluminously in the *Smart Set*.

It was not long into his career as a reviewer that Mencken began using the novels, tales, and treatises that appeared relentlessly month after month as occasions for his increasingly trenchant criticisms of American culture and society. The follies of religion, always a favorite topic, were dissected in his reviews of Howells's *The Leatherwood God*, Lewis's *Elmer Gantry*, and a number of other novels; Winston Churchill's *A Far Country* offered an excuse for Mencken to expatiate on the deficiencies of the American political system in terms strikingly reminiscent of his later treatise, *Notes on Democracy*; the work of Cabell and Ellen Glasgow allowed for one more exposé of the absence of culture in the South, a theme most provocatively expressed in "The Sahara of the Bozart" (*Prejudices: Second Series*); and, in one of the most celebrated of his reviews, his raptures over Lewis's *Babbitt* led inexorably to a condemnation of the American *bourgeoisie*. It should not be assumed that Mencken was merely finding, in these and other works, convenient excuses for spouting off on his *bêtes noires*; instead, he saw well that every work of literature had broader social, political, and cultural implications, and his own developing theories of life and society impelled an examination of these implications that took him unapologetically beyond the narrow bounds of literary criticism.

The one area in which Mencken is conventionally thought to be deficient is the criticism of poetry. While he embraced many of the more daring novelists of the 1920s, he remained cool to most of the Modernist poets who made their reputations at the same period. Mencken's taste was always for lyric: the simple, delicate lyrics of Sara Teasdale; his fellow Baltimorean Lizette Woodworth Reese; the California poet George Sterling (whose poems he used frequently in the *Smart Set*, although he never reviewed any of Sterling's poetry volumes); John McClure, the early Robinson Jeffers, and the like. This apparent insensitivity to the more daring poetry of his day has led to accusations of Mencken's lack of competence as a poetry critic. Vincent Fitzpatrick has flatly declared: "As a critic of poetry, Mencken can be dismissed outright."[5] I am not prepared to agree with so harsh a verdict, but this book is not the place to argue the matter. Because of space restrictions, I have entirely omitted Mencken's reviews of poetry.

It was easy for Mencken to poke harmless fun at the many self-published poetasters of his day, as well as at the metrical eccentricities of the Imagists, Vorticists, and other radicals; but on the whole he merely passed over in silence many of the Modernist poets of the 1920s. He praises Ezra Pound's *Lustra* (*Smart Set*, June 1918), but his sole comment on T. S. Eliot's *Prufrock and Other Observations* (1917) is that it is "extremely exhilarating,"[6] and he never bothered to review *The Waste Land* (1922). William Carlos Williams similarly goes almost unmentioned in the nearly two million words of Mencken's collected reviews. As early as 1912, Mencken felt the need to devote at least one column a year in the *Smart Set* to poetry, and in the course of these columns he covered an enormous number of titles; on one occasion (May 1916) he resorted to an alphabetical list of poets, with brief comments on their new books. But he had given up the practice by the early 1920s—at exactly the time when the "new" poetry was beginning to flourish—and in the *American Mercury* he devoted only two columns in ten years (October 1925 and June 1926) to an omnibus review of poetry. In the latter he remarked that the radicalism of the previous decade had declined into a "general orthodoxy": experiments in meter and diction had seemed to subside, and in his judgment the more orthodox work of Jeffers, Masters, and Vachel Lindsay represented the best verse of the period.

Mencken no doubt relished his position as arbiter of letters, although it becomes evident that after a decade or so of reviewing hundreds, perhaps thousands, of books in the *Smart Set* the effort to consume so many good, bad, and dreadful volumes was becoming something of a chore. The very titles of some of his later columns—"Book Article No. 158" (January 1922), "The Niagara of Novels" (April 1922), "The Coroner's Inquest" (September 1922)—point to a growing weariness. When, at the end of 1923, the owners of the *Smart Set* resolved to make the magazine more "popular"— catering exactly to that half-illiterate audience he so frequently derided— Mencken realized that his days with the magazine were numbered. He and George Jean Nathan had edited it since November 1914, but their departure in December 1923 led seamlessly to the first issue of the *American Mercury* in January 1924, which featured Mencken's column "The Library." In accordance with the general tenor of the new magazine, Mencken reviewed far fewer novels and concentrated on works of history, politics, philosophy, religion, and social criticism. Accordingly, a good many of the significant novels and novelists of the period pass unnoticed. Of Ernest Hemingway's works, Mencken reviewed only *Men without Women, A Farewell to Arms,* and *Death in the Afternoon.* However, he frequently discussed literary matters in his weekly contributions to the *Chicago Sunday Tribune* (1924–28), and his review of Fitzgerald's *The Great Gatsby* in that paper is far more exhaustive and perspicacious than his brief notice in the *American Mercury.*

By the time Mencken retired from the *American Mercury* at the end of 1933, his reviewing career was largely over. He wrote scattered reviews for the *Nation,* the *Baltimore Evening Sun,* and other periodicals; as author of *The American Language* and its supplements, he had become a leading authority on American philology, and he regularly reviewed other such works in both scholarly and popular magazines. But his assessment of the mainstream of American literature was at an end. And yet, he could rest assured that he had done his duty: his relentless championing of Dreiser, Lewis, Cather, Cabell, Anderson, and Fitzgerald had helped to establish them as leading writers of their time, and his equally relentless lampooning of the "trade goods" of the best-selling novelists of the day had relegated these confections to the aesthetic oblivion they deserved. He had played his part—and it was a significant part—in establishing the American literary canon, and all that remained was to confirm his judgments. In large part, posterity has done exactly that.

⚑ A Note on This Edition

I have reprinted Mencken's book reviews from their original appearances in the *Smart Set, American Mercury,* and other magazines and newspapers, even in those few instances in which the reviews were reprinted (usually with extensive revisions) in later books by Mencken. I have made no alterations in the texts save the correction of a few obvious typographical errors, the elimination of the publishing information Mencken habitually supplies, and the uniform use of italics rather than quotation marks for book titles. Some factual errors by Mencken (such as his persistently erroneous citation of the title of F. Scott Fitzgerald's *The Beautiful and Damned*) have been preserved. I provide full bibliographical information at the end of each selection. Mencken's *Smart Set* columns bore individual titles, usually referring to the featured book under review; in the *American Mercury* the column was uniformly titled "The Library," with separate titles for the book or group of books under review (these titles have been placed in parentheses following the page citation). Any cuts or abridgments within the texts are indicated by ellipses within brackets. Mencken himself frequently used ellipses for a certain type of emphasis; any ellipses not enclosed in brackets are his own.

Because Mencken had a penchant for name-dropping, it seemed best to prepare a glossary of names mentioned in the text. This glossary lists all names cited in the reviews except those of well-known literary or historical figures. Even some of these figures are included in the glossary in order to point the reader to Mencken's writings about them. In some cases I have found it easier to supply a note elucidating certain names (usually nonliterary ones) mentioned in passing.

In the glossary and notes, I have frequently cited and quoted Mencken's reviews of books by the authors he mentions. References to these reviews are highly abbreviated; full bibliographical information on them can be found in Betty Adler's *H.L.M.: The Mencken Bibliography* (Baltimore: Enoch Pratt Free Library/Johns Hopkins University Press, 1961), pp. 162–268.

I use the following abbreviations in the text, notes, and glossary:

AM   = *American Mercury*
BES   = *Baltimore Evening Sun*
CST   = *Chicago Sunday Tribune*
HLM = H. L. Mencken
P1–6 = *Prejudices: First Series–Sixth Series* (1919–27)
SS   = *Smart Set*

Most of my research was conducted at the New York Public Library and the New York University Library. I am grateful to the librarians at these institutions for their unfailingly courteous assistance. I am deeply indebted to Scott Connors and Douglas A. Anderson for supplying copies of some of the texts included in this book. I have learned much about Mencken from Ray Stevens, S. L. Harrison, Richard J. Schrader, and other members of the Mencken Society.

H. L. Mencken

on American Literature

The Travails of a
Book Reviewer

1

Eight Years of Reviewing

I nursed a secret hope that last month's article would bring me a wreath of ivy from the Authors' League of America, or, at all events, an invitation to guzzle *vin rouge* with the Poetry Society, for it was not only intrinsically meritorious, but it also had a certain historical and military interest, for it was my one hundredth mensual discourse in this place. No such celebration of the anniversary having been forthcoming, I herewith recall it myself. It is not often, on this bleak western front of civilization, that a critic holds a trench so long. The hazards of the trade are numerous and flabbergasting. The authors one puts to the torture have a habit of making furious and unexpected reprisals; the publishers undertake countless counter-offensives; there come fearful squawks from Old Subscribers when their prejudices are violated or their pet fictioneers are nailed to the wall; even the best of editors, in the midst of such a din, grows skittish at times, and wonders if a change of critics would not help his digestion. All in all, a harsh and forbidding life, and yet, after eight and a third years, I still pursue it, and if all goes well I hope to print my thousandth article in February, 1991. In those eight and a third years I have served under four editors, not including myself; I have grown two beards and shaved them off; I have eaten 3,086 meals; I have made more than $100,000 in wages, fees, refreshers, tips and bribes; and I have written 510,000 words about books and not about books; I have received, looked at, and thrown away nearly 3,000 novels; I have been called a fraud 700 times, and blushed at the proofs; I have had more than 200 invitations to lecture before women's clubs, chautauquas, Y.M.C.A.'s, chambers of commerce, Christian Endeavor societies, and lodges of the Elks; I have received 150 pounds of letters of sweet flattery; I have myself written and published eight books, and reviewed them all favorably;[1] I have had seventeen proposals of marriage from lady poets; I have been indicted by grand juries eight times; I have discovered thirty bogus geniuses; I have been abroad three and a half times, and learned and forgotten six foreign languages; I have attended 62 weddings, and spent nearly $200 for wedding presents; I have gained 48 pounds in weight and lost 18 pounds, and have grown bald and gray; I have been converted by the Rev. Dr. Billy Sunday, and then recanted and gone back to the devil; I have worn out nine suits of clothes; I have narrowly escaped marriage four times; I have had lumbago and neuralgia; I have taken to horn-rimmed spectacles; I have eluded the white-slave traders; I have fallen downstairs twice; I have undergone nine surgical operations; I have read the *Police Gazette* in the barbershop every week; I have shaken hands with Dr. Wilson; I have upheld the banner of the ideal; I have kept the faith, in so far as I could make out what it was; I have loved and lied; I have got old and sentimental; I have been torpedoed without warning.

Ah, the wonder and glory of life! The precession of the equinoxes! The mystery of tears and laughter! The toxic gurgle of a kiss! The way flowers shoot up, and horned cattle gambol in the fields! Eight and a third years seems a short while, and yet it has fetched me out of youth into middle age, and left my heart as bulged and battered as a gladiator's ear. Eight and a third years ago *Floradora*[2] was still the rage, and the *New Republic* was unheard of, and Pilsner came in by every ship, and the muckrakers yet drove a fine trade, and Dr. Wilson was happy and untempted at Princeton, and Major-General Roosevelt was a simple colonel of cavalry d. R. a. D., and Diaz was on deck in Mexico, and beefsteak was still 23 cents a pound, and God was in His heaven, and all was well with the world. Where are the charming young authoresses who came to *The Smart Set* office in the autumn of 1908, the cuties who tripped in with their ingratiating smiles and their manuscripts under their arms; the sweet ones who were startled to find that a critic of the bozart could be so toothsome a youth, and so beautifully polite? Married, thirty, fat, sour, abhorrent! Where are the poets who sent in notice that I was a *schuft*, and that their dithyrambs would survive my snickers? Dried up, blown away, forgotten, accursed! Where are the new geniuses who inflamed the skies that year—the revolutionary novelists, the novel soothsayers? Done, desolated, damned! Where are all the Great Thinkers that Col. Roosevelt used to introduce with such loud whoops—the faunal naturalists, the Pastor Wagners, the Warrington Dawsons, the exotic poets? Passed on, alas, passed on! I remember great vogues, excitements, turmoils—for Bergson, for W. B. Trites, for Eucken, for Gorky, for Maeterlinck, for Arnold Bennett, for Leonard Merrick, for Chesterton, for Mathilde Serao, for Synge, for H. G. Wells, for William James, for Alfred Noyes, for Robert W. Service, for Signorina Montessori, for Ellen Key, for Chekoff, for Dr. Cook, for that poetizing jail-bird out West (I have even forgotten his name!) . . . *Dominus dedit, Dominus abstulit! Mais où sont les neiges d'antan! . . . Wein nicht, Süsschen, 's giebt gar kein Use! . . .*

I glance back through my first compositions for this sodality and find some strange things. For example, this in the initial article: "Mary Roberts Rinehart is a new writer." Again, a solemn tirade against the platitudinousness of Upton Sinclair: evidently news in 1908. Yet again, good counsel to Mlle. Marie Corelli: "I should advise her to spend six months in the chorus of a Broadway operetta." Operetta? They still existed eight and a third years ago! . . . In No. 2, a long hymn to Joseph Conrad, the opening anthem of a cantata yet going on. Conrad, in 1908, was scarcely more than a name on this side of the water, and only a hushed whisper on the other side. All of his greatest stories had been written, but they had dogged about from publisher's office to publisher's office, and each successive book had come out with a new imprint. Run your eye down the list: Macmillan, Appleton, Dodd-Mead, Scribner, Doubleday, McClure, Putnam—seven different publishers for his first seven books! He was a long time getting down, but down he went in the end. To-day his works are offered to cognoscenti in an elegant series of navy-blue, limp-leather volumes: very roycrofty,[3] indeed. I am almost tempted to lay in a set. Not only does it soothe the cultured eye, but it would also save wear and tear of the first editions, which are now soaring in value. My natural sagacity, which functions in profane affairs as well as in *belles lettres*, led me to accumulate them while they still sold at par, and they now fortify me against the *Canis lupus. Almayer's Folly*, published at six shillings, is worth from $25 to $35, according to your passion for it. *The Nigger of the Narcissus*, in good condition, would probably bring more. Even so recent a book as *Some Reminiscences*, published in 1912, carries a premium of $10 or $12. The whole set was offered a year or so ago for $150. I doubt that it could be brought together to-day for less than $225. The graft of book reviewers, if they have foresight, is thus seen to be very fair. A forward-looker, I have acquired wealth, and eat and drink, perhaps, more than is strictly decent.

And Dreiser! Back in 1908 only *Sister Carrie* was behind him, and even *Sister Carrie* was but little known, for the first edition had been suppressed by a snuffling publisher, and the second edition had but recently reached the book-stalls. That first edition is now so rare that collectors bid against one another for every stray copy that shows itself. It would be a good idea to hunt up the old plates and print a forgery; nine collectors out of ten have been pleasantly deceived by the forged first edition of Thackeray's *Second Funeral of Napoleon*.[4] Such risks add to the charm of book collecting, for every professor of the art believes firmly that he himself is beyond being fooled, and so it joys him to think of the swindles perpetrated on the other fellow. Incidentally, I know a dealer who lately bought a fine copy of the original *Sister Carrie* for twenty-five cents. He found it in a junk-shop, and leaped from the place like an archdeacon stung by wasps the moment the transaction was closed. Human-like, he couldn't help boasting about his coup, and so I was able, on juridic grounds, to beat him down to a couple of dollars for the prize. I in my turn then emitted oxygen, whereupon a kind friend, unsuccessful in his own hunt for the book, affably accepted it from me as a present. I had, of course, another copy. I shall leave it to some orphan asylum when I die, and so help to save Dreiser from hell. The Comstocks, as I write, bawl for his blood on the ground that Eugene Witla, in *The "Genius,"* is a mammal, and occasionally looses a big, big damn.[5] By the time this article is printed, he may be safely roosting in some kindly jail, with leisure to read his own books. If he gets more than six months he will have time to finish them. Then, perhaps, he will fall to work upon a novel in strict accord with the prevailing Methodist canon—a novel whose males confine their carnalities to sly glances at servant girls, and to fighting their way into Billy Sunday meetings "for men only," and to the diligent study of such literature as *What a Girl of 45 Should Know*, and II Samuel, xi, 2–27. . . .[6]

I am often asked if I enjoy my job, and reply frankly that I do. There is, at all events, constant variety in it; a surprise is always around the corner; that is a dull month which doesn't produce two or three genuinely interesting books. I glance back over eight and a third years and recall such things as Sudermann's *The Indian Lily*, and Anatole France's *The Revolt of the Angels*, and Lord Dunsany's *The Book of Wonder*, and Arnold Bennett's *The Old Wives' Tale*, and Dreiser's *The Titan*, and H. G. Wells' *Ann Veronica*, and Mrs. Wharton's *Ethan Frome*, and Max Beerbohm's *Zuleika Dobson*, and Conrad's *Victory*—I glance back and decide at once that my time has not been wasted.[7] It is a superlative pleasure to dredge such glowing and memorable books out of the stream of drivel and commonplace, the endless avalanche of balderdash by the Oppenheims and the Chamberses, the Bindlosses and Hall Caines, the Corellis and Phillpottses, the jitney Richard Harding Davises and second-table O. Henrys. Sound literature, indeed, is being produced in this, our age. The rate of emission of good books is more rapid than ever before. Moreover, it seems to me that discrimination is increasing, despite the flood of shoddy wares. There is still a vast market for such sentimental slobber as one finds in the *Pollyannas* and *Bambis*,[8] but it is no longer mistaken for great art, as was done with the slobber of Dickens. We have as many boob-thrillers and mountebanks as ever before, but we do not revere Hall Caine as Bulwer-Lytton was revered. We yet have rages for sensational poets, but they do not last as long as the rage for Byron, nor do so many folk succumb to them. Puritanism still wars upon all art among us, but its arm grows weak and the devices on its banners are laughed at. I doubt that any truly first-rate book has gone unrecognized for twenty years past; I doubt that any first-rate book has gone unpublished. If a new Samuel Butler should print a new *Erewhon* to-morrow, even the *Nation* would be aware of it within a year.

The United States, of course, produces relatively little sound writing of its own, but it has at least grown eagerly hospitable to the sound writing that is produced elsewhere. Our thirst for foreign novelties, in truth, is almost as avid as the Germans'. Scarcely a month goes by that some new Selma Lagerlöf or Leonid Andreyieff or Emil Verhaeren or Mathilde Serao or Henri Bergson is not discovered, devoured and hymned. The Americanos got down Ibsen long before the English; the first performance of an Ibsen play in English, indeed, was given in Louisville back in 1882. They embraced Synge while the Dublin mob was yet heaving benches at him. They saw the first adequate performances of Shaw. They were bemused by the moonshine of Maeterlinck before France gave him a thought. They are hot for English novelists who are scarcely heard of at home. . . . One of the causes of this alacrity of welcome, perhaps, lies in the somewhat appalling mediocrity of our domestic produce in beautiful letters. Our books, in the main, lack genuine distinction; they just miss arousing the imagination. The country, for example, is full of novelists who have shown promise and then failed. Robert Herrick is one. He began auspiciously, but to-day he wallows in claptrap. His trouble is plain enough: he is clever, but not profound; he has facility, but he lacks ideas. Edith Wharton is another. She rose to the peak of *Ethan Frome* and then settled down into a valley of fustian. A third is Robert Grant. He flew all the signals of great talent—and then hauled them in. Howells, James Lane Allen, John Luther Long, Hamlin Garland and the rest of that elder company have run their race. Churchill has succumbed to the national platitudinousness. Miss Cather and Mrs. Watts have yet to strike twelve. Stephen French Whitman, Ernest Poole, Henry Milner Rideout, Owen Johnson and a dozen others of their quality seem to be done for; the lure of the *Saturday Evening Post* has finished most of them.

But let us not wail and gnash our teeth. We still have Dreiser, and despite *The "Genius,"* he will probably do his best work hereafter. He is the one novelist among us who shows no response whatever to the variable winds of public favor; he hacks out his path undeterred by either praise or blame; a sort of blind fury of creation seems to move him. And we still have two or three other men who are sound artists, and yet as American as trading stamps or chewing gum: Booth Tarkington, George Ade, Harry Leon Wilson. All have yielded themselves to temptation; all have stooped for the shekel. And yet, when everything has been said, Ade's *Fables in Slang* come near being the best comic writing of our time in any language, and Tarkington's *Penrod* is a book that will long outlive Tarkington, and

Wilson has done things in *Bunker Bean* and again in *Ruggles of Red Gap* that belong to satire at its best, and hint clearly at what he could do on a larger scale if he would only spit on his hands and make the effort. ["The Books of the Irish," *SS* 51, no. 3 (March 1917): 141–44.]

Books I Have Not Read

All the bones in my body are intact. I have never broken humerus or radius, femur or tibia. In consequence, I have never been laid up with nothing to do, and in consequence of that consequence I have never read *Alice in Wonderland*. It seems somehow indecent, and yet it is a fact. Of course, I know what the book is about—one acquires such knowledge, in literate society, by a sort of osmosis—and I probably quote it as often as another, but I have never actually read it, and shall probably never do so until I come down upon the ice in my senility and go to bed for six weeks with a cracked hip. When I finish it, I shall read *The Pilgrim's Progress*, another book that I have never so much as opened. Years ago I made up my mind to read it, but presently the late Major General Roosevelt began quoting it, and he scared me off: I was already privy to the singular badness of his taste in books. After *The Pilgrim's Progress*, I'll tackle *The Dunciad*, and then *Wuthering Heights*, and then *The Brothers Karamazov*, and then the Bhagavad Gita, and then Ibsen's *Kejser og Galilaeer*, and then Gibbon's *Decline and Fall*. I once tried *The Brothers Karamazov* on board ship, but it made me so sleepy that I turned from it to Morley's *Life of Gladstone*, borrowed from the ship library—a potent soporific, but not as effective in my case as Dostoevsky. Of large reaches of George Meredith I am densely ignorant; of George Eliot I am almost wholly so. I tried to read *Adam Bede* at the age of twelve, and it bored me so fearfully that I had to give it up, and have never gone back to it. Yet less than a year later I was reading *Henry Esmond*, and enjoying it. *Sartor Resartus* was beyond my comprehension when I attempted it, probably at fourteen, and it gave me such a distaste for Carlyle that I was beyond thirty-five before I could read *The French Revolution*. I was actually nearly forty when I first read *Frederick the Great*. It was worth waiting for: a stupendous piece of work, never sufficiently to be praised. I must have picked up a lot of Carlyle from the air in my twenties, for when I read him at last he seemed like an old friend. No living man is to be mentioned in the same breath with old Thomas. There was in him something of the austere magnificence, the remote and awe-inspiring massiveness, of his own heroes. Think of a Frederick done by a Carlyle! A Ulysses done by a Homer!

There is a tremendous amount of tosh written about books. All the Hamilton Wright Mabies, Matthew Arnolds and James Russell Lowells praise the same celebrated works, and often they are dull and fly-blown. If I have to go to hell for it, I must here set down my conviction that much of *The Divine Comedy* is piffle. So is nine-tenths of Byron. Byron fascinated me at fifteen; to-day he makes me laugh. He was a sort of premature Greenwich Villager, and would have been snickered into obscurity if he had not been a noble lord. There are books by Anatole France that make me snore, for example, *Le Crime de Sylvestre Bonnard.* I can read Tolstoi, a fearful old ass, but not Turgenev, apparently a man of sense. Pope's *Essay on Man* seems to me to be comparable to a piano piece by Eduard Holst. As for Browning, his poetry classifies itself in my mind with the New Thought: it is cacophonous as poetry and puerile as philosophy. Browning, so far as I have been able to make out, never had an idea that was beyond the comprehension of a schoolmarm. His so-called complexity is merely stupidity. Washington Irving I can't read. Prescott I can get through, for his story is always hair-raising, but his style is that of a United States Senator. Poe's tales, with a few exceptions, seem tedious to me, and much of his poetry strikes me as hollow jingling, but his criticism is my delight. Cooper appears to me to be separated by but little from the dime-novelists. Emerson is an agreeable old dodo—a sort of vast hopper of borrowed and undigested ideas, many of them idiotic. That Carlyle viewed him with respect is one of the great mysteries of letters. But didn't Mark Twain venerate Howells? And hasn't Joseph Conrad praised Henry James? Hawthorne, Whitman, Melville, even Bierce—here we encounter nobler fowl. But nothing has ever been written in America to surpass *Huckleberry Finn.* It is rather more than a mere book; it is almost a whole literature. ["From the Diary of a Reviewer," *SS* 66, no. 1 (September 1921): 141–42.]

On Reviewing

The longer I live the more thoroughly I become convinced that criticism is anything but an exact science. The things I remember chiefly, looking back over my own somewhat longish service in the critical trenches, are not my occasional sound judgments, but my far more frequent imbecilities—some of them, seen in retrospect, quite astounding. I have often misunderstood men grossly, and I have misrepresented them when I understood them, sacrificing sense to make a phrase. Here, of course, is where even the most conscientious critic often goes aground; he is apt to be an artist before he is a scientist, and the impulse to create something passionately is stronger in him than the impulse to state something accurately. As for me, I am not noticeably conscientious. But I do not apologize for the lack. Is any other critic now in practise in America? I can recall none. Certainly those who, in the exercise of their office, perform upon my own books are not much better in this respect than I am. A good many of them denounce me violently, simply because they disagree with my politics. Others, less prejudiced, fall into profound errors as to my aims, and credit me constantly with ideas that are as abhorrent to me as they would be to a Methodist bishop. What is the remedy for this distressing piling up of nonsense? Perhaps the best way out would be for every writer to attempt a clear statement of his own ideas, confining himself to fundamentals. The thing is often done by painters and sculptors. I have before me half a dozen catalogues of art exhibitions by new men—one-man shows of novel stuff. Each of the exhibitors prints a preface over his sign manual explaining just what he is about—often, alas, somewhat muddily, for artists seldom know how to write, but always earnestly and sometimes very indignantly. I find such expositions very interesting and instructive. Even when one of them is downright idiotic it at least sets forth the useful fact that the author is an idiot.

As for me, my literary theory, like my politics, is based chiefly upon one main idea, to wit, the idea of freedom. I am, in brief, a libertarian of the most extreme variety, and know of no human right that is one-tenth as valuable as the simple right to utter what seems (at the moment) to be the truth. Take away this right, and none other is worth a hoot; nor, indeed, can any other long exist. Debauched by that notion, it follows necessarily that I can be only an indifferent citizen of a democratic state, for democracy is grounded upon the instinct of inferior men to herd themselves in large masses, and its principal manifestation is their bitter opposition to all free thought. In the United States, in fact, I am commonly regarded as a violent anti-patriot. But this is simply because most of the ideas upon which American patriotism bases itself seem to me to be obviously sentimental and nonsensical—that is, they have, for me at least, no intelligible relation to the visible facts. I do not object to patriotism when it is logically defensible. On the contrary, I respect it as a necessary corollary to the undeniable inequality of races and peoples. Its converse, internationalism, appears to me to be almost insane. What an internationalist says, stripping it of rhetoric, is simply that a lion is no more than a large rat.

My literary criticism has been almost exclusively devoted to attacking and trying to break down the formal ideas, most of them wholly devoid of logical content, which formerly oppressed the art of letters in the United States very severely, and still hang about its flanks—ideas of form and method, of aim and purpose, of mere fashion and propriety. This attack, carried on for many years, has got me the name of a mere professional ruffian: I am constantly accused, and sometimes quite honestly, of tearing down without building up, of murdering a theory without offering in its place a new and better theory. But it must be plain enough that the objection, however earnestly made, is quite without merit. My business, considering the state of the society in which I find myself, has been principally to clear the ground of mouldering rubbish, to chase away old ghosts, to help set the artist free. The work of erecting a new structure belongs primarily to the artist as creator, not to me as critic. It may be (and, alas, it is often the case!) that after he has been set free it turns out that he actually has nothing worth hearing to say. (I could name names, but refrain in decency.) But it is certainly better to utter even nonsense as a free man than to keep on repeating formulæ like a boy in school.

Here the astute reader may file a caveat: if I am so hot for freedom, then why do I belabor fellows whose sole crime, at bottom, is that they express their honest ideas in a banal and oleaginous manner? The answer is simple: it is not their sole crime. I do not belabor them for expressing their own ideas; I belabor them for trying to prevent other men expressing *theirs*—that is, for trying to set up standards and taboos that hinder the free play of the creative impulse. This effort seems to me to be intrinsically immoral, however exalted the purpose behind it. The essence of sound art is freedom. The artist must be allowed his impish impulse, his revolt, his perversity. He stands in a fundamental opposition to Philistine correctness; if he is bound by it he is nothing. But I by no means engage to agree with him: all I ask is that no one oppose him with weapons foreign to the world he inhabits, *e.g.*, the ballot, the policeman's club, the schoolmaster's rattan, the bishop's mitre. I am even against proscriptions on purely æsthetic grounds. Thus when Miss Lowell and her friends essayed to set up the doctrine that the only decent way to write poetry was the way they personally wrote it, and that all exponents of other ways were ignoramuses—when this theory appeared in learned groves and barber-shops I joined the professors in opposing it. But the great majority of such attacks upon freedom are not made by revolutionists, but by advocates of an established order: for one Futurist who launches bulls like a pope there are a hundred pedagogues who issue proscriptions like an American Attorney-General—for one Miss Lowell there are whole herds of Comstocks. Thus my critical labors, in the main, have been on the side of the younger generation. I have protested *sforzando* against the schoolmastering of letters—against setting the artist in bondage to his inferiors. For this service, I am convinced, I shall be rewarded by a just and intelligent God when I have been translated from these sordid scenes. If it turns out that I am in error about it, then I confess frankly that I shall be very greatly disappointed. ["The Monthly Feuilleton," *SS* 69, no. 4 (December 1922): 140–41.]

Fifteen Years of Book Reviewing

I began to write these book articles for *The Smart Set* in November, 1908—that is, the first of them appeared in the magazine for that month. Since then, counting this one, I have composed and printed no less than one hundred and eighty-two—in all, more than nine hundred thousand words of criticism. An appalling dose, certainly! How many books have I reviewed, noticed, praised, mocked, dismissed with lofty sneers? I don't know precisely, but probably fully two thousand. But how many have I *read*? Again I must guess, but I should say at least twice as many. What? Even so. The notion that book reviewers often review books without having read them is chiefly a delusion; it may happen on newspapers, but certainly not on magazines of any pretensions. I remember printing notices of a number of books that were so dull, at least to me, that I couldn't get through them, but in every such case I printed the fact frankly, and so offered no complete judgment. Once, indeed, I read part of a book, wrote

and printed a notice denouncing it as drivel, and then, moved by some obscure, inner necessity, returned to it and read it to the end.[9] This experience gave me pause and taught me something. One cylinder of my
vanity—the foul passion that is responsible for all book reviewers above the
rank of slaves, as it is for all actor-managers, Presidents and archbishops—
urged me to stick to my unfavorable notice, but the other cylinder urged
me to make handsome amends. I did the latter, and trust that God will not
forget it. I trust, too, that He will not overlook my present voluntary with-
drawal from this pulpit. The insurance actuaries say that my expectation of
life is exactly twenty-five years; in twenty-five years I might write and print
three hundred more articles—another million and a half words. If I now
resign the chance and retire to other scenes, then perhaps it may help me
a few inches along the Eight-Fold Path. Men have been made saints for
less.

Among the thousands of letters that have come to me from my customers and the public generally during the fifteen years of my episcopate
have been a great many of a uræmic and acerbitous flavor, and not a few
of these have set up the doctrine that whoever nominated me for my job
was an idiot. To this day, curiously enough, I don't know who he was. At
the time the poisoned pen was offered to me I was not in practise as a literary critic, and I had not, in fact, done much book reviewing. My actual
trade was that of an editorial writer on a provincial newspaper, then in sad
decay, and the subjects that I was told off to treat were chiefly (a) foreign
politics, a topic then disdained by most American editorial writers, and (b)
such manifestations of the naïve and charming communal life of the Republic as are now grouped under the general head of Babbittry. I had a
good time in that newspaper job, and invented a large vocabulary of terms
of abuse of my countrymen; a number of these terms have since passed
into the American language and are now used even by Babbitts. But I
never reviewed books save when the literary critic of the paper was drunk,
and that was not often. Some years before I had been the dramatic critic,
but that office was already filled by another, to the great relief of the local
Frohmans.[10] Those were the palmy days of Augustus Thomas, Clyde Fitch
and the dramatized novel. Mansfield was still the emperor of the American stage, Nazimova was a nine-days' wonder, Belasco was almost universally regarded as a Master Mind, and the late Joseph Jefferson[11] still

wobbled around the provinces with his tattered scenery and his company of amateurish sons, sons-in-law, cousins and second cousins. I am fond of recalling (to the disquiet of Comrade Nathan, who believed in the Belasco hocus-pocus so late as 1907, and once actually praised Nazimova's Nora in *A Doll's House*) that my observations upon these half-forgotten worthies brought many an indignant manager to the business office of my paper, and filled me with a fine sensation of bellicose sagacity. Some time ago I unearthed a bundle of clippings of my old dramatic notices, and their general sapience amazed and enchanted me. It was like meeting a precious one of 1902 and finding her still slim and sweet, with night-black hair and eyes like gasoline pools on wet asphalt. Once, aroused to indignation by my derision of his mumming, Mansfield wrote me a letter denouncing me as an ass and inviting me to dinner. But I was not quite ass enough to accept his invitation. The fashionable way to fetch an anarchistic provincial critic in those days was to hire him as a press-agent; it is, in fact, still done. But I always had a few dollars in my pocket, and so resisted the lure. But by and by I tired of the theatre, and took to writing facetious editorials, many of which were never printed. To this day I dislike the showhouse, and never enter it if I can help it.

But to return to my story. The assistant editor of *The Smart Set*, in 1908, was the late Norman Boyer, with whom, eight years before, I had worked as a police reporter in Baltimore. One day I received a polite note from him, asking me to wait upon him on my next visit to New York. I did so a few weeks later; Boyer introduced me to his chief, Fred Splint, and Splint forthwith offered me the situation of book reviewer to the magazine, with the rank and pay of a sergeant of artillery. Whose notion it was to hire me—whether Boyer's, or Splint's, or some anonymous outsider's—I was not told, and do not know to this day. I had never printed anything in the magazine; I had not, in fact, been doing any magazine work since 1905, when I abandoned the writing of short-stories, as I had abandoned poetry in 1900. But Splint engaged me with a strange and suspicious absence of parley, Boyer gave me an armful of books, the two of us went to Murray's for lunch (I remember a detail: I there heard the waltz, "Ach, Frühling, wie bist du so schön!" for the first time), and in November of the same year my first article appeared in this place. I have not missed an issue since. But now I shuffle off to other scenes.

Glancing back over the decade and a half, what strikes me most forcibly is the great change and improvement in the situation of the American imaginative author—the novelist, poet, dramatist and writer of short stories. In 1908, strange as it may seem to the literary radicals who roar so safely in Greenwich Village to-day, the old tradition was still powerful, and the young man or woman who came to New York with a manuscript which violated in any way the pruderies and prejudices of the professors had a very hard time getting it printed. It was a day of complacency and conformity. Hamilton Wright Mabie was still alive and still taken seriously, and all the young pedagogues who aspired to the critical gown imitated him in his watchful stupidity. This camorra had delivered a violent wallop to Theodore Dreiser eight years before, and he was yet suffering from his bruises; it was not until 1911 that he printed *Jennie Gerhardt*. Miss Harriet Monroe and her gang of new poets were still dispersed and inarticulate; Miss Amy Lowell, as yet unaware of Imagism, was writing polite doggerel in the manner of a New England schoolmarm; the reigning dramatists of the nation were Augustus Thomas, David Belasco and Clyde Fitch; Miss Cather was imitating Mrs. Wharton; Hergesheimer had six years to go before he'd come to *The Lay Anthony*; Cabell was known only as one who provided the text for illustrated gift-books; the American novelists most admired by most publishers, by most readers and by all practising critics were Richard Harding Davis, Robert W. Chambers and James Lane Allen. It is hard, indeed, in retrospect, to picture those remote days just as they were. They seem almost fabulous. The chief critical organ of the Republic was actually the Literary Supplement of the New York *Times*. The *Dial* was down with diabetes in Chicago; the *Nation* was made dreadful by the gloomy humors of Paul Elmer More; the *Bookman* was even more saccharine and sophomoric than it is to-day; the *Freeman*, the *New Republic* and the *Literary Review*[12] were yet unheard of. When the mild and *pianissimo* revolt of the middle 90's—a feeble echo of the English revolt—had spent itself, the Presbyterians marched in and took possession of the works. Most of the erstwhile *revoltés* boldly took the veil—notably Hamlin Garland. The American Idealism now preached so pathetically by Prof. Dr. Sherman and his fellow fugitives from the Christian Endeavor belt was actually on tap. No novel that told the truth about life as Americans were living it, no poem that departed from the old patterns, no play that had the merest ghost of an idea in it had a chance. When, in 1908, Mrs. Mary Roberts Rinehart printed a conventional mystery story which yet managed to have a trace of sense in it, it caused a sensation. (I reviewed it, by the way, in my first article.) And when, two years later, Dr. William Lyon Phelps printed a book of criticism in which he actually ranked Mark Twain alongside Emerson and Hawthorne, there was as great a stirring beneath the college elms as if a naked fancy woman had run across the campus. If Hergesheimer had come into New York in 1908 with *Cytherea* under his arm, he would have worn out his pantaloons on publishers' benches without getting so much as a polite kick. If Eugene O'Neill had come to Broadway with *The Emperor Jones* or *The Hairy Ape*, he would have been sent to Edward E. Rose to learn the elements of his trade. The devilish and advanced thing, in those days, was for a fat lady star to give a couple of matinées of Ibsen's *A Doll's House*.

A great many men and a few women addressed themselves to the dispersal of this fog. Some of them were imaginative writers who found it simply impossible to bring themselves within the prevailing rules; some were critics; others were young publishers. As I look back, I can't find any sign of concerted effort; it was, in the main, a case of each on his own. The more contumacious of the younger critics, true enough, tended to rally 'round Huneker, who, as a matter of fact, was very little interested in American letters, and the young novelists had a leader in Dreiser, who, I suspect, was quite unaware of most of them. However, it was probably Dreiser who chiefly gave form to the movement, despite the fact that for eleven long years he was silent. Not only was there a useful rallying-point in the idiotic suppression of *Sister Carrie;*[13] there was also the encouraging fact of the man's massive immovability. Physically and mentally he loomed up like a sort of headland—a great crag of basalt that no conceivable assault seemed able to touch. His predecessor, Frank Norris, was of much softer stuff. Norris, had he lived longer, would have been wooed and ruined, I fear, by the Mabies, Boyntons and other such Christian critics, as Garland had been wooed and ruined before him. Dreiser, fortunately for American letters, never had to face any such seduction. The critical schoolmarms, young and old, fell upon him with violence the moment he appeared above the horizon of his native steppe, and soon he was the storm center of a battle-royal that lasted nearly twenty years. The man himself was solid, granitic,

without nerves. Very little cunning was in him and not much bellicose enterprise, but he showed a truly appalling tenacity. The pedagogues tried to
scare him to death, they tried to stampede his partisans, and they tried to
put him into Coventry and get him forgotten, but they failed every time.
The more he was reviled, sneered at, neglected, the more resolutely he
stuck to his formula. That formula is now every serious American novelist's
formula. They all try to write better than Dreiser, and not a few of them
succeed, but they all follow him in his fundamental purpose—to make the
novel true. Dreiser added something, and here following is harder; he
tried to make the novel poignant—to add sympathy, feeling, imagination
to understanding. It will be a long while before that aim is better achieved
than he achieved it in *Jennie Gerhardt.*

To-day, it seems to me, the American imaginative writer, whether he
be novelist, poet or dramatist, is quite as free as he deserves to be. He is free
to depict the life about him precisely as he sees it, and to interpret it in any
manner he pleases. The publishers of the land, once so fearful of novelty,
are now so hospitable to it that they constantly fail to distinguish the novelty that has hard thought behind it from that which has only some Village
mountebank's desire to stagger the *booboisie.* Our stage is perhaps the
freest in the world—not only to sensations, but also to ideas. Our poets get
into print regularly with stuff so bizarre and unearthly that only Christian
Scientists can understand it. The extent of this new freedom, indeed, is so
great that large numbers of persons appear to be unable to believe in it;
they are constantly getting into sweats about the few taboos and inhibitions that remain, for example, those nourished by Comstockery. But the
importance and puissance of Comstockery, I believe, is quite as much
overestimated as the importance and puissance of the objurgations still
hurled at sense and honesty by the provincial prophets of American Idealism, the Genius of America, and other such phantasms. The Comstocks,
true enough, still raid an occasional book, particularly when their funds
are running low and there is need to inflame Christian men, but that their
monkeyshines ever actually *suppress* a book of any consequence I very
much doubt. The flood is too vast for them. Chasing a minnow with desperate passion, they let a whole school of whales go by. In any case, they
confine their operations to the single field of sex, and it must be plain that
it is not in the field of sex that the hottest battles against the old American

tradition have been fought and won. *Three Soldiers* was far more subversive of that tradition than all the stories of sex ever written in America — and yet *Three Soldiers* came out with the imprint of one of the most respectable of American publishers, and was scarcely challenged. *Babbitt* scored a victory that was still easier, and yet more significant, for its target was the double one of American business and American Christianity; it set the whole world to laughing at two things that are far more venerated in the United States than the bodily chastity of women. Nevertheless, *Babbitt* went down so easily that even the alfalfa *Gelehrten* joined in whooping for it, apparently on the theory that praising Lewis would make the young of the national species forget Dreiser. Victimized by their own craft, the *Gelehrten* thus made a foul attack upon their own principles, for if their principles did not stand against just such anarchistic books, then they were without any sense whatever, as was and is, indeed, the case.

I shall not rehearse the steps in the advance from *Sister Carrie*, suppressed and proscribed, to *Babbitt*, swallowed and hailed. The important thing is that almost complete freedom now prevails for the serious artist — that publishers stand ready to print him, that critics exist who are competent to recognize him and willing to do battle for him, and that there is a large public eager to read him. What use is he making of his opportunity? Certainly not the worst use possible, but also certainly not the best. He is free, but he is not yet, perhaps, worthy of freedom. He lets the popular magazine, the movie and the cheap-John publisher pull him too hard in one direction; he lets the vagaries of his politics pull him too hard in another. In my first article in this place I predicted the destruction of Upton Sinclair the artist by Upton Sinclair the visionary and reformer. Sinclair's bones now bleach upon the beach. Beside them repose those of many another man and woman of great promise — for example, Winston Churchill. Floyd Dell is on his way — one novel and two doses of Greenwich Village psychology. Hergesheimer writes novelettes for the *Saturday Evening Post*. Willa Cather has won the Pulitzer Prize — a transaction comparable to the election of Charles W. Eliot to the Elks. Masters turns to prose fiction that somehow fails to come off. Dreiser, forgetting his trilogy, experiments rather futilely with the drama, the essay, free verse. Fuller renounces the novel for book reviewing. Tarkington is another Pulitzer prizeman, always on the verge of first-rate work but always falling short by an inch. Many of the White Hopes of ten or fifteen years ago perished in the war, as surely victims of its slaughter as Rupert Brooke or Otto Braun; it is, indeed, curious to note that practically every American author who moaned and sobbed for democracy between the years 1914 and 1919 is now extinct. The rest have gone down the chute of the movies.

But all this, after all, may signify little. The shock troops have been piled up in great masses, but ground is cleared for those that follow. Well, then, what of the youngsters? Do they show any sign of seizing their chance? The answer is yes and no. On the one hand there is a group which, revolving 'round the *Bookman,* talks a great deal and accomplishes nothing. On the other hand, there is a group which, revolving 'round the *Dial, Broom* and the *Little Review,* talks even more and does even less. But on the third hand, as it were, there is a group which says little and saws wood. I have, from time to time, pointed out some of it members in this place. There seems to be nothing in concert between them, no sign of a formal movement, with its *blague* and its bombast, but all of them have this in common: that they owe both their opportunity and their method to the revolution that followed *Sister Carrie.* Most of them are from the Middle West, but they are distinct from the Chicago crowd, now degenerated to posturing and worse. They are sophisticated, disillusioned, free from cant, and yet they have imagination. The raucous protests of the evangelists of American Idealism seem to have no more effect upon them than the advances of the Expressionists, Dadaists and other such café-table prophets. Out of this dispersed and ill-defined group, I believe, something will come. Its members are those who are free from the two great delusions which, from the beginning, have always cursed American letters: the delusion that a work of art is primarily a moral document, that its purpose is to make men better Christians and more docile cannon-fodder, and the delusion that it is an exercise in logic, that its purpose is to prove something. These delusions, lingering beyond their time, are responsible for most of the disasters visible in the national literature to-day—the disasters of the radicals as well as those of the 100 per cent dunderheads. The writers of the future, I hope and believe, will carefully avoid both of them.

Inasmuch as I was immersed from the start in the struggle that I have briefly described, it is but natural that my critical treatises should have seemed, to many worthy souls, unduly tart, and even, in some cases, extravagantly abusive and unjust. But as I re-examine them in these closing days of my pastorate, I can't escape the feeling that that view of them is itself somewhat bilious. Tart, yes. But unjust—well, certainly not often. If I regret anything, it is that I have been, more than once, unduly tolerant. The spectacle of a man hard and earnestly at work is one that somehow moves me; I am often blinded to the falseness of his purpose by the agony of his striving. It is a sentimentality that quickly damages critical honesty, and I have succumbed to it more than once. I have overpraised books, and I have applauded authors incautiously and too soon. But, as the Lord God Jahveh is my judge and I hope in all humility to be summoned to sit upon His right hand upon the dreadful and inevitable Day of Judgment, when all hearts are bared and virtue gets its long-delayed reward, I most solemnly make my oath that, with the single exception noted on a previous page, I can't remember a time when I ever printed a slating that was excessive or unjust. The quacks and dolts who have been mauled in these pages all deserved it; more, they all deserved far worse than they got. If I lost them customers by my performances I am glad of it. If I annoyed and humiliated them I am glad of it again. If I shamed any of them into abandoning their quackery—but here I begin to pass beyond the borders of probability, and become a quack myself.

Regarding false art, cheap cant, pious skullduggery, dishonest pretense—regarding all these things my position is this: that their practitioners have absolutely no rights that anyone is bound to respect. To be polite to them is not to be tolerant; it is simply to be silly. If a critic has any duty at all, save the primary duty to be true to himself, it is the public duty of protecting the fine arts against the invasion of such frauds. They are insidious in their approach; they know how to cajole and deceive; unchallenged, they are apt to bag many victims. Once they are permitted to get a foothold, however insecure, it becomes doubly hard to combat them. My method, therefore, has been to tackle them at first sight and with an axe. It has led to some boisterous engagements, and, I sincerely hope, to a few useful unmaskings. So engaged, I do not hesitate to admit that I have been led by my private tastes quite as much as by any sense of professional duty. The man who tries to subjugate beautiful letters to the puerile uses of some bucolic moral scheme, or some nonsensical notion of the national destiny, or some petty variety of new-fangled politics is a man who is congenitally and incurably offensive to me. He has his right, true enough, to be heard, but that right is not properly exercised in the field of *belles lettres.*

A hundred times, during these fifteen years, I have been made aware painfully of a great gap in our domestic *apparatus criticus,* and I still wonder that no competent clerk of letters has ever thought to fill it. I allude to the lack of a comprehensive and intelligent history of American literature. Why does it remain unwritten? The existing books are all either conventional texts for the instruction of schoolboys, or histories of single periods, *e.g.,* Tyler's excellent work on the Colonial literature and Pattee's unimaginative but nevertheless often shrewd monograph on the period from 1870 to 1900.[14] The Cambridge History of American Literature by no means meets the need.[15] It is, in detail, accurate enough, and it shows some original exploration of the sources, but its defect is that it does not indicate the direction of the main currents, nor the non-literary forces behind them — that it is too much a series of essays on salient men, and views them only too often as phenomena in vacuo. Whole sections of the field are not entered at all — and often they are extremely interesting sections. Many of them are along the borders, with religion, politics or race enmity just over the fence. So far as I know, no literary historian, writing about Poe, has ever thrown up the fact that he came to manhood just as Andrew Jackson mounted the tin throne at Washington. Yet it seems to me to be a fact of capital importance; it explains many things about Poe that are otherwise inexplicable.

Poe, indeed, is a colossus who has never had a competent historian. His biographers have spent themselves upon vain efforts to find out the truth about his periodical drunkenness and his banal love affairs; meanwhile, the question of his artistic origins, like the question of his influence, is passed over with a few platitudes. The current doctrine in the highschools seems to be that he was a superb poet and the inventor of the short story, or, at all events, of the tale of mystery and horror. He was actually neither. Nine-tenths of his poetry is so artificial that it is difficult to imagine even college tutors reading it voluntarily; as for his tales, they have long since passed over to the shelf of juveniles. But Poe was nevertheless a man with a first-rate head on him, and it seems to me that he proved it abundantly in his criticism, which the pedagogues now neglect. This criticism was not only revolutionary in its own time; it would have continued to seem revolutionary, had it been read, down to a few years ago. Who could imagine anything more subversive of the professorial categories— more direct, clear and hard-hitting, more fatal to literary cheese-mongers, more disconcerting to every hollow pretense and quackery. How did Poe come to write it? What set him on the track? And by what process was the whole body of it so neatly buried the moment he gasped out his last breath?

The equally strange case of Emerson I have discussed more than once in the past, but an adequate treatise upon him, alive and dead, yet remains to be written. It was obviously Emerson's central aim in life to liberate the American mind—to set it free from the crippling ethical obsessions of Puritanism, to break down herd thinking, to make liberty more real on the intellectual plane than it could ever be on the political plane. It is his tragic fate to be mouthed and admired to-day chiefly by persons who have entirely misunderstood his position—in brief, by the heirs and assigns of the very prigs and dullards he spent his whole life opposing. Certainly it would be difficult to imagine a greater irony than this. Emerson paved the way for every intellectual revolt that has occurred since his time, and yet he has always been brought into court, not as a witness for the rebels, but as a witness for the militia and the police. Three-fourths of the books and monographs written about him depict him as a sort of primeval Dr. Frank Crane; he was actually the first important American to give a hand to Whitman. . . . And Whitman himself! Who will work up the material so laboriously and competently unearthed by Prof. Holloway? . . . Who, indeed, will write the first history of American literature that fits such men as Poe, Emerson and Whitman into their true places, and reveals the forces that shaped them, and describes accurately the heritage that they left to their countrymen? . . . I ask the question and pass on.

SOLI DEO GLORIA!

["Fifteen Years," SS 72, no. 4 (December 1923): 138–44]

Establishing
the Canon

Chapter

2

Mark Twain

Albert Bigelow Paine, *Mark Twain:
A Biography* (1912)

W

hat is the origin of the prejudice against
humor? Why is it so dangerous, if you would
keep the public confidence, to make the
public laugh?

Is it because humor and sound sense are essentially antagonistic? Has humanity found by experience
that the man who sees the fun of life is unfitted to deal
sanely with its problems? I think not. No man had
more of the comic spirit in him than William Shakespeare, and yet his serious reflections, by the sheer
force of their sublime obviousness, have pushed their
way into the race's arsenal of immortal platitudes. So,
too, with Æsop, and with Lincoln and Johnson, to
come down the scale. All of these men were humorists, and yet all of them performed prodigies of
indubitable wisdom. And contrariwise, many an undeniable pundit has had his guffaw. Huxley, if he had

not been the greatest intellectual duellist of his age, might have been its greatest wit. And Beethoven, after soaring to the heights of tragedy in the first movement of the Fifth Symphony, turned to the divine fooling, the irresistible bull-fiddling of the *scherzo*.

No, there is not the slightest disharmony between sense and nonsense, humor and respectability, despite the almost universal tendency to assume that there is. But, why, then, that widespread error? What actual fact of life lies behind it, giving it a specious appearance of reasonableness? None other, I am convinced, than the fact that the average man is far too stupid to make a joke.

He may *see* a joke and *love* a joke, particularly when it floors and flabbergasts some person he dislikes, but the only way he can himself take part in the priming and pointing of a new one is by acting as its target. In brief, his personal contact with humor tends to fill him with an accumulated sense of disadvantage, of pricked complacency, of sudden and crushing defeat; and so, by an easy psychological process, he is led into the idea that the thing itself is incompatible with true dignity of character and intellect. Hence his deep suspicion of jokers, however their thrusts. "What a damphool!"—this same half-pitying tribute he pays to wit and butt alike. He cannot separate the virtuoso of comedy from his general concept of comedy itself, and that concept is inextricably mixed with memories of foul ambuscades and mortifying hurts. And so it is not often that he is willing to admit any wisdom in a humorist, or to condone frivolity in a sage.

In all this, I believe, there is a plausible explanation of the popular, and even of the critical attitude toward the late Samuel Langhorne Clemens (Mark Twain). Unless I am so wholly mistaken that my only expiation lies in suicide, Mark was the noblest literary artist who ever set pen to paper on American soil, and not only the noblest artist, but also one of the most profound and sagacious philosophers. From the beginning of his maturity down to his old age he dealt constantly and earnestly with the deepest problems of life and living, and to his consideration of them he brought a truly amazing instinct for the truth, an almost uncanny talent for ridding the essential thing of its deceptive husks of tradition, prejudice, flubdub and balderdash. No man, not even Nietzsche, ever did greater execution against those puerilities of fancy which so many men mistake for religion, and over which they are so eager to dispute and break heads. No

man had a keener eye for that element of pretense which is bound to in-
trude itself into all human thinking, however serious, however painstaking, however honest in intent. And yet, because the man had humor as
well as acumen, because he laughed at human weakness instead of weeping over it, because he turned now and then from the riddle of life to the
joy of life—because of this habit of mind it is the custom to regard him
lightly and somewhat apologetically, as one debarred from greatness by
unfortunate infirmities.

William Dean Howells probably knew him better than any other
human being, but in all that Howells has written about him one is conscious of a conditioned admiration, of a subtle fear of allowing him too
much merit, of an ineradicable disinclination to take him quite seriously.[1]
The Mark that Howells draws is not so much a great artist as a glorious *en-
fant terrible*. And even William Lyon Phelps, a hospitable and penetrating
critic, wholly loose of orthodox shackles—even Phelps hems and haws a
bit before putting Mark above Oliver Wendell Holmes, and is still convinced that *The Scarlet Letter* is an incomparably finer work of art than
Huckleberry Finn.[2]

Well, such notions will die hard, but soon or late, I am sure, they will
inevitably die. So certain am I, indeed, of their dying that I now formally
announce their death in advance, and prepare to wait in patience for the
delayed applause. In one of his essays Dr. Phelps shows how critical opinion of Mark has gradually evolved from scorn into indifference, and from
indifference into toleration, and from toleration into apologetic praise,
and from apologetic praise into hearty praise. The stage of unqualified enthusiasm is coming—it has already cast its lights before England—and I
am very glad to join the lodge as a charter member. Let me now set down
my faith, for the literary archeologists of day after to-morrow:

I believe that *Huckleberry Finn* is one of the great masterpieces of the
world, that it is the full equal of *Don Quixote* and *Robinson Crusoe*, that it
is vastly better than *Gil Blas*, *Tristram Shandy*, *Nicholas Nickleby* or *Tom
Jones*. I believe that it will be read by human beings of all ages, not as a
solemn duty but for the honest love of it, and over and over again, long
after every book written in America between the years 1800 and 1860, with
perhaps three exceptions, has disappeared entirely save as a classroom fos-
sil. I believe that Mark Twain had a clearer vision of life, that he came

nearer to its elementals and was less deceived by its false appearances, than any other American who has ever presumed to manufacture generalizations, not excepting Emerson. I believe that, admitting all his defects, he wrote better English, in the sense of cleaner, straighter, vivider, saner English, than either Irving or Hawthorne. I believe that four of his books — *Huck, Life on the Mississippi, Captain Stormfield's Visit to Heaven,* and *A Connecticut Yankee* — are alone worth more, as works of art and as criticisms of life, than the whole output of Cooper, Irving, Holmes, Mitchell, Stedman, Whittier and Bryant. I believe that he ranks well above Whitman and certainly not below Poe. I believe that he was the true father of our national literature, the first genuinely American artist of the blood royal.

Such is my feeling at the moment, and such has been my feeling for many a moon. If any gentleman in the audience shares it, either wholly or with qualifications, then I advise him to buy and read the biography of Mark lately published by Albert Bigelow Paine, for therein he will find an elaborate, painstaking and immensely interesting portrait of the man, and sundry shrewd observations upon the writer.

Not that I agree with Paine in all his judgments. Far from it, indeed. It seems to me that he gets bogged hopelessly when he tries to prove that *The Innocents Abroad* is a better book than *A Tramp Abroad,* that he commits a crime when he puts *Joan of Arc* above *Huck Finn,* and that he is too willing to join Howells and other such literary sacristans in frowning down upon Mark's clowning, his weakness for vulgarity, his irrepressible maleness. In brief, Paine is disposed, at times, to yield to current critical opinion against what must be his own good sense. But when you have allowed for all this — and it is not obtrusive — the thing that remains is a vivid and sympathetic biography, a book with sound merit in every chapter of it, a mountain of difficulties triumphantly surmounted, a fluent and excellent piece of writing. Paine tells everything that is worth hearing, whether favorable to Mark or the reverse, and leaves out all that is not worth hearing. One closes the third volume with unbounded admiration for the industry of the biographer, and with no less admiration for his frankness and sagacity. He has given us a rich and colorful book, presenting coherently a wise selection from a perfect chaos of materials. The Mark Twain that emerges from it is almost as real as Huckleberry Finn.

And what a man that Mark Twain was! How he stood above and apart from the world, like Rabelais come to life again, observing the human comedy, chuckling over the eternal fraudulence of man! What a sharp eye he had for the bogus, in religion, politics, art, literature, patriotism, virtue! What contempt he emptied upon shams of all sorts—and what pity! Mr. Paine reveals for us very clearly, by quotation and exposition, his habitual attitude of mind. He regarded all men as humbugs, but as humbugs to be dealt with gently, as humbugs too often taken in and swindled by their own humbuggery. He saw how false reasoning, false assumptions, false gods had entered into the very warp and woof of their thinking; how impossible it was for them to attack honestly the problems of being; how helpless they were in the face of life's emergencies. And seeing all this, he laughed at them, but not often with malice. What genuine indignation he was capable of was leveled at life itself and not at its victims. Through all his later years the riddle of existence was ever before him. He thought about it constantly; he discussed it with everyone he knew; he made copious notes of his speculations. But he never came to any soothing custom made conclusion. The more he examined life, the more it appeared to him to be without meaning, and even without direction; the more he pondered upon the idea of God, the more a definite idea of God eluded him. In the end, as Mr. Paine tells us, he verged toward a hopeless pessimism. Death seemed to him a glad release, an inestimable boon. When his daughter Jean died, suddenly, tragically, he wrote to her sister: "I am so glad she is out of it and safe—safe!"

It is this reflective, philosophizing Clemens who stands out most clearly in Mr. Paine's book. In his own works, our glimpses of him are all too brief. His wife and his friends opposed his speculations, perhaps wisely, for the artist might have been swallowed up in the sage. But he wrote much to please himself and left a vast mass of unpublished manuscript behind him. Certainly it is to be hoped that these writings will see the light, and before long. One book described by Mr. Paine, "Three Thousand Years Among the Microbes,"[3] would appear to be a satire so mordant and so large in scale that his admirers have a plain right to demand its publication. And there should be a new edition, too, of his confession of doubt, *What Is Man?* of which a few copies were printed for private distribution in 1905. Yet again we have a right to ask for most if not all of his unpublished stories and sketches, many of which were suppressed at the behest of Mrs. Clemens, for reasons no longer worth considering. There is good ground for believing that his reputation will gain rather than suffer by the publication of these things, and in any case it can withstand the experiment, for *Huck Finn* and *Life on the Mississippi* and the *Connecticut Yankee* will remain, and so long as they remain there can be no question of the man's literary stature. He was one of the great artists of all time. He was the full equal of Cervantes and Molière, Swift and Defoe. He was and is the one authentic giant of our national literature. ["The Burden of Humor," *SS* 39, no. 2 (February 1913): 151–54]

The older I grow the more I am convinced that Mark was, by long odds, the largest figure that ever reared itself out of the flat, damp prairie of American literature. He was great absolutely, but one must consider him relatively to get at the measure of his true greatness. Put him beside Emerson, or Whitman, or Hawthorne, or even Poe; he was palpably the superior of all of them. What ailed the whole quartette was a defective contact with their environment, an aloofness from the plain facts of life, a sort of incurable otherworldliness. Emerson was always half lost in the shadows; toward the end of his life they closed upon him completely. The ideas that he spoke for, in the main, were ideas borrowed from men in far lands, and for all his eloquence he never got into them any sense of their pressing importance to the men of his own country. He was the academic theorist *par excellence*. He inhabited a world of mystical abstractions. The very folks who yielded most readily to his soughing phrases were furthest from grasping their exact import; to this day he is chiefly the philosopher, not of men who think clearly and accurately, but of half-educated dolts whose thinking is all a mellow and witless booziness. A man of extraordinary mental equipment and of even more extraordinary nobility of character, he failed both as a great teacher and as a great artist because of his remoteness from the active, exigent life that he was a part of. Set here in the America of the nineteenth century, begirt by politics, railways and commercial enterprise (and no less by revivals, cuspidors and braggadocio), he carried on his inquiries in the manner of a medieval monk, and his conclusions showed all the nebulousness that one associates with the monkish character. To this day his speculations have had no appreciable influence upon American

ways of thought. His only professed disciples, in fact, are the votaries of
what is called the New Thought, and these idiots libel him quite as absurdly as the Methodists, say, burlesque Christ.

The intellectual foreignness and loneliness of Hawthorne, Whitman
and Poe is scarcely less noticeable. They lived in the republic, but were
anything but of it. Hawthorne concerned himself with psychological problems that were not only inordinately obscure and labored, but even archaic; his enterprise, in his chief work, might almost be called an attempt
to psychoanalyze the dead. It would be ridiculous to say that there was anything in his books that was characteristic of his time and his country. The
gusto of a man thoroughly at home in his surroundings was simply not in
him, and it is surely not surprising to hear that while he was physically
present in America he lived like a hermit, and that his only happiness was
found abroad. Whitman was even more solitary. The democracy he
dreamed of was simply a figment of his imagination; it had no more relation to the reality sprawling before him than the Sermon on the Mount
has to the practical ethic of the average Christian ecclesiastic. His countrymen, recognizing the conflict, regarded him generally as a loafer and a
scoundrel, and it was only after foreign enthusiasts began to cry him up
that he emerged from the constant threat of going to jail. As for Poe, he was
almost the complete antithesis of a great national artist. In the midst of the
most sordid civilization ever seen on earth and in the face of a population
of utter literalists, he devoted himself grandly to *héliogabalisme*.4 His countrymen, in the main, were quite unaware of his stature while he lived.
They regarded Cooper and Irving as incomparably greater artists, and
such eighth-raters as N. P. Willis as far cleverer men. When they went to
the works of Poe at all they went to them as, a generation later, they went
to Barnum's circus—that is, as to an entertainment fantastic and somehow
discreditable—one to be enjoyed now and then, but not too often. The
Baptist critic, Rufus W. Griswold, accurately expressed the national view;
his judgment was not challenged for years. An American boy of 1848 who
had conceived the ambition of becoming a second Poe would have been
caned until his very pantaloons took fire.

At the bottom of this isolation of Poe and Whitman and Hawthorne
and Emerson there was, of course, the dense ignorance of a nation in a
very backward state of culture; a Beethoven or a Mozart or an El Greco,

set down amid the same scenes, would have got the same cold shoulder. But the fault, obviously, was not all on one side; the men themselves lacked something. What that something was I have already indicated. It may be described briefly as responsiveness, observation, aliveness, a sense of reality, a joy in life. Around them roared a great show; it was dramatic, thrilling, unprecedented; above all, it was intensely amusing. And yet they were as unconscious of it as so many deaf men at a combat of brass bands. Only Whitman seemed to have the slightest notion that anything was going on—and Whitman mistook the show for a great sacrament, a cheap and gaudy circus for a sort of Second Coming of Christ. Well, such lofty detachment is not the habit of great artists. It was not the habit of Shakespeare, or of Cervantes, or of Goethe, or of Pushkin, or of Thackeray, or of Balzac. More important to our present purpose, it was not the habit of Mark Twain. Mark was the first of our great national artists to be wholeheartedly and enthusiastically American. He was the first to immerse himself willingly and with gusto in the infinitely picturesque and brilliant life of his time and country. He was the first to understand the common man of his race, and to interpret him fairly, honestly and accurately. He was the first to project brilliantly, for the information and entertainment of all the world, the American point of view, the American philosophy of life, the American character, the American soul. He would have been a great artist, I believe, even on the high-flung plane of Emerson or Hawthorne. He would have been *konzertmeister* even among the *umbilicarii*. But being what he was, his greatness was enormously augmented. He stands to-day at the head of the line. He is the one indubitable glory of American letters.

The bitter, of course, goes with the sweet. To be an American is, unquestionably, to be the noblest, the grandest, the proudest mammal that ever hoofed the verdure of God's green footstool. Often, in the black abysm of the night, the thought that I am one awakens me like a blast of trumpets, and I am thrown into a cold sweat by contemplation of the fact. I shall cherish it on the scaffold; it will console me in hell. But, as I have said, there is no perfection under heaven, and so even an American has his small blemishes, his scarcely discernible weaknesses, his minute traces of vice and depravity. Mark, alas, had them: he was as thoroughly American as a Knight of Pythias, a Wheeling stogie or Prohibition. One might almost exhibit his effigy in a museum as the archetype of the *Homo Americanus*.

And what were these stigmata that betrayed him? In chief, they were two in number, and both lay at the very foundation of his character. On the one hand, there was his immovable moral certainty, his firm belief that he knew what was right from what was wrong, and that all who differed from him were, in some obscure way, men of an inferior and sinister order. And on the other hand, there was his profound intellectual timorousness, his abiding fear of his own ideas, his incurable cowardice in the face of public disapproval. These two characteristics colored his whole thinking; they showed themselves in his every attitude and gesture. They were the visible signs of his limitation as an Emersonian Man Thinking, and they were the bright symbols of his nationality. He was great in every way that an American could be great, but when he came to the border of his Americanism he came to the end of his greatness.

The true Mark Twain is only partly on view in his actual books—that is, in his printed books. To get the rest of the portrait you must go to Paine's exhaustive and fascinating biography—a work so engrossing as a character study that, despite its three volumes and more than 1,700 pages, I have gone through it three times. The real Mark was not the amiable jester of the white dress suit, the newspaper interviews and the after-dinner speeches. He was not the somewhat heavy-handed satirist of A *Tramp Abroad* and *Tom Sawyer*. He was not even the extraordinarily fine and delicate artist of *Joan of Arc* and *Huckleberry Finn*. Nay, he was a different bird altogether—an intensely serious and even lugubrious man, an iconoclast of the most relentless sort, a man not so much amused by the spectacle of life as appalled by it, a pessimist to the last degree. Nothing could be more unsound than the Mark legend—the legend of the light-hearted and kindly old clown. Study the volumes of Paine and you will quickly discern its unsoundness. The real Mark was a man haunted to the point of distraction by the endless and meaningless tragedy of existence—a man whose thoughts turned to it constantly, in season and out of season. And to think, with him, was to write; he was, for all his laziness, the most assiduous of scribblers; he piled up notes, sketches of books and articles, even whole books, about it, almost mountain high.

Well, why did these notes, sketches, articles and books get no further? Why do most of them remain unprinted, even to-day? You will find the answer in a prefatory note that Mark appended to *What Is Man?* published privately in 1905. I quote it in full:

The studies for these papers were begun twenty-five or twenty-seven years ago. The papers were written seven years ago. I have examined them once or twice per year since and found them satisfactory. I have just examined them again, and am still satisfied that they speak the truth. Every thought in them has been thought (and accepted as unassailable truth) by millions upon millions of men—and concealed, kept private. Why did they not speak out? Because they dreaded (*and could not bear*) the disapproval of the people around them. Why have I not published? The same reason has restrained me, I think. I can find no other.

Imagine a man writing so honest and excellent a book, imagine him examining it and re-examining it and always finding it good—and yet holding off the printing of it for twenty-five years, and then issuing it timorously and behind the door, in an edition of 250 copies, none of them for sale! Even his death did not quench his fear. His executors, taking it over as part of his goods, withheld the book for five years more—and then printed it very discreetly, with the betraying preface omitted! Surely it would be impossible in the literature of any other civilized country since the Middle Ages to find anything to match that long hesitation. Here was a man of the highest dignity in the national letters, a man universally recognized to be their chief living adornment, and here was a book into which he had put the earnest convictions of his lifetime, a book carefully and deliberately written, a book representing him more accurately than any other, both as artist and as man—and yet it had to wait thirty-five years before it saw the light of day! An astounding affair, in all conscience—but thoroughly American, Messieurs, thoroughly American! Mark knew his countrymen. He knew their intense suspicion of ideas, their blind hatred of heterodoxy, their bitter way of dealing with dissenters. He knew how, their pruderies outraged, they would turn upon even the gaudiest hero and roll him in the mud. And knowing, he was afraid. He "dreaded the disapproval of the people around him." And part of that dread, I suspect, was peculiarly internal. In brief, Mark himself was also an American, and he shared the national horror of the unorthodox. His own speculations always half appalled him. He was not only afraid to utter what he believed; he was even a bit timorous about *believing* what he believed.

The weakness takes a good deal from his stature. It leaves him radiating a subtle flavor of the second-rate. With more courage, he would have gone a great deal further, and left a far deeper mark upon the intellectual history of his time. Not, perhaps, intrinsically as artist. He got as far in that direction as possible for a man of his training to go. *Huckleberry Finn* is a truly stupendous piece of work—perhaps the greatest novel ever written in English. And it would be difficult to surpass the sheer artistry of such things as *A Connecticut Yankee, Captain Stormfield, Joan of Arc* and parts of *A Tramp Abroad.* But there is more to the making of literature than the mere depiction of human beings at their obscene follies; there is also the play of ideas. Mark had ideas that were clear, that were vigorous, and that had an immediate appositeness. True enough, most of them were not quite original. As Prof. Schoenemann, of Harvard, has lately demonstrated, he got the notion of *The Mysterious Stranger* from Adolf Wilbrandt's *Der Meister von Palmyra;*[5] much of *What Is Man?* you will find in the forgotten harangues of Ingersoll; in other directions he borrowed right and left. But it is only necessary to read either of the books I have just mentioned to see how thoroughly he recast everything he wrote; how brilliantly it came to be marked by the charm of his own personality; how he got his own peculiar and unmatchable eloquence into the merest statement of it. When, entering these regions of his true faith, he yielded to a puerile timidity— when he sacrificed his conscience and his self-respect to the idiotic popularity that so often more than half dishonored him—then he not only did a cruel disservice to his own permanent fame, but inflicted genuine damage upon the national literature. He was greater than all the others because he was more American, but in this one way, at least, he was less than them for the same reason. . . .

Well, there he stands—a bit concealed, a bit false, but still a colossus. As I said at the start, I am inclined year by year to rate his achievement higher. In such a work as *Huckleberry Finn* there is something that vastly transcends the merit of all ordinary books. It has a merit that is special and extraordinary; it lifts itself above all hollow standards and criteria; it seems greater every time I read it. The books that gave Mark his first celebrity do not hold up so well. "The Jumping Frog" still wrings snickers, but, after all, it is commonplace at bottom; even an Ellis Parker Butler might have conceivably written it. *The Innocents Abroad,* re-read to-day, is largely tedious. Its humors are artificial; its audacities are stale; its eloquence belongs to the fancy journalism of a past generation. Even *Tom Sawyer* and *A Tramp*

Abroad have long stretches of flatness. But in *Huckleberry Finn*, though he didn't know it at the time and never quite realized it, Mark found himself. There, working against the grain, heartily sick of the book before it was done, always putting it off until to-morrow, he hacked out a masterpiece that expands as year chases year. There, if I am not wrong, he produced the greatest work of the imagination that These States have yet seen. ["Mark Twain," SS 60, no. 2 (October 1919): 139–43]

Edgar Allan Poe

Joseph Wood Krutch, *Edgar Allan Poe: A Study in Genius* (1926)

Strange though it may seem, this is the first book on Poe that offers anything approaching a rational and convincing account of him. His critics in the past, almost unanimously, have been diverted from the business by the fascinating phenomenon of his drunkenness. To some it has been a sinister external force, like smallpox or jury duty, dissuading him from his high concerns, and so crippling his genius. To others it has been the mainspring of his life, and proof sufficient of his unfitness to be admired by Christian men and women. Mr. Krutch, following a somewhat faint lead by Dr. John W. Robertson,[6] puts it finally into its proper place. Poe was a drunkard intermittently and by orgy, as he was a bounder intermittently and by orgy. The habit was a symptom, not a cause, and even as a symptom it was trivial, though it brought him to the grave. Strapped to the water-wagon, with a ton of Bibles to hold him down, he would have been precisely the same Poe. He came into the world bearing bizarre stigmata, and the Weird Sisters fanned him in the cradle. The visible universe scarcely touched him. He inhabited a universe of his own, with red glares lighting it, implacable clouds hedging it round, and preposterous fauna roving its evil groves. He was, in his way, a patriotic citizen of it—what might be called a 100 per cent Fantastic. He delighted in its occult sins, its drug-store smells. But there were times, too, when he longed pathetically to get out of it, and now and then these longings took the form of overt flights. But always he was turned back. Always the world of fact rebuffed and terrified him, and he returned anew to his world of charnel-house dreams.

Mr. Krutch's study of him is full of shrewd observation and plausible speculation. The ordinary tests of literary criticism, of course, are not to be applied to Poe. He was *sui generis*—or he was simply a poor mountebank, and not worth studying. Mr. Krutch finds, however, that psychology can account for him. His complexes were genuinely complex, but nevertheless they fit into the categories. More, they flow naturally out of the circumstances of his unstable youth: the dreadful death of his mother, his equivocal and painful position in the house of the Allans, his humiliating difficulties at the University of Virginia, his service as a common soldier, his abject poverty. All of his early life was a struggle against inferiorities. He saw himself as one distinguished and superior; the reality brought him very near to the gutter. Mr. Krutch believes that even his first literary enterprises were no more than parts of his general flight mechanism. He turned to the pen as to a sort of surrogate for the lost sword of the Virginia cavalier, snatched from his hand by Allan. He would show the cock-eyed world! And when genius alone failed to amaze it, he resorted readily to gaudy lying. Thus his grandfather, the lowly profiteer, became a hero of the Revolution. And thus he himself became a mysterious political agent in Russia, and a comrade of Byron in Greece.

It was his mother's death, penniless and among not too friendly strangers, that left the deepest mark upon him. It not only made him a fugitive from a too cruel world; it also made him incapable of ordinary human love. His marriage was so preposterous as to be almost pathological. Virginia Clemm was a child scarcely come to adolescence; moreover, she was next door to an idiot. Mr. Krutch believes that Poe married her as a device of safety. So long as she was there he was secure, to that extent, against other women. Her incapacity as wife did not daunt him. It was, indeed, her incapacity as wife that chiefly attracted him, for in women as sexual objects he took no interest. There is no hint of carnal love in any of his stories; he was a Parsifal if there ever was one on this earth. When, toward the end of his own life, Virginia died, his affairs of the heart at once took on a grotesque and impossible character. He engaged himself to several women at once, and most of them were fantastic blue-stockings, as devoid of sexual charm as so many lady embalmers. Women stirred him only when they were in decay, and even then they did not stir his hormones. His heroines all suffer from phagocytolysis, and he approaches them on his knees.

Mr. Krutch shows clearly how vain is the effort to detach Poe from his work, or his work from Poe. The man simply poured himself into his writings. They have only the remotest sort of contact with anything external to his own singular personality. They are full of the strange horrors that beset him; there is little in them else. The effort to pigeon-hole them, carried on for years by humorless professors, is manifestly vain. There was only one Poe, and the tragic turmoil within him was his beginning and his end. In certain moods all of us can understand him; in other moods even his fondest partisans must find him only absurd. The man wrote abominably. Some of his most celebrated stories are done in a Johnsonese that would have disgraced the late Mr. Harding. His poetry is popular in proportion as it justifies Emerson's sneer: to wit, that it consists of jingles. But Poe himself remains. There is something titanic in his tragedy. It breaks through his ornate and rococo sentences; it overwhelms his nonsensical theories and idle pedantries; it gives an austere dignity to even his worst jingles. It will always bring a crowd to his booth—a crowd fascinated and yet a bit uneasy. There have been far greater artists, but there have been few more glamorous men. ["The Mystery of Poe," *Nation* 122 (March 17, 1926): 289–90]

Ralph Waldo Emerson

Régis Michaud, *Emerson: The Enraptured Yankee* (1930)

It took a Frenchman to write this amusing and instructive book. An American can never regard the dreadful writhings and belchings of the Puritan soul with the right detachment: either he tries to prove absurdly that the bean-burning theologians were Great Thinkers, or he succumbs to indignation and denounces than as mere swindlers and scoundrels. M. Michaud, though he has lived in the United States a long while and can eat without upset all the Heinz 57 varieties, is still thoroughly Gallic at heart, and so he is able to enjoy Emerson immensely without either being taken in by him or losing patience with him. His book is not a biography, nor even a work of criticism. It is simply a character sketch of one of the most fantastic worthies ever come to growth on American soil. As such, it is extraordinarily penetrating, ingenious and diverting. I know of no treatise on Emerson that is better. I know of no other, indeed, that is so good.

It is one of the mysteries of American life that Rotary has never discov-

ered Emerson. His so-called philosophy, even more than that of Elbert
Hubbard, seems to be made precisely for the luncheon-table idealists.
There is in it an almost incomparable sweep of soothing generalities, a vast
marshalling of sugary and not too specific words, a wholesale assurance, a
soaring optimism. It sets up a magnificent glow without adding any destructive heat. I can imagine nothing better suited to the spiritual needs of
used-car dealers, insurance underwriters, trust company vice-presidents,
bath-fixture magnates, and the like, gathered together in the sight of God
to take cheer from one another and hoist the Republic along its rocky
road. Its effect upon the circulation is as powerful as that of dioxyphenol
ethanol-methylamine. And yet the Rotarians neglect this powerful medicine for the feeble philtres of Hubbard, and gulp the even more watery pe-
runas[7] of Roger W. Babson, Bishop Manning and Rabbi Stephen S. Wise
as chasers!

M. Michaud is plainly surprised by this blindness. As he points out
over and over again, Emerson was always very careful to keep idealism
within the bounds of American respectability. He incited to hope, optimism, enterprise, enthusiasm, but never to any downright violation of
decorum. Did he preach the sacredness of the individual, the kingship of
the lonely soul? Then he always stopped short of Thoreau's corollary that
it was unnecessary to pay taxes. Did he view theologians with a fishy eye,
and distrust their mumbo-jumbo of sacraments and ceremonials? Then he
still found it discreet and decent to go to church on Sunday. Did he call
for frank words, honest exultations, dancing with arms and legs? Then he
knew how to be cautious when it came to Walt Whitman. And did he
praise the simple life and renounce luxury? Then it was always from the
security of an ample income. In this last field, indeed, the student scarcely
detects any difference between his philosophy and that of Arthur Brisbane.
"One can read between the lines," says Michaud, "that in Emerson's eyes
the poor, like the sick, are rogues, that the capitalists are the real 'representative men,' that all compensation which pays in specie is divine, and
that Wall Street is the true temple of the Over-Soul."

If this is not a philosophy made for enlightened American business
men, then I am surely no tailor of the psyche. But, as I say, they pass it over
for inferior goods, and so leave it to the New Thoughters and the New Hu-

manists. Both, alas, make a sad hash of it. The New Thoughters force it into a miscegenation with deep breathing, umbilicular contemplation and other borrowings from the heathen Hindus, and the New Humanists try to ram it into the mold of Calvinism. Emerson, if he were alive to-day, would feel uncomfortable in either camp. He was, for all his ventures into interstellar space, far too realistic a Yankee to believe that reading the Bhagavad-Gita could wake his solar plexus or give him second sight, and he owed far too much to the Romantic movement to countenance the Humanists' saucy denunciations of Rousseau. He was, indeed, the real founder of Romanticism in America, though he took his Rousseau at third hand. It was precisely from Romanticism that he got the ammunition for his revolt against Calvinism. And now the New Humanists try to make a Calvinist of him, as the New Thoughters try to make him a Muggletonian![8] ["The Library," AM 21, no. 2 (October 1930): 251–52 ("The Moonstruck Pastor")]

Henry James

Julia Bride (1909)

Henry James, it would appear, is clearing his shelves of shopworn stock and remnants of odd lengths—a sensible and even laudable enterprise. One of the latter appears on the current book list under the appellation of *Julia Bride* and in a gorgeous red cover. It seems to be made up of the first and second chapters of a novel begun in high spirits and terminated in sudden despair. That novel, I am convinced, had Mr. James but labored resolutely to the end of it, would have gone thundering down the dim corridors of time as one of the most delightful to his credit, for the two chapters he now gives to the world are in his very best manner. In spirit and humor, in indirection and ambuscade, in ingenuity and insight, and even in actual theme, they recall *What Maisie Knew*.

The Maisie of this limbless trunk of a story is a young woman of vast charm, whose social progress is hampered by a somewhat disconcerting history. Her mamma, also a lady of charm, is a triple divorcee, and she herself has been engaged no less than half a dozen times. These facts confront her gloomily when a young man of rich but extremely respectable parentage begins to take notice of her. How is she to gloss over and minimize her ghastly past? She begins by tackling her mamma's second husband. Will he be a dear, and suffer the story to be circulated that mamma simply had to leave him, he being an insufferable brute? Gladly, he says—but the fact of the matter is that he thinks of marrying again himself, and the highly virtuous object of his devotion is to be won only upon the theory that mamma was the brute. Julia, staggered, turns to one of her six young men. Will he assure the opulent but moral eligible that there was never any engagement, and so inoculate him with the idea that the five others were also mere gossip? He consents to undertake the office, not only willingly, but even wildly. He will visit the opulent eligible at once, and take his fiancée with him, for there is a successor to Julia in his affections. And then poor Julia begins to doubt the expediency of the whole maneuver. This ex-lover, indeed, is plainly inflamed by the idea of making social capital out of the encounter with the young millionaire.

Here the story ends, with Julia weeping mournfully. It's a pity that Mr. James lost heart. What a novel the history of Julia's battle against the slings and arrows of outrageous fortune, with victory at the end, would have made! ["George Bernard Shaw as a Hero," SS 30, no. 1 (January 1910): 156]

The Finer Grain (1910)

The James book is a collection of five short stories, published under the title of *The Finer Grain*. In the first of them, "The Velvet Glove," we see how John Berridge, a brilliant young American dramatist, "tastes in their fullness the sweets of success." Lolling at his ease in Paris, he is sought out by a young lord—just *what* lord we never find out—who talks to him eloquently about a princess—name also unknown—who yearns to meet him. Berridge glows; he is in full reaction against the democracy of his native soil; it will please him vastly to rub noses with this blooded and exquisite creature. But alas and alack, what bitterness awaits! The princess it turns out has literary ambitions. She has written gushy best-sellers under the name of "Amy Evans." She wants Berridge to do a log rolling preface for her next one. The poor fellow, aghast, backs away. "Why write romances?" he demands. "You *are* Romance. . . . Don't attempt such base things. Leave those to us. Only live. Only be. *We'll* do the rest." And then he kisses her and takes to his heels, a disillusioned and suffering man. A good story. A story capitally told. Easy reading? Perhaps not. But a lot of very fine music, it may be recalled, is not easy listening. ["A Stack of Novels," SS 33, no. 3 (March 1911): 161–62]

The Outcry (1911)

Henry James—good old Henry! Here he is with another of his fugues: *The Outcry*, the tale of a belted earl who proposes to sell certain incomparable handpainted oil paintings, heirlooms of his belted race, to Mr. Breckenridge Bender, an American art wolf, and thereby provokes, from the patriot gullets of his countrymen, the outcry aforesaid. The Jacobin syntax was never more complex, never more baroque. To find its like, in all the realm of artistic endeavor, you must go to that passage in *Ein Heldenleben* which ties twenty-four themes in a knot,⁹ or to the façades of Polish churches in mining towns. Don't ask me to expound it, defend it! There would be a job for the Doctor Subtilissimus himself. But let me assure you meanwhile that *The Outcry*, for all the cruel cacophony of its style, is yet a story with curiously interesting people in it, and a number of incisive observations upon them, and with the wind of wit blowing through it from end to end. ["Conrad, Bennett, James et al.," SS 36, no. 1 (January 1912): 158]

Theodore Dreiser

Jennie Gerhardt (1911)

If you miss reading *Jennie Gerhardt*, by Theodore Dreiser, you will miss the best American novel, all things considered, that has reached the book counters in a dozen years. On second thought, change "a dozen" into "twenty-five." On third thought, strike out everything after "counters." On fourth thought, strike out everything after "novel." Why back and fill? Why evade and qualify? Hot from it, I am firmly convinced that *Jennie Gerhardt* is the best American novel I have ever read, with the lonesome but Himalayan exception of *Huckleberry Finn*, and so I may as well say it aloud and at once and have done with it. Am I forgetting *The Scarlet Letter*, *The Rise of Silas Lapham* and (to drag an exile unwillingly home) *What Maisie Knew*? I am not. Am I forgetting *McTeague* and *The Pit*? I am not. Am I forgetting the stupendous masterpieces of James Fenimore Cooper, beloved of the pedagogues, or those of James Lane Allen, Mrs. Wharton and Dr. S. Weir Mitchell, beloved of the women's clubs and literary monthlies? No. Or *Uncle Tom's Cabin* or *Rob o' the Bowl* or *Gates Ajar* or *Ben Hur* or *David Harum* or *Lewis Rand* or *Richard Carvel?*[10] No. Or *The Hungry Heart* or Mr. Dreiser's own *Sister Carrie?* No. I have all these good and bad books in mind. I have read them and survived them and in many cases enjoyed them.

And yet in the face of them, and in the face of all the high authority, constituted and self-constituted, behind them, it seems to me at this moment that *Jennie Gerhardt* stands apart from all of them, and a bit above them. It lacks the grace of this one, the humor of that one, the perfect form of some other one; but taking it as it stands, grim, gaunt, mirthless, shapeless, it remains, and by long odds, the most impressive work of art that we have yet to show in prose fiction—a tale not unrelated, in its stark simplicity, its profound sincerity, to *Germinal* and *Anna Karenina* and *Lord Jim*—a tale assertively American in its scene and its human material, and yet so European in its method, its point of view, its almost reverential seriousness, that one can scarcely imagine an American writing it. Its personages are few in number, and their progress is along a path that seldom widens, but the effect of that progress is ever one of large movements and large masses. One senses constantly the group behind the individual, the natural law behind the human act. The result is an indefinable impression of bigness, of epic dignity. The thing is not a mere story, not a novel in the ordinary American meaning of the word, but a criticism and an interpretation of life—and that interpretation loses nothing in validity by the fact that its burden is the doctrine that life is meaningless, a tragedy without a moral, a joke without a point. What else have Moore and Conrad and Hardy been telling us these many years? What else does all the new knowledge of a century teach us? One by one the old ready answers have been disposed of. To-day the one intelligible answer to the riddle of aspiration and sacrifice is that there is no answer at all.

"The power to tell the same story in two forms," said George Moore not long ago, "is the sign of the true artist." You will think of this when you read *Jennie Gerhardt,* for in its objective plan, and even in its scheme of subjective unfolding, it suggests *Sister Carrie* at every turn. Reduce it to a hundred words, and those same words would also describe that earlier study of a woman's soul, with scarcely the change of a syllable. Jennie Gerhardt, like Carrie Meeber, is a rose grown from turnip seed. Over each, at the start, hangs poverty, ignorance, the dumb helplessness of the Shudra —and yet in each there is that indescribable something, that element of essential gentleness, that innate, inward beauty which levels all caste barriers and makes Esther a fit queen for Ahasuerus. And the history of each, reduced to its elements, is the history of the other. Jennie, like Carrie, escapes from the physical miseries of the struggle for existence only to taste the worse miseries of the struggle for happiness. Not, of course, that we have in either case a moral, maudlin fable of virtue's fall; Mr. Dreiser, I need scarcely assure you, is too dignified an artist, too sane a man, for any such banality. Seduction, in point of fact, is not all tragedy for either Jennie or Carrie. The gain of each, until the actual event has been left behind and obliterated by experiences more salient and poignant, is rather greater than her loss, and that gain is to the soul as well as to the creature. With the rise from want to security, from fear to ease, comes an awakening of the finer perceptions, a widening of the sympathies, a gradual unfolding of the delicate flower called personality, an increased capacity for loving and living. But with all this, and as a part of it, there comes, too, an increased capacity for suffering—and so in the end, when love slips away and the empty years stretch before, it is the awakened and supersentient woman that pays for the folly of the groping, bewildered girl. The tragedy of Carrie and Jennie, in brief, is not that they are degraded but that they are lifted up, not that they go to the gutter but that they escape the gutter.

But if the two stories are thus variations upon the same somber theme, if each starts from the same place and arrives at the same dark goal, if each shows a woman heartened by the same hopes and tortured by the same agonies, there is still a vast difference between them, and that difference is the measure of the author's progress in his art. *Sister Carrie* was a first sketch, a rough piling-up of observations and impressions, disordered and often incoherent. In the midst of the story of Carrie, Mr. Dreiser paused to tell the story of Hurstwood—an astonishingly vivid and tragic story, true enough, but still one that broke the back of the other. In *Jennie Gerhardt* he falls into no such overelaboration of episode. His narrative goes forward steadily from beginning to end. Episodes there are, of course, but they keep their proper place, their proper bulk. It is always Jennie that holds the attention; it is in Jennie's soul that every scene is ultimately played out. Her father and mother, Senator Brander the god of her first worship, her daughter Vesta and Lester Kane, the man who makes and mars her—all these are drawn with infinite painstaking, and in every one of them there is the blood of life. But it is Jennie that dominates the drama from curtain to curtain. Not an event is unrelated to her; not a climax fails to make clearer the struggles going on in her mind and heart.

I have spoken of reducing *Jennie Gerhardt* to a hundred words. The thing, I fancy, might be actually done. The machinery of the tale is not complex; it has no plot, as plots are understood in these days of "mystery" stories; no puzzles madden the reader. It is dull, unromantic poverty that sends Jennie into the world. Brander finds her there, lightly seduces her, and then discovers that, for some strange gentleness within her, he loves her. Lunacy—but he is willing to face it out. Death, however, steps in; Brander, stricken down without warning, leaves Jennie homeless and a mother. Now enters Lester Kane—not the villain of the books, but a normal, decent, cleanly American of the better class, well to do, level-headed, not too introspective, eager for the sweets of life. He and Jennie are drawn together; if love is not all of the spirit, then it is love that binds them. For half a dozen years the world lets them alone. A certain grave respectability settles over their relation; if they are not actually married, then it is only because marriage is a mere formality, to be put off until to-morrow. But bit by bit they are dragged into the light. Kane's father, dying with millions, gives him two years to put Jennie away. The penalty is poverty; the reward is wealth—and not only wealth itself, but all the pleasant and well remembered things that will come with it: the lost friends of other days, a sense of dignity and importance, an end of apologies and evasions, good society, the comradeship of decent women—particularly the comradeship of one decent woman. Kane hesitates, makes a brave defiance, thinks it over—and finally yields. Jennie does not flood him with tears. She has made progress in the world, has Jennie; the simple faith of the girl has given way to the pride and poise of the woman. Five years later Kane sends for her. He is dying. When it is over, Jennie goes back to her lonely home, and there, like Carrie Meeber before her, she faces the long years with dry eyes and an empty heart. "Days and days in endless reiteration, and then—"

A moral tale? Not at all. It has no more moral than a string quartet or the first book of Euclid. But a philosophy of life is in it, and that philosophy is the same profound pessimism which gives a dark color to the best that we have from Hardy, Moore, Zola and the great Russians—the pessimism of disillusion—not the jejune, Byronic thing, not the green sickness of youth, but that pessimism which comes with the discovery that the riddle of life, despite all the fine solutions offered by the learned doctors, is essentially insoluble. One can discern no intelligible sequence of cause and effect in the agonies of Jennie Gerhardt. She is, as human beings go, of the nobler, finer metal. There is within her a great capacity for service, a great capacity for love, a great capacity for happiness. And yet all that life has to offer her, in the end, is the mere license to live. The days stretch before her "in endless reiteration." She is a prisoner doomed to perpetual punishment for some fanciful, incomprehensible crime against the gods who make their mirthless sport of us all. And to me, at least, she is more tragic thus than Lear on his wild heath or Prometheus on his rock.

Nothing of the art of the literary lapidary is visible in this novel. Its form is the simple one of a panorama unrolled. Its style is unstudied to the verge of barrenness. There is no painful groping for the exquisite, inevitable word; Mr. Dreiser seems content to use the common, even the commonplace coin of speech. On the very first page one encounters "frank, open countenance," "diffident manner," "helpless poor," "untutored mind," "honest necessity" and half a dozen other such ancients. And yet in the long run it is this very *naïveté* which gives the story much of its impressiveness. The narrative, in places, has the effect of a series of unisons in music—an effect which, given a solemn theme, vastly exceeds that of the most ornate polyphony. One cannot imagine *Jennie Gerhardt* done in the gypsy phrases of Meredith, the fugual manner of James. One cannot imagine that stark, stenographic dialogue adorned with the brilliants of speech. The thing could have been done only in the way that it has been done. As it stands, it is a work of art from which I for one would not care to take anything away—not even its gross crudities, its incessant returns to C major. It is a novel that depicts the life we Americans are living with extreme accuracy and criticises that life with extraordinary insight. It is a novel, I am convinced, of the very first consideration. ["A Novel of the First Rank," SS 35, no. 3 (November 1911): 153–55]

The Financier (1912)

Theodore Dreiser's new novel, *The Financier,* shows all of the faults and peculiarities of method that gave a rude, barbarous sort of distinction to his *Sister Carrie* and *Jennie Gerhardt,* those arresting tales of yesteryear. The man does not write as the other novelists of his day and generation write, and, what is more, he does not make any effort to do so, or to have any feeling that such an effort would be worth while. You may read him for page after page, held spellbound by his people and their doings, and yet not find a single pretty turn of phrase, or a single touch of smartness in dialogue, or a single visible endeavor to stiffen a dull scene into drama, or any other such application of artifice or art.

For all the common tricks of writing, in truth, he reveals a degree of disdain amounting almost to denial. He never "teases up" a situation to make it take your breath; he never hurries over something difficult and static in order to get to something easy and dynamic; he never leads you into ambuscades of plot or sets off stylistic fireworks; he never so much as takes the trouble to hunt for a new adjective when an old one will answer as well. In brief, his manner is uncompromisingly forthright, elemental, grim, gaunt, bare. He rolls over the hills and valleys of his narrative at the same patient, lumbering gait, surmounting obstacles by sheer weight and momentum, refusing all short cuts, however eminently trod, as beneath his contempt, and turning his back resolutely upon all the common lifts by the way.

But do I give the impression that the result is dullness, that all this persistent, undeviating effort leads to nothing but a confused and meaningless piling up of words? Then I have described it very badly, for the net effect is precisely the opposite. Out of chaos, by that unceasing pounding, order finally emerges. Out of the disdain of drama comes drama stirring and poignant. Out of that welter of words step human beings, round, ruddy, alive. In other words, Dreiser accomplishes at last, for all his muddling, what men with a hundred times his finesse too often fail to accomplish, and that is, an almost perfect illusion of reality. You may say that he writes with a hand of five thumbs, and that he has no more humor than a hangman, and that he loves assiduity so much that he often forgets inspiration altogether, and you may follow up all of these sayings by ample provings, but in the end you will have to admit that Carrie Meeber is far more real than nine-tenths of the women you actually know, and that old Gerhardt's veritable existence is no more to be doubted than the existence of Père Goriot.

If *The Financier*, on a first reading, leaves a less vivid impression than the two books preceding it, then that apparent falling off is probably due to two things, the first being that its principal character is a man and that in consequence he must needs lack some of the fascinating mystery and appeal of Carrie and Jennie; and the second being that the story stops just as it is beginning (for all its 780 pages!), and so leaves the reader with a sense of incompleteness, of a picture washed in but not wholly painted. Final judgment, indeed, will be impossible until the more important second volume is put beside this first, for it is there that the real drama of Frank Cowperwood's life will be played out. But meanwhile there can be no doubt whatever of the author's firm grip upon the man, nor of his astute understanding of the enormously complex interplay of personalities and events against which the man is projected.

This Cowperwood is meant, I suppose, to be a sort of archetype of the American money king, and despite a good many little deviations he is probably typical enough. The main thing to remember about him is that he is anything but a mere chaser of the dollar, that avarice as a thing in itself is not in him. For the actual dollar, indeed, he has no liking at all, but only the toleration of an artist for his brushes and paint-pots. What he is really after is power, and the way power commonly visualizes itself in this mind is as a means to beauty. He likes all things that caress the eye—a fine rug, an inviting room, a noble picture, a good horse, a pretty woman, particularly a pretty woman. There is in him what might be called an aloof voluptuousness, a dignified hedonism. He is not so much sensual as sensitive. A perfect eyebrow seems to him to be something worth thinking about, soberly and profoundly. The world, in his sight, is endlessly curious and beautiful.

And with this over-development of the æsthetic sense there goes, naturally enough, an under-development of the ethical sense. Cowperwood has little more feeling for right and wrong, save as a setting or a mask for beauty, than a healthy schoolboy. When a chance offers to make a large sum of money by an alliance with political buccaneers, he takes it without the slightest question of its essential virtue. And when, later on, the bucca-neers themselves lay open for pillage, he pillages them with a light heart. And as with means, so with ends. When Aileen Butler, the daughter of his partner and mentor, old Edward Malia Butler, the great political contrac-tor—when Aileen comes his way, radiant and tempting, he debauches her without a moment's thought of consequences, and carries on the affair under old Butler's very nose.

The man is not vicious; a better word for him would be innocent. He has no sense of wrong to Aileen, nor of wrong to Butler, nor even of wrong to the wife of his youth. The only idea that takes clear form in his mind is the idea that Aileen is extremely pleasing, and that it would be a ridiculous piece of folly to let her charms go to waste. Even when he is the conquered instead of the conqueror, not much feeling that an act of conquest can have a moral content appears in him. Old Butler, discovering his affair with Aileen, knocks over his financial house of cards and railroads him to prison, but he shows little rancor against Butler, and less against the oblig-ing catchpolls of the law, but only a vague discontent that fate should bring him such hardships, and take him away from beauty so long.

This term in prison is a salient event in Cowperwood's life, but it can-not be said that it is a turning point. He comes out into the Philadelphia of the early seventies with all his old determination to beat the game. He has been defeated once, true enough, but that defeat has taught him a lot that easy victory might have left unsaid, and he has full confidence that he will win next time. And win he does. Black Friday[11] sees him the most pitilessly ursine of bears, and the next day sees him with a million. He is now on his feet again and able to choose his cards carefully and at leisure. With the ut-most calm he divorces his wife, tucks Aileen under his arm, and sets out for Chicago. There, where the players are settling down for the wildest game of money ever played in the world, he will prove that luck in the long run is with the wise. And there, in the second volume of this history, we shall see him at the proving.

An heroic character, and not without his touches of the admirable. Once admit his honest doubts of the workaday moralities of the world, and at once you range him with all the other memorable battlers against fate, from Prometheus to Etienne Lantier.[12] The achievement of Dreiser is found in this very fact: that he has made the man not only comprehen-

sible, but also a bit tragic. One is conscious of a serene dignity in his chicaneries, and even in his debaucheries, and so his struggle for happiness
becomes truly moving. I am not alluding here to that cheap sympathy
which is so easily evoked by mere rhetoric, but to that higher sympathy
which grows out of a thorough understanding of motives and processes of
mind. This understanding Dreiser insures. Say what you will against his
solemn and onerous piling up of words, his slow plodding through jungles
of detail, his insatiable lust for facts, you must always admit that he gets his
effect in the end. There are no sudden flashes of revelation; the lights are
turned on patiently and deliberately, one by one. But when the thing is
done at last the figure of the financier leaps out amazingly, perfectly mod-
eled, wholly accounted for.

So with the lesser personages, and particularly with Aileen and her father. Old Butler, indeed, is worthy to stand just below the ancient Gerhardt, by long odds the most real of Dreiser's creatures, not even excepting
Carrie Meeber and Hurstwood. You remember Gerhardt, of course, with
his bent back, his squirrel's economies, his mediæval piety and his pathetic
wonderment at the deviltries of the world? Well, Butler is a vastly different
man, if only because he is richer, more intelligent, and more powerful, but
still, in the end, he takes on much of that reality and all of that pathos, raging homerically but impotently against an enemy who eludes him and
defies him and has broken his heart.

And so, too, with the background of the story. I can imagine nothing
more complex than the interplay of finance and politics in war time and
during the days following, when the money kings were just finding themselves and graft was just rising to the splendor of an exact science. And yet
Dreiser works his way through that maze with sure steps, and leaves order
and understanding where confusion reigned. Of tales of municipal corruption we have had a-plenty; scarcely a serious American novelist of to-
day, indeed, has failed to experiment with that endless and recondite
drama. But what other has brought its prodigal details into better sequence
and adjustment, or made them enter more vitally and convincingly into
the characters and adventures of his people? Those people of Dreiser's, indeed, are never the beings in vacuo who populate our common romances.
We never see them save in contact with a vivid and fluent environment, reacting to its constant stimuli, taking color from it, wholly a part of it.

So much for *The Financier*. It is the prologue rather than the play. The real tragi-comedy of Cowperwood's struggle for power and beauty will be played out in Chicago, and of its brilliancy and mordacity we have abundant earnest. Dreiser knows Chicago as few other men know it; he has pierced to the very heart of that most bewildering of cities. And, what is more, he has got his secure grip upon Cowperwood. ["Dreiser's Novel," *New York Times Review of Books*, November 10, 1912, p. 654]

The Titan (1914)

After all, Dr. Munyon is quite right: there is yet hope.[13] Sometimes, of course, it is hard to discern, almost impossible to embrace. Sweating through the best-sellers of the moment, shot from the presses in a gaudy cataract, one can scarcely escape a mood of intense depression, a bleak æsthetic melancholia. What is to become of a nation which buys such imbecile books by the hundred thousand, and not only buys them, but reads them, and not only reads them, but enjoys them, gabbles about them, takes them seriously, even pays reverence to them as literature?

Publishers get rich printing that sort of "literature," and then use their money to bludgeon and browbeat all authors who try to do anything better. Imagine a young American bobbing up with a new *Germinal*, or a new *Lord Jim*, or a new *Brothers Karamazov*: what a job he would have getting it between covers! But let him rise shamelessly out of the old bog of mush, dripping honey and buttermilk, and at once there is silver in his palm and praise in his ear. The Barabbases fight for him, playing one another all kinds of sharp tricks; the newspapers record his amours, his motor accidents and his table talk; the literary monthlies print his portrait (in golf togs) opposite that of Gerhart Hauptmann; the women's clubs forget Bergson and the white slave trade to study his style. In the end, he retires to Palm Beach or Tuscany with a fortune, and so becomes a romantic legend, half genius and half god.

But, as I started out to say, there is yet a glimmer of hope. A small class of more civilized readers begins to show itself here and there; a few daring publishers risk a dollar or two on fiction of an appreciably better sort; the literary monthlies forget their muttons long enough to say a kind word for Joseph Conrad; now and then a genuine artist is seen in the offing. Fate, alas, conspires with stupidity to keep the number down. Frank Norris died just as he was getting into his stride; David Graham Phillips was murdered by a lunatic at the very moment of his deliverance; a dozen others, after diffident bows, have disappeared in ways just as mysterious. But there remains Theodore Dreiser, patient, forthright, earnest, plodding, unswerving, uncompromising—and so long as Dreiser keeps out of jail there will be hope.

Four long novels are now behind him, and in every one of them one sees the same grim fidelity to an austere artistic theory, the same laborious service to a stern and rigorous faith. That faith may be put briefly into two articles: (*a*) that it is the business of a novelist to describe human beings as they actually are, unemotionally, objectively and relentlessly, and not as they might be, or would like to be, or ought to be; and (*b*) that his business is completed when he has so described them, and he is under no obligation to read copybook morals into their lives, or to estimate their virtue (or their lack of it) in terms of an ideal goodness. In brief, the art of Dreiser is almost wholly representative, detached, aloof, unethical: he makes no attempt whatever to provide that pious glow, that mellow sentimentality, that soothing escape from reality, which Americans are accustomed to seek and find in prose fiction. And despite all the enormous advantages of giving them what they are used to and cry for, he has stuck resolutely to his program. In the fourteen years since *Sister Carrie* he has not deviated once, nor compromised once. There are his books: you may take them or leave them. If you have any respect for an artist who has respect for himself, you may care to look into them; if not, you may go to the devil.

In all this, Dreiser runs on a track parallel to Conrad's; the two men suggest each other in a score of ways. Superficially, of course, they may seem to be far apart: the gorgeous colors of Conrad are never encountered in Dreiser. But that difference lies almost wholly in materials; in ideas and methods they are curiously alike. To each the salient fact of life is its utter meaninglessness, its sordid cruelty, its mystery. Each stands in amazement before the human tendency to weigh it, to motivate it, to see esoteric significances in it. Nothing could be more profoundly agnostic and unmoral than Conrad's *Lord Jim* or Dreiser's *Jennie Gerhardt*. In neither book is there the slightest suggestion of a moral order of the world; neither novelist has any blame to hand out, nor any opinion to offer as to the justice or injustice of the destiny he describes. It is precisely here, indeed, that both take their departure from the art of fiction as we of English speech commonly know it. They are wholly emancipated from the moral obsession that afflicts our race; they see the human comedy as a series of inexplicable and unrepresentative phenomena, and not at all as a mere allegory and Sunday school lesson. If art be imagined as a sort of halfway station between science and morals, their faces are plainly turned toward the hard rocks of science, just as the faces of the more orthodox novelists are turned toward pansy beds of morals.

Conrad tells us somewhere that it was Flaubert who helped him to formulate his theory of the novel, with Turgenieff and the other Russians assisting. The influences that moulded Dreiser are not to be stated with such certainty. Here and there one happens upon what seem to be obvious tracks of Zola, but Dreiser, if I remember rightly, has said that he knows the Frenchman only at second hand. Did the inspiration come through Frank Norris, Zola's one avowed disciple in America? Against the supposition stands the fact that *Sister Carrie* followed too soon after *McTeague* to be an imitation of it—and besides, *Sister Carrie* is a far greater novel, in more than one way, than *McTeague* itself. Perhaps some earlier and lesser work of Norris's was the model that the younger man followed, consciously or unconsciously. Norris was his discoverer, and in a sense, his patron saint, battling for him valiantly when the firm of Doubleday, Page & Co. achieved immortality by suppressing *Sister Carrie*. (Some day the whole of this tale must be told. The part that Norris played proved that he was not only a sound critic, but also an extraordinarily courageous and unselfish friend.) But whatever the fact and the process, Dreiser has kept the faith far better than Norris, whose later work, particularly *The Octopus*, shows a disconcerting mingling of honest realism and vaporous mysticism. In Dreiser there has been no such yielding. His last book, *The Titan*, is cut from exactly the same cloth that made *Sister Carrie*. Despite years of critical hammering and misunderstanding, and a number of attacks of a sort even harder to bear, he has made no sacrifice of his convictions and done no treason to his artistic conscience. He may be right or he may be wrong, but at all events he has gone straight ahead.

The Titan, like *Sister Carrie*, enjoys the honor of having been suppressed after getting into type. This time the virtuous act was performed by Harper & Brothers, a firm which provided mirth for the mocking back in the nineties by refusing the early work of Rudyard Kipling. The passing years work strange farces. To-day the American publisher of Kipling is the firm of Doubleday, Page & Co., which suppressed *Sister Carrie* — and *Sister Carrie*, after years upon the town, is now on the vestal list of the Harpers, who bucked at *The Titan!* The grotesque comedy should have been completed by the publication of the latter work by Doubleday, Page & Co., but of this delectable fourth act we were unluckily deprived. Life, alas, is seldom quite artistic. Its phenomena do not fit snugly together, like squares in a checkerboard. But nevertheless the whole story of the adventures of his books would make a novel in Dreiser's best manner — a novel without the slightest hint of a moral. His own career as an artist has been full of the blind and unmeaning fortuitousness that he expounds.

But what of *The Titan* as a work of art? To me, at least, it comes closer to what I conceive to be Dreiser's ideal than any other story he has done. Here, at last, he has thrown overboard all the usual baggage of the novelist, making short and merciless shrift of "heart interest," "sympathy" and even romance. In *Sister Carrie* there was still a sop, however little intended, for the sentimentalists: if they didn't like the history of Carrie as a study of the blind forces which determine human destiny, they could wallow in it as a sad, sad love story. Carrie was pathetic, appealing, melting; she moved, like Marguerite Gautier,[14] in an atmosphere of agreeable melancholy. And Jennie Gerhardt, of course, was merely another Carrie — a Carrie more carefully and objectively drawn, perhaps, but still one to be easily mistaken for a "sympathetic" heroine of the best-sellers. Readers jumped from *The Prisoner of Zenda*[15] to *Jennie Gerhardt* without knowing that they were jumping ten thousand miles. The tear jugs were there to cry into; the machinery seemed to be the same. Even in *The Financier* there was still a hint of familiar things. The first Mrs. Cowperwood was sorely put upon; Cowperwood himself suffered injustice, and pined away in a dungeon.

But no one, I venture to say, will ever make the same mistake about *The Titan* — no one, not even the youngest and fairest, will ever take it for a sentimental romance. Not a single appeal to the emotions is in it; it is a purely intellectual account, as devoid of heroics as a death certificate, of a strong man's savage endeavors to live out his life as it pleases him, regardless of all the subtle and enormous forces that seek to break him to a rule. There is nothing in him of the conventional outlaw; he does not wear a red sash and bellow for liberty; from end to end he issues no melodramatic defiance of the existing order. The salient thing about him is precisely his avoidance of all such fine feathers and sonorous words. He is no hero at all, but merely an extraordinary gamester—sharp, merciless, tricky, insatiable. One stands amazed before his marvelous resourcefulness and daring, his absolute lack of conscience, but there is never the slightest effort to cast a romantic glamour over him, to raise sympathy for him, to make it appear that he is misunderstood, unfortunate, persecuted. Even in love he is devoid of the old glamour of the lover. Even in disaster he asks for no quarter, no generosity, no compassion. Up or down, he is sufficient unto himself.

The man is the same Cowperwood who came a cropper in *The Financier*, but he has now reached middle age, and all the faltering weakness and irresolutions of his youth are behind him. He knows exactly what he wants, and in the Chicago of the early eighties he proceeds to grab it. The town is full of other fellows with much the same aspirations, but Cowperwood has the advantage over them that he has already fallen off his wall and survived, and so he lacks that sneaking fear of consequences which holds them in check. In brief, they are brigands with one eye on the *posse comitatus*, while he is a brigand with both eyes on the swag. The result, as may be imagined, is a combat truly homeric in its proportions—a combat in which associated orthodoxy in rapine is pitted against the most fantastic and astounding heterodoxy. The street railways of Chicago are the prize, and Cowperwood fights for control of them with all the ferocity of a hungry hyena and all the guile of a middle-aged serpent. His devices are staggering and unprecedented, even in that town of surprises. He makes a trial of every crime in the calendar of roguery, from blackmail to downright pillage. And though, in the end, he is defeated in his main purpose, for the enemy takes the cars, he is yet so far successful that he goes away with a lordly share of the profits, and leaves behind him a memory like that of a man-eating tiger in an Indian village.

A mere hero of melodrama? A brother to Monte Cristo and Captain Kidd? A play-acting superman, stalking his gorgeous heights? Far from it, indeed. The very charm of the man, as I have hinted before, lies in his utter lack of obvious charm. He is not sentimental. He is incapable of attitudinizing. He makes no bid for that homage which goes to the conscious outlaw, the devil-of-a-fellow. Even in his amours, which are carried on as boldly and as copiously as his chicaneries, there is no hint of the barbered Don Juan, the professional scourge of virtue. Cowperwood pursues women unmorally, almost innocently. He seduces the wives and daughters of friends and enemies alike; there is seldom any conscious purpose to dramatize and romanticize the adventure. Women are attractive to him simply because they represent difficulties to be surmounted, problems to be solved, personalities to be brought into subjection, and he in his turn is attractive to women simply because he transcends all that they know, or think they know, of men. There must be at least a dozen different maids and wives in his story, and in one way or another they all contribute to his final defeat, but there is nothing approaching a grand affair. At no time is a woman hunt the principal business before him. At no time does one charmer blind him to all others. Even at the close, when we see him genuinely smitten, an easy fatalism still conditions his eagerness, and he waits with unflagging patience for the victory that finally rewards him.

Such a man, described romantically, would be undistinguishable from the wicked earls and seven-foot guardsmen of Ouida and the Duchess.[16] But described realistically, with all that wealth of minute and apparently inconsequential detail which Dreiser piles up so amazingly, he becomes a figure astonishingly vivid, lifelike and engrossing. He fits into no *a priori* theory of conduct or scheme of rewards and punishments; he proves nothing and teaches nothing; the motives which move him are never obvious and frequently unintelligible. But in the end he seems genuinely a man — a man of the sort that we see about us in the real world — not a transparent and simple fellow, reacting docilely according to a formula, but a bundle of complexities and contradictions, a creature oscillating between the light and the shadow, a unique and, at bottom, inexplicable personality. It is here that Dreiser gets farthest from the wallowed rut of fiction. The Cowperwood he puts before us is not the two-dimensional cut-out, the facile jumping jack, of the ordinary novel, but a being of three dimensions and innumerable planes — in brief, the impenetrable mystery that is man. The makers of best-sellers, if they could imagine him at all, would seek to account for him, explain him, turn him into a moral (*i.e.*, romantic) equation. Dreiser is content to describe him.

Naturally enough, the lady reviewers of the newspapers have been wholly flabbergasted by the book. Unable to think of a character in a novel save in terms of the characters in other novels, they have sought to beplaster Cowperwood with the old, old labels. He is the Wealthy Seducer, the Captain of Industry, the Natural Polygamist, the Corruptionist, the Franchise Grabber, the Bribe Giver, the Plutocrat, the Villain. Some of them, intelligent enough to see that not one of these labels actually fits, have interpreted the fact as a proof of Dreiser's incapacity. He is denounced for creating a Cowperwood who is not like other capitalists, not like other lawbreakers, not like other voluptuaries—that is to say, not like the capitalists, lawbreakers and voluptuaries of Harold MacGrath, E. Phillips Oppenheim and Richard Harding Davis. And one hears, too, the piping voice of outraged virtue: a man who chases women in his leisure and captures a dozen or so in twenty years is ungentlemanly, un-American, indecent— and therefore ought not to be put into a book. But I do not think that Dreiser is going to be stopped by such piffle, nor even by the more damaging attacks of smug and preposterous publishers. He has stuck to his guns through thick and thin, and he is going to stick to them to the end of the chapter. And soon or late, unless I err very grievously, he is going to reap the just reward of a sound and courageous artist, just as George Meredith reaped it before him, and Joseph Conrad is beginning to reap it even now. ["Adventures among the New Novels," SS 43, no. 4 (August 1914): 153–57]

The "Genius" (1915)

On page 703 of Theodore Dreiser's new novel, The "Genius," the gentleman described by the title, Eugene Tennyson Witla by name, is on his way to a Christian Scientist to apply for treatment for "his evil tendencies in regard to women." Remember the place: page 703. The reader, by this time, has hacked and gummed his way through 702 large pages of fine print: 97 long chapters: more than 300,000 words. The stage-hands stand ready to yank down the curtain; messieurs of the orchestra, their minds fixed eagerly upon malt liquor, are up to their hips in the finale; the weary nurses are swabbing up the operating room; the learned chirurgeons are wiping their knives upon their pantaloons; the rev. clergy are swinging into the benediction; the inexorable embalmer waits in the ante-chamber with his unescapable syringe, his Mona Lisa smile. . . . And then, at this painfully hurried and impatient point, with the *coda* already under weigh and even the most somnolent reaching nervously for his goloshes, Dreiser halts the whole show to explain the origin, nature and inner meaning of Christian Science, and to make us privy to a lot of chatty stuff about Mrs. Althea Johns, the lady-like healer, and to supply us with detailed plans and specifications of the joint, lair or apartment-house in which this fair sorceress lives, works her miracles, trims her boobs,[17] and has her being!

Believe me, I do not spoof. Turn to page 703 and see for yourself. There, while the fate of Witla waits and the bowels of patience are turned to water, we are instructed and tortured with the following particulars about the house:

1. That it was "of conventional design."
2. That there was "a spacious areaway" between its two wings.
3. That these wings were "of cream-colored pressed brick."
4. That the entrance between them "was protected by a handsome wrought-iron door."
5. That to either side of this door was "an electric lamp support of handsome design."
6. That in each of these lamp supports there were "lovely cream-colored globes, shedding a soft lustre."
7. That "inside was the usual lobby."
8. That in the lobby was the usual elevator.
9. That in the elevator was the usual "uniformed negro elevator man."
10. That this negro elevator man (name not given) was "indifferent and impertinent."
11. That a telephone switchboard was also in the lobby.
12. That the building was seven stories in height.

Such is novel-writing as Dreiser understands it—a laborious and relentless meticulousness, an endless piling up of small details, an almost furious tracking down of ions, electrons and molecules. One is amazed and flabbergasted by the mole-like industry of the man, and no less by his lavish disregard for the ease and convenience of his readers. A Dreiser novel, at least of the later canon, cannot be read as other novels are read, *e. g.*, on a winter evening or a summer afternoon, between meal and meal, travelling from New York to Boston. It demands the attention for at least a week, and uses up the strength for at least a month. If, tackling The *"Genius,"* one were to become engrossed in the fabulous manner described by the newspaper reviewers and so find oneself unable to put it down and go to bed before the end, one would get no sleep for three days and three nights. A man who can prove that he has read such a novel without medical assistance should be admitted to the *Landwehr* at once, without thesis or examination, and perhaps even given the order *pour la mérite.* A woman of equal attainments is tough enough to take in washing or to sing Brunnhilde. . . .

And yet, and yet—well, here comes the inevitable "and yet." For all his long-windedness, for all his persistent refusal to get about his business, for all his mouthing of things so small that they seem to be nothings, this Dreiser is undoubtedly a literary artist of very respectable rank, and nothing proves it more certainly than this, the last, the longest and one is tempted to add the damnedest of his novels. The thing is staggering, alarming, maddening—and yet one sticks to it. It is rambling, formless, chaotic—and yet there emerges out of it, in the end, a picture of almost blinding brilliancy, a panorama that will remain in the mind so long as memory lasts. Is it necessary to proceed against the reader in so barbarous a manner? Is there no way of impressing him short of wearing him out? Is there no route to his consciousness save laparotomy? God knows. But this, at all events, is plain: that no other route is open to Dreiser. He must do his work in his own manner, and his oafish clumsiness and crudeness are just as much a part of it as his amazing steadiness of vision, his easy management of gigantic operations, his superb sense of character. One is familiar with stylist-novelists, fellows who tickle with apt phrases, workers in psychological miniature, carvers of cameos. Here is one who works with a steam-shovel, his material being a county. Here is a wholesaler in general merchandise. Here, if such a fellow as Henry James be likened to a duellist, is the Hindenburg of the novel.

And what have we, precisely, in the story of Eugene Tennyson Witla? A tale enormous and indescribable—the chronicle, not only of Witla's own life, but also of the lives of a dozen other persons, some of them of only the slightest influence upon him. And what sort of man is this Witla?

In brief, an artist, but though he actually paints pictures and even makes a success of it, not the artist of conventional legend, not a moony fellow in a velvet coat. What the story of Witla shows us, in truth, is very much the same thing that the story of Frank Cowperwood, in *The Financier* and *The Titan*, showed us, to wit, the reaction of the artistic temperament against the unfavorable environment of this grand and glorious republic. If a Wagner or a Beethoven were born in the United States to-morrow it is highly improbable that he would express himself in the way that those men did; if a Raphael or a Cézanne, it is even more unlikely. The cause thereof is not that we disesteem music and painting, but that we esteem certain other arts infinitely more, particularly the art of creating vast industrial organisms, of bringing the scattered efforts of thousands of workers into order and coherence, of conjuring up huge forces out of spent and puny attractions and repulsions. Witla, as I have said, tries conventional art; he even goes to Paris and sets up as a genius of Montmartre. But his creative instinct and intelligence are soon challenged by larger opportunities; he is too thoroughly an American to waste himself upon pictures to hang upon walls. Instead he tackles jobs that better fit his race and time, and so, after a while, we see him at the head of a mammoth publishing house, with irons in half a dozen other fires—a boss American with all the capacity for splendor that goes with the species.

The chief apparent business of the story, indeed, is to show Witla's rise to this state of splendor, and its corrupting effect upon his soul. To this extent Dreiser plays the moralist: he, too, is an American, and cannot escape it altogether. Witla mounts the ladder of riches rung by rung, and at each rise he yields more and more to the lavishness surrounding him. He acquires fast horses, objects of art, the physical comforts of a sultan. His wife, out of Wisconsin, is hung with fragile and costly draperies; his home is a thing for the decorator to boast about; his very office has something of the luxurious gaudiness of a bordello. Bit by bit he is conquered by this pervasive richness, this atmosphere of gorgeous ease. His appetite increases as dish follows dish upon the groaning table that fate has set for him; he acquires, by subtle stages, the tastes, the prejudices, the point of view of a man of wealth; his creative faculty, disdaining its old objects, concentrates itself upon the moulding and forcing of opportunities for greater and greater acquisitions. And so his highest success becomes his deepest degradation, and we see the marks of his disintegration multiply as he approaches it. He falls, indeed, almost as fast as he rises. It is a collapse worthy of melodrama. (Again the moral note!)

I say that this rise and fall make the chief business of the story, but that, of course, is only externally. Its inner drama presents a conflict between the two Witlas—the artist who is trying to create something, however meretricious, however undeserving his effort, and the sentimentalist whose longing is to be loved, coddled, kept at ease. This conflict, of course, is at the bottom of the misery of all men who may be truly said to be conscious creatures—that is, of all men above the grade of car conductor, barber, waiter or Sunday-school superintendent. On the one hand there is the desire to exert power, to do something that has not been done before, to bend reluctant material to one's will, and on the other hand there is the desire for comfort, for well-being, for an easy life. This latter desire, nine times out of ten, perhaps actually always, is visualized by women. Women are the conservatives and conservators, the enemies of hazard and innovation, the compromisers and temporizers. That very capacity for mothering which is their supreme gift is the greatest of all foes to masculine enterprise. Most men, alas, yield to it. In the common phrase, they marry and settle down—i. e., they give up all notion of making the world over. This resignationism usually passes for happiness, but to the genuine artist it is quite impossible. He must go on sacrificing ease to aspiration and aspiration to ease, thus vacillating abominably and forever between his two irreconcilable desires. No such man is ever happy, not even in the moment of his highest achievement. Life, to him, must always be a muddled and a tragic business. The best he can hope for is a makeshift and false sort of contentment.

This is what Eugene Tennyson Witla comes to in the end. Women have been the curse of his life, from the days of his nonage onward. Forced into their arms constantly by an irresistible impulse, an unquenchable yearning for their facile caresses, he has been turned aside as constantly from his higher goals and led into smoother and broader paths. Good, bad and indifferent, they have all done him harm. His own wife, clinging to him pathetically through good and evil report, always ready to take him back after one of his innumerable runnings amuck, is perhaps his greatest enemy among them. She is always ten yards behind him, hanging on to his coat-tails, trying to drag him back. She is fearful when he needs daring, stupid when he needs stimulation, virtuously wifely when the thing he craves is wild adventure. But the rest all fail him, too. Seeking for joy he finds only bitterness. It is the gradual slowing down of the machine, mental and physical, that finally brings him release. Slipping into the middle forties he begins to turn, almost imperceptibly at first, from the follies of his early manhood. When we part from him at last he seems to have found what he has been so long seeking in his little daughter. The lover has merged into the father.

It is upon this tale, so simple in its main outlines, that Dreiser spills more than 300,000 long and short words, most of them commonplace, many of them improperly used. His writing, which in *The Titan* gave promise of rising to distinction and even to something resembling beauty, is here a mere dogged piling up of nouns, adjectives, verbs, adverbs, pronouns and particles, and as devoid of æsthetic quality as an article in the *Nation*. I often wonder if he gets anything properly describable as pleasure out of his writing—that is, out of the actual act of composition. To the man who deals in phrases, who gropes for the perfect word, who puts the way of saying it above the thing actually said, there is in writing the constant joy of sudden discovery, of happy accident. But what joy can there be in rolling up sentences that have no more life or beauty in them, intrinsically, than so many election bulletins? Where is the thrill in the manufacture of such a paragraph as that I have referred to above, in which the apartment-house infested by Mrs. Althea Johns is described as particularly as if it were being offered for sale? Or in the laborious breeding of such guff as this, from Book I, Chapter IV:

> The city of Chicago—who shall portray it! This vast ruck of life that had sprung suddenly into existence upon the dank marshes of a lake shore.

But why protest and repine? Dreiser writes in this banal fashion, I dessay, because God hath made him so, and a man is too old, at my time of life, to begin criticising the Creator. But all the same it may do no harm to point out, quite academically, that a greater regard for fairness of phrase and epithet would be as a flow of Pilsner to the weary reader in his journey

across the vast deserts, steppes and pampas of the Dreiserian fable. Myself
no voluptuary of letters, searching fantodishly for the rare tit-bit, the suc-
culent morsel, I have yet enough sensitiveness to style to suffer damnably
when all style is absent. And so with form. The well-made novel is as irritating as the well-made play—but let it at least have a beginning, a middle
and an end! Such a confection as The "Genius" is as shapeless as a
Philadelphia pie-woman. It billows and rolls and bulges out like a cloud of
smoke, and its internal organization is as vague. There are episodes that,
with a few chapters added, would make very respectable novels. There are
chapters that need but a touch or two to be excellent short stories. The
thing rambles, staggers, fumbles, trips, wobbles, straggles, strays, heaves,
pitches, reels, totters, wavers. More than once it seems to be foundering, in
both the equine and the maritime senses. The author forgets it, goes out to
get a drink, comes back to find it smothering. One has heard of the tree so
tall that it took two men to see to the top of it. Here is a novel so huge that
a whole shift of critics is needed to read it. Did I myself do it all alone? By
no means. I read only the first and last paragraphs of each chapter. The rest
I farmed out to my wife and children, to my cousin Ferd, and to my pastor
and my beer man.

Nathless, as I have before remarked, the composition hath merit. The
people in it have the fogginess and impenetrability of reality; they stand before us in three dimensions; their sufferings at the hands of fate are genuinely poignant. Of the situations it is sufficient to say that they do not seem
like "situations" at all: they unroll aimlessly, artlessly, inevitably, like actual
happenings. A weakness lies in the background: New York is vastly less interesting than Chicago. At all events, it is vastly less interesting to Dreiser,
and so he cannot make it as interesting to the reader. And no wonder.
Chicago is the epitome of the United States, of the New World, of youth. It
shows all the passion for beauty, the high striving, the infinite curiosity, the
unashamed hoggishness, the purple romance, the gorgeous lack of humor
of twenty-one. Save for San Francisco, it is the only American city that has
inspired a first-rate novel in twenty-five years. Dreiser's best books, Sister
Carrie, Jennie Gerhardt and The Titan, deal with it. His worst, The Financier, is a gallant but hopeless effort to dramatize Philadelphia—a superb subject for a satirist, but not for a novelist. In The "Genius" he makes
the costly blunder of bringing Witla from Chicago to New York. It would

have been a better story, I venture, if that emigration had been left out of it.
. . . ["A Literary Behemoth," *SS* 47, no. 4 (December 1915): 150–54]

A Hoosier Holiday (1916)

The similarity between the fundamental ideas of Joseph Conrad and
those of Theodore Dreiser, so often exhibited to the public gape in this
place, is made plain beyond all shadow of cavil by the appearance of
Dreiser's *A Hoosier Holiday*, a volume of mingled reminiscence, observation, speculation and confession of faith. Put the book beside Conrad's *A
Personal Record* (Harper, 1912), and you will find parallels from end to end.
Or better still, put it beside Hugh Walpole's little volume, *Joseph Conrad*,
in which the Conradean metaphysic is condensed from the novels even
better than Conrad has done it himself: at once you will see how the two
novelists, each a worker in the elemental emotions, each a rebel against
the prevailing cocksureness and superficiality, each an alien to his place
and time, touch each other in a hundred ways.

"Conrad," says Walpole (himself a very penetrating and competent
novelist), "is of the firm and resolute conviction that life is too strong, too
clever and too remorseless for the sons of men." And then, in amplifica-
tion: "It is as though, from some high window, looking down, he were able
to watch some shore, from whose security men were forever launching little cockleshell boats upon a limitless and angry sea . . . From his height he
can follow their fortunes, their brave struggles, their fortitude to the very
end. He admires that courage, the simplicity of that faith, but his irony
springs from his knowledge of the inevitable end." . . . Substitute the name
of Dreiser for that of Conrad, with *A Hoosier Holiday* as text, and you will
have to change scarcely a word. Perhaps one, to wit, "clever." I suspect that
Dreiser, writing so of his own creed, would be tempted to make it "stupid,"
or, at all events, "unintelligible." The struggle of man, as he sees it, is more
than impotent; it is meaningless. There is, to his eye, no grand ingenuity,
no skillful adaptation of means to end, no moral (or even dramatic) plan
in the order of the universe. He can get out of it only a sense of profound
and inexplicable *dis*order, of a seeking without a finding. There is not only
no neat programme of rewards and punishments; there is not even an
understandable balance of causes and effects. The waves which batter the

cockleshells change their direction at every instant. Their navigation is a vast adventure, but intolerably fortuitous and inept—a voyage without chart, compass, sun or stars . . .

So at bottom. But to look into the blackness steadily, of course, is almost beyond the endurance of man. In the very moment that its impenetrability is grasped the imagination begins attacking it with pale beams of false light. All religions, I dare say, are thus projected from the soul of man, and not only all religions, but also all great agnosticisms. Nietzsche, shrinking from the horror of that abyss of negation, revived the Pythagorean concept of *der ewigen Wiederkunft*[8]—a vain and blood-curdling sort of comfort. To it, after a while, he added explanations almost Christian—a whole repertoire of whys and wherefores, aims and goals, aspirations and significations. Other seers have gone back even further: the Transcendentalists stemmed from Zeno of Elea. The late Mark Twain, in an unpublished work, toyed with a characteristically daring idea: that men are to some unimaginably vast and incomprehensible Being what the unicellular organisms of his body are to man, and so on *ad infinitum*. Dreiser occasionally dallies with much the same notion; he likens the endless reactions going on in the world we know, the myriadal creation, collision and destruction of entities, to the slow accumulation and organization of cells *in utero*. He would make us specks in the insentient embryo of some gigantic Presence whose form is still unimaginable and whose birth must wait for eons and eons. Again, he turns to something not easily distinguishable from philosophical idealism, whether out of Berkeley or Fichte it is hard to make out—that is, he would interpret the whole phenomenon of life as no more than an appearance, a nightmare of some unseen sleeper or of men themselves, an "uncanny blur of nothingness"—in Euripides' phrase, "a tale told by an idiot, dancing down the wind." Yet again, he talks vaguely of the intricate polyphony of a cosmic orchestra, cacophonous to our dull ears. Finally, he puts the observed into the ordered, reading a purpose in the displayed event: "life was intended as a spectacle, it was intended to sting and hurt" . . . But these are only gropings, and not to be read too critically. From speculations and explanations he always returns, Conrad-like, to the bald fact: to "the spectacle and stress of life." The bolder flights go with the puerile solutions of current religion and morals. Even more than Conrad, he sees life as a struggle in which man is not only

doomed to defeat, but denied any glimpse or understanding of his antagonist. His philosophy is an agnosticism that has almost got beyond curiosity.
What good would it do us, he asks, to know? In our ignorance and helplessness, we may at least get a slave's comfort out of cursing the gods. Suppose we saw them striving blindly too, and pitied them?

The function of poetry, says F. C. Prescott, in *Poetry and Dreams* (a
book so modest and yet so searching that it will be years before the solemn
donkeys of the seminaries ever hear of it), is to conjure up for us a vivid
picture of what we want, but cannot get.[19] The desire is half of the story,
but the inhibition is as plainly the other half, and of no less importance. It
is this element that gives its glamour to tragedy; the mind seizes upon the
image as a substitute for the reality, and the result is the psychical *kathar-
sis* described by Aristotle. It is precisely by the same process that Dreiser
and Conrad get a profound and melancholy poetry into their books. Floating above the bitter picture of what actually is, there is always the misty but
inordinately charming picture of what might be or ought to be. Here we
get a clue to the method of both men, and to the secret of their capacity for
reaching the emotions. All of Conrad's brilliant and poignant creatures are
dreamers who go to smash upon the rocks of human weakness and stupidity — Kurtz, Nostromo, Lord Jim, Almayer, Razumov, Heyst, even Whalley
and M'Whirr. And so with Carrie Meeber, Jennie Gerhardt, Frank Cowperwood and Eugene Witla. They are not merely vivid and interesting figures; they are essentially tragic figures, and in their tragedy, despite its
superficial sordidness, there is a deep and ghostly poetry. "My task," said
Conrad once, "is, by the power of the printed word, to make you hear, to
make you feel — it is, above all, to make you *see.*" Comprehension, sympathy, pity — these are the things he seeks to evoke. And these, too, are the
things that Dreiser seeks to evoke. The reader does not arise from such a
book as *Sister Carrie* with a smirk of satisfaction, as he might from a novel
by Howells or James; he leaves it infinitely touched . . .

Mr. Walpole, in his little book, is at pains to prove that Conrad is neither realist nor romanticist, but an intricate combination of both. The thesis scarcely needs support, or even statement: *all* imaginative writers of the
higher ranks are both. Plain realism, as in the early Zola, simply wearies us
by its futility; plain romance, if we ever get beyond youth, makes us laugh.
It is their artistic combination, as in life itself, that fetches us — the subtle

projection of the muddle that is living against the orderliness that we reach out for—the eternal war of aspiration and experience—the combat of man and his destiny. As I say, this contrast lies at the bottom of all that is vital and significant in imaginative writing; to argue for it is to wade in platitudes. I speak of it here simply because the more stupid of Dreiser's critics—and what author has ever been hoofed by worse asses!—insist upon seeing him and denouncing him as a realist, and as a realist only. One of them, for example, has lately printed a long article maintaining that he is blind to the spiritual side of man altogether, and that he accounts for his characters solely by some incomprehensible "theory of animal behaviour." Could one imagine a more absurd mouthing of a phrase? One is almost staggered, indeed, by such critical imbecility, even in a college professor. The truth is, of course, that all of Dreiser's novels deal fundamentally with the endless conflict between this "animal behaviour" and the soarings of the spirit—between the destiny forced upon his characters by their environment, their groping instincts, their lack of courage and resourcefulness, and the destiny they picture for themselves in their dreams. This is the tragedy of Carrie Meeber and Jennie Gerhardt. The physical fact of their "seduction" (they are willing enough) blasts them doubly, for on the one hand it brings down upon them the conventional burden of the pariah, and on the other hand the worldly advancement which follows widens their aspiration beyond their inherent capacities, and so augments their unhappiness. It is the tragedy, too, of Cowperwood and Witla. To see these men as mere melodramatic Don Juans is to fall into an error almost unimaginably ridiculous. The salient fact about them, indeed, is that they are *not* mere Don Juans—that they are men in whom the highest idealism strives against the bonds of the flesh. Witla, passion-torn, goes down to disaster and despair. It is what remains of the wreck of his old ideals that floats him into peace at last. As for Cowperwood, we have yet to see his actual end—but how plainly its shadows are cast before! Life is beating him, and through his own weakness. There remains for him, as for Lord Jim, only the remnant of a dream.

With so much ignorant and misleading criticism of him going about, the appearance of A *Hoosier Holiday* should be of service to Dreiser's reputation, for it shows the man as he actually is, stripped of all the scarlet trappings hung upon him by horrified lady reviewers, male and female.

The book, indeed, is amazingly naïf. Slow in tempo, discursive, medita-tive, it covers a vast territory, and lingers in far fields. One finds in it an al-most complete confession of faith, artistic, religious, even political. And not infrequently that confession comes in the form of somewhat discon-certing confidences—about the fortunes of the house of Dreiser, the dis-persed Dreiser family, the old neighbors in Indiana, new friends made along the way. As readers of A *Traveller at Forty*[20] are well aware, Dreiser knows little of reticence, and is no slave to prudery. In that earlier book he described the people he encountered exactly as he saw them, without for-getting a vanity or a wart. In A *Hoosier Holiday* he goes even further: he speculates about them, prodding into the motives behind their acts, won-dering what they would do in this or that situation, forcing them painfully into laboratory jars. They become, in the end, not unlike characters in a novel; one misses only the neatness of a plot. Strangely enough, the one personage of the chronicle who remains dim throughout is the artist, Franklin Booth, Dreiser's host and companion on the long motor ride from New York to Indiana, and the maker of the book's excellent pictures. One gets a brilliant etching of Booth's father, and scarcely less vivid por-traits of Speed, the chauffeur; of various persons encountered on the way, and of friends and relatives dredged up out of the abyss of the past. But of Booth one learns little save that he is a Christian Scientist and a fine figure of a man. There must have been much talk during those two weeks of ca-reening along the high-road, and Booth must have borne some part in it, but what he said is very meagrely reported, and so he is still somewhat vague at the end—a personality sensed, but scarcely apprehended.

However, it is Dreiser himself who is the chief character of the story, and who stands out from it most brilliantly. One sees in the man all the special marks of the novelist: his capacity for photographic and relentless observation, his insatiable curiosity, his keen zest in life as a spectacle, his comprehension of and sympathy for the poor striving of humble folks, his endless mulling of insoluble problems, his recurrent Philistinism, his im-patience of restraints, his suspicion of messiahs, his passion for physical beauty, his relish for the gaudy drama of big cities, his incurable Ameri-canism. The panorama that he enrolls runs the whole scale of the colors; it is a series of extraordinarily vivid pictures. The sombre gloom of the Pennsylvania hills, with Wilkes-Barré lying among them like a gem; the

procession of little country towns, sleepy and a bit hoggish; the flash of
Buffalo, Cleveland, Indianapolis; the gargantuan coal-pockets and ore-
docks along the Erie shore; the tinsel summer resorts; the lush Indiana
farm-lands, with their stodgy, bovine people—all of these things are
sketched in simply, and yet almost magnificently. I know, indeed, of no
book which better describes the American hinterland. Here we have no
idle spying by a stranger, but a full-length representation by one who
knows the thing he describes intimately, and is himself a part of it. Almost
every mile of the road travelled has been Dreiser's own road in life. He
knew those unkempt Indiana towns in boyhood; he wandered in the Indiana woods; he came to Toledo, Cleveland, Buffalo as a young man; all the
roots of his existence are out there. And so he does his chronicle *con
amore*, with many a sentimental dredging up of old memories, old hopes
and old dreams.

Strangely enough, for all the literary efflorescence of the Middle West,
such pictures of it are very rare. I know, in fact, of no other on the same
scale. It is, in more than one way, the heart of America, and yet it has gone
undescribed. Dreiser remedies that lack with all his characteristic labori-
ousness and painstaking. When he has done with them, those drowsy villages and oafish country towns have grown as real as the Chicago of *Sister
Carrie* and *The Titan*. One sees a land that blinks and naps in the sunshine
like some great cow, udders full, the cud going—a land of Dutch fatness
and contentment—a land, despite its riches, of almost unbelievable stupidity and immobility. We get a picture of a typical summer afternoon;
mile after mile of farms, villages, little towns, the people sleepy and empty
in mind, lolling on their verandas, killing time between trivial events, shut
off from all the turmoil of the world. What, in the end, will come out of
this over-fed, too-happy region? Ideas? Rebellions? The spark to set off
great wars? Or only the silence of decay? In Ohio industry has already invaded the farms; chimneys arise among the haystacks. And so farther west.
But in Indiana there is a back-water, a sort of American Midi, a neutral
ground in the battles of the nation. It has no art, no great industry, no dom-
inating men. Its literature, in the main, is a feeble romanticism for flappers
and fat women. Its politics is a skeptical opportunism. It is not stirred by
great passions. It knows no heroes. . . . What will be the end of it? Which
way is it heading?

Save for passages in *The Titan*, *A Hoosier Holiday* marks the high tide
of Dreiser's writing—that is, as sheer writing. His old faults are in it, and
plentifully. There are empty, brackish phrases enough, God knows—
"high noon" among them. But for all that, there is an undeniable glow in
it; it shows, in more than one place, an approach to style; the mere wholesaler of words has become, in some sense, a connoisseur, even a voluptuary. The picture of Wilkes-Barré girt in by her hills is simply done, and
yet there is imagination in it and touches of brilliance. The sombre beauty
of the Pennsylvania mountains is vividly transferred to the page. The towns
by the wayside are differentiated, swiftly drawn, made to live. There are excellent sketches of people—a courtly hotelkeeper in some God-forsaken
hamlet, his self-respect triumphing over his wallow; a group of babbling
Civil War veterans, endlessly mouthing incomprehensible jests; the half-
grown beaux and belles of the summer resorts, enchanted and yet a bit
staggered by the awakening of sex; Booth *père* and his sinister politics; broken and forgotten men in the Indiana towns; policemen, waitresses, farmers, country characters; Dreiser's own people—the boys and girls of his
youth; his brother Paul, the Indiana Schneckenburger and Francis Scott
Key, author of "On the Banks of the Wabash";[21] his sisters and brothers; his
beaten, hopeless, pious father; his brave and noble mother. The book is
dedicated to this mother, now long dead, and in a way it is a memorial to
her, a monument to affection. Life bore upon her cruelly; she knew
poverty at its lowest ebb and despair at its bitterest; and yet there was in her
a touch of fineness that never yielded, a gallant spirit that faced and fought
things through. *Une âme grande dans un petit destin:* a great soul in a small
destiny! One thinks, somehow, of the mother of Gounod. . . . Her son has
not forgotten her. His book is her epitaph. He enters into her presence with
love and with reverence and with something not far from awe. . . .

In sum, this record of a chance holiday is much more than a mere
travel book, for it offers, and for the first time, a clear understanding of the
fundamental faiths and ideas, and of the intellectual and spiritual background no less, of a man with whom the future historian of American literature will have to deal at no little length. Dreiser, as yet, has not come
into his own. In England his true stature has begun to be recognized, and
once the war is over I believe that he will be "discovered," as the phrase is,
in Germany and Russia, and perhaps in France. But in his own country he

is still denied and belabored in a manner that would be comic were it not
so pathetically stupid. The college professors rail and snarl at him in the
Nation and the *Dial*; the elderly virgins of the newspapers represent him
as an iconoclast, an immoralist, an Anti-Christ, even a German spy; the
professional moralists fatuously proceed to jail him because his Witlas and
his Cowperwoods are not eunuchs—more absurdly still, because a few
"God damns" are scattered through the 736 crowded pages of *The "Genius."* The Puritan fog still hangs over American letters; it is formally de-
manded that all literature be made with the girl of sixteen in mind, and
that she be assumed to be quite ignorant of sex. And the orthodox teachers
sing the hymn that is lined out. In Prof. Fred Lewis Pattee's *History of
American Literature Since 1870*, just published, there is no mention of
Dreiser whatever! Such novelists as Owen Wister, Robert W. Chambers
and Holman F. Day are mentioned as "leaders"; substantial notices are
given to Capt. Charles King, Blanche Willis Howard and Julian
Hawthorne; five whole pages are dedicated to F. Marion Crawford; even
Richard Harding Davis, E. P. Roe and "Octave Thanet" are soberly estimated. But not a line about Dreiser! Not an incidental mention of him!
One recalls Richardson's *American Literature*, with its contemptuous dismissal of Mark Twain.[22] A sapient band, these college professors!

But the joke, of course, is not on Dreiser, but on the professors themselves, and on the host of old maids, best-seller fanatics and ecstatic Puritans who support them. Time will bring the Indianan his revenge, and
perhaps he will yield to humor and help time along. A Dreiser novel with
a Puritan for its protagonist would be something to caress the soul—a full-
length portrait of the Eternal Pharisee, a limning of the Chemically Pure,
done scientifically, relentlessly, affectionately. Dreiser knows the animal
from snout to tail. He could do a picture that would live. . . . ["The Creed
of a Novelist," *SS* 50, no. 2 (October 1916): 138–43]

An American Tragedy (1925)

Whatever else this vasty double-header may reveal about its author, it
at least shows brilliantly that he is wholly devoid of what may be called literary tact. A more artful and ingratiating fellow, facing the situation that

confronted him, would have met it with a far less difficult book. It was ten years since he had published his last novel, and so all his old customers, it is reasonable to assume, were hungry for another—all his old customers and all his new customers. His publisher, after a long and gallant battle, had at last chased off the Comstocks. Rivals, springing up at intervals, had all succumbed—or, what is the same thing, withdrawn from the Dreiser reservation. The Dreiser cult, once grown somewhat wobbly, was full of new strength and enthusiasm. The time was thus plainly at hand to make a ten strike. What was needed was a book full of all the sound and solid Dreiser merits, and agreeably free from the familiar Dreiser defects—a book carefully designed and smoothly written, with no puerile clichés in it and no maudlin moralizing—in brief, a book aimed deliberately at readers of a certain taste, and competent to estimate good workmanship. Well, how did Dreiser meet the challenge? He met it, characteristically, by throwing out the present shapeless and forbidding monster—a heaping cartload of raw materials for a novel, with rubbish of all sorts intermixed— a vast, sloppy, chaotic thing of 385,000 words—at least 250,000 of them unnecessary! Such is scientific salesmanship as Dreiser understands it! Such is his reply to a pleasant invitation to a party!

By this time, I suppose, you have heard what it is all about. The plot, in fact, is extremely simple. Clyde Griffiths, the son of a street preacher in Kansas City, revolts against the piety of his squalid home, and gets himself a job as bellboy in a gaudy hotel. There he acquires a taste for the luxuries affected by travelling Elks, and is presently a leader in shop-girl society. An automobile accident, for which he is not to blame, forces him to withdraw discreetly, and he proceeds to Chicago, where he goes to work in a club. One day his father's rich brother, a collar magnate from Lycurgus, N.Y., is put up there by a member, and Clyde resolves to cultivate him. The old boy, taking a shine to the youngster, invites him to Lycurgus, and gives him a job in the factory. There ensues the conflict that makes the story. Clyde has hopes, but very little ready cash; he is thus forced to seek most of his recreation in low life. But as a nephew to old Samuel Griffiths he is also taken up by the Lycurgus *haut ton*. The conflict naturally assumes the form of girls. Roberta Alden, a beautiful female operative in the factory, falls in love with him and yields herself to him. Almost simultaneously

Sondra Finchley, an even more beautiful society girl, falls in love with him and promises to marry him. Clyde is ambitious and decides for Sondra. But at that precise moment Roberta tells him that their sin has found her out. His reply is to take her to a lonely lake and drown her. The crime being detected, he is arrested, put on trial, convicted, and electrocuted.

A simple tale. Hardly more, in fact, than the plot of a three page story in *True Confessions*. But Dreiser rolls it out to such lengths that it becomes, in the end, a sort of sequence of serials. The whole first volume, of 431 pages of small type, brings us only to the lamentable event of Roberta's pregnancy. The home life of the Griffithses in Kansas City is described in detail. We make intimate acquaintance with the street preacher himself, a poor fanatic, always trusting in the God who has fooled him incessantly, and with his pathetic, drab wife, and with his daughter Esta, who runs away with a vaudeville actor and comes home with a baby. There ensues a leisurely and meticulous treatise upon the life of the bellboys in the rococo Green-Davidson Hotel—how they do their work, what they collect in tips, how they spend their evenings, what sort of girls they fancy. The automobile accident is done in the same spacious manner. Finally, we get to Lycurgus, and page after page is devoted to the operations of the Griffiths factory, and to the gay doings in Lycurgus society, and to the first faint stirrings, the passionate high tide, and the disagreeable ebb of Clyde's affair with Roberta. So much for Volume I: 200,000 words. In Volume II we have the murder, the arrest, the trial and the execution: 185,000 more.

Obviously, there is something wrong here. Somewhere or other, there must be whole chapters that could be spared. I find, in fact, many such chapters—literally dozens of them. They incommode the action, they swamp and conceal the principal personages, and they lead the author steadily into his weakness for banal moralizing and trite, meaningless words. In *The "Genius"* it was *trig* that rode him; in *An American Tragedy* it is *chic*. Did *chic* go out in 1896? Then so much the better! It is the mark of an unterrified craftsman to use it now—more, to rub it in mercilessly. Is Freudism stale, even in Greenwich Village? Ahoy, then, let us heave in a couple of bargeloads of complexes—let us explain even judges and district attorneys in terms of suppressions! Is the "chemic" theory of sex somewhat flyblown? Then let us trot it out, and give it a polishing with the dish-rag!

Is there such a thing as sound English, graceful English, charming and beautiful English? Then let us defy a world of scoundrels, half Methodist and half æsthete, with such sentences as this one:

> The "death house" in this particular prison was one of those crass erections and maintenances of human insensibility and stupidity principally for which no one primarily was really responsible.

And such as this:

> Quite everything of all this was being published in the papers each day.

What is one to say of such dreadful bilge? What is one to say of a novelist who, after a quarter of a century at his trade, still writes it? What one is to say, I feel and fear, had better be engraved on the head of a pin and thrown into the ocean: there is such a thing as critical *politesse*. Here I can only remark that sentences of the kind I have quoted please me very little. One of them to a page is enough to make me very unhappy. In *An American Tragedy* — or, at all events, in parts of it — they run to much more than that. Is Dreiser actually deaf to their dreadful cacophony? I can't believe it. He can write, on occasion, with great clarity, and even with a certain grace. I point, for example, to Chapter XIII of Book III, and to the chapter following. There is here no idiotic "quite everything of all," and no piling up of infirm adverbs. There is, instead, straightforward and lucid writing, which is caressing in itself and gets the story along. But elsewhere! . . .

Thus the defects of this gargantuan book. They are the old defects of Dreiser, and he seems to be quite unable to get rid of them. They grow more marked, indeed, as he passes into middle life. His writing in *Jennie Gerhardt* was better than his writing in *The "Genius,"* and so was his sense of form, his feeling for structure. But what of the more profound elements? What of his feeling for character, his capacity to imagine situations, his skill at reaching the emotions of the reader? I can only say that I see no falling off in this direction. *An American Tragedy*, as a work of art, is a colossal botch, but as a human document it is searching and full of a solemn dignity, and at times it rises to the level of genuine tragedy. Especially the second volume. Once Roberta is killed and Clyde faces his fate, the thing begins to move, and thereafter it roars on, with ever increasing impetus, to the final terrific smash. What other American novelist could have done the trial as well as Dreiser has done it? His method, true enough, is the simple, bald one of the reporter—but of *what* a reporter! And who could have handled so magnificently the last scenes in the death-house? Here his very defects come to his aid. What we behold is the gradual, terrible, irresistible approach of doom—the slow slipping away of hopes. The thing somehow has the effect of a tolling of bells. It is clumsy. It lacks all grace. But it is tremendously moving.

In brief, the book improves as it nears its shocking climax—a humane fact, indeed, for the reader. The first volume heaves and pitches, and the second, until the actual murder, is full of psychologizing that usually fails to come off. But once the poor girl is in the water, there is a change, and thereafter *An American Tragedy* is Dreiser at his plodding, booming best. The means are often bad, but the effects are superb. One gets the same feeling of complete reality that came from *Sister Carrie*, and especially from the last days of Hurstwood. The thing ceases to be a story, and becomes a harrowing reality. Dreiser, I suppose, regards himself as an adept at the Freudian psychology. He frequently uses its terms, and seems to take its fundamental doctrines very seriously. But he is actually a behaviorist of the most advanced wing. What interests him primarily is not what people think, but what they do. He is full of a sense of their helplessness. They are, to him, automata thrown hither and thither by fate—but suffering tragically under every buffet. Their thoughts are muddled and trivial—but they can feel. And Dreiser feels with them, and can make the reader feel with them. It takes skill of a kind that is surely not common. Good writing is far easier.

The Dreiserian ideology does not change. Such notions as he carried out of the experiences of his youth still abide with him at fifty-four. They take somewhat curious forms. The revolt of youth, as he sees it, is primarily a revolt against religious dogmas and forms. He is still engaged in delivering Young America from the imbecilities of a frozen Christianity. And the economic struggle, in his eye, has a bizarre symbol: the modern American hotel. Do you remember Carrie Meeber's first encounter with a hotel beefsteak in *Sister Carrie*? And Jennie Gerhardt's dumb wonder before the splendors of that hotel in which her mother scrubbed the grand staircase? There are hotels, too, and aplenty, in *The Titan* and *The "Genius"*; toward the end of the latter there is a famous description, pages long, of the lobby of a New York apartment house, by the Waldorf-Astoria out of the Third avenue car-barn. It was a hotel that lured Jennie (like Carrie before her) to ruin, and it is a hotel that starts Clyde Griffiths on his swift journey to the chair. I suggest a more extensive examination of the matter, in the best Dreiser-Freud style. Let some ambitious young *Privat Dozent* tackle it.

So much for *An American Tragedy*. Hire your pastor to read the first volume for you. But don't miss the second! ["The Library," *AM* 7, no. 3 (March 1926): 379–81 ("Dreiser in 840 Pages")]

Willa Cather

Alexander's Bridge (1912)

Alexander's Bridge, by Willa S. Cather, has the influence of Edith Wharton written all over it, and there is no need for the canned review on the cover to call attention to the fact—the which remark, let me hasten to add, is not to be taken as a sneer but as hearty praise, for the novelizing novice who chooses Mrs. Wharton as her model is at least one who knows a hawk from a handsaw, an artist from an artisan. The majority of beginners in this our fair land choose E. Phillips Oppenheim or Marie Corelli; if we have two schools, then one is the School of Plot and the other is the School of Piffle. But Miss Cather, as I have said, is intelligent enough to aim higher, and the thing she offers must be set down a very promising piece of writing. Its chief defect is a certain triteness in structure. When Bartley Alexander, the great engineer, discovers that he is torn hopelessly between a genuine affection for his wife, Winifred, and a wild passion for his old flame, Hilda Burgoyne, it seems a banal device to send him out on his greatest bridge a moment before it falls, and so drown him in the St. Lawrence. This is not a working out of the problem, it is a mere evasion of the problem. In real life how would such a man solve it for himself? Winifred, remember, is in Boston and Hilda is in London, and business takes Bartley across the ocean four or five times a year. No doubt the authentic male would let the situation drift. In the end he would sink into the lean and slippered pantaloon by two firesides, a highly respectable and

reasonably contented bigamist (unofficially of course), a more or less successful and satisfied wrestler with fate. Such things happen. I could tell
you tales. But I tell them not. All I do is to throw out the suggestion that
the shivering of the triangle is far from inevitable. Sometimes, for all the
hazards of life, it holds together for years. But the fictioneers are seldom
content until they have destroyed it by catastrophe. That way is the
thrilling way, and more important still, it is the easy way.

Aside from all this, Miss Cather gives a very good account of herself indeed. She writes carefully, skillfully, artistically. Her dialogue has life in it
and gets her story ahead. Her occasional paragraphs of description are full
of feeling and color. She gives us a well drawn picture of the cold
Winifred, a better one of the emotional and alluring Hilda and a fairly
credible one of Bartley himself—this last a difficult business, for the genius
grows flabby in a book. It is seldom, indeed, that fiction can rise above second rate men. The motives and impulses and processes of mind of the superman are too recondite for plausible analysis. It is easy enough to
explain how John Smith courted and won his wife, and even how William
Jones fought and died for his country, but it would be impossible to explain (or, at any rate, to convince by explaining) how Beethoven wrote the
Fifth Symphony, or how Pasteur reasoned out the hydrophobia vaccine, or
how Stonewall Jackson arrived at his miracles of strategy. The thing has
been tried often, but it has always ended in failure. Those supermen of fiction who are not mere shadows and dummies are supermen reduced to
saving ordinariness. Shakespeare made Hamlet a comprehensible and
convincing man by diluting that half of him which was Shakespeare by a
half which was a college sophomore. In the same way he saved Lear by
making him, in large part, a silly and obscene old man—the blood brother
of any average ancient of any average English taproom. Tackling Cæsar,
he was rescued from disaster by Brutus's knife. George Bernard Shaw, facing the same difficulty, resolved it by drawing a composite portrait of two
or three London actor-managers and half a dozen English politicians. ["A
Visit to a Short Story Factory," SS 38, no. 4 (December 1912): 156–57]

The Song of the Lark (1915)

There is nothing new in the story that Willa Sibert Cather tells in The
Song of the Lark; it is, in fact, merely one more version, with few changes,

of the ancient fable of Cinderella, probably the oldest of the world's love stories, and surely the most steadily popular. Thea Kronborg begins as a Methodist preacher's daughter in a little town in Colorado, and ends as Sieglinde at the Metropolitan Opera House, with a packed house "roaring" at her and bombarding her with "a greeting that was almost savage in its fierceness." As for Fairy Princes, there are no less than three of them, the first a Galahad in the sooty overalls of a freight conductor, the second a small town doctor with a disagreeable wife, and the third Mr. Fred Otterburg, the *Bierkronprinz.*

But if the tale is thus conventional in its outlines, it is full of novelty and ingenuity in its details, and so the reading of it passes very pleasantly. Miss Cather, indeed, here steps definitely into the small class of American novelists who are seriously to be reckoned with. Her *Alexander's Bridge* was full of promise, and her *O Pioneers* showed the beginnings of fulfilment.[23] In *The Song of the Lark* she is already happily at ease, a competent journeyman. I have read no late novel, in fact, with a greater sense of intellectual stimulation. Especially in the first half, it is alive with sharp bits of observation, sly touches of humor, gestures of that gentle pity which is the fruit of understanding. Miss Cather not only has a desire to write; she also has something to say. Ah, that the former masked less often as the latter! Our scriveners are forever mistaking the *cacoethes scribendi* for a theory of beauty and a rule of life. But not this one. From her book comes the notion that she has thought things out, that she is never at a loss, that her mind is plentifully stored. I commend her story to your affable attention—at least the first half of it. ["Partly about Books," SS 48, no. 1 (January 1916): 306–7]

My Antonia (1918)

The Cather story, *My Antonia*, was reviewed somewhat briefly in this place last month. It well deserves another notice, for it is not an isolated phenomenon, an extraordinary single book like Cahan's *The Rise of David Levinsky*, or Masters's *Spoon River Anthology*, but merely one more step upward in the career of a writer who has labored with the utmost patience and industry, and won every foot of the way by hard work. She began, setting aside certain early experiments, with *Alexander's Bridge* in 1912—a book strongly suggesting the influence of Edith Wharton and yet thoroughly individual and newly thought out. Its defect was one of locale and people: one somehow got the feeling that Miss Cather was dealing with things at second-hand, that she knew her personages a bit less intimately than she should have known them. This defect, I venture to guess, impressed itself upon the author herself. At all events, she abandoned New England, in her next novel, for the Middle West, and in particular for the Middle West of the last great immigrations—a region far better known to her. The result was *O Pioneers*, a book of very fine achievement and of even finer promise. Then came *The Song of the Lark* in 1915—still more competent, more searching and convincing, better in every way. And now, after three years, comes *My Antonia*, a work in which improvement takes a sudden leap—a novel, indeed, that is not only the best done by Miss Cather herself, but also one of the best that any American has ever done, East or West, early or late. It is simple; it is honest; it is intelligent; it is moving. The means that appear in it are means perfectly adapted to its end. Its people are unquestionably real. Its background is brilliantly vivid. It has form, grace, good literary manners. In a word, it is a capital piece of writing, and it will be heard of long after the baroque balderdash now touted on the "book pages" is forgotten.

It goes without saying that all the machinery customary to that balderdash is charmingly absent. There is, in the ordinary sense, no plot. There is no hero. There is, save as a momentary flash, no love affair. There is no apparent hortatory purpose, no show of theory, no visible aim to improve the world. The whole enchantment is achieved by the simplest of all possible devices. One follows a poor Bohemian farm girl from her earliest teens to middle age, looking closely at her narrow world, mingling with her friends, observing the gradual widening of her experience, her point of view—and that is all. Intrinsically, the thing is sordid—the life is almost horrible, the horizon is leaden, the soul within is pitifully shrunken and dismayed. But what Miss Cather tries to reveal is the true romance that lies even there—the grim tragedy at the heart of all that dull, cow-like existence—the fineness that lies deeply buried beneath the peasant shell. Dreiser tried to do the same thing with both Carrie Meeber and Jennie Gerhardt, and his success was unmistakable. Miss Cather succeeds quite as certainly, but in an altogether different way. Dreiser's method was that of tremendous particularity—he built up his picture with an infinity of little strokes, many of them superficially meaningless. Miss Cather's method inclines more to suggestion and indirection. Here a glimpse, there a turn of phrase, and suddenly the thing stands out, suddenly it is as real as real can be—and withal moving, arresting, beautiful with a strange and charming beauty. . . . I commend the book to your attention, and the author no less. There is no other American author of her sex, now in view, whose future promises so much. . . . ["Mainly Fiction," SS 58, no. 3 (March 1919): 140–41]

Youth and the Bright Medusa (1920)

Youth and the Bright Medusa [. . .] is made up of eight stories, and all of them deal with artists. It is Miss Cather's peculiar virtue that she represents the artist in terms of his own thinking—that she does not look *at* him through a peep-hole in the studio-door, but looks *with* him at the life that he is so important and yet so isolated and lonely a part of. One finds in every line of her writing a sure-footed and civilized culture; it gives her an odd air of foreignness, particularly when she discusses music, which is often. Six of her eight stories deal with musicians. One of them, "Coming, Aphrodite!" was published in this great moral periodical last August. Another, "Scandal," was printed in *The Century* during the Spring, to the envious rage of Dr. Nathan, who read it with vast admiration and cursed God that it had escaped these refined pages. Four others were reprinted from *The Troll Garden*, a volume first published fifteen years ago. These early stories are excellent, particularly "The Sculptor's Funeral," but Miss Cather has learned a great deal since she wrote them. Her grasp upon character is firmer than it was; she writes with much more ease and grace; above all, she has mastered the delicate and difficult art of evoking the feelings. A touch of the maudlin lingers in "Paul's Case" and in "A Death in the Desert." It is wholly absent from "Coming, Aphrodite!" and "Scandal," as it is from *My Antonia*. These last indeed show utterly competent workmanship in every line. They are stories that lift themselves completely above the level of current American fiction, even of good fiction. They are the work of a woman who, after a long apprenticeship, has got herself into the front rank of American novelists, and is still young enough to have her best writing ahead of her. I call *My Antonia* to your attention once more. It is the finest thing of its sort ever done in America. ["Chiefly Americans," SS 63, no. 4 (December 1920): 139–40]

One of Ours (1922)

Miss Willa Cather's *One of Ours* divides itself very neatly into two halves, one of which deserves to rank almost with *My Antonia* and the other of which drops precipitately to the level of a serial in the *Ladies' Home Journal*. It is the first half that is the good one. Here Miss Cather sets herself a scene that she knows most intimately and addresses herself to the interpretation of characters that have both her sympathy and her understanding. The scene is the prairie-land of Nebraska; the characters are the emerging peasants of that region—no longer the pathetic clods that their fathers were, and yet but half rescued from mud, loneliness and Methodist demonology. Her protagonist is one who has gone a bit further along the upward path than most of the folks about him—young Claude Wheeler, son of old Nat, the land-hog. Claude's mother was a schoolteacher, and if the dour religion of the steppes had not paralyzed her faculties in youth, might have developed into a primeval Carol Kennicott.[24] As it is, she can only hand on the somewhat smudgy torch to Claude himself—and it is his effort to find a way through the gloom by its light that makes the story. Defeat and disaster are inevitable. The folks of Frankfort are not stupid, but beyond a certain point their imaginations will not go. Claude, fired by a year at the State University, tries to pass that point, and finds all that he knows of human society in a conspiracy against him—his father, his brothers, the girl he falls in love with, even his poor old mother. He yields bit by bit. His father fastens him relentlessly to the soil; his wife binds him in the chains of Christian Endeavor; his mother can only look on and sigh for she knows not what.

Then comes the war, and deliverance. The hinds of that remote farm-land are easy victims of the prevailing propaganda. They see every event of the first two years of the struggle in the terms set by the Associated Press and the *Saturday Evening Post*. Comes 1917, and they begin flocking to the recruiting-offices, or falling cheerfully upon the patriotic business of badgering their German neighbors. Claude is one of the first to volunteer, and presently he finds himself on the way to France. Months of hope and squalor in the mud, and his regiment goes forward. A brush or two, and he is a veteran. Then, one morning, a German bullet fetches him in the heart. . . . He has found the solution to the riddle of his life in this soldier's death. A strange fish out at Frankfort, Neb., his world misundertanding and by his world misunderstood, he has come to his heroic destiny in this far-flung trench. It was the brilliant end, no doubt, of many another such groping and uncomfortable man. War is the enemy of the fat and happy, but it is kind to the lonesome. It brings them into kinship with their kind, it fills them with a sense of high usefulness—and it obliterates the benign delusion at last in a swift, humane and workmanlike manner.

What spoils the story is simply the fact that a year or so ago a young soldier named John Dos Passos printed a novel called *Three Soldiers*. Until *Three Soldiers* is forgotten and fancy achieves its inevitable victory over fact, no war story can be written in the United States without challenging comparison with it—and no story that is less meticulously true will stand up to it. At one blast it disposed of oceans of romance and blather. It changed the whole tone of American opinion about the war; it even changed the recollections of actual veterans of the war. They saw, no doubt, substantially what Dos Passos saw, but it took his bold realism to disentangle their recollection from the prevailing buncombe and sentimentality. Unluckily for Miss Cather, she seems to have read *Three Soldiers* inattentively, if at all. The war she depicts has its thrills and even its touches of plausibility, but at bottom it is fought out, not in France, but on a Hollywood movie-lot. Its American soldiers are idealists engaged upon a crusade to put down sin; its Germans are imbeciles who charge machine-guns six-deep, in the manner of the war dispatches of the New York *Tribune*. There is a lyrical nonsensicality in it that often grows half pathetic; it is precious near the war of the standard model of lady novelist.

Which Miss Cather surely is not. When she walks ground that she knows, her footstep is infinitely light and sure. Nothing could exceed the skill with which she washes in that lush and yet desolate Nebraska landscape—the fat farms with their wood-lots of cottonwood, the villages with their grain-elevators and church-spires, the long, burning lines of straight railroad track. Nor is there any other American novelist who better comprehends the soul of the American farmer-folk—their slow, dogged battle with the soil that once threatened to make mere animals of them, their slavery to the forms and superstitions of a barbaric theology, their heroic struggle to educate and emancipate their children, their shy reaching out for beauty. To this profound knowledge Miss Cather adds a very great technical expertness. She knows how to manage a situation, how to present a character, how to get poetry into the commonplace. I give you an example from *One of Us*. In one chapter Claude visits a German family named Erlich, and one of the other guests is a remote cousin of the house, a cele-brated opera-singer. She is there but a day or two and we see her for but a few moments, but when she passes on she remains almost as vivid as Claude himself. It is excellent writing, and there is a lot more of it in the first half of the book. But in the second half good writing is not sufficient to conceal the underlying unreality. It is a picture of the war, both as idea and as spectacle, that belongs to Coningsby Dawson and 1915, not to John Dos Passos and 1922. ["Portrait of an American Citizen," *SS* 69, no. 2 (October 1922): 140–41]

A Lost Lady (1923)

Miss Cather's *A Lost Lady* has the air of a first sketch for a longer story. There are episodes that are described without being accounted for; there is at least one place where a salient character is depicted in the simple outlines of a melodrama villain. But this vagueness, I suspect, is mainly deliberate. Miss Cather is not trying to explain her cryptic and sensational Mrs. Forrester in the customary omniscient way of a novelist; she is trying, rather, to show us the effects of the Forrester apparition upon a group of simple folk, and particularly upon the romantic boy, Niel Herbert. How is that business achieved? It is achieved, it seems to me, very beautifully. The story has an arch and lyrical air; there is more genuine romance in it than in half a dozen romances in the grand manner. One gets the effect of a scarlet tanager invading a nest of sparrows—an effect not incomparable to that managed by Hergesheimer in *Java Head*. But to say that *A Lost Lady* is as sound and important a work as *My Antonia*—as has been done, in fact, more than once in the public prints—is to say something quite absurd. It is excellent stuff, but it remains a bit light. It presents a situation, not a history. ["The Library," *AM* 1, no. 2 (February 1924): 253 ("Three Volumes of Fiction")]

The Professor's House (1925)

Miss Cather, in *The Professor's House*, shows all the qualities that one has learned to expect of her. Her observation is sharp and exact; she is alert to the tragedy of every-day life; she sees her people, not in vacuums, but against a definite background; above all, she writes in clear, glowing and charming English. I know of no other American novelist, indeed, whose writing is so certain of its effects, and yet so free from artifice. She avoids both the elaborate preciosities of Cabell and Hergesheimer and the harsh uncouthness of Dreiser and Anderson. She has, obviously, a good ear, and apprehends the world as symphony more than as spectacle. Her defect is a somewhat uncertain grasp of form; her stories often seem to run away with her. It is apparent even in *My Antonia*; in *The Professor's House* it comes dangerously near being fatal. Tom Outland's story, 75 pages long, almost breaks the back of the story of Professor St. Peter. It is, in itself, a story of singular power, and it is essential to what goes before it and yet more essential to what follows after; nevertheless, the feeling persists that throwing it in so boldly and baldly is bad workmanship—that the business might have been managed with far more nicety. One submits to the shock only because the book as a whole is so beautifully written—because the surface is so fine and velvety in texture that one half forgets the ungraceful structure beneath.

In brief, *The Professor's House* is a study of the effects of a purple episode upon a dull life—perhaps more accurately, of the effects of a purple episode upon a life that is dull only superficially, with purple glows of its own deep down. Professor St. Peter is a teacher of history, and spends half his life at work upon one monumental monograph. His subject is the early Spanish adventurers; he writes about them in the attic room of a colorless house in an inland college town, with the neighborhood seamstress for company. Into his quiet circle there pops suddenly a romantic youth from the very land of the ancient conquistadors—a fellow curious and mysterious, half hind and half genius. A few years, and he is gone again. But not from the professor's memory—not from his heart. Tom Outland lives on there, though his bones lie somewhere in France. (Once more, alas, Miss Cather hears the bugles of 1917!) . . . Not, perhaps, much of a story. Rather obvious. But how skillfully written! How excellent in its details! What an ingratiating piece of work! ["The Library," *AM* 6, no. 3 (November 1925): 380 ("Fiction Good and Bad")]

Death Comes for the Archbishop (1927)

There is a curious likeness between these two stories [*Death Comes for the Archbishop* and Harvey Fergusson's *Wolf Song*], though they are separated by some sharp contrasts. Both have to do with the taming of the Old Southwest, and both are character sketches rather than tales. The scene of each is the north central desert region of New Mexico, lying about Santa Fé and Taos, and each deals with the conflict between the old barbaric Mexican civilization and the new order. In *Wolf Song* the time is a century ago, and the old civilization, meeting the hard rush of a wild man from Yankeedom, floors and tames him. In *Death Comes for the Archbishop*, which begins on an Autumn afternoon in 1851, the fortunes of war go the other way. Here the antagonist, true enough, is not a Yankee mountain man; he is, indeed, not a Yankee at all, but a French priest. But it is the vast momentum of the new Republic that lies behind him when he flings himself upon what remains of the ancient Spanish *raj*, and it is a tight and well-ordered Yankee archdiocese that he leaves to his successors, and another that his chief of staff carves out of the mountain wilds to the northward.

I part from the Cather story with a certain regret that the author did nor make this chief of staff the hero of it, instead of the gentler Monsignor Jean Marie Latour. Latour is a charming fellow, but only too often he stiffens into the austere and somewhat fatiguing attitudes of a plaster saint. Nor once does he show any heat of honest archiepiscopal passion. There is pertinacity in him, and patience and understanding, and a steady if mild glow of zeal for the True Faith, but no steel. When rough work is to be done he turns naturally to Father Joseph Vaillant, indomitable vicar, gifted cook, hearty drinker, untiring traveler, and heavy weight champion of the Lord. Father Joseph should have been the apostolic delegate to those wilds, and Father Jean Marie a village *curé* back in Auvergne, tending his placid garden and reading and rereading his dusty books. But the desires of God, published through a committee of three Cardinals, all of them somewhat hazy about New Spain, run otherwise, and so it is not until late in life that Father Joseph puts on a mitre of his own. What a gaudy glimpse we have of him in Colorado, policing the miners! What a story gone to waste!

But of the story that is told there is little complaint to be made. At times, it seems to me, Miss Cather takes the somewhat naïve view of a bishop's business that belongs properly, not to a novelist, but to a highly devoted member of the Sodality of the Blessed Virgin, and so her narrative drops to the level of a pious tale. But that is not often. If there is a devotee hidden in her, there is also an immensely skillful story-teller. What could be more dramatic, more waggish, more thoroughly amusing than the episode of Fray Baltazar and his tragic end on lonely Acoma? Here, indeed, is a tale informed with all the high humor and washed with all the brilliant color of *The Three-Cornered Hat*.[25] The writing throughout is in Miss Cather's best manner. In her English there is no ornateness, but it is surely not monotonous. She has a fine feeling for the beauty of simple words. Her style flows in a quiet, unrestrained, melodious, almost Mozartian manner. She has done stories far richer in content, but she has never exceeded *Death Comes for the Archbishop* as a piece of writing. ["The Library," *AM* 12, no. 4 (December 1927): 508–9 ("The Desert Epic")]

Sherwood Anderson

Windy McPherson's Son (1916)

[. . .] *Windy McPherson's Son*, by Sherwood Anderson, [is] a first novel that holds out unmistakable promise. The figure of Sam McPherson, financier and romanticist, dominates it from the first page to the last; all the other characters, though some of them are very deftly drawn, are unimportant save as they react upon him. We follow him from his boyhood in a little Iowa town, overshadowed by the drunkenness and clownishness of his father, to his youth as a pushing young business man in Chicago, his maturity as a manipulator of men and money, and into the psychic break-up his middle age. As in Dreiser's *The Titan* the essential conflict of the drama is within the man himself. On the one hand there is his homeric energy, his determination to get on, the sheer clang and rattle of him, and on the other hand there is the groping sentimentality that beats him at the height of his success. He and his wife fall out almost absurdly: she can't have a child. But behind that bald fact one senses a dream that is grand and even noble, and it is the harsh awakening from it that shakes McPherson out of his world, and sets him adrift at forty, a waster, a drunkard and a chaser of chimeras. This catastrophe, it seems to me, is managed weakly. An air of unreality, even of improbability, gets into it. Nevertheless, one somehow picks up something of the author's own belief in it, and at bottom, I daresay, it is soundly enough imagined. Turn to Crile,[26] and you will find much the same picture of the devastating effect of an accumulation of violent impressions and sensations, a too rapid gathering of experience. But whatever its fault here, the book at least lifts itself far out of the common rut. It is written forcefully, earnestly, almost passionately. There is the gusto of a true artist in it. I suspect that we shall hear much more about this Mr. Anderson. ["The Creed of a Novelist," SS 50, no. 2 (October 1916): 144]

Marching Men (1917)

Anderson's Marching Men starts off brilliantly, but toward the end he begins to load it with dubious sociological ideas, as he loaded Windy McPherson's Son, and so it loses some of its early vitality. In brief, it is the history of Norman McGregor, a youth from the Pennsylvania mining region who goes to Chicago, studies law, sets up shop as a prophet, and organizes the floating workers out there into regiments of industrial soldiers. The idea is that of Kipling's McAndrews: "Law, Order, Duty an' Restraint, Obedience, Discipline!"[27] Above all, discipline. The regular tramp, tramp, tramp of rank after rank, the subtle strength of the drilled man, the mob made one and irresistible. Thus the plan. But the end, the aim? Here, alas, McGregor is less explicit, and with him his creator. I put down the book with the wish that Mr. Anderson had not brought the prophet out of Coal Creek. There he is brilliantly projected against a background as real as the landscape you see out of your window. There, and not in the last chapters, is the proof that Mr. Anderson is a novelist with something to say. ["Critics Wild and Tame," SS 53, no. 4 (December 1917): 143]

Winesburg, Ohio (1919)

[. . .] the Anderson book [is] a collection of short stories of a new order, including at least half a dozen of a very striking quality. This Anderson is a man of whom a great deal will be heard hereafter. Along with Willa Sibert Cather, James Branch Cabell and a few others, he belongs to a small group that has somehow emancipated itself from the prevailing imitativeness and banality of the national letters and is moving steadily toward work that will do honor to the country. His first novel, *Windy McPherson's Son*, printed in 1916, had plenty of faults, but there were so many compensating merits that it stood out clearly above the general run of the fiction of its year. Then came *Marching Men*, another defective but extremely interesting novel, and then a book of dithyrambs, *Mid-American Chants*.[28] But these things, for all their brilliant moments, did not adequately represent Anderson. The national vice of ethical purpose corrupted them; they were burdened with *Tendenz*. Now, in *Winesburg, Ohio*, he throws off that handicap. What remains is pure representation — and it is representation so vivid, so full of insight, so shiningly life-like and glowing, that the book is lifted into a category all its own. Nothing quite like it has ever been done in America. It is a book that, at one stroke, turns depression into enthusiasm.

In form, it is a collection of short stories, with common characters welding them into a continued picture of life in a small inland town. But what short stories! Compare them to the popular trade goods of the Gouverneur Morrises and Julian Streets, or even to the more pretentious work of the Alice Browns and Katharine Fullerton Geroulds. It is the difference between music by a Chaminade and music by a Brahms. Into his brief pages Anderson not only gets brilliant images of men and women who walk in all the colors of reality; he also gets a profound sense of the obscure, inner drama of their lives. Consider, for example, the four-part story called "Godliness." It is fiction for half a page, but after that it seems indubitable fact — fact that is searching and ferret-like — fact infinitely stealthy and persuasive — the sort of fact that suddenly changes a stolid, inscrutable Captain MacWhirr into a moving symbol of man in his struggle with the fates. And then turn to "Respectability," and to "The Strength of God," and to "Adventure," and to "The Teacher." Here one gets all the joy that goes with the discovery of something quite new under the sun — a new order of short story, half tale and half psychological anatomizing, and vastly better than all the kinds that have gone before. Here is the goal that *The Spoon River Anthology* aimed at, and missed by half a mile. Allow everything to the imperfection of the form and everything to the author's occasional failure to rise to it: what remains is a truly extraordinary book, by a man of such palpably unusual talent that it seems almost an impertinence to welcome him. ["Novels, Chiefly Bad," *SS* 59, no. 4 (August 1919): 140]

Poor White (1920)

Of all American novelists, past or present, Sherwood Anderson is probably the one whose struggles to express himself are the most interesting. Even more than Dreiser he is beset by devils that make the business difficult for him. What ails him primarily is the fact that there are two Andersons, sharply differentiated and tending to fall into implacable antagonisms. One is the artist who sees the America of his day as the most cruel and sordid, and yet at the same time as the most melodramatic and engrossing of spectacles—the artist enchanted by the sheer barbaric color of it all, and eager to get that color into living pages—the artist standing, as it were, above the turmoil, and intent only upon observing it accurately and representing it honestly, feelingly and unhindered. The other is a sort of uncertain social reformer—one appalled by the muddle of ideas and aspirations in the Republic, and impelled to do something or say something, however fantastic, however obvious, to help along the slow and agonizing process of reorganization—in brief, a typical American of the more reflective sort, full of inchoate visions and confused indignations. The combat between the two was visible in Anderson's first novel, *Windy McPherson's Son*, a book that started off so vigorously and brilliantly as a work of art that most readers overlooked its subsequent transformation into a furious but somewhat unintelligent tract. In *Marching Men*, after a brief struggle, the second Anderson won hands down, and the thing degenerated into formal prophecy, often hard to distinguish, toward the end, from burlesque. This defeat, however, did not destroy the first Anderson, the artist Anderson; on the contrary, it seems to have stimulated him enormously. In *Winesburg, Ohio*, which followed, he drove his enemy quite off the field. The result was a book of high and delicate quality, a book uncorrupted by theories and moral purposes, a book that stands clearly above anything of its sort in latter-day American literature, saving only Dreiser's *Twelve Men*.[29] It will be appreciated at its true worth, I believe, in the years to come. At the moment its peculiar excellencies are obscured by its very unusualness—its complete departure from all the customary methods and materials of prose fiction among us. Study it, and you will get some smell of the fiction of the future. If the great American novelists visioned by Carl Sandburg[30] ever escape from Chautauqua and Atlanta, they will learn much more from *Winesburg* than ever they learn from Howells and Henry James.

In *Poor White*, Anderson's latest book, there is a sort of compromise, but with most of the advantages going to the artist. It, too, has its ideas, its theory, but that theory relates itself to the demonstrable facts of the past and not to the shadowy possibilities of the future, as was the case in *Marching Men*. What Anderson seeks to set forth is the demoralizing effect of the introduction of the factory system into the rural Middle West. It came at a time when the old struggle with the soil had reached success. The land was under the yoke; the yokels were secure at last, and learning to take their ease, and beginning to feel around for new enterprises; the day was one which might have seen the birth of an art and a civilization. But then came the factory, and with it a revival of the sordid combat. Rich farmers, ripe to hear ideas, to hatch aspirations, to dream dreams, now became stockholders in tile-factories and shingle-mills, and at once plunged back into their old hoggishness. The countryside was polluted, the towns were made hideous, the people were poisoned with ignoble aims. Worse, this new struggle was not a self-limiting disease, like the old struggle against Indians, wolves, cyclones, mud and tree-stumps. There could be no end to it. One factory would bring another factory. One success would breed an insatiable thirst for another and larger success. Thus Arcady succumbed to Youngstown and Zanesville, and the pioneer, a poet as well as a peasant, ceased to be either, and became a filthy manufacturer of muck and money.

Anderson lights up the process by carrying an imaginative and unchanging man through it. This man is Hugh McVey, a dreamer of the machines. His dreams attract the fathers of the factory system; they can be converted into money; he is dragged out of his ivory tower and put to labor in a machine-shop. But he never really succumbs. To him his successive inventions—preposterous potato-planters, coal-unloaders and other such ghastly monsters—always remain far more visions than realities. In the end he fades gently from the scene, uncomprehended and forgotten by the usurers he has enriched. A curious love affair is his final experiment.

The girl is a peasant suffering all the pangs of the newly intellectual. She grasps ineptly at a culture that always eludes her. One wonders what she and McVey will make of life, the one so eager and the other so melancholy and resigned. The answer would be clearer if McVey himself were clearer. I have a notion that Anderson makes his unlikeness to the general a bit too pronounced; Norris fell into the same error in *The Octopus*. It is hard to imagine a man so absolutely out of contact with his environment—so enchanted by his visions that he scarcely sees John Doe and Richard Roe on the street. But McVey, after all, is only a sort of chorus to the main drama. That drama is set forth with a tremendous meticulousness and a tremendous force. The people who enter into it have a superb reality. There is a great brilliancy of detail. More, the inner structure of the thing is sound; Anderson has learned how to hold himself upon the track. Altogether, the best novel that he has done—not better than *Winesburg* certainly, but far better than *Marching Men* and *Windy McPherson's Son*. The Anderson promise begins to be fulfilled. Here is a serious novelist who must be taken seriously.... ["Chiefly Americans," SS 63, no. 4 (December 1920): 138–39]

The Triumph of the Egg (1921)

Some of the salient defects of Sherwood Anderson are still visible in his latest book, *The Triumph of the Egg*, notably his liking for unresolved dissonances and his frequent groping for ideas that elude him. The primary purpose of the author is plainly realistic, but he is so often brought up by riddles defying his solution that the illumination he effects is sometimes no more than a series of brief flashes of pale light. Nevertheless, there is no denying the intrinsic force of this strange book. It simply makes a mock of all attempts at analysis. There it is—absolutely original, creepily fantastic, almost shocking in its sudden brilliances; you may take it, or you may leave it. But I doubt that even the most intransigent pedagogue will make any attempt hereafter to dispose of Anderson with a mere gesture of dismissal. His importance must now be patent even to professors of English. No other American writer of to-day has come nearer to evoking the essential tragedy of American life, or brought to its exhibition a finer or bolder imagination. One of the most curious things about him is his isolation, his freedom from any sign of imitativeness. So far as I can make out, he had no forerunners—and I doubt that he ever has many followers. The general stream of American writing flows on at a great distance from him, leaving him to lurk in his back-water unchallenged. What he is producing there, at its best, belongs to the very first literature of the country to-day. It is work that is quite unlike any other man's work, and it is full of a strange beauty and an unmistakable power. ["Frank Harris and Others," SS 67, no. 2 (February 1922): 143]

Many Marriages (1922–23)

Sherwood Anderson's *Many Marriages*, his first long story in three years, exemplifies very forcibly two of the faults that I have often mentioned in discussing him in this place in the past: first, his apparent inability to manage the machinery of a sustained narrative, and second, his tendency to grow vague and nonsensical when he abandons simple representation and ventures into the field of what is called ideas. It seems to me that no writer now in practise in America can write a better short story than Anderson. He not only sees into character with sharp and awful eyes; he is also extraordinarily adept at handling a simple situation. If any better short story than "I Am a Fool" has been printed in English for five years past, then it must be "I Want to Know Why"—and both of them are by Anderson. But when he tackles a novel, as he has now done four times, he begins to wobble after he has hauled his protagonist through the opening situation, and before the end he usually tries to reinforce his fading story with ideational flights that have nothing clearly and necessarily to do with it and are commonly only defectively rational and intelligible, and so the whole thing goes to pot. This failing spoiled *Windy McPherson's Son*, which began brilliantly; it spoiled *Marching Men*, which began yet more brilliantly; it spoiled *Poor White*, which held up until very near the end; it now spoils *Many Marriages*, which starts out better, even, than any of the others.

The problem before Anderson here is to depict and account for a dramatic episode in the life of a hitherto commonplace man, one John Webster, a washing-machine manufacturer in a small Wisconsin town—his desertion of his wife and daughter, and his elopement with one Natalie Swartz, a dull, uncharming girl in his office, daughter to a small German saloonkeeper and an Irish *Saufschwester*. The bald episode is handled with great deftness and plausibility. The successive steps are not only fully accounted for; they also take on an air of inevitability; one feels, like Webster himself, that he is moved by forces beyond him, that he could not turn back if he would. Natalie is as unappetizing as a lady embalmer; every vestige of prudence in him bids Webster to halt; nevertheless, he is drawn into his banal and ruinous romance by invisible and irresistible chains. But, having got so far, Anderson is not content to shut down and call it a day. Instead, he proceeds to outfit Webster with a stock of theories and intuitions that are as vague as the ideas of a New Thought healer—ideas by Freud out of Greenwich Village, by the Doukobors[31] out of the behaviorist psychology—and presently he ceases altogether to be John Webster, of Wisconsin, and becomes a character in a play by Maeterlinck.

What, in brief, is his fundamental notion? As I understand it, peering for its outlines through the hazes surrounding it, it is the notion that men and women are in bondage to their bodies—that they will never be genuinely free until they get rid of the shames laid as burdens upon Mother Eve. To the end of getting rid of them before departing with Natalie, Webster strips off his union suit and parades before his wife and daughter in the uniform of an artist's model. His wife, shocked beyond endurance by this spectacle and by his statement that, when he first had the honor of viewing her, she was in the same state herself, retires to the next room and swallows a dose of poison. But his daughter, perhaps because she not only hears the words reported to us by the author, but also has the advantage of seeing his facial expression and gestures, seems to understand him and agree with him. Finally, his exposition completed, he resumes his clothes, leaves the house, and proceeds upon his adulterous journey with Natalie, whose drunken mother, having denounced her unjustly for unchastity for years, is now confronted at last with the proof that nature, in the long run, always imitates art—in brief, that lying about a dog makes him bite.

This theory of somatic servitude that Webster expounds is, as I say, extremely nebulous and tantalizing. I am what may be called a professional consumer of ideas; I have read Immanuel Kant, and followed him; I have even read Mary Baker G. Eddy and followed her; but the Websterian exegesis, I must confess, is mainly beyond me. In so far as it is intelligible to me at all, it seems to be simply the old doctrine that we'd all blush less and be happier if we went naked; in so far as it gets past that point it casts itself into terms of a metaphysic that I am frankly not privy to. But even more puzzling than its own intrinsic substance is the question of its applicability to the situation before us. Let us grant that Webster's wife is hopeless—that not even an act of God could make her rise to the philosophizing of her husband. It thus appears reasonable that he should leave her. But why should he run off with Natalie, who is apparently ten times worse? Is it because Natalie is a simpler and more innocent animal than his wife, and will thus refrain from plaguing him with inhibitions, as his wife has done? Then why seek to adorn that elemental fact with so formidable a soliloquy and so startling a dumb-show? And if, unknown to us, there is something in Natalie that attracts a philosopher—if she is actually a more seemly mate for poor John than Mrs. Webster—then why not show what that something is? . . .

Well, perhaps I labor the thing too hard. The inexplicable, after all, occurs in life every day; it belongs in novels, along with everything else that is real. But when it plays so important a rôle that any reader not gifted with clairvoyance must needs halt and scratch his nose—when the distraction that it presents breaks down an otherwise well-ordered and interesting narrative, and reduces reading to a bewildered sort of speculation —then there is excuse for filing a polite caveat. Anderson is so accurate an observer of the inner weaknesses and aspirations of man, and particularly of the more simple varieties of man, and he has so fine a gift for setting forth his observations in a succinct, novel and effectively dramatic manner that it is irritating to see him leaving the light for the shadows, and blundering absurdly in regions where the roads, even when they exist, are obviously not on his map. *Many Marriages* is boldly planned and it is full of brilliant detail, but as a whole it seems to me to be the author's worst failure. The opaque theorizing of Greenwich Village is in it. If there is a lesson in it, it is the lesson that Freud should have made sure that his customers were familiar with the elements of high school physiology before he began instructing them in his non-Euclidian psychology. ["Some New Books," *SS* 71, no. 3 (July 1923): 138–39]

Horses and Men (1923)

Sherwood Anderson dedicates his new book of short stories to Theodore Dreiser and prints a short but eloquent hymn to the elder novelist as

a sort of preface. A graceful acknowledgment of a debt that must be obvious to every reader of current American fiction. What Dreiser chiefly contributed to the American novel, next after his courageous destruction of its
old taboos, was a sense of the tragedy that may play itself out among the
lowly. The lowly, of course, had been familiar figures in our fiction for
many years; the most popular of all American novels of the middle period,
indeed, had had a hero who was an actual slave. But even the authors of
text-books of literature for undergraduates must be aware by this time that
Mrs. Stowe never actually saw into the soul of Tom—that she simply
dressed up a dummy and then somewhat heavily patronized it. The same
patronage continued unbroken until Dreiser wrote *Sister Carrie*. In that
book, for the first time, a girl of the Chandala[32] suddenly became real.
Dreiser did not patronize her in the slightest. Instead, he tried to see her
exactly as she was, to understand her secret soul, to *feel* with her. It was a
new kind of novel among us, and after the Comstocks, the college tutors
and other such imbeciles had tried in vain to dispose of it, it began to have
an influence. To-day that influence is visible in stories as widely different
otherwise as Miss Cather's *My Antonia* and Anderson's *Many Marriages*,
Tarkington's *Alice Adams* and Elliot H. Paul's *Impromptu*.

    Horses and Men, indeed, is largely a set of variations on Dreiserian
themes, though mere imitation, of course, is nowhere visible. The book
represents a sort of reaction from the elaborate and often nonsensical psychologizing of *Many Marriages*. In other words, Anderson here returns to
earth—specifically, to the rural Ohio that he knows so well, and to the
odd, pathetic peasants whose aspirations he sees into so clearly. I put the
first story in the volume, "I Am a Fool," beside the most esteemed confections of the day, and call confidently for judgment. If it is not enormously
better than anything ever done by Katherine Mansfield, Arthur Machen or
any other such transient favorite of the women's clubs, then I am prepared
to confess freely that I am a Chinaman. There is a vast shrewdness in it;
there is sound design; there is understanding; above all, there is feeling.
Anderson does not merely tell a story; he evokes an emotion, and it is not
maudlin. So in "An Ohio Pagan," a story scarcely less adept and charming—the tale of a simple youth to whom going to school is a tragedy almost as poignant as the nationalization of men would be to an archbishop.
And so, too, in "The Sad Horn Blowers," in "Unused," and in "The Man's

Story." These are short stories of the very first rank. They are simple, moving, and brilliantly vivid. Another such volume and all of us will begin to forget the Wisconsin washing-machine manufacturer and his occult posturing in the altogether. ["The Library," *AM* 1, no. 2 (February 1924): 252 ("Three Volumes of Fiction")]

Dark Laughter (1925)

Sherwood Anderson, like Conrad, seems unable to stand still. His whole career has been a history of seeking, of experimentation, of hard effort. More than once, groping for ideas that somehow eluded him, he has come to grief. There was the early case of *Marching Men*. There was the recent case of *Many Marriages*. But in *Dark Laughter*, it seems to me, he has at last found his method, and achieved his first wholly satisfying book. It is, in essence, extremely simple in plan, and even bald. A man and a woman, each married, meet by chance, and are presently in flight together. An obvious story? Its merit lies precisely in the fact that it is *not* obvious. What Anderson seeks to convey is the fundamental irrationality of the whole proceeding. He shows the two propelled into each other's arms by forces that are quite beyond them—not great cosmic currents, turned on by the angels, but a complex series of trivial impulses, arising out of the dullness of every day. John Stockton, a second-rate newspaper reporter, flees from life in two rooms with a banal wife, and goes to work, idiotically enough, in a wheel factory. It is in a small Ohio town, and the owner of the factory has a wife. She and John float together like leaves gliding down a stream. It is scarcely a love affair, as such things are understood. There is no grotesque Freudian machinery. John and Aline Grey simply collide in the void. When they depart together it somehow seems impossible and unreal. But are such things clearly real in actual life? Are they rationalized before the fact—or after?

"The only thing I could possibly write about," says one of the minor characters in the tale, "would be just about this stuff I am always giving you—about impotence, what a lot of it there is." It is a statement of Anderson's own limitation, and of the sources of his peculiar merit. The fatuous omniscience of the average novelist is not in him. He does not set out to tell you exactly why his characters do this or that; he is content to show them doing it. What he offers, beyond that, is mere speculation—often vague enough, but sometimes vastly more illuminating than cocksure explanations. I don't think he is altogether successful with Aline, but certainly he has never done a more brilliant and searching portrait than that of Stockton. Nor has he ever managed his background with greater skill or finer feeling. Nor has he ever bespattered it with more striking minor personages. The book, in brief, shows him coming to a genuine mastery of his manner. It is not the manner of any other novelist ever heard of. It has defects, disadvantages, even absurdities. But if the central purpose of a novelist is to make his people breathe and move, then surely Anderson has come to be one of the most adept of the craft in practise among us. ["The Library," AM 6, no. 3 (November 1925): 379–80 ("Fiction Good and Bad")]

Tar: A Midwest Childhood (1926)

Anderson's book, like most of his work, is uneven. There are chapters wherein his philosophizings over the experiences and aspirations of his youth become so thin as to be almost puerile; worse, there are repetitions in his story, and much of its material has been used in other places, sometimes much more effectively. But there are also chapters that show him at his very best—subtle, penetrating and incomparably romantic. I point to Chapter XV, the story of Mame Thompson, the circus-man's daughter, and to Chapter XII, the story of the old woman dead in the snow. The latter, in a slightly different form, was printed as "Death in the Woods" in *The American Mercury* for last September. It is a truly superb piece of writing, beautifully conceived and very skillfully executed. Let it stand as an answer to those reviewers who still maintain that Anderson doesn't know what he is about. I think he knows very well what he is about. But sometimes he tries to do his work with insufficient materials, and sometimes he is flabbergasted by technical problems that lie beyond his ingenuity. His air of amateurishness is one of his most valuable assets. In part it represents a very real deficiency. There is nothing of Cabell's virtuosity about him, nor anything of Hergesheimer's high sophistication. He is still a boy gaping at the world, and it often puzzles him. But I think his timorous, half uncertain manner is precisely suited to the sort of thing he tries to do. The omniscience of the more professional and workmanlike novelist would spoil him. I hope he remains the amateur so long as he writes. ["The Library," AM 10, no. 3 (March 1927): 382–83 ("Literary Confidences")]

James Branch Cabell

Out in Chicago, the only genuinely civilized city in the New World, they take the fine arts seriously, and get into such frets and excitements about them as are raised nowhere else save by baseball, murder, political treachery, foreign wars and romantic loves. Boston is too solemn for such frenzies, and too idiotic; the æsthetic passion, up there, has been quenched by the hose of Harvard; the typical Boston æsthete is a professor, and hence an embalmer. As for New York, its artistic activities are dominated by the publishers of bad books, sellers of eighth-rate (and usually bogus) paintings, and social pushers (often Jews and always bouncers) who patronize music for the advertising that is in it. The other towns are vacuums. Huneker is temporarily in Philadelphia, but not a fluid ounce of Philadelphia is in Huneker. In San Francisco George Sterling is left blooming alone; the Baptists have chased out all other friends of beauty and the devil. St. Louis? Mention Orrick Johns and Zoë Akins and you have said all; Sara Teasdale has moved to New York. Detroit, Minneapolis, Milwaukee, New Orleans, Baltimore, Washington, Los Angeles, Denver, the Indiana towns? To ask is to answer. The life of such fat and stupid places is absolutely devoid of artistic interest; a contrapuntist or a dry-point etcher, dumped into any of them, would be jailed as a Bolshevik. And an artistic question, raised publicly in any of them, would get about as much attention as a problem in quaternions, semasiology or honor.

But not in Chicago. Out there they not only produce artists in such number that the produce of all the rest of the nation is surpassed; they also debate the mysteries and snares of the bozart with astounding fervor and copiousness. Dramatic criticism, in New York, is a trade of the chautauqua-minded; the most esteemed critics are such pious gushers and sobbers as Clayton Hamilton and the late William Winter. In Chicago the business gets the best talent of the town, which is the best talent of the country. And so with music, and painting, and the squeezing of mud, and books. Only one New York newspaper prints a literary supplement that anyone above a Greek bus boy can read without pain; in Chicago every last paper has one. In New York the chief music critics are merely ambulent card indexes; in Chicago they are musicians. In New York (and Boston no less)—

But what I started out to do was to call attention to the uproarious critical battle that has been going on in Chicago of late over James Branch

Cabell—a battle full of tremendous whoops, cracks, wallops and devil-tries, with critic pulling the nose of critic, and volunteers going over the top in swarms, and the air heavy with ink, ears, typewriters, adjectives, chair legs and strophes from the Greek Anthology. And the question, what is it? One of morals—Cabell vs. the Comstocks? Nay. One of sales—Cabell as a best-seller? Nay. One of patriotism, politics? Cabell as a Socialist, a forward-looker, a wilful one, an agent of the Wilhelmstrasse? Nay again. The question is simply one of style. Is Cabell a great stylist, imbecilely overlooked and neglected by the connoisseurs of the republic, or is he simply a flashy fellow, a dexterous but essentially hollow trickster? This is the problem that keeps those young Chicagoans up at night, and sets them to writing against one another in high astounding terms, and fills their papers with articles columns long. A question of style—and within one verst of the stockyards! Almost one fancies the world bumped by a flying asteroid, and the Chicago river suddenly turned into the Seine!

Well, it was a long time coming, and I am delighted to see it here at last. For this Cabell, soon or late, was bound to make his splash; the one danger was that it would come half a century after his death and burial. I roll back through my yellowing files and find dithyrambs upon his deft mastery of words so long ago as June, 1909—praises for his "artist's feeling for form and color," his "musician's feeling for rhythm," the high distinction of his style, "a quality as rare in American novels as Christian charity in a Christian bishop."[33] Nor was I first, or alone. His *The Eagle's Shadow* had arrested the discreet back in 1904; he had been in the magazines, including this one. But somehow the esteem that he thus came into took on a sort of esoteric quality; he was admired by enough to make a creditable *Minyan*, but it was in silence and behind the door. The newspaper critics, looking for juicy, oleaginous romance, couldn't find it in his books. The professors who write for the literary weeklies and monthlies never heard of him. He passed into a state of half-fabulous disembodiment, sensed but not quite apprehended. And meanwhile he kept on writing books, both in prose and in verse.

Now, by dint of the sudden roughhouse on the lake shore, he is pulled out of his shadow, and exhibited before the national calciums. What stands revealed is an artist, as artists go among us, of the first consideration —a man of novel and ingenious ideas, a penetrating ironist, a shrewd and infectious laugher, a delicate virtuoso of situation, an anatomist of character, one who sees into the eternal tragi-comedy of hope and striving, above all, a highly accomplished doctor of words. It is this last talent which stands above all the others, and sets him off from the whole herd of native novelists. He puts into writing an indefatigable effort and a quite unusual fastidiousness. There is not merely the right word; there is, far more importantly, the right cadence, the right rhythm. He could no more concoct a stumbling sentence than he could concoct a "glad" book. What he has to say, in the last analysis, is always secondary; his first consideration goes to the way it is said. The result, of course, is sometimes an appearance of hardness, of over-laboring. Accustomed in the current books to a mode of writing that is sluttishly loose and unstudied—to a style suggesting, more than anything else, a pie-woman in a Mother Hubbard—one feels, at times, a great tightness in this elaboration of effort. But nine times out of ten its success disposes of its strangeness. In it there is a satisfaction that is rare and charming. It is writing in the manner of a proficient and self-respecting journeyman.

What distinguishes Cabell's matter, as opposed to his manner, is simply his ironical detachment, his ethical sophistication, his complete removal from all the puerile blather that passes for profundity in the modern novel. What is the "idea"—the "message," as the lady critics put it—in such a book as *The Cream of the Jest* or *The Rivet in Grandfather's Neck?* Simply the pathetic hollowness of all "ideas"—the sheer fortuitousness and meaninglessness of the comedy, the eternal helplessness and donkeyishness of man. Here we have old materials, familiar situations, commonplace romance— and yet as skilfully worked over, as brilliantly made new, as the blood-tub melodrama in the tales of Joseph Conrad. Is it mystifying, as certain reviewers have set up, that Cabell should go back to the Eighteenth Century, and even beyond? Surely not. What he seeks in those old days is the drama of man and woman rid of its current swathings of convention and illusion—a drama made simple and almost abstract. His characters are thus rid of non-essentials; they become Pierrots and Pierrettes. A somewhat puzzling business, to readers saturated with mere timeliness, concreteness, news interest. But not puzzling, after all, if we look beneath the surface, and see the Pierrot that is in every man of us, and the Pierrette that is in every woman.

If you are not familiar with the books of Cabell, take a look. He is an

original, and he will be talked of hereafter. ["A Sub-Potomac Phenomenon," SS 55, no. 4 (August 1918): 138–40]

The Cream of the Jest (1917)

The Cabell book is another quite unusual composition, half novel and
half essay in psychology, and with excellent writing in it from cover to
cover. In ground plan it is an attempt to lay bare the secret soul of Felix
Kennaston, a successful novelist—not the Bovaryan pseudo-soul visible to
his wife and his neighbors, but that esoteric spirit which transcends time
and space, and has its adventures in the super-world of the imagination.
Outwardly, Kennaston is a discreet and reputable man—a convinced
monogamist, a dutiful householder, a docile Presbyterian. But within him
there dwells an adventurer who ranges the whole of the visible universe,
and a lover who has found his heart's desire. So much for the framework of
the story. Upon it Mr. Cabell hangs the loot of much intellectual maraud-
ing—brilliant bits of irony, penetrating reflections upon faiths and ideas, a
whole agnostic philosophy. It would be difficult to match the book in
American fiction; it has, from first to last, a French smack; one constantly
hears overtones that suggest Anatole France and J. K. Huysmans. A thing
obviously written *con amore*, joyously, without regard to markets. The
reader it will attract is precisely the reader most worth attracting. It is not a
popular novel, not a story, not a mere time-killer; it is a piece of literature.
["Critics Wild and Tame," SS 53, no. 4 (December 1917): 143]

Beyond Life (1919)

The row over James Branch Cabell, intermittently breaking out, with
gradually increasing choler, for a year or so past, should be vastly stimulated by his new book, *Beyond Life*, for in it, instead of attempting to pla-
cate his detractors, he deliberately has at them with all arms. Is art
representation? A thousand times, Pish! Art is a dream of perfection, art is
a projection of fancy, art is a "rumor of dawn," art is an escape from life!
Down with all the dolts who merely set up cameras and squeeze bulbs!
Down, again, with the donkeys who mount soap-boxes and essay to read
morals into life, to make it logical and mathematical, to rationalize it, to

explain it. The thing is not to be rationalized and explained at all—that is the eternal charm of it. It is to be admired, experimented with, toyed with, wondered at. Itself a supreme adventure, it is the spring and end of all other adventure—especially of the ever-entrancing adventure into ideas. And, above all, let us not get into wraths about it—let us not torture ourselves with the maudlin certainties that make for indignation. Life is a comedy to him, etc., etc. . . . Say that the Walpolean spirit is in Cabell, and you have described him perhaps as accurately as it may be done. His frequent ventures into the eighteenth century are not accidental, but inevitable. It was the century of sentiment, but it was also, in its top layers, the century of a fine and exhilarating skepticism. This skepticism is what chiefly gives character to Cabell, and sets him off so sharply from an age of oafish faiths, of imbecile enthusiasms, of unearthly and innumerable sure cures, of incredible credulities. This is the thing in him that outrages the simple-minded, and causes them to fall upon him furiously, not merely for what they conceive to be sins æsthetical, but also for what appears to their disordered ire as a vague and sinister inner depravity. To laugh at certainty as he laughs at it is inordinately offensive to the right-minded, and in the course of time, as the war upon intelligence makes progress, it will probably become jailable.

Yet there he holds the fort, disdainfully convinced that artificiality is the only true reality. And there he fashions books in a hard and brilliant style—the last word in artful and arduous craftsmanship among us— Paterism somehow humanized and made expansive. I wonder what the amazed old maids, male and female, of the newspapers will call *Beyond Life*—novel, book of essays, or *apologia pro vita sua?* If novel, then it is a strange novel indeed, for there is but one character, and he talks steadily from page 23 to the end. If book of essays, then where are the essays?— surely these rolling discourses are nothing of the sort. And if *apologia*, then why not an occasional apology? The college professors of the literary weeklies, with their dusty shelf of pigeon-holes, have work for them here. As for the rest of us, all we need do is read on, enjoying the fare as we go. What is it? In brief, excellent reading—shy, insinuating learning; heterodoxy infinitely gilded; facts rolled out in fragile thinness and cut into pretty figures; above all, a sure and delicate sense of words, a style at once exact and undulate, very caressing writing.

In detail, much shrewd discussion of this and that, with many a flash of sound criticism. The chapter on Christopher Marlowe has interested me more than any other. To how many of us, in these later days, does Marlowe remain a living figure in English letters? Hasn't he been condemned, for a century past, to the literature books—and hideously disemboweled and mummified by imbecile birchmen, editors of "school editions," mouthers of dead inanities. To the majority, even of the literate, he survives perhaps as a mere phrase: "Marlowe's mighty line."[34] (Once launching it idiotically at an American dramatist, I found that he thought I meant Julia.)[35] And yet what a man he was!—what a superb virtuoso of English!—what a colossal master of rhythm and color and verbal dynamics! Shakespeare learned a great deal more from him than any of the professors suspect, and debased not a little of it in the learning. The phrases we all use as rubber-stamps, the philosophizings that endear the Bard to the general, are simply platitudes done into second-hand Marlowese. As for Marlowe himself, he disdained platitudes—and thus doomed himself to perish. His one concern was with the noble music that lies in words. He was stylist first, last and forever. Drunk upon nouns, verbs, adjectives, adverbs, pronouns, prepositions and conjunctions, he forgot his audience, forgot his characters, forgot his very drama. But what divine roars and whispers of sound remain upon those neglected pages, despite all the notes of the pedagogues! What a work he achieved! . . . But Cabell makes it plain. And other things too. A singular and fascinating book. ["Mainly Fiction," SS 58, no. 3 (March 1919): 142–43]

Jurgen (1919)

Of literary reputations a number of distinct varieties are to be distinguished. There is, first of all, the sort of reputation that is high both vertically and horizontally—the sort that tends to convert itself into a racial myth, unchallenged and even unexamined—to wit, the reputation of a Shakespeare, a Goethe, a Molière, a Dante, a Schiller, or, to drop a peg or two, a Tolstoi, a Hugo or a Mark Twain. Secondly, there is the kind that has a wide base but dissolves in sniffs above—the reputation of a Brieux, a Harold Bell Wright, a Lew Wallace, a Richard Harding Davis, an Elbert Hubbard, a Conan Doyle or a D'Annunzio. Thirdly, there is the kind that is brilliant above but shadowy below—the reputation of a Henry James, a

Huysmans, a Lafcadio Hearn, a Schnitzler, a Joseph Conrad or a George Gissing. Fourthly, there is the kind that is shadowy up and down—a thing less of public bruitings than of cautious whispers—a diffident, esoteric, Hugo-Wolfish variety—*e. g.*, the reputation of a Max Stirner, an Henri Becque, a Marie Henri Beyle or an Ambrose Bierce. . . .

Bierce is dead, and in America, at least, the post is vacant. I have a fancy that James Branch Cabell will enter into enjoyment of its prerogatives and usufructs. All efforts to make him popular will fail inevitably; he is far too mystifying a fellow ever to enchant the simple folk who delight in O. Henry, Kathleen Norris and Henry van Dyke. Moreover, he writes too well; his English is too voluptuous to be endured; there is nothing ingratiatingly mushy and idiotic about it. Nor is he likely to be embraced by such *intelligentsia* as disport in the literary weeklies and the women's clubs, for he is not a Deep Thinker, but a Scoffer, and, worse, he scoffs at Sacred Things, including even American Ideals. Nay, there is no hope for Cabell in either direction. If he ever had a chance, his new book, *Jurgen*, has ruined it. *Jurgen*, estimated by current American standards, whether of the boobery or of the super-boobery, is everything that is abhorrent. On the negative side, it lacks all Inspiration, all Optimism, all tendency to whoop up the Finer Things; it moves toward no shining Goal; it even neglects to denounce Pessimism, Marital Infidelity, Bolshevism, the Alien Menace and German *Kultur*. And on the positive side it piles up sins unspeakable: it is full of racy and mirthful ideas, it is brilliantly written, it is novel and daring, it is ribald, it is heretical, it is blasphemous, it is Rabelaisian. Such a book simply refuses to fit into the decorous mid-Victorian pattern of American letters. It belongs to some outlandish literature, most probably the French. One might imagine it written by a member of the French Academy, say Anatole France. But could one imagine it written by a member of the American Academy of Arts and Letters, say Bliss Perry? The thought is not only fantastic; it is almost obscene.

Cabell came near sneaking into refined society, a few years ago, as a novelist. Several of his novels, like the earlier pieces of Hergesheimer, trembled on the verge of polite acceptance. Both writers were handicapped by having ears. They wrote English that was delicately musical and colorful—and hence incurably offensive to constant readers of Rex Beach, Thomas H. Dixon, and the New York *Times*. Hergesheimer finally atoned for his style by mastering the popular novelette formula; thereafter he was in the *Saturday Evening Post* and the old maids who review books for the newspapers began to praise him. A few weeks ago I received an invitation to hear him lecture before a Browning Society; in a year or two, if he continues to be good, he will be elected to membership in the National Institute of Arts and Letters, in full equality with Ernest Poole, Oliver Herford, Henry Sydnor Harrison and E. W. Townsend, author of *Chimmie Fadden*. Cabell, I fear, must resign himself to doing without the accolade. *Beyond Life* spilled many a bean; beneath its rumblings one discerned more than one cackle of satanic laughter. *Jurgen* wrecks the whole beanery. It is a compendium of backward-looking and wrong-thinking. It is a devil's sonata, an infernal *Kindersinfonie* for slap-stick, seltzer-siphon and bladder-on-a-string. . . . And, too, for the caressing violin, the lovely and melancholy flute. How charmingly the fellow writes! What a hand for the slick and slippery phrase he has! How cunningly he winds up a sentence, and then flicks it out with a twist of the wrist—a shimmering, dazzling shower of nouns, verbs, adjectives, adverbs, pronouns and prepositions! . . .

It is curious how often the gift of irony is coupled with pedantry. Think of old François and his astounding citations from incredible authorities— almost like an article in a German medical journal. Or of Anatole France. Or of Swift. Cabell, in *Jurgen*, borrows all the best hocus-pocus of the professors. He reconstructs an imaginary medieval legend with all the attention to detail of the pundits who publish college editions of *Aucassin et Nicolette*; until, toward the end, his own exuberance intoxicates him a bit, he actually makes it seem a genuine translation. But his Jurgen, of course, is never a medieval man. No; Jurgen is horribly modern. Jurgen is you and I, or you and me, as you choose. Jurgen is the modern man in reaction against a skepticism that explains everything away and yet leaves everything inexplicable. He is the modern man in doubt of all things, including especially his own doubts. So his quest is no heroic enterprise, though it takes him over half the earth and into all the gaudiest and most romantic kingdoms thereof, for the thing that he seeks is not a great hazard and an homeric death but simply ease and contentment, and what he comes to in the end is the discovery that they are nowhere to be found, not even in the arms of a royal princess. Jurgen acquires the shirt of Nessus and the magical sword Caliburn; he becomes Duke of Logreus, Prince Consort in Cocaigne, King of Eubonia, and Emperor of Noumaria; he meets and loves the incomparable Guenevere in the moonlight on the eve of her marriage to King Arthur; he unveils the beauty of Helen of Troy; he is taught all the ineffable secrets of love by Queen Anaïtis; he becomes a great poet; he sees strange coasts; he roams the whole universe. But in the end, he returns sadly to a world "wherein the result of every human endeavor is transient and the end of all is death," and takes his old place behind the counter of his pawnshop, and resumes philosophically his interrupted feud with his faded wife, Dame Lisa.

In brief, a very simple tale, and as old in its fundamental dolorousness as arterio sclerosis. What gives it its high quality is the richness of its detail—the prodigious gorgeousness of its imagery, the dramatic effectiveness of its shifting scenes, the whole glow and gusto of it. Here, at all events, it is medieval. Here Cabell evokes an atmosphere that is the very essence of charm. Nothing could be more delightfully done than some of the episodes—that of Jurgen's meeting with Guenevere in the Hall of Judgment, that of his dialogue with old King Gogyrvan Gawr, that of his adventure with the Hamadryad, that of the ceremony of the Breaking of the Veil, that of his invasion of the bed-chamber of Helen of Troy. The man who could imagine such scenes is a first-rate artist, and in the manner of their execution he proves the fact again. Time and again they seem to be dissolving, shaking a bit, going to pieces—but always he carries them off. And always neatly, delicately, with an air. The humor of them has its perils; to Puritans it must often seem shocking; it might easily become gross. But here it is no more gross than a rose-window. . . . Toward the end, alack, the thing falls down. The transition from heathen Olympuses and Arcadies to the Christian Heaven and Hell works an inevitable debasement of the comedy. The satire here ceases to be light-fingered and becomes heavy-handed: "the religion of Hell is patriotism, and the government is an enlightened democracy." It is almost like making fun of a man with inflammatory rheumatism. Perhaps the essential thing is that the book is a trifle too long. By the time one comes to Calvinism, democracy and the moral order of the world one has begun to feel surfeited. But where is there a work of art without a blemish? Even Beethoven occasionally misses fire. This *Jurgen*, for all such ifs and buts, is a very fine thing. It is a great pity that it was not written in French. Done in English, and printed in These States, it somehow suggests Brahms scoring his Fourth

Symphony for a jazz band and giving it at an annual convention of the Knights of Pythias. ["The Flood of Fiction," SS 61, no. 1 (January 1920): 138–40]

Figures of Earth (1921)

For reasons peculiarly personal, I find it impossible to praise the new Cabell *opus*, *Figures of Earth*, in high, astounding terms, but I may as well confess at once that this impediment gives me very little real difficulty, for the book seems to me to lie a good way below *Jurgen*, both in conception and in execution. To begin with, the quest of Manuel the swineherd is intrinsically less gaudy and glamorous than the quest of Jurgen the pawnbroker; the things he searches for in the world are less alluring than the things that Jurgen seeks, and he looks for them in narrower fields and among less amusing folk. It follows inevitably that his adventures are less various and exhilarating. Who, among all the twice and thrice-born men that he encounters, is to be mentioned in the same breath with Gogyrvan Gawr, King of Glathion and father to the delectable Guenevere? And where, among all his colloquies with the beings of both worlds, is there a debate so gorgeous as that which Jurgen has with Gogyrvan in the thirteenth chapter of his saga? Alas, you may open any chapter of *Jurgen* at random, and find things not to be matched in *Figures of Earth*—the ceremonial of the breaking of the veil, the episode with the hamadryad, the scenes in the palace of Queen Anaïtis, the journey with the ghost of Queen Sylvia Tereu, the visit to Hell, the last palaver with Dame Lisa. The whole story of Manuel is on a smaller scale; there is more of the fairy tale in it and less of Rabelais; its humor seems to me to be more obvious and less penetrating. Is the influence of Comstockery to blame for the difference? Perhaps in part. In more than one place the effort to bring a medieval tale within the limits laid down by the blue-noses is evident enough; often, indeed, the author pokes fun at the idiotic Presbyterian barriers that hedge him in. But that is only part of the story. The primary fact is that *Figures of Earth* is planned upon a smaller scale than *Jurgen*, and that it lacks the epical sweep and swagger of that masterpiece. Cabell is still enormously fantastic and whimsical; his satire is often as sharp as a needle; he has all his old skill at putting words together in mellifluous sequences. But there are no high points, no ascents to the grand manner, no passages for the full orchestra. From end to end of the book I find nothing comparable to that memorable buffoonery in *Jurgen* beginning: "The religion of Hell is patriotism, and the government is an enlightened democracy."

So much for the prosecution. What remains is a very excellent piece of writing—a book that would stand out brilliantly if the vast shadow of *Jurgen* were not upon it. I know of no man writing English to-day who handles the language with quite the same feeling for its smallest rhythms that Cabell shows; not even George Moore is his peer in that department. It is, in fact, a charming experience to read him for the sheer music that is in him, regardless of what he is driving at. His sentences follow one another like shadows, slyly, fleetly and beautifully. The raucous word, the clumsy phrase—these things seem to be quite beyond him; it is a literal fact that he is absolutely never guilty of them. His method, in other hands, might easily degenerate to sweetness; in truth, it always does when some lesser man attempts it. But he rolls along from end to end of a longish book without faltering once—without once falling into ineptitude or banality. For anyone to write such English is as rare as for anyone to write music like Mozart or Haydn; for an American to do it is little short of a miracle. We produce few stylists of any sort. All eyes, in a moral republic, are upon content; if the doctrine of the scrivener is pure his manner is taken for granted. But here is an author who has so perfected manner that it makes content seem secondary, and even negligible; Cabell on the Constitution, or the eight-hour day, or the initiative and referendum would be charming, just as the average American, even on the Kamasutram, would be dull. I have told you that *Figures of Earth* is not up to his high mark, but I defy you to begin it without sliding through it to the end, easily and delightedly. ["The Land of the Free," SS 65, no. 1 (May 1921): 142–43]

The High Place (1923)

The High Place is in the manner of the celebrated *Jurgen*, and all the ground that the author seemed to lose in the first successor to *Jurgen*, to wit, *Figures of Earth*, is here recovered in a handsome style, with some gains further on. *The High Place*, indeed, is far more competently put together than *Jurgen*. The fundamental idea is simpler; the structure is less complex and dispersed. In brief, the melancholy story of a dream come true. Florian de Puysange has a vision in youth of the perfect maiden,

Melior. Her beauty is beyond all other conceivable beauty; she is perfect as the seraphim are perfect. But not unattainable! Florian hacks his way to her through dragons and monsters; he employs magicians to aid him; he is helped both by the Devil and by a holy saint. In the end he wins his Melior, and discovers—That she is a shrew? No; nothing so obvious. He discovers that she is an unbearable and incurable bore.

The tale has charm almost without measure. It is clear-running, it is ingenious, and it is full of truly delightful detail. Mr. Cabell was never more shrewd, sardonic, iconoclastic, daring. He has made a romance that is captivating in itself, and yet remains a devastating *reductio ad absurdum* of all romance. It is as if the species came to perfect flower in a bloom that poisoned itself. I praise it no more, but pass on to its defects, of which there are two. The first issues out of the fact that the author appears to be down with a bad case of pronounophobia; in particular, the pronouns of the third person seem to affright him. The result is a multiplicity of such sentences as this one: "Thus it was not until the coming of Spring that Florian rode away from the Hôtel de Puysange, wherein he had just passed the first actually unhappy period of Florian's life." Why not "his" for the second "Florian"? The sentence is botched as it stands—and a botched sentence in Cabell stands out as brilliantly as a good one in D. H. Lawrence. A worse defect comes at the very end of the book. Cabell brings it up to a logical and delightful finale, and then tacks on a banal chapter explaining that Florian's adventures in two worlds have been but the fancies of a dream—that he has never actually wooed, won and married the incomparable Melior, that he is still a romantic boy asleep under a magic tree. It is almost as bad as if he had added a moral chapter advocating the World Court and the Coolidge idealism. Still worse, he prints a second appendix hinting plainly that Florian has been called back to life and youth in order to open the way for a sequel. Such crimes against sense and decency are too gross to be punished in literary courts. If there is a secular arm in Virginia, let Cabell be handed over to it. ["The Library," *AM* 1, no. 3 (March 1924): 380–81 ("Three Gay Stories")]

Straws and Prayer-Books (1924)

Ostensibly, this extremely lively and amusing book is a sort of epilogue to all of Cabell's other books—a final summing-up by an author who grows weary of the pen, and is about to lay it down. But let the Cabellistas hold their fears and protests! Cabell is not only *not* going to quit the trade he so brilliantly adorns; he here offers overwhelming proof that he'll *never* quit it—that is, so long as there is breath in him and he can stagger to his desk on two sticks. To do so would be as impossible for him as it would be for a movie actor to give up wenching. He is moved toward it by an irresistible impulse and desire, nearly amounting to a tropism. The true artist, indeed, is almost completely the creature of instinct; the Good Citizen is quite right in viewing him somewhat suspiciously, as a fellow defectively broken to correct living. A young man may choose rationally between entering a bank and embracing the tallow business, or even between entering a bank and studying law or taking holy orders, but when he goes in for any of the fine arts it is a sign that God, in His infinite wisdom, has put a ring into his nose, and that the pull at the other end is far beyond his volition and control. Beethoven did not write his music by a logical process; he wrote it by a process comparable to the fine, free, nonsensical jumping of a grasshopper.

Cabell goes into all this at length in his book, and then enters upon a consideration of the nature of art itself. He balks at calling it a criticism of life, apparently because that definition of it has been worn threadbare by pedants, but he is soon saying much the same thing in different words. Art, he maintains, is, in its essence, "an evasion of the distasteful." The artist is "simply one who does not like the earth he inhabits." For the laws of nature "his admiration has always been remarkably temperate, and with the laws of society he has never had any patience whatever." In other words, art is an escape from life. The artist seeks to create an ideal world that is measurably more beautiful and more comfortable than this dreadful world we live in. His value to society lies in the fact that he cannot monopolize it, once he has created it. Anyone with the yearning is free to enter its pearly gates and graze upon its field of asphodel. Cabell himself has led a happy horde that way. He calls his world Poictesme, and he has not only planted it with asphodel but also peopled it with rare and charming folk. They are more real to thousands than Cabell himself. But the friends they make are, in a way, his friends too. Thus the artist leaves his mark upon his time and attains to happiness. Thus, by making life more bearable to strangers, he makes it more bearable to himself.

Straws and Prayer-Books is a fine piece of work, beautifully designed and delicately wrought. It is the composition of one of the soundest artists this great Christian land has yet produced. ["The Library," *AM* 3, no. 4 (December 1924): 509–10 ("Cabell")]

Something about Eve (1927)

"Every marriage," says Gerald Musgrave, "gets at least one man into trouble—and it is not always the bridegroom." The text may serve as good as another for *Something about Eve*. Gerald, like all of the Cabell heroes, goes on a quest, and again like all of them, he returns from it sadly at fifty-eight, his neck scarred indelibly by the marks of that sinister rope which disguises itself as the naked female arm, and his shoulders burned and cicatrized by female tears. *So geht's in die Welt!* The story comes down to us from time immemorial, and in the form of a thousand tragedies, but Cabell prefers to view it (with sound sense) as comedy, and in the present version of it he adorns it with all the blooms of his singularly lively and corrosive wit. Who can match him at his diabolical best? If you have a candidate, then bring him on to equal the treatise on the articles of war for married ladies and their lovers, in the fourth chapter of *Something about Eve*.

As year chases year the position of Cabell gradually solidifies, and it becomes manifest that his place among the American writers of his time, seen in retrospect, will be at the first table. It used to be the fashion to speak of him as an imitator of Anatole France, but that folly seems to be passing out. There are, in fact, few signs in his books that France has influenced him, save perhaps in non-essentials. His point of view is the result, not of viewing the world from Paris, but of viewing it from Virginia. No more thorough American lives and has his being among us. It was the grotesque quasi-civilization in which, coming to manhood, he found himself that sent him flying to Poictesme, and it is that civilization which he depicts from his exile there. The articles of war that I have mentioned would be unintelligible to a Frenchman, and I fancy that they would also puzzle an Englishman, whose traditional answer to adultery on his premises is a suit in equity. But they must ring true to every American, and especially to every American who has lived in the charming wilderness below Wilmington, Del. The observation in them is of the first degree of accuracy, and they are set forth with all the lovely enchantment of a Vienna waltz.

The Cabellian style shows no sign of playing out. It is still caressingly dulcet, but it is by no means sing-songy. There is steel in it as well as attar of roses. It is capable of a phrase that stings as well as of a phrase that lulls. Cabell clings to certain mannerisms that, I confess, greatly irritate me— for example, his curious avoidance of pronouns, his piling up of proper names—, but that clinging is less amorous and irritating than it used to be—or maybe I have got used to it. In *Something about Eve* the narrative flows in beautiful cadences. There is no harsh improvising in it; it is all thought out to the last place of decimals. Cabell has done better books: I nominate *The High Place* at once. But few of his books are better done. ["The Library," AM 12, no. 4 (December 1927): 510 ("A Comedy of Fig-Leaves")]

F. Scott Fitzgerald

This Side of Paradise (1920)

The best American novel that I have seen of late is [. . .] the product of a neophyte, to wit, F. Scott Fitzgerald. This Fitzgerald has taken part in *The Smart Set*'s display of literary fireworks more than once, and so you are probably familiar with his method.[36] In *This Side of Paradise* he offers a truly amazing first novel—original in structure, extremely sophisticated in manner, and adorned with a brilliancy that is as rare in American writing as honesty is in American statecraft. The young American novelist usually reveals himself as a naïve, sentimental and somewhat disgusting ignoramus— a believer in Great Causes, a snuffler and eye-roller, a spouter of stale philosophies out of Kensington drawing-rooms, the doggeries of French hack-drivers, and the lower floor of the Munich Hofbräuhaus. Nine times out of ten one finds him shocked by the discovery that women are not the complete angels that they pretend to be, and full of the theory that all of the miners in West Virginia would become instantly non-luetic, intelligent and happy if Congress would only pass half a dozen simple laws. In brief, a fellow viewing human existence through a knot-hole in the floor of a Socialist local. Fitzgerald is nothing of the sort. On the contrary, he is a highly civilized and rather waggish fellow—a youngster not without sentiment, and one even cursed with a touch or two of pretty sentimentality, but still one who is many cuts above the general of the land. More, an artist—an apt and delicate weaver of words, a clever hand, a sound workman. The first half of the story is far better than the second half. It is not that Fitzgerald's manner runs thin, but that his hero begins to elude him. What, after such a youth, is to be done with the fellow? The author's solution is anything but felicitous. He simply drops his Amory Blaine as Mark Twain dropped Huckleberry Finn, but for a less cogent reason. But down to and including the episode of the love affair with Rosalind the thing is capital, especially the first chapters. Not since Frank Norris's day has there been a more adept slapping in of preliminaries. ["Books More or Less Amusing," SS 62, no. 4 (August 1920): 140]

The Beautiful and Damned (1922)

F. Scott Fitzgerald's *The Beautiful and the Damned* is an *adagio* following the *scherzo* of *This Side of Paradise*. It starts off ingratiatingly and disarmingly, with brilliant variations upon the theme of the *scherzo*, but pretty soon a more sombre tune is heard in the bull-fiddles, and toward the end there is very solemn music, indeed—music that will probably give a shock to all the fluffier and more flapperish Fizgeraldistas. In brief, a disconcerting peep into the future of a pair of the amiable children dealt with in *This Side of Paradise*. Here we have Gloria Gilbert, the prom angel, graduating into a star of hotel dances in New York, and then into a wife, and then into the scared spectator of her husband's disintegration, and then, at the end, into a pathetic trembler on the brink of middle age. And here we have Anthony Patch, the gallant young Harvard man, sliding hopelessly down the hill of idleness, incompetence, extravagance and drunkenness. It is, in the main, Anthony's story, not Gloria's. His reactions to her, of course—to her somewhat florid charm, her acrid feminine cynicism, her love of hollow show and hollower gayety, her fear of inconvenient facts—are integral parts of the intricate machinery of his decay, but one feels that he would have decayed quite rapidly without her, whatever may be said for the notion that a wife of another sort might have saved him. There is little that is vicious about Anthony; he is simply silly—the fearful product of ill-assorted marriages, a quite typical American of the third generation from shirt-sleeves. The forthright competence of his old grandfather, Adam J. Patch, the millionaire moralist, has been bred out of the strain. Into it have come dilutions from a New England blue-stocking and worse. He is hopeless from birth.

The waters into which this essentially serious and even tragic story bring Fitzgerald seemed quite beyond the ken of the author of *This Side of Paradise*. It is thus not surprising to find him navigating, at times, rather cautiously and ineptly. The vast plausibility that Dreiser got into the similar chronicle of Hurstwood is not there; one often encounters shakiness, both in the imagining and the telling. Worse, the thing is botched at the end by the introduction of a god from the machine: Anthony is saved from the inexorable logic of his life by a court decision which gives him, most unexpectedly and improbably, his grandfather's millions. But allowing for all that, it must be said for Fitzgerald that he discharges his unaccustomed and difficult business with ingenuity and dignity. Opportunity beckoned him toward very facile jobs; he might have gone on rewriting the charming romance of *This Side of Paradise* for ten or fifteen years, and made a lot of money out of it, and got a great deal of uncritical praise for it. Instead, he tried something much more difficult, and if the result is not a complete success, it is nevertheless near enough to success to be worthy of respect. There is fine observation in it, and much penetrating detail, and the writing is solid and sound. After *This Side of Paradise* the future of Fitzgerald seemed extremely uncertain. There was an air about that book which suggested a fortunate accident. The shabby stuff collected in *Flappers and Philosophers* converted uncertainty into something worse. But *The Beautiful and the Damned* delivers the author from all those doubts. There are a hundred signs in it of serious purpose and unquestionable skill. Even in its defects there is proof of hard striving. Fitzgerald ceases to be a *Wunderkind*, and begins to come into his maturity. ["The Niagara of Novels," SS 67, no. 4 (April 1922): 140–41]

The Great Gatsby (1925)

Scott Fitzgerald's new novel, *The Great Gatsby*, is in form no more than a glorified anecdote, and not too probable at that. The scene is the Long Island that hangs precariously on the edges of the New York City ash dumps—the Long Island of gaudy villas and bawdy house parties. The theme is the old one of a romantic and preposterous love—the ancient *fidelis ad urnum* motif reduced to a macabre humor. The principal personage is a bounder typical of those parties—a fellow who seems to know every one and yet remain unknown to all—a young man with a great deal of mysterious money, the tastes of a movie actor and, under it all, the simple sentimentality of a somewhat sclerotic fat woman.

This clown Fitzgerald rushes to his death in nine short chapters. The other performers in the *Totentanz* are of a like, or even worse, quality. One of them is a rich man who carries on a grotesque intrigue with the wife of a garage keeper. Another is a woman golfer who wins championships by cheating. A third, a sort of chorus to the tragic farce, is a bond salesman—symbol of the New America! Fitzgerald clears them all off at last by a triple butchery. The garage keeper's wife, rushing out upon the road to escape her husband's third degree, is run down and killed by the wife of her lover. The garage keeper, misled by the lover, kills the lover of the lover's wife—the Great Gatsby himself. Another bullet, and the garage keeper is also reduced to offal. Choragus fades away. The crooked lady golfer departs. The lover of the garage keeper's wife goes back to his own consort. The immense house of the Great Gatsby stands idle, its bedrooms given over to the bat and the owl, its cocktail shakers dry. The curtain lurches down.

This story is obviously unimportant and, though, as I shall show, it has its place in the Fitzgerald canon, it is certainly not to be put on the same shelf with, say, *This Side of Paradise*. What ails it, fundamentally, is the plain fact that it is simply a story—that Fitzgerald seems to be far more interested in maintaining its suspense than in getting under the skins of his people. It is not that they are false; it is that they are taken too much for granted. Only Gatsby himself genuinely lives and breathes. The rest are mere marionettes—often astonishingly lifelike, but nevertheless not quite alive.

What gives the story distinction is something quite different from the management of the action or the handling of the characters; it is the charm and beauty of the writing. In Fitzgerald's first days it seemed almost unimaginable that he would ever show such qualities. His writing, then, was extraordinarily slipshod—at times almost illiterate. He seemed to be devoid of any feeling for the color and savor of words. He could see people clearly and he could devise capital situations, but as writer *qua* writer he was apparently little more than a bright college boy. The critics of the Re-public were not slow to discern the fact. They praised *This Side of Paradise* as a story, as a social document, but they were almost unanimous in de-nouncing it as a piece of writing.

It is vastly to Fitzgerald's credit that he appears to have taken their caveats seriously, and pondered them to good effect. In *The Great Gatsby* the highly agreeable fruits of that pondering are visible. The story, for all its basic triviality, has a fine texture, a careful and brilliant finish. The ob-vious phrase is simply not in it. The sentences roll along smoothly, sparklingly, variously. There is evidence in every line of hard and intelli-gent effort. It is a quite new Fitzgerald who emerges from this little book, and the qualities that he shows are dignified and solid. *This Side of Par-adise*, after all, might have been merely a lucky accident. But *The Great Gatsby*, a far inferior story at bottom, is plainly the product of a sound and stable talent, conjured into being by hard work.

I make much of this improvement because it is of an order not often witnessed in American writers, and seldom, indeed, in those who start off with a popular success. The usual progression, indeed, is in the opposite direction. Every year first books of great promise are published—and every year a great deal of stale drivel is printed by the promising authors of year before last. The rewards of literary success in this country are so vast that, when they come early, they are not unnaturally somewhat demoralizing. The average author yields to them readily. Having struck the bull's-eye once, he is too proud to learn new tricks. Above all, he is too proud to tackle hard work. The result is a gradual degeneration of whatever talent he had at the beginning. He begins to imitate himself. He peters out.

There is certainly no sign of petering out in Fitzgerald. After his first experimenting he plainly sat himself down calmly to consider his defi-ciencies. They were many and serious. He was, first of all, too facile. He could write entertainingly without giving thought to form and organiza-tion. He was, secondly, somewhat amateurish. The materials and methods of his craft, I venture, rather puzzled him. He used them ineptly. His books showed brilliancy in conception, but they were crude and even ig-norant in detail. They suggested, only too often, the improvisations of a pianist playing furiously by ear, but unable to read notes.

These are the defects that he has now got rid of. *The Great Gatsby*, I seem to recall, was announced a long while ago. It was probably several years on the stocks. It shows, on every page, the results of that laborious effort. Writing it, I take it, was painful. The author wrote, tore up, rewrote, tore up again. There are pages so artfully contrived that one can no more imagine improvising them than one can imagine improvising a fugue. They are full of little delicacies, charming turns of phrase, penetrating second thoughts. In other words, they are easy and excellent reading—which is what always comes out of hard writing.

Thus Fitzgerald, the stylist, arises to challenge Fitzgerald, the social historian, but I doubt that the latter ever quite succumbs to the former. The thing that chiefly interests the basic Fitzgerald is still the florid show of modern American life—and especially the devil's dance that goes on at the top. He is unconcerned about the sweatings and sufferings of the nether herd; what engrosses him is the high carnival of those who have too much money to spend, and too much time for the spending of it. Their idiotic pursuit of sensation, their almost incredible stupidity and triviality, their glittering swinishness—these are the things that go into his notebook.

In *The Great Gatsby*, though he does not go below the surface, he depicts this rattle and hullabaloo with great gusto and, I believe, with sharp accuracy. The Long Island he sets before us is no fanciful Alsatia; it actually exists. More, it is worth any social historian's study, for its influence upon the rest of the country is immense and profound. What is vogue among the profiteers of Manhattan and their harlots to-day is imitated by the flappers of the Bible Belt country clubs weeks after next. The whole tone of American society, once so highly formalized and so suspicious of change, is now taken largely from frail ladies who were slinging hash a year ago.

Fitzgerald showed the end products of the new dispensation in *This Side of Paradise*. In *The Beautiful and the Damned* he cut a bit lower. In *The Great Gatsby* he comes near the bottom. Social leader and jailbird, grand lady and kept woman, are here almost indistinguishable. We are in an atmosphere grown increasingly levantine. The Paris of the Second Empire pales to a sort of snobbish chautauqua; the New York of Ward McAllister[37] becomes the scene of a convention of Gold Star Mothers. To find a parallel for the grossness and debauchery that now reign in New York one must go back to the Constantinople of Basil I. ["Scott Fitzgerald and His Work," *Chicago Sunday Tribune*, May 3, 1925, Magazine Section, pp. 1, 3]

Sinclair Lewis

Main Street (1920)

After all, Munyon was probably right: there is yet hope. Perhaps Emerson and Whitman were right too; maybe even Sandburg is right.[38] What ails us all is a weakness for rash over-generalization, leading to shooting pains in the psyche and delusions of divine persecution. Observing the steady and precipitate descent of promising postulants in beautiful letters down the steep, greasy chutes of the *Saturday Evening Post*, the *Metropolitan*, the *Cosmopolitan* and the rest of the Hearst and Hearstoid magazines, we are too prone, ass-like, to throw up our heads and bawl that all is lost, including honor. But all the while a contrary movement is in progress, far less noted than it ought to be. Authors with their pockets full of best-seller money are bitten by high ambition, and strive heroically to scramble out of the literary Cloaca Maxima. Now and then one of them succeeds, bursting suddenly into the light of the good red sun with the foul liquors of the depths still streaming from him, like a prisoner loosed from some obscure dungeon. Is it so soon forgotten that Willa Cather used to be one of the editors of *McClure's*? That Dreiser wrote editorials for the *Delineator* and was an editor of dime novels for Street & Smith? That Huneker worked for the *Musical Courier*? That Amy Lowell imitated George E. Woodberry and Felicia Hemans? That E. W. Howe was born a Methodist? That Sandburg was once a Chautauqua orator? That Cabell's first stories were printed in *Harper's Magazine*? . . . As I say, they occasionally break out, strange as it may seem. A few months ago I recorded the case of Zona Gale, emerging from her stew of glad books with *Miss Lulu Bett*. Now comes another fugitive, his face blanched by years in the hulks, but his eyes alight with high purpose. His name is Sinclair Lewis, and the work he offers is a novel called *Main Street* . . .

This *Main Street* I commend to your polite attention. It is, in brief, good stuff. It presents characters that are genuinely human, and not only genuinely human but also authentically American; it carries them through a series of transactions that are all interesting and plausible; it exhibits those transactions thoughtfully and acutely, in the light of the social and cultural forces underlying them; it is well written, and full of a sharp sense of comedy, and rich in observation, and competently designed. Superficially, the story of a man and his wife in a small Minnesota town, it is actually the typical story of the typical American family—that is, of the family in its first stage, before husband and wife have become lost in father and mother. The average American wife, I daresay, does not come quite so close to downright revolt as Carol Kennicott, but that is the only exaggeration, and we may well overlook it. Otherwise, she and her Will are triumphs of the national normalcy—she with her vague stirrings, her unintelligible yearnings, her clumsy gropings, and he with his magnificent obtuseness, his childish belief in meaningless phrases, his intellectual deafness and near-sightedness, his pathetic inability to comprehend the turmoil that goes on within her. Here is the essential tragedy of American life, and if not the tragedy, then at least the sardonic farce; the disparate cultural development of male and female, the great strangeness that lies between husband and wife when they begin to function as members of society. The men, sweating at their sordid concerns, have given the women leisure, and out of that leisure the women have fashioned disquieting discontents. To Will Kennicott, as to most other normal American males, life remains simple; do your work, care for your family, buy your Liberty Bonds, root for your home team, help to build up your lodge, venerate the flag. But to Carol it is far more complex and challenging. She has become aware of forces that her husband is wholly unable to comprehend, and that she herself can comprehend only in a dim and muddled way. The ideas of the great world press upon her, confusing her and making her uneasy. She is flustered by strange heresies, by romantic personalities, by exotic images of beauty. To Kennicott she is flighty, illogical, ungrateful for the benefits that he and God have heaped upon her. To her he is dull, narrow, ignoble.

Mr. Lewis depicts the resultant struggle with great penetration. He is far too intelligent to take sides—to turn the thing into a mere harangue against one or the other. Above all, he is too intelligent to take the side of Carol, as nine novelists out of ten would have done. He sees clearly what is too often not seen—that her superior culture is, after all, chiefly bogus—that the oafish Kennicott, in more ways than one, is better than she is. Her war upon his Philistinism is carried on with essentially Philistine weapons. Her dream of converting a Minnesota prairie town into a sort of Long Island suburb, with overtones of Greenwich Village and the Harvard campus, is quite as absurd as his dream of converting it into a second Minneapolis, with overtones of Gary, Ind., and Paterson, N. J. When their conflict is made concrete and dramatic by the entrance of a *tertium quid*, the hollow-ness of her whole case is at once made apparent, for this *tertium quid* is a Swedish trousers-presser who becomes a moving-picture actor. It seems to me that the irony here is delicate and delicious. This, then, is the end-product of the Maeterlinck complex! Needless to say, Carol lacks the courage to decamp with her Scandinavian. Instead, she descends to sheer banality. That is, she departs for Washington, becomes a war-worker, and rubs noses with the suffragettes. In the end, it goes without saying, she re-turns to Gopher Prairie and the hearth-stone of her Will. The fellow is at least honest. He offers her no ignominious compromise. She comes back under the old rules, and is presently nursing a baby. Thus the true idealism of the Republic, the idealism of its Chambers of Commerce, its Knights of Pythias, its Rotary Clubs and its National Defense Leagues, for which Washington froze at Valley Forge and Our Boys died at Chateau Thierry — thus this genuine and unpolluted article conquers the phoney idealism of Nietzsche, Edward W. Bok, Dunsany, George Bernard Shaw, Margaret An-derson, Mrs. Margaret Sanger, Percy Mackaye and the I.W.W.[39]

But the mere story, after all, is nothing; the virtue of the book lies in its packed and brilliant detail. It is an attempt, not to solve the American cul-tural problem, but simply to depict with great care a group of typical Americans. This attempt is extraordinarily successful. The figures often re-main in the flat; the author is quite unable to get that poignancy into them which Dreiser manages so superbly; one seldom sees into them very deeply or feels with them very keenly. But in their externals, at all events, they are done with uncommon skill. In particular, Mr. Lewis represents their speech vividly and accurately. It would be hard to find a false note in the dialogue, and it would be impossible to exceed the verisimilitude of the various extracts from the Gopher Prairie paper, or of the sermon by a Methodist dervish in the Gopher Prairie Wesleyan cathedral, or of a speech by a boomer at a banquet of the Chamber of Commerce. Here Mr. Lewis lays on with obvious malice, but always he keeps within the bounds of probability, always his realism holds up. It is, as I have said, good stuff. I have read no more genuinely amusing novel for a long while. The man who did it deserves a hearty welcome. His apprenticeship in the cellars of the tabernacle was not wasted. . . . ["Consolation," *SS* 64, no. 1 (January 1921): 138–40]

Babbitt (1922)

The theory lately held in Greenwich Village that the merit and success of *Main Street* constituted a sort of double-headed accident, probably
to be ascribed to a case of mistaken identity on the part of God—this theory blows up with a frightful roar toward the middle of *Babbitt*. The plain
truth is, indeed, that *Babbitt* is at least twice as good a novel as *Main Street*
was—that it avoids all the more obvious faults of that celebrated work, and
shows a number of virtues that are quite new. It is better designed than
Main Street; the action is more logical and coherent; there is more imagination in it and less bald journalism; above all, there is a better grip upon
the characters. If Carol Kennicott, at one leap, became as real a figure to
most literate Americans as Jane Addams or Nan Patterson; then George F.
Babbitt should become as real as Jack Dempsey or Charlie Schwab.[40] The
fellow simply drips with human juices. Every one of his joints is movable
in all directions. Real freckles are upon his neck and real sweat stands out
upon his forehead. I have personally known him since my earliest days as
a newspaper reporter, back in the last century. I have heard him make
such speeches as Cicero never dreamed of at banquets of the Chamber of
Commerce. I have seen him marching in parades. I have observed him
advancing upon his Presbyterian tabernacle of a Sunday morning, his
somewhat stoutish lady upon his arm. I have watched and heard him
crank his Buick. I have noted the effect of alcohol upon him, both before
and after Prohibition. And I have seen him, when some convention of
Good Fellows was in town, at his innocent sports in the parlors of brothels,
grandly ordering wine at $10 a round and bidding the professor play
"White Wings."

To me his saga, as Sinclair Lewis has set it down, is fiction only by a
sort of courtesy. All the usual fittings of the prose fable seem to be absent.
There is no plot whatever, and very little of the hocus-pocus commonly
called development of character. Babbitt simply grows two years older as
the tale unfolds; otherwise he doesn't change at all—any more than you or
I have changed since 1920. Every customary device of the novelist is absent. When Babbitt, revolting against the irksome happiness of his home,
takes to a series of low affairs with manicure girls, grass-widows and ladies
even more complaisant, nothing overt and melodramatic happens to him.

He never meets his young son Teddy in a dubious cabaret; his wife never discovers incriminating correspondence in his pockets; no one tries to blackmail him; he is never present when a joint is raided. The worst punishment that falls upon him is that his old friends at the Athletic Club—cheats exactly like himself—gossip about him a bit. Even so, that gossip goes no further; Mrs. Babbitt does not hear it. When she accuses him of adultery, it is simply the formal accusation of a loving wife: she herself has absolutely no belief in it. Moreover, it does not cause Babbitt to break down, confess and promise to sin no more. Instead, he lies like a major-general, denounces his wife for her evil imagination, and returns forthwith to his carnalities. If, in the end, he abandons them, it is not because they torture his conscience, but because they seem likely to hurt his business. This prospect gives him pause, and the pause saves him. He is, beside, growing old. He is 48, and more than a little bald. A night out leaves his tongue coated in the morning. As the curtain falls upon him he is back upon the track of rectitude—a sound business man, a faithful Booster, an assiduous Elk, a trustworthy Presbyterian, a good husband, a loving father, a successful and unchallenged fraud.

Let me confess at once that this story has given me vast delight. I know the Babbitt type, I believe, as well as most; for twenty years I have devoted myself to the exploration of its peculiarities. Lewis depicts it with complete and absolute fidelity. There is irony in the picture; irony that is unflagging and unfailing, but nowhere is there any important departure from the essential truth. Babbitt has a great clownishness in him, but he never becomes a mere clown. In the midst of his most extravagant imbecilities he keeps both feet upon the ground. One not only sees him brilliantly; one also understands him; he is made plausible and natural. As an old professor of Babbittry I welcome him as an almost perfect specimen—a genuine museum piece. Every American city swarms with his brothers. They run things in the Republic, East, West, North, South. They are the originators and propagators of the national delusions—all, that is, save those which spring from the farms. They are the palladiums of 100% Americanism; the apostles of the Harding politics; the guardians of the Only True Christianity. They constitute the Chambers of Commerce, the Rotary Clubs, the Kiwanis Clubs, the Watch and Ward Societies, the Men and Religion Forward Movements, the Y.M.C.A. directorates, the Good Citizen Leagues.

They are the advertisers who determine what is to go into the American newspapers and what is to stay out. They are the Leading Citizens, the speakers at banquets, the profiteers, the corruptors of politics, the supporters of evangelical Christianity, the peers of the realm. Babbitt is their archetype. He is no worse than most, and no better; he is the average American of the ruling minority in this hundred and forty-sixth year of the Republic. He is America incarnate, exuberant and exquisite. Study him well and you will know better what is the matter with the land we live in than you would know after plowing through a thousand such volumes as Walter Lippmann's *Public Opinion*.[41] What Lippmann tried to do as a professor, laboriously and without imagination, Lewis has here done as an artist with a few vivid strokes. It is a very fine piece of work indeed.

Nor is all its merit in the central figure. It is not Babbitt that shines forth most gaudily, but the whole complex of Babbittry, Babbittism, Babbittismus. In brief, Babbitt is seen as no more than a single member of the society he lives in—a matter far more difficult to handle, obviously, than any mere character sketch. His every act is related to the phenomena of that society. It is not what he feels and aspires to that moves him primarily; it is what the folks about him will think of him. His politics is communal politics, mob politics, herd politics; his religion is a public rite wholly without subjective significance; his relations to his wife and his children are formalized and standardized; even his debaucheries are the orthodox debaucheries of a sound business man. The salient thing about him, in truth, is his complete lack of originality—and that is precisely the salient mark of every American of his class. What he feels and thinks is what it is currently proper to feel and think. Only once, during the two years that we have him under view, does he venture upon an idea that is even remotely original—and that time the heresy almost ruins him. The lesson, you may be sure, is not lost upon him. If he lives, he will not offend again. No thought will ever get a lodgment in his mind, even in the wildest deliriums following bootleg gin, that will offer offense to the pruderies of Vergil Gunch, president of the Boosters' Club, or to those of old Mr. Eathorne, president of the First State Bank, or to those of the Rev. Dr. John Jennison Drew, pastor of the Chatham Road Presbyterian church, or to those of Prof. Pumphrey, head of the Zenith Business College, or even to those of Miss McGoun, the virtuous stenographer. He has been rolled through the mill. He emerges the very model and pattern of a forward-looking, right-thinking Americano.

As I say, this *Babbitt* gives me great delight. It is shrewdly devised; it is adeptly managed; it is well written. The details, as in *Main Street*, are extraordinarily vivid—the speech of Babbitt before the Zenith Real Estate Board, the meeting to consider ways and means of bulging the Chatham Road Sunday-school, the annual convention of the real-estate men, Babbitt's amour with the manicure-girl, the episode of Sir Gerald Doak, the warning visit when Babbitt is suspected of liberalism, the New Thought meeting, the elopement of young Theodore Roosevelt Babbitt and Eunice Littlefield at the end. In all these scenes there is more than mere humor; there is searching truth. They reveal something; they mean something. I know of no American novel that more accurately presents the real America. It is a social document of a high order. ["Portrait of an American Citizen," SS 69, no. 2 (October 1922): 138–40]

Arrowsmith (1925)

Of Sinclair Lewis' technical skill it is unnecessary to speak. The fellow, indeed, has a vast cunning at the art he adorns and staggers—far more than any of the high-toned English novelists who swarm across the ocean to instruct and patronize Yankee blighters. If he would pull himself together, translate his very sure instincts into plain propositions, and put them on paper, the result would be the best treatise on novel-writing ever heard of. His *Babbitt* is not only an extremely engaging story, full of grotesque and devastating humors; it is also, in structure, the very model of a modern novel. It hangs together admirably. It moves, breathes, lives. From the first page to the last there is not the slightest faltering in direction or purpose. If you think that planning a novel so adeptly is an easy job, then try to do it yourself. Try, indeed, to write *any* book—that is, of more than a hundred pages. What you will inevitably discover, to your dismay, is that the author's worst peril is that of getting lost in his own manuscript—of standing blinded and gasping in the middle, unable to discern either one end or the other. Lewis never falls into that difficulty, or, if he does, he always surmounts it with great aplomb. Even in *Main Street*, vast in area, crowded with people and flabby in design, he never got lost for an instant. And even in *Arrowsmith*, treading unfamiliar and arduous ground and constantly confronted by technical problems of a complicated and onerous sort, he never wobbles. Once the thing gets under way—and it gets under way toward the bottom of the first page—it thunders on in a straight line to an inescapable conclusion. There are episodes, true enough. There is what the musicians call passage work. There are moments of voluptuous lingering, as over stuff too sweet to be left behind. But there is never any uncertainty in design. There is never any wavering in theme or purpose.

That theme, in brief, is the burden which lies upon any man, in our highly materialistic society, who gives over his life to the pursuit of truth—not only the indifference and contempt which he must face, but also the positive opposition which he must face. The public theory, of course, is that the tide runs the other way. Haven't we two or three hundred universities, more than all Europe and all Asia, and don't all of them devote at least a part of their funds to keeping scholars? Aren't there scores of great foundations for research, maintained gloriously by Baptists in the oil business, Rotarians in the chewing tobacco business, Harvard graduates in the bond business? Doesn't the government itself provide three thousand jobs for scientists? Are not thousands more employed by the States, the cities, the correspondence schools, the rolling mills, the manufacturers of vaccines, tooth-pastes, oleomargarine, sheep washes, wall-papers, ready-mixed paints? All true, and yet the tragic fact remains. What ails every one of these undertakings for the fostering of science is that, whatever its pretensions on the label, it is utilitarian in the bottle—that its primary aim is to back the scientist into a comfortable stall and milk him like a cow. This is true even of the most pretentious of the scientific foundations: the glorified Babbitts who sit on their boards are all hot for "practical" results, and judge every aspiring Virchow or Rayleigh[42] by the ease and rapidity with which he reaches them. It is true especially of the universities, which have been converted of late into mere breeding pens for industrial laboratory slaves and "research" workers, *i.e.*, kept scientists, *i.e.*, anti-scientists. The State universities in the Middle West have gone the whole hog; they frankly put the professor of swine husbandry and his colleague of ice-cream making above the forlorn fellows who presume to inquire into such useless subjects as philology and archeology. Even in the East the thing has rolled a long way. Harvard, like Kansas and Michigan, now trains bookkeepers, pig-iron salesmen, and liars to write bond circulars; the Johns Hopkins was but lately offering courses in choir leading and motor troubles. Do the medical schools remain? Alas, no. Their old aim of breeding competent doctors is now abandoned, and they devote themselves to teaching brisk young fellows how to invent new sure cures for chilblains and psoriasis, and so provide the "director of public relations" with something to hand out to the newspaper boys, and so attract the favorable notice of illiterates with millions for endowments. It used to be football; now it is quackery.

Yet scientists remain among us. They are hatched every year, sometimes in low life. The passion which animated Johannes Müller and Karl Ludwig[43] penetrates, curiously, to the remotest reaches of the land. Of our two native-born Nobel prize-winners—both workers in pure science—one was born in an Illinois village and the other in a suburb of Philadelphia.[44] But what is the national machinery for rescuing such fellows from their surroundings, and helping them to develop their powers? Is it effective? Does it work? The thesis of *Arrowsmith* is that it doesn't—that, on the contrary, it opposes and hobbles them—that most of its help goes to quacks. Nearly five hundred pages are devoted to that thesis—five hundred pages of riotous and often barbarous humor, yet always with a sharp undertone of irony in it, always with a bitter flavor. Lewis, in brief, preaches. Well, if this be preaching let us have more of it! For it has the strange aim, for preaching, of combating fraud and obscurantism, of getting at and hymning the truth. It has a moral, but there is in it no snuffling moralizing. Arrowsmith is no peerless Florestan, standing against the Philistines. He shares all their weaknesses. He is almost as bad as they are—but not quite. In the end, after long and dreadful battles, some ending with his defeat outright and some with his surrender, he escapes by flight. So "science" goes marching on, its banners flying, Babbitts clearing the way, a mule-load of gold every ten paces. And Martin, saved at last, woos science-without-the-quotation-marks in his austere retreat, rid at last of all urging to get "practical" results.

The book has interested me immensely. It is well thought out and executed with great skill. Whether or not there is a popular success in it I don't know: perhaps the passages which set forth a bacteriologist's problems will balk more readers than one. Neither do I know who should get the credit for the highly skillful management of detail—Lewis or his collaborator, Dr.

Paul H. De Kruif, himself a bacteriologist.[45] Perhaps De Kruif deserves most of it. Did he invent Dr. Almus Pickerbaugh, the forward-looking health commissioner? If so, then he is a reporter of the highest imaginative type. Pickerbaugh exists everywhere, in almost every American town. He is the quack who flings himself melodramatically upon measles, chicken pox, whooping cough—the organizer of Health Weeks and author of prophy-lactic, Kiwanian slogans—the hero of clean-up campaigns—the scientific beau ideal of newspaper reporters, Y.M.C.A. secretaries, and the pastors of suburban churches. He has been leering at the novelists of America for years, and yet Lewis and De Kruif were the first to see and hail him. They have made an almost epic figure of him. He is the Babbitt of this book—far more charming than Arrowsmith himself, and far more real. Arrow-smith fails in one important particular: he is not typical, he is not a good American. I daresay that many a reader, following his struggles with the seekers for "practical" results, will sympathize frankly with the latter. After all, it is not American to prefer honor to honors; no man, pursuing that folly, could ever hope to be president of the United States. Pickerbaugh will cause no such lifting of eyebrows. Like Babbitt, he will be recognized instantly and enjoyed innocently. Within six weeks, I suspect, every health officer in America will be receiving letters denouncing him as a Picker-baugh. Thus nature imitates art. ["The Library," *AM* 4, no. 4 (April 1925): 507–9 ("'Arrowsmith'")]

Elmer Gantry (1927)

For the third time Lewis knocks one clear over the fence. Does it go higher and further than *Main Street* and *Babbitt*? I am inclined to think so. *Main Street* was superb in detail, but the book did not hang together, and its ending was vague and somewhat baffling. *Babbitt* was a magnifi-cent character sketch, but more often than not—as, for example, in the episode of Babbitt's transient yielding to Liberal heresies—that sketch went outside the bounds of the typical Americano. I can find no such flaws in *Elmer Gantry*. The story is beautifully designed, and it moves with the inevitability of a fugue. It is packed with observation, all fresh, all shrewd, all sound. There is gargantuan humor in it, and there is also something not far from moving drama. It is American from the first low cackle of the prologue to the last gigantic obscenity—as American as goose-stepping or the mean admiration of mean things. And out of it leaps the most vivid and loving, the most gaudy and glorious, the most dreadful and perfect portrait of a man of God that has got between covers since Rabelais painted Friar John.

In limning it, it seems to me, Lewis shows a great discretion, and no little self-restraint. The temptation to make the thing a mere lampoon and the man himself a simple and obvious hypocrite must have been very considerable, but there is no sign of yielding to it. Elmer Gantry is essentially a sincere man: that, indeed, is precisely the worst horror of his personality. He not only believes in all the fundamental imbecilities of evangelical Christianity; he also believes, and more especially, in his own magical gifts. When he mounts the pulpit and begins to vomit forth the immemorial bilge of his order a sort of mystical ecstasy falls upon him, and as the morons in front of him respond with their hosannas he feels himself to be veritably a spokesman of the All Highest. His occasional doubts—and he has them, of course, as even the Pope must have them on blue days—are never searching and never lasting. They play about superficialities: they concern only the machinery of his hocus-pocus, not its essence. In his most rationalistic moments the ancient Kansan faith keeps its hold upon him. He believes fully that the pathological phenomenon known as conversion is a genuinely transcendental experience, and that a half-wit who has gone through it is materially improved. He even swallows the archaic and barbarous ethical code that goes with the madhouse psychology and jungle theology. Personally, he slips through it more than once, but never deliberately, never knavishly. What may be called, to descend to theological slang, his conscience is ever alert and never tolerant. He laments his debauching of Lulu, the deacon's daughter, as honestly and as poignantly as he laments his periodical infidelities to Prohibition. In his sight there is nothing ignoble in these treasons to Revelation: they signify only that he is yet short of Christian perfection—that the Devil, eyeing him in some alarm, has been at pains to trip him. He resolves every time to sin no more, and as the years creep upon him he finds it easier and easier. When we leave him in the end he has been riding the water-wagon for a long time, in secret as well as in public, and the last of his mistresses has just been driven out, and there is no sign that she is ever to have a successor.

To do him thus, as I say, took no little self-discipline. It took even more to keep the general fable from bulging over the shadowy line that separates the evangelical verities from sheer burlesque. A civilized man, viewing a Kansas Baptist or Methodist, is urged to laugh by a process almost as irresistible as that which prompts a galled jade to wince. The theory that such poor oafs are the special pride and concern of the Infinite Power that hung the nebulæ in the heavens and set the electrons to spinning in the atom — this theory is of the very juice and essence of humor. If it is not comical, then neither is the spectacle of Coolidge in the White House comical. But Lewis is shrewd enough to see that comedy can never lie wholly in the object: its main part must ever be in the eye of the beholder. His effort is thus not simply to parade his preposterous dunderheads before his gallery, but also to search their hearts. What he finds there is not something special and peculiar, but only the ancient folly of mankind. They are not comical to themselves, but sober beyond measure, and even a bit tragic. Their struggles with the theological puerilities that beset them are as real as Leibnitz's struggles with the differential calculus. The Hell they fear is near and yawning, and stoked with genuine brimstone. The Heaven they yearn for, though it may be only a sublimated Kansas, is as grand and glorious in their sight as the fields of asphodel that enchanted the Greeks. Lewis has done them mercilessly, but yet with decent feeling. There is not a downright rogue among them. From yokel deacons to gaudy Bishops they all follow a star.

In structure the story is extremely simple. Gantry's native tastes are anything but ecclesiastical. His fancy, indeed, turns him toward the law, but the prayers of his pious mother, combined with the effects of whiskey upon his hot blood, jockey him into holy orders. There is a slip at one point, and he puts in a couple of years selling agricultural implements. But the black eyes of the Rev. Sharon Falconer, the female evangelist, draw him back into the Kingdom, and he is presently serving her as assistant exhorter, business manager, and lover. So far he has been a Baptist. But when Sharon passes on to bliss eternal God sends Elmer into the path of the Right Rev. Wesley R. Toomis, Bishop of the Zenith Area of the Methodist Episcopal Church North, and that holy man, discerning his possibilities, recruits him for the Wesleyan pastorate. His chronicle thereafter is one of almost uninterrupted success. He has all the talents that

Methodists admire in their clergy. He knows how to coo and he knows how to yell. A handsome man, with the figure of an ice-wagon driver and the hearty affability of a realtor, he shines alike in pastoral visiting and in the heroic exercises of the sacred desk. Acquiring a rich (though unfortunately frigid) wife in his first meagre charge, he passes on successively to better and better cures, until in the end he is in New York, a Methodist colossus, able to make and break even Bishops and with the whole country in the hollow of his hand. His masterpiece is a Methodist holding company to take over the Anti-Saloon League, the Lord's Day Alliance, the Board of Temperance, Prohibition and Public Morals and every other such engine of reform. He will be the boss of this celestial trust, and as such he will tell Senators when to back and Presidents when to fill.

Such is the outline. The merit of the thing lies in its detail. Here there is a truly immense accumulation of observation, and almost invariably its accuracy is obvious. There is seldom, if ever, a false note. The transaction recorded always has the air of a transaction actually seen. The labor of getting all that stuff together must have been enormous. Lewis sweeps the whole field of evangelical thought, prying into its most obscure vagaries. Multitudes of minor characters troop across the scene, everyone real, everyone carefully observed. There are no lay figures, no mere mobs. In certain of the more important episodes, it seems to me, he goes far beyond anything visible in *Main Street* or *Babbitt*. I point, for example, to the business of Gantry's conversion. It is done riotously, but the thing could scarcely be more true. There is, again, the episode of Gantry's approach to the beautiful and elusive Sharon Falconer—a little masterpiece of dialogue. The book is packed with such things, and especially the earlier parts. Toward the end it flags a bit, but only a bit. The final scenes, departing, as they do, from the normalcy that has prevailed so far, lose the overwhelming reality of what has gone before, but nevertheless Lewis has managed them with striking skill. *Gantry*, I believe, will consolidate and improve his position in his craft. Was *Main Street* merely a lucky shot, and *Babbitt* only a bravura piece? In the light of *Elmer Gantry* such notions begin to look silly. The man actually has a tremendous talent. He is, within his bounds, an artist of the first calibre. No other American novelist, living or dead, has ever come to closer grips with the essential Americano, or depicted him with more ferocious brilliancy. The three works of

his main canon are all shot through with defects, but in spite of these defects they remain almost incomparable. Put beside them, the average
novel seems trivial and futile. His colleagues spend themselves upon riddles of personality. He depicts a civilization.

The possible effects of *Elmer Gantry* are incalculable. Like *Main
Street* and *Babbitt* before it, it may give the language a new term of oppro-
brium, and so color the whole stream of the national thought. I speak as
one who has devoted many years to preaching its fundamental thesis—
that the Methodist dervishes who, through such agencies as the Anti-
Saloon League, now seek to run the United States are men deficient in
both intelligence and character, and that their power is inimical to everything rationally describable as civilization. The same sort of preaching has
been done by many other men, most of them of far more eloquence and
influence than I can pretend to. Its net effect, so far, has been precisely nil:
the Methodists, despite the melodramatic failure of Prohibition, are more
powerful in the government than they ever were before. It would be as
hard, indeed, to imagine Dr. Coolidge flouting them as it would be to
imagine him eloping with a Follies girl. Well, here comes Lewis with the
case against them put into the form of a fable—more, a fable not too serious—an indictment in *scherzo* form. I am no prophet, but it seems to be
quite possible that this simple (but far from idle!) tale may accomplish at
one stroke what ten billion kilowatt hours of argument and invective have
failed to accomplish. It may awaken the Americano to the dangers of
the Methodist tyranny, as *Babbitt* awakened him to the imbecility of the
Rotary-Kiwanis blather. In six months every Wesleyan spouter in the land
may be jeered at as a Gantry, as every gabby tradesman is now sneered at
as a Babbitt. The book may turn out a bugle-blast to topple over the evangelical wall, now so high and frowning. It may be the bomb foreordained
to blow up the citadel. For there is a power in the imagination that indignation can never show. Its works enchant—and enchantment is vastly
more than conviction. I confess frankly that I envy the man who possesses
it. Especially I envy Lewis, for he has left a mark upon his time that will
loom up wider and blacker, in the years to come, than the marks of a thousand Coolidges. Coolidge, I believe, will be remembered only as a foot-
note to Lewis' fancy. He will go down into history, perhaps, as only half

real—by Babbitt out of Main Street. ["The Library," *AM* 10, no. 4 (April 1927): 506–8 ("Man of God: American Style")]

Dodsworth (1929)

This somewhat sombre work, I daresay, will give a great deal of comfort to Lewis's enemies, who seem to be extremely numerous, especially among rival novelists. It has faults so obvious that they stand out like sore thumbs, and so gross that they must cause even the most faithful partisan to cough sadly behind his hand. In brief, what Lewis attempts to do is to depict the disintegration of a marriage. It begins in the safe harbor of Zenith City, flourishes there for nearly twenty years, and then goes swiftly to wreck amid the decadent carnalities of Europe. The lady crosses the Atlantic eastward a virtuous wife; she comes back an incorrigible antinomian, with three lovers behind her and a long series of others looming ahead. Her husband, all the while, trails along. Her first slip shocks him and her second enrages him, but after that he learns to bear it. When we part from them at last, he has given her up as hopeless, and his eyes flicker toward a sweetie of his own.

Two defects mar the story, and both of them are of capital importance. The first lies in the fact that the woman is never rationally accounted for—that her adulteries, like the social pushing that inspires them, seem gratuitous and senseless. The second has to do with her husband. Lewis first shows that he is intelligent, and then pictures him playing the complete fool. I am not arguing here that real people do not do things irrationally or that intelligent men are above folly: all I am arguing is that the novelist gets into dangerous waters when he puts such folks into his book. We somehow expect him to show us something beyond their bald externals, their overt acts. We assume unconsciously that he must know a great deal about them that is not on the surface, else he would not write about them at all. We look for him to organize their acts into a coherent drama. It seems to me that, in the present case, Lewis has not done this as persuasively as he ought to have done it. His Fran Dodsworth plainly puzzles him. His Sam Dodsworth is alive one moment, and a stuffed shirt the next.

The worst holes in the book are where the two come together. Some of the dialogues between them are simply impossible. They harangue each other in the manner of actors in a bad play. Nothing comes out of these harangues. When one of them is over there is no more light upon the underlying motives of the parties—nor even, indeed, upon their feelings —than there was when it began. Fran has merely made a disingenuous and improbable speech, and Sam has replied to it in correct but hollow phrases. If these dialogues were missing altogether the story would be better than it is. Lewis would still fail to account logically for Fran's follies and Sam's complacence, but he would at least avoid disconcerting the reader by accounting for them in unplausible ways. Strike out all the connubial gabble, and try it for yourself. It seems to me that the story gains momentum instantly, and loses the air of false philosophizing which now damages it.

So much for its defects. Its merits are many and should not be overlooked. There are passages which show Lewis at his best—unctuous, ingenious, penetrating and devastating. No novelist in practise among us observes so accurately, or has so vast a talent for putting what he sees into pungent phrases. He is, by long odds, the best reporter ever heard of—not, as incompetent critics so often allege, because he is only a reporter, but because he is so much more than a reporter. Babbitt shaving, Dr. Kennicott operating, Gantry drunk—these are little masterpieces that no rival has ever matched. The quality of complete reality is in them, but they are also informed by imagination. There are plenty of things of the same kind in *Dodsworth*—the ante-nuptial dinner at the grandiose Norddeutscher-Lloyd home of old Herman Voelker; the encounter between Sam and Alec Kynance, boss of the great Unit Automotive Company; the grand drunk with Tub Pearson in Paris; the palaver with Matey Pearson in the bathroom. There is vastly more than good reporting in such episodes; one senses in them, also, something that is a kind of poetry.

Lewis's observation is always fresh, trenchant and full of the color of his peculiarly biting and charming personality. Whatever his defects as an explorer of the soul of man, he is at least a master professor of man's behavior. Somewhere in *Dodsworth* there is a passage on the horrors of travel—the lonely evenings in flabby hotels, the dismaying struggles with enigmatical languages, the vain effort to emerge from the tourist's harness and live as the people live. It is short, but it is well-nigh perfect. The whole folly of gadding about is made obvious and appalling. Everyone who has done any travelling will recognize the truth of every word. But it remained

for Lewis to fetch those words out of the reservoir of common knowledge, and arrange them consummately, just as it remained for him to
make visible the Main Street that all of us knew, and to give a habitation
and a name to the Babbitt who was everywhere. He is, in such matters,
facile princeps. No other contemporary novelist, not even the early
Wells, has dredged more memorable stuff out of the illimitable stock of
what-everyone-knows. The joy of recognition is not the only joy that a
work of art can engender, but it is surely one of the most agreeable and
satisfying, and Lewis is unsurpassed at evoking it. Put beside him, most
other novelists seem to be incarcerated in ivory towers, with the actual
world far away.

It is my belief, frequently set forth at length, to the ire alike of sturdy
100% Americans and tender æsthetes, that his work will probably endure,
at all events as long as any other fiction of the Coolidge *Aufklärung* en-
dures. As everyone knows, it is irritatingly uneven. From the best scenes of
Babbitt to the worst of *Mantrap*[46] there is a drop as dizzy as that from a
string quartette to a movie. Within the limits of a single book he can manage to be both incomparably good and unbelievably bad. I point to *Arrowsmith*. I point to *Dodsworth*. The chief defect of *Elmer Gantry* is that very
variability. *Gantry*, to be sure, is never quite as false as the critics who dislike it say it is, but certainly it is sometimes false enough. But equally certainly it is basically and prevailingly true. Elmer Gantrys not only exist;
they are as common, almost, as George F. Babbitts. I have known personally at least a dozen of them. There is a touch of Gantry, indeed, in every
evangelical pastor, and not a few of them are far worse than Elmer at his
worst.

The opposition to his history, as Lewis sets it forth so magnificently, is
psychological, and lies within the cortices of those who voice it so rau-
cously. The trouble with them is that, despite the spread of atheism and
antinomianism, they are still authentic Americanoes, and hence born with
a reverence for theologians. It takes at least two generations, and usually
three or four, to breed out that folly. The leaders of the anti-Lewis camorra
are simply unable to throw it off. *Elmer Gantry* outrages them, not in
proportion as it is false, but in proportion as it is true. They would not
dislike it so much if it were actually as flimsy that they pretend to think it
is. I do not denounce these gentlemen for their weakness; I merely point
it out. After all, every man must be something, and in America it is quite

natural for many men to be Americans. But I do not share their apparent belief that being Americans makes them trustworthy critics of works of art. The national talent lies in other directions. It is the special gift of our people, not to differentiate swiftly and certainly between the false and the true, whether in art or in philosophy, but to love and venerate the sweet. The ideal, to them, is always a shade more convincing than the real. If they lacked their gift, then life in the Republic, to most of them, would be unendurable.

Lewis has been bathed in more bad criticism than any other novelist of his time and country. His books, beginning with *Main Street,* have always encountered the subjective hostility that I have just described, and so they have been exposed to a great deal of mauling. He himself has aided the business, for he is a dreadful ham as a critic, and yet he insists, ever and anon, upon putting on the critical chasuble. It is sad. It is deplorable. Once, if my agents do not lie, he concocted the preposterous theory that he was himself a Babbitt. I can imagine nothing less true. Lewis's lingering Americanism, such as it is, actually belongs to Main Street, not to the Zenith City Club. One might fancy him going back to Gopher Prairie and settling down behind the pumps of a quiet service station, but he could no more turn himself into a big town realtor than he could turn himself into an archbishop. His essential rusticity shows itself in his humor, which is as far from Broadway wise-cracking as it is from the Greek anthology. The actual Babbitts know better. They rank him, being numskulls, with Trotsky and Karl Marx, Ingersoll and Tom Paine. If they were subtler they would put him with Sockless Jerry Simpson[47]—and Mark Twain.

But here I wander into an autopsy on the man, whereas the sole business of a reviewer, if what I hear is true, is with his books. The Lewis books, it seems to me, are sufficiently excellent to make their weaknesses more than tolerable. *Dodsworth,* to be sure, is mainly flabby, but what of *Babbitt?* The more I abandon myself to prayer and meditation, the more I am convinced that it is a genuinely first-rate piece of work. There is in it the lusty reality of things actually seen, and there is in it, too, something else— the vaguely poetical quality that I was mentioning a little while back. Lewis is anything but a mere caricaturist; he is, indeed, the precise opposite of a caricaturist. He is too humane and romantic a man to make his people worse than they are, or even as bad as they are; he always manages to make them a bit better. In *Dodsworth* that habit helps to bring him to grief. He is so obviously eager to make his wretched Fran Dodsworth a victim, not of her own inherent rascality, but of forces beyond her, that he succeeds only in making her false. His Sam Dodsworth is better, but still not quite plausible. Let him spit on his hands at once and begin another book. If he can produce a *Babbitt*, a *Main Street* or an *Elmer Gantry* now and then, he is entitled to his intervening *Dodsworths*. ["The Library," AM 16, no. 4 (April 1929): 506–8 ("Escape and Return")]

Ann Vickers (1933)

Compared to *Babbitt* and the larger part of *Elmer Gantry*, this study of a lady uplifter's struggles and ecstasies is surely no great shakes, but there is still enough good stuff in it to lift it above the general. There are, indeed, some gaudy and wholly Lewisonian scenes in it—for example, those laid in the female seminary where Ann acquires the humanities, and those laid in the suffragette bastile where she is grounded in good works—and they are numerous enough to take some of the curse off the flubdub that lies between. For flubdub it is, alas, alas. And if, shocked, you say, "It cannot, it shall not be!," then consider this:

> I will have my child, as I have my man! A working woman has a right to her child and her lover. Oh, I don't suppose she has any specific *right*. Probably there are no "rights"—only the chance of having good glands and good luck. But whatever the philosophy of it may be, I'm going to have, Barney and I are going to have, our daughter!

Is this burlesque? Is it to be taken in the spirit of the sermons of Dr. Gantry, the luncheon addresses of Mr. Babbitt? If so, then Mr. Lewis has concealed that ribald and filthy purpose with a kind of artfulness verging upon false pretenses. The whole context, in fact, points the other way: it indicates only too plainly that the speech is to be read quite seriously. Not a hint of the *New Yorker* is there; the mood is one of moral indignation, recalling the worst raptures of the *New Republic*. What would a prudent man do, hearing such words from a female in real life? He would grab his hat and run like hell. But here we must stay for more:

> By the grace of God Amen in our Christian nation wherein we rage not as the Heathen but under the gentle teachings of Jesus do combine in one grand union for the purpose of gently murdering skinny old colored mammies let us now sing the Land of the Free and the Home of the Brave—

It is not Ann who is talking now, but the author himself! He goes on:

> Just as it is felony to help a condemned murderer cheat the state of its beloved blood-letting by passing poison to him, so that he may die decently and alone, with no sadistic parade of priests and guards and reporters, so it is a crime to assist a woman condemned to the tittering gossip that can be worse than death by helping her to avoid having what is quaintly known as an "illegitimate baby"— as though one should speak of an "illegitimate mountain" or an "illegitimate hurricane."

But enough of this sad wind-music! I can account for it only on the ground that Lewis, in the course of writing his book, fell in love with his heroine, and developed a senile yen to steal her away from Judge Bernard Dow Dolphin, the last and most he of her lovers. Certainly the creator of Babbitt, in a normal state of mind, would never have been fooled by her. He would have seen that, like any other lady uplifter, she was inescapably a character in comedy, and dealt with her as such. But here he takes her with deadly seriousness, and his slapstick is reserved for the low scoundrels who try to thwart and baffle her. He even keeps a straight face at the end, when she throws up the Uplift for love, and settles down to police her sixth beau, third lover, and second husband. This is her parting Message:

> I think that soil where the rose-bushes are planted is wretched. You ought to put in enormous quantities of fertilizer.

And here is the reply of an ex-Catholic, an ex-Tammany leader, an ex-Justice of the Supreme Court of New York, and an ex-convict at Sing Sing:

> Of course, I'll do what you think.

But let us not yield to the voluptuousness of vain repining. Lewis is still Lewis, even under the fumes of Social Justice. In detail there is many a dish of Lewisonian richness—not as much, of course, as in the works of the author's major canon, but still enough to write his name all over the book. As I have said, the scenes in the female seminary are capital, and out of them emerges a Miss Eula Towers who fades much too soon: I was in hopes to the last page that she would return, for she is much better observed than Ann. The suffragettes, too, are all brilliantly real, with their Amazonian rough-house by day and their virgin whisperings under the eaves at night. Dr. Agatha Snow, Dr. Merribel Peaselee, Miss Ardence Benescoten, Dr. Addington Slenk, Mitzi Brewer, Mrs. Emily Allen Aukett, Miss Mamie Bogardus, Mrs. Dudley Cowxes, Mrs. Ethelinda St. Vincent —the very names are enough to inflame the Lewis addict.

I lament that we learn so little about Captain Lafayette Resnick, the cynical Jewish warrior who has the honor of relieving Ann of her extraordinarily oppressive virginity. He is brought to life, like Dogberry, in fifty words, but then he begins to fade out, and by the time he achieves his foul purpose he is hardly more than a shadow. Ann's other followers go the same route: the campus Nietzsche, Glenn Hargis; the pallid lawyer, Lindsay Atwell; the boisterous charity-monger, J. Russell Spaulding (he becomes her first husband); even Judge Dolphin, the bewhiskered troglodyte who gets her into so pathological a state of mind that she sees a *curved* street in Baltimore. His Honor shows high promise at his first entrance: one begins to hope that a genuine American judge is to make his début in American fiction at last. But presently he flickers and is out. Oh, wurra, wurra!

All the while it is manifest that Ann was really made for Lewis: she is almost as perfect a symbol of American buncombe and futility as Gantry or Babbitt. But she simply gets away from him. Her fol-de-rol enchants him; he swallows it without a grunt; he begins to babble it himself. Not, of course, that he lacks lucid intervals. Now and then he breaks away from the hussy, and takes a cold and scientific look at her. If the whole book were such a look it would be a masterpiece; as it is, it is a kind of patchwork, partly very good, but mainly bad. I am in hopes that Lewis, in the quiet years to come, will do Ann over, as I am in hopes that he will rewrite the last 30,000 words of *Elmer Gantry*. She deserves it, he deserves it, and the nobility and gentry deserve it. Let him keep her to her anthro-pophagous trade to the end, and turn her inside out. Certainly the lady up-lifter must be got into the national records, with not a wart gilded. She cries aloud for embalming, as the college president cries aloud, and the union leader (A. F. of L. model), and the police captain.

If Lewis lets these pearls of the American *Kultur* escape him, then they will never be done, for none of his imitators shows a hundredth part of his skill at seeing into such people. They have all tried to match Babbitt, and they have all failed. The idea that Lewis himself is simply a mimic is as id-iotic as the old doctrine that Richard Mansfield was simply a character actor. He is, in fact, a novelist of really extraordinary talents, and at his best—say in parts of *Main Street, Elmer Gantry* and *Arrowsmith*, and in nearly all of *Babbitt*—he is unsurpassed. ["The Library," AM 38, no. 3 (March 1933): 382–83 ("A Lady of Vision")]

John Dos Passos

Three Soldiers (1921)

Published three years ago, or even two years ago, John Dos Passos' *Three Soldiers* would have been suppressed out of hand, and the author hurried to Leavenworth or Atlanta, with a Federal judge bawling obscene farewells to him from the bench. Even as it stands, it shows the marks of a good deal of discreet trimming; in fact, the publishers admit openly, over their sign manual, that they induced Mr. Dos Passos to tone it down some-what before he departed for Europe and safety, and that they themselves continued the process after he had left. Nevertheless, the thing still has enough frankness to make it stand clearly above the general level of Amer-ican novels. It is a serious attempt to picture the war, not as it appeared to newspaper editorial writers denouncing the Hun, or to bankers' commit-tees forcing Liberty Loans on the yokels at a personal profit of 3 or 4%, or to sentimental women parading the streets in grotesque uniforms, or to four-minute spellbinders in movie parlors, but to three young men who ac-tually served in it, as the author did himself. It is a picture somehow dis-concerting. The theory of the time was that service would be of great spiritual and intellectual benefit to the conscripts, whatever the risk to their skins—that it would elevate and mellow them to be parts of so

knightly an organization as the Army, and to take part in so noble a cause
as the struggle to preserve democracy, the Word of God, and the French
and English loans. But the fact seems to be that the Army quickly acquired
the tone, not of a crusade of Geoffrey de Bouillons, but of a Billy Sunday
revival, a chautauqua, a convention of Rotary Clubs, a woman-flogging
session of the Ku Klux Klan. In other words, most of the efforts of its man-
agers were devoted, not to making the conscripts gallant and brave, but
simply to making them swallow all sorts of childish piffle about the enemy.
The aim, it would seem, was to augment their resolution by scaring them
to death—by trying to make them believe that if they ever fell into the
hands of that enemy they would be relieved of their ears and teeth, beaten
with clubs, and boiled in oil. The ideal soldier, by this system, was the one
who most quickly acquired the imbecility of a Y.M.C.A. secretary or a college professor working for the Creel-Wilson-Hog Island press bureau.[48]

It is an unfortunate fact—to be deplored, I hope, by future historians
—that the American people got so little of spiritual value out of the war. I
am a firm believer in war, and regard it as the most effective of all antidotes
to the sickly sordidness of Christian civilization. It lifts men above all their
usual puerile fears and uncertainties, and gives them something to be genuinely afraid of; it brings out qualities of a rare and lofty variety, wholly
obscured by the daily routine of life. But it must be obvious that it is possible to enter even a great and brilliant war in a manner so discreditable that
all of the advantages of the enterprise will be lost. It was in this way that the
United States entered the war of 1914–1918. We hung back for three long
years, meanwhile robbing the Allies in a manner unparalleled in history.
We hid behind a neutrality that was dishonest and knavish. Then we
marched in against a foe already beset by odds of at least two to one, and
gave him the *coup de grace* at odds of at least four to one. Meanwhile, the
great majority of Americans who were liable to military duty tried to get
out of it, and those who succeeded devoted themselves riotously to plun-
der. Not only the so-called profiteers fought for the loot; the honest laboring man, within the limits of his opportunities, was just as eager. And over
all we had a *Kriegherr* who drenched the world with streams of pious
balderdash so sickening that even our allies began to gag. In brief, a war
with no more gallantry in it than a lynching, and no more dignity than an
auction sale. Is it any wonder that its chief psychic effect has been the

horizontal degradation of the whole American people, so that they become bywords in the world for hypocrisy and sharp-dealing, and so far forget the ideas the Fathers of the Republic fought for that they accept any invasion of their old liberties, however gross, with scarcely a protest?

Mr. Dos Passos takes three young Americans, each typical of a large class, and shows their progress through this great machine. It is not a pleasant picture; I do not recommend the book for lazy reading on a Sabbath afternoon. But a passion for the truth is plainly there, and with it an imagination that makes that truth live. ["Variations upon a Familiar Theme," *SS* 66, no. 4 (December 1921): 143–44]

Streets of Night (1923)

Mr. Dos Passos, in *Streets of Night,* abandons the heroes of democracy and their innocent swineries for the lavender strivings of the Young Intellectuals, two of them male and one female. The trouble with his story is that he fails to make their doings logically credible—that the natural mooniness of youth is permitted to pass into something indistinguishable from lunacy. The result is a feeling, at least in this reader, that the whole thing is futile—that it throws no light whatever upon the soul struggles it professes to illuminate. A novelist, true enough, is not bound to explain his characters completely; he need not pretend to omniscience. But he must at least explain them enough to make their conduct intelligible and plausible; he must hold them on some kind of track, however feebly. This, it seems to me, Mr. Dos Passos fails to do. His fable is simply a series of puerile and often improbable episodes in the lives of two silly boys and an even sillier girl, ending with the suicide of one of them and the spiritual collapse of the other two. The Young Intellectual deserves a far more scientific and exhaustive treatment. He represents the high, fine spray of a wave of revolt that is probably running deeper in the Republic than most observers seem to think. His current proceedings are often somewhat clownish, but at the bottom of him there is a sound instinct, and as the general level of civilization rises in America he will grow in dignity and influence. Harold Stearns has already discussed his case at length in the form of a political manifesto; what remains is to put him into a novel. Mr.

Dos Passos, whose ineptitudes were already painfully visible in *Three Soldiers*, is not up to the business. It calls for a less grave and humorless reporter, and one with far more ingenuity. If Sinclair Lewis could only lay eggs and hatch young of his own kind there would be hope; he himself is probably too old for the job. But maybe Harvard or Yale is nourishing, even now, the performer foreordained. ["The Library," AM 2, no. 3 (July 1924): 380–81 ("Rambles in Fiction")]

Ernest Hemingway

A *Farewell to Arms* (1929)

Mr. Hemingway's *Farewell to Arms* is a study of the disintegration of two youngsters under the impact of war. The man, Frederic Henry, is a young American architect, turned into a lieutenant of the Italian Ambulance; the woman is Catherine Barkley, a Scotch nurse. They meet just after Catherine has lost her fiancé, blown to pieces on the Western front, and fall into each other's arms at once. For six months they dodge about between Milan and the Italian front, carrying on their affair under vast technical difficulties. Henry is badly wounded; the Italians, broken, retreat in a panic; earth and sky are full of blood and flames. Finally a baby is on its way, and the pair escape to Switzerland. There Catherine dies in childbirth, and Henry wanders into space. "It was like saying good-bye to a statue. After a while I went out and left the hospital and walked back to the hotel in the rain."

The virtue of the story lies in its brilliant evocation of the horrible squalor and confusion of war—specifically, of war *à la Italienne*. The thing has all the blinding color of a Kiralfy spectacle.[49] And the people who move through it, seen flittingly in the glare, are often almost appallingly real. But Henry and Catherine, it seems to me, are always a shade less real than the rest. The more they are accounted for, the less accountable they become. In the end they fade into mere wraiths, and in the last scene they scarcely seem human at all. Mr. Hemingway's dialogue, as always, is fresh and vivid. Otherwise, his tricks begin to wear thin. The mounting incoherence of a drunken scene is effective once but not three or four times. And there is surely no need to write such vile English as this: "The last mile or two of the new road, where it started to level out, *would be able* to be shelled steadily by the Austrians." ["The Library," *AM* 19, no. 1 (January 1930): 127 ("Fiction by Adept Hands")]

Death in the Afternoon (1932)

Mr. Hemingway has been before the public for ten years and in that time he has published seven books. He has been praised very lavishly, but has somehow failed to make his way into the first rank of living American authors. Nevertheless, he has made some progress in that direction, and his last novel, A *Farewell to Arms*, was unquestionably his best. In the present book, which is not fiction but fact, his characteristic merits and defects are clearly revealed. It is, on the one hand, an extraordinarily fine piece of expository writing, but on the other hand it often descends to a gross and irritating cheapness. So long as the author confines himself to his proper business, which is that of describing the art and science of bullfighting, he is unfailingly clear, colorful and interesting. Unfortunately, he apparently finds it hard to so confine himself. Only too often he turns aside from his theme to prove fatuously that he is a naughty fellow, and when he does so he almost invariably falls into banality and worse. The reader he seems to keep in his mind's eye is a sort of common denominator of all the Ladies' Aid Societies of his native Oak Park, Ill. The way to shock this innocent grandam, obviously, is to have at her with the ancient four-letter words. Mr. Hemingway does so with moral industry; he even drags her into the story as a character, to gloat over her horror. But she is quite as much an intruder in that story as King George V would be, or Dr. Irving Babbitt, or the Holy Ghost, and the four-letter words are as idiotically incongruous as so many boosters' slogans or college yells.

Mr. Hemingway's main purpose in *Death in the Afternoon* is to describe bullfighting as he has observed it in Spain. He admits frankly that he enjoys it, and he conveys a good deal of that enjoyment to the reader. The sport is brutal, but there is no evidence that it is any more brutal than football. The common American idea, I suppose, is that the bull is a senile and sclerotic beast with no chance against the matador, but Mr. Hemingway shows that this is very far from the truth. The bull, in fact, is always a youngster, and he is selected for his stamina and warlike enterprise. If he shows no pugnacity the fight is a flop, and the fans indicate their discontent by bombarding the matador with empty bottles. Moreover, the matador is not permitted to kill his antagonist in the safest way possible, which would probably also be the easiest. On the contrary, he must expose himself deliberately to the maximum of risk, and his rank in his profession is determined very largely by his ingenuity in devising new hazards, and his courage in facing them. When the formal jousting prescribed by the canon is over and he prepares to kill, he must approach the bull so closely and so openly that a miscalculation of half an inch may well cost him his life.

Mr. Hemingway has seen hundreds of fights, and no less than 3,000 bulls have been dispatched before his eyes. He has cultivated bullfighters and studied the immense literature of their mystery, and at one time he even ventured into the ring himself. Thus he knows everything about bullfighting that anyone save an actual matador can hope to learn, and this large and particular knowledge is visible on every page of his book. No better treatise on the sport has ever been written in English, and there is not much probability that better ones are to be had in Spanish. The narrative is full of the vividness of something really seen, felt, experienced. It is done simply, in English that is often bald and graceless, but it is done nevertheless with great skill. Take out the interludes behind the barn, for the pained astonishment of the Oak Park *Damenverein*, and it would be a really first-rate book. Even with the interludes it is well worth reading. Not many current books unearth so much unfamiliar stuff, or present it so effectively. I emerge cherishing a hope that bullfighting will be introduced at Harvard and Yale, or, if not at Harvard and Yale, then at least in the Lynching Belt of the South, where it would offer stiff and perhaps ruinous competition to the frying of poor blackamoors. Years ago I proposed that brass bands be set up down there for that purpose, but bullfights would be better. Imagine the moral stimulation in rural Georgia if an evangelist came to town offering to fight the local bulls by day and baptize the local damned by night!

Mr. Hemingway's main text fills about half of his book. There follows a series of excellent full-page photographs of bullfighters in action, including several which show the bull getting the better of it. There is also an elaborate and amusing glossary of bullfighting terms, running to nearly a hundred pages, and at the end is a calendar of the principal bullfights of Spain and Latin-America, for the convenience of tourists. A four-page note on Sidney Franklin, the Brooklyn matador, completes the book. Señor Franklin first came to fame in Mexico, but of late he has been enjoying great success in Spain. Mr. Hemingway says that "he kills easily and well. He does not give the importance to killing that it merits, since it is easy for him and because he ignores the danger." But ignoring it has not enabled him to avoid it, for he has been gored twice, once very badly. Mr. Hemingway describes his principal wounds in plain English. They will give the Oak Park W.C.T.U.[50] another conniption fit. The Hemingway boy is really a case. ["The Library," *AM* 27, no. 4 (December 1932): 506–7 ("The Spanish Idea of a Good Time")]

Some Worthy
Second-Raters

3

Ambrose Bierce

In the Midst of Life (1891; rpt. 1918)

A nother reprint is *In the Midst of Life*, a collection of stories by Ambrose Bierce. I am informed that it is the first of a series planned to
extend to five or six volumes and to include all the
writings of Bierce that seem worth preserving. His
Complete Works, in twelve volumes, are far too garru-
lous and unconsidered. Preparing them for the press
in his last days he heaved in a great deal of stuff that
was stupid and unreadable—forgotten newspaper editorials, epigrams upon nobodies long since dead, ancient wheezes, half-baked sketches, all the trivial
lumber of a busy journalist's clipping drawer. The result was that the twelve volumes, instead of improving
his celebrity, as his friends counted upon them doing,
actually revived the doctrine that he was a dull fellow
and much overestimated.

   The truth about Bierce, I believe, is that he was a
good deal damaged by the excessive praises of his partisans, some of whom gravely ranked him with the
great masters of English prose and put him in the first

place among American writers. A careful study of his writing shows that he ill deserved that gigantic encomium. He wrote skillfully, clearly, nicely, but always a bit tightly, always somewhat like an unusually talented college professor. The full savor of English is not in his prose. One misses the true gusto of the language, the native wildness, the gypsy quality. I can find no music in his style. Put beside that of Thackeray it is hard and artificial. Put beside that of Macaulay or Huxley or even Stevenson, it is cold and paltry. A purist of the most extravagant sort, he carried his prejudice against a vulgar looseness of expression so far that his writing, more than once, came to be indistinguishable from an exercise in "correct English," and so the life oozed out of it and it grew stiff and disagreeable.

Nor was he the great story-teller that his admirers have sought to make him out. In the present volume some of his very best work in fiction is undoubtedly presented, and yet a re-reading of it leaves one cold. All he could achieve was a surprising anecdote, and very often the surprise was banal enough—a Federal soldier shooting his Confederate father, an officer accused of cowardice throwing away his life in some fantastic act of heroism.[1] No genuine play of character is in these stories. The men they set before us, with precious few exceptions, are mere lay figures. They are moved about to make the plot, to prepare the surprise, to shock the uncritical reader; one learns nothing from them or of them; they remain almost marionettes at the end. And this even in the best of the stories, capital thrillers though they may be. In the worst one finds naught save a somewhat childish ingenuity, a feeble talent for raising the hair, melodrama reduced to scenarios.

But was Bierce, then, a false alarm? Nay, turn first to his epigrams, and particularly to *The Devil's Dictionary*. There you will find the most brilliant stuff, first and last, that America has ever produced. There you will find the true masterpiece of the one genuine wit that These States have ever seen. There you will wallow in Bierce, and wallowing, lament that he ever tried to be an Edgar Allan Poe. ["Suite Elegiaque," SS 57, no. 2 (October 1918): 144]

Carey McWilliams, *Ambrose Bierce: A Biography* (1929)

This is the fourth biography of Bierce to appear within the space of a year[2]—certainly a sufficient proof that interest in him, for long confined to

a small sect of *Feinschmecker*, has begun to be general. It is by long odds
the best of the four, not only because it presents a great deal of important
material that the others lack, but also because its point of view is more ju-
dicious.

Mr. C. Hartley Grattan's *Bitter Bierce*, the first life to be published,
contained some shrewd criticism, but its principal conclusion remained
somewhat dubious; moreover, the biographical portions stood on shaky
ground. Dr. Danziger's *Portrait* dealt with Danziger far more than it dealt
with Bierce, and Danziger turned out to be an extremely unimportant and
uninteresting person. So, in a measure, with Mr. Neale's *Life*: he had a lot
to say about Bierce that was not familiar, but he stopped too often to boast
about Neale. Mr. McWilliams avoids all of these follies. He has gone to
immense pains to unearth his facts, he sets them forth in a clear manner,
and when he pauses to philosophize upon them he speaks very sensibly.
Altogether, he has done an admirable piece of work. There are still some
holes in the record—no one really knows, for example, how or where
Bierce died—, but in so far as making it complete was humanly possible
Mr. McWilliams has done so, and he has added no gratuitous speculations
of his own.

He dissents sharply from Mr. Neale's interesting theory that Bierce was
not really killed in Mexico, as is commonly believed, but went to the
Grand Canyon of the Colorado and there committed suicide. The new evidence, apparently unknown to Neale, seems to make that theory unten-
able. Not only is it now certain that Bierce really entered Mexico; it is
known that he wrote home from there, and a record of his letters, though
not the texts thereof, was preserved by his friend and secretary, Miss Carrie Christiansen. This record, shortly before Miss Christiansen's death,
passed to Bierce's daughter, Mrs. Helen Isgrigg, and by her it was placed
in Mr. McWilliams' hands. It shows that her father was in the State of Chi-
huahua, on December 16, 1913, that he was in contact with a body of Mexican troops—whether of the loyal army or of the rebels does not
appear—and that he was expecting to proceed soon to Torreón, where
there was fighting. After that—silence. Where and when he was killed (or
died otherwise) is not known. Four or five circumstantial stories are in circulation, but all of them fall far short of persuasiveness. But if Bierce actually reached the front, as now seems overwhelmingly probable, it becomes
almost impossible to believe that he later returned to the United States,

and, making his way to the Grand Canyon, there committed suicide. And it becomes equally impossible to believe, as many persons have believed in California, that he died in an asylum for the insane at Napa.

Mr. McWilliams clears off many other legends about Bierce, and in general brings him down from the region of fable and gives him reality. The old whispers about Mrs. Bierce are shown to be without ground, the various fantastic stories about the death of Bierce's son, Day, are disposed of by relating the plain facts, and there are a dozen or more other such salutary services to the truth. The man who emerges is far more interesting and charming than the old fee-faw-fum. He was not, it appears, the appalling cynic that trembling young reporters used to admire. On the contrary, he was "one of the most idealistic men that his generation produced in America"—in fact, "a great moral force, . . . for he would not lie, and truth alone mattered to him. It came to mean more than beauty; . . . it came to be the paramount value of his life."

His rages were quite natural to such a character. Doomed to live in a country in which, by God's will, honesty is rare, courage is still rarer, and honor is almost unknown, he found his pruderies outraged at every step. So he fell upon the current mountebanks, great and small, in a Berserker fury, seeking thus to sooth and secure his own integrity. That integrity, so far as I can make out, was never betrayed by compromise. Right or wrong, Bierce always stuck to the truth as he saw it. He was magnificently decent. It cost him something, but he never wavered.

I suspect that his death came just in time. Suppose he had survived into the war years: would he have stood pat, or would he have allowed the prevailing blather to fetch him? His private philosophy, of course, was all against it. He was violently opposed to democracy, and held all its heroes in contempt. Somewhere in the present book Mr. McWilliams records his blistering opinion of the absurd jenkins, Walter Hines Page; and in another place he is denounced in his turn by that other exponent of bogus idealism, Franklin K. Lane.[3] But would he have resisted the full pressure, once it was turned on in 1917? I am not so sure. Mark Twain, plainly enough, would have succumbed at once: his death in 1910 spared a candid world some very painful scenes. Bierce, of course, would have been harder to run amok, but that he would have held out to the end is not to be put down as certain. Thus I find myself rather glad that the Mexicans disposed of him in 1913, before the great test really confronted him. If he had held on to the common sense and common decency of his life-long devotion the professional patriots of the time would have badgered him cruelly, and if he had compromised ever so little it would have been a sad and shameful thing. ["The Library," *AM* 19, no. 2 (February 1930): 251–52 ("Bierce Emerges from the Shadows")]

Edith Wharton
The Hermit and the Wild Woman (1908)

Mrs. Edith Wharton's new volume of short stories, *The Hermit and the Wild Woman,* is one of those genteel and well-made books which seem to presuppose a high degree of culture and no little personal fastidiousness in the reader. I have read Conrad and Kipling on the deck of a smelly tramp steamer, with my attire confined to a simple suit of pajamas, and somehow, the time, the place and the garb seemed in no wise indecent; but after I had passed the first story in Mrs. Wharton's book, I began to long for a velvet smoking jacket and a genuine Havana substitute for my corncob pipe. That is to say, the main concern of this charming and excellent writer is with the doings and meditations of ultra-civilized folks. The mental processes of an artist losing faith in his work, of a statesman tortured by an indiscreet wife, of a social climber reaching higher and higher—these are the problems in psychology that engage her. Her Hermit and her Wild Woman, true enough, are savages, but after all, they are mere figures of speech, and one feels that she means them to typify far more complex persons. In all the other stories we are frankly above the level of those who sweat and swear. It is not especially fashionable persons that she draws, for she knows well enough that fashionable persons often have elemental minds. A fairly accurate notion of her field may be derived from the thought that her average hero would suffer acutely on hearing a ragged entrance of the wood wind, or on suddenly encountering, by some mischance, a portrait in crayon. Of such are the people of her stories, and it is needless to say that she pictures them with a sure and artistic hand. ["A Road Map of the New Books," *SS* 27, no. 1 (January 1909): 157–58]

Ethan Frome (1911)

The virtue of *Ethan Frome* is the somewhat uncommon virtue of dignity—of that dignity which belongs to sound, conscientious, thoughtful execution. In design the thing is far from impeccable. Mrs. Wharton, in truth, begins downright clumsily. The narrative proper is hidden behind a sort of prologue—a device unnecessary and fruitful of difficulties. But once she gets into that narrative, once the bad start is over, the rest of the tale is managed with such grace and skill, with such nice balance and care for detail, that one quickly forgets the artificiality of its beginning. We have here, in brief, an excellent piece of writing. Mrs. Wharton has seldom given better evidence of her craftsmanship. The dismal story of Ethan Frome, the lorn New England farmer; of his silent sacrifices for his insane mother, his hypochondriac wife; of his pitiful yearning for little Mattie Silver; of his endless, hopeless struggle with the unyielding soil; of the slow decay and death of his hopes, his ambitions, his lingering joy in life—this story, as it is set down, gathers the poignancy of true tragedy. One senses the unutterable desolation of those Northern valleys, the meaningless horror of life in those lonely farmhouses. A breath of chill Norwegian wind blows across the scene. There is in Ethan some hint of Alfred Allmers, of Hjalmar Ekdal.[4] He is the archetype of an American we have been forgetting, in our eagerness to follow the doings of more pushful and spectacular fellows. He is the American whom life has passed over like the lightnings, leaving him hurt and mute by the roadside. ["An Overdose of Novels," SS 35, no. 4 (December 1911): 151]

The Reef (1912)

Let me [. . .] pass on to Mrs. Wharton, whose *The Reef* is so far below *Ethan Frome* that it seems to be by a different novelist. Here we have the story of a dashing young American diplomat (the Indiana *motif*—the Siegfried of our national romance!) who stops off in Paris with Sophie Viner on his way to court the widowed Anna Leath. George Darrow's intentions are honorable; he is sorry for poor Sophie and plans to do no more than take her to a few theaters. But the affair goes much further than that, and so he is given a great shock later on, when he finds Sophie installed in the Leath chateau as governess to Anna's little daughter—and *fiancée* to Anna's stepson! No doubt you can imagine the rest: how suspicions began to circulate, how Sophie breaks down and confesses, how the stepson rages and Anna weeps, and how, in the end, it is all smoothed over nicely and George and Anna make up. A tawdry story, almost bad enough for a bestseller, but relieved and embellished, of course, by Mrs. Wharton's keen wit, her skillful management of situation, her dramatic sense, her finished and admirable craftsmanship. However, I cannot recommend it as a fair specimen of her work, nor even as a passable specimen. That would be unjust to you, and more unjust to Mrs. Wharton. ["The Burden of Humor," *SS* 39, no. 2 (February 1913): 157]

The Age of Innocence (1920)

John Galsworthy's *In Chancery* and Edith Wharton's *The Age of Innocence* are very much alike. Both deal ironically with the tyranny of convention in past eras, and in each the dramatic conflict is supplied by a somewhat scandalous divorce—in the case of the Galsworthy story, by two divorces, or, more accurately, by a divorce and a half. Galsworthy's scene is the London of Boer War days—Victorian England at its last gasp. Mrs. Wharton's is the New York of the 70's, with the old aristocracy at grips with the new plutocracy. It grieves me, as a patriot, to have to say that Galsworthy tells his story much more amusingly and competently than Mrs. Wharton tells hers. It is by no means a story of any force or poignancy, but it has entertaining characters (brought over from *The Man of Property* and *Indian Summer of a Forsyte*), and there is a great deal of humor in the detail of it, and much excellent writing. Mrs. Wharton's writing, on the contrary, is probably the worst that she has ever done. It is, of course, not bad in the sense that Dreiser's writing is often bad, but it lacks all character, all distinction: any literate person might have done it. Worse, her story is full of anachronisms. If we believe that Newland Archer went to hear Christine Nilsson in *Faust* at the Academy of Music, then it is hard to believe that he was simultaneously reading Huysmans, Bourget and Vernon Lee, for Nilsson gargled her way to fame between 1870 and 1872, and Huysmans did not print *Marthe* until 1876, and Bourget was absolutely unheard of until 1874, and Vernon Lee, in 1872, was but sixteen years old. No, I am not professorial: I simply apply a realistic test to a story that pretends to be meticulously realistic. . . . But a readable story, none the less, and not without its moments. A long-practised and competent novelist wrote it, but certainly not a novelist on a high tide of creative gusto. It droops more than once. It is a bit weary. . . . ["The Anatomy of Ochlocracy," *SS* 64, no. 2 (February 1921): 143]

William Dean Howells

New Leaf Mills (1913)

More and more unearthly grow the heroes and heroines of our current Thackerays and Dostoevskys. A while back, as you may recall, the Hon. Will Levington Comfort, a clever fellow, was asking us to listen to the melancholy, metaphysical harangues of one Andrew Bedient, ship's cook and New Thought—all about Mystic Motherhood, the Third Lustrous Dimension, the Big Deep, the Bhagavad Gita and other such trappings and delusions of the Zeitgeist. Then came John Masefield, with a bacteriologist fighting the sleeping sickness on the shores of the Upper Congo. And then came A. E. W. Mason, with an explorer homesick for the pemmican and chilblains of the Antarctic. And after Mason came H. G. Wells, with a millionaire physicist laid up with a broken leg in the Labrador hinterland; and A. Conan Doyle, with a mad, rip-snorting Barnum of *pterichthyidæ* and *mastodontinæ*; and Edith Wharton, with a soiled maiden who blabbed the story of her own folly; and Gerhart Hauptmann, with a German stage-door Johnnie; and Alfred Ollivant, with a Cockney tanner dying of tuberculosis; and George Moore, with himself. Finally, no longer than a month ago, there was Elizabeth Robins, with a heroine trapped by White Slavers and sold into gilded but hideous captivity.5 [. . .]

This Howells hero is the most fearsome of them all, at least to my private taste. Given a lonely heath and a dark night, I would rather meet a Christian Endeavor leader or even a Vice Crusader than a Swedenborgian. I do not defend this dread intellectually: I know very well, in fact, that the average Swedenborgian is a harmless fellow, that the average

Dunkard or hard shell Baptist is ten times as dangerous. But there falls upon me from my lost youth the shadow of Swedenborg's *Heaven and Hell*, read dutifully by a boy too eager to believe in all apparently serious books, and the lingering relic of that cruel perplexity and stupefaction is the aforesaid skittishness. A man bears forever the scars of such early tortures. If I revile Chopin to-day, denouncing him absurdly as a perjurer, a fop and a sucker of eggs, then blame it on my struggles with the banal scales of the *Valse du petit chien*, Op. 64, No. 1, in the year 1890—so long, long ago! And if I am cold to Poe, then blame the Poeomaniacs who haunted my schooldays in Poe-ridden Baltimore, mixing pifflish local pride with more pifflish literary criticism. And if I am unjust to the Swedenborgians, then collect the fine from Swedenborg.

But for all this, I am free to admit that the Howells book, *New Leaf Mills* by name, is the best, and by long odds, of all the fictions of the current boiling, if only because it shows the ease and fluency of a veteran hand. The ancient Howells, indeed, has every virtue that one demands of a first-rate journeyman. He lays out his work with precision, he selects the proper tools with care, and he proceeds to the actual labor with calm and confidence. There is never any sense of difficulties slowly battered down; there is never any heaving and blowing; there is never any wasted effort. The less experienced craftsman, however talented, seldom produces any such effect of perfect facility, of magnificent adroitness, of ready virtuosity. You can feel that lesser fellow laboring damnably in spots; you can see him overburdened with inspiration in other spots. He is never content to let well enough alone: he is always impatient to put in everything he can think of, to gild his lily until it shines like a set of false teeth. Not so the venerable and consummate Howells. He doesn't waste upon one book the stuff that might serve for two books, or three books. He never surges over the strict limits of his frame. He never drags in extraneous persons and events, merely because he knows about them and is eager to show it. In brief he composes prose fiction (not to mention other things) much as old Johann Sebastian Bach used to compose fugues—with the end in sight from the very beginning, and a straight line connecting the two points. Not, of course, that he is as towering a genius as Johann Sebastian—nor, indeed, as relentless a formalist. But there is still something suggestively

Bachian about his stark, sophisticated method, and particularly about his careful economy of materials.

The scene of *New Leaf Mills* is the rural Ohio of the year or two following the Mexican War, and the Swedenborgian hero is one Owen Powell. Scratch an Emmanuel Mover and you will find a Psychical Researcher; scratch a Psychical Researcher and you will find a Vegetarian, and if not a Vegetarian, then a Eugenist. So with the Swedenborgians: their interest in archangels is always accompanied by other enthusiasms. This Powell is also an Abolitionist and a Communist. His dream is of a little Utopia in the wilderness, a pastoral Paradise of a dozen or more families, with plenty of hams in the smokehouse, plenty of children in the dooryards, and a friendly welcome for all strangers, white or black, free or fugitive. He interests two of his brothers in the enterprise, and with money supplied by one of them—he is a pathetic bankrupt himself—he buys a small flour mill. This is to be the beginning and corner stone of his roseate colony. Until things settle a bit, he will keep on grinding wheat, but eventually he will change the flour mill into a paper mill, and paper-making will become the central industry of a busy and happy community—a community spread out over a whole countryside and basking in the plenty of the Lord. Thus the dream of Owen Powell, Swedenborgian.

Alas for its fulfilment! Fate is against it, indeed, from the start. The rude hinds of the vicinage are but little impressed by communism, and even less by Swedenborgianism. They laugh at Owen behind his back, and mingled with their guffaws is a subtle distrust of one dissenting from the prevalent theology. In the case of one of them, Overdale, the practical miller at the mill, this distrust takes the form of open hostility. Overdale is a gloomy and churlish ignoramus, eternally full of bad whiskey, and it is only accident that keeps him from an actual attempt upon Owen's life. But even worse than these outward handicaps upon the great enterprise are handicaps within. Owen is not the man to carry such things through. He lacks the hard sagacity, the unsentimental common sense. Working day and night, he yet accomplishes nothing. His wife and children wallow in a three-room hut while their new house progresses by inches—and then stops progressing altogether. The paper machinery never arrives; the necessary converts are never made; the desert refuses to blossom. In the end, poor Owen goes back to the city, hopeful still, but a failure unutterable. As he passes from the scene he is preparing to take over a Swedenborgian bookstore and start a Swedenborgian monthly.

The perfect type of the fantastic visionary and chronic incompetent. We of to-day are prone to forget the part played by such benign asses in the early history of the republic. We remember only the pioneer who was successful—the flinty, indomitable fellow who faced the sunset and tamed the wilderness. We forget the vast company of dreamers and impossibilists who hung at his heels—founders of empires that come to nothing, preachers of outlandish and incomprehensible religions, believers in brummagem millenniums, the grotesque white crows and black swans of the humdrum East. Their bones are scattered from end to end of our West Country; they pushed over the Alleghenies but a few miles behind the trappers and railsplitters. Something of their childish faith in the incredible still lingers in our people; nowhere else on earth is it so easy to launch a new political panacea or a new invention in theology. Our progress, in its main current, may be wholly materialistic and even sordid, but upon that current there has always floated a froth of divine folly. Only in the United States is it possible to imagine such a puerile thing as the New Thought becoming a widespread and important cult, with a whole literature to interpret it, and agents to defend it upon the floor of the national legislature, and millions of fools trying to live according to its gratuitous and incoherent tenets, and thousands of prophets and mad mullahs fattening upon the fools.

It is this typically American weakness for the sonorous, this national defect of character, that Mr. Howells has sought to describe and illumine in *New Leaf Mills*, and his success is unmistakable. True enough, he has not gone very far; he has not ploughed too deeply and scientifically into the psychology of Owen Powell. But so far as he has actually gone, he has carried sympathy and understanding with him. He has made the man real, and what is more, he has made him pitiful. One somehow leaves the chronicle with a fellow feeling for this preposterous amateur theologian, dreaming his vain dreams, groping through his endless shadows, bruised and beaten by the oafs of his gray world. And there is poignancy, too, in the picture of the dreamer's wife, for Ann Powell shares all of the penalties of

Owen's dreaming without quite sharing his dream. Her feet are ever on the earth. She knows the precise difference between a stony hillside and the Elysian Fields. And yet she sticks to the poor fool, her lord and master, to the very end, easing the agonies of his disillusion, bravely striving for a way out. A pair of careful, lifelike, appealing portraits. A tale with something of youth's freshness and earnestness in it, for all the author's three score and sixteen years. A useful model for those young novelists who have not yet learned the value of careful planning, ruthless selection and straightforward, simple writing. ["A Nietzschean, a Swedenborgian and Other Queer Fowl," SS 40, no. 2 (June 1913): 145–47]

The Leatherwood God (1916)

Politeness must be mingled delicately with criticism in dealing with The Leatherwood God, by William Dean Howells, for it is the work of a man of eighty, and much high striving is behind him, and not a little sound accomplishment. On the whole, a superficial novelist, and not to be mentioned in the same breath with such men as Clemens, Dreiser and Norris, Dr. Howells has yet concocted three or four novels that belong to the top of the third rank, and at least one, The Rise of Silas Lapham, that is a valuable and permanent contribution to our national literature. On the whole, a somewhat romantic and unintelligible critic, with a great gift for discovering bogus geniuses, he has nevertheless done some useful pioneering, notably for Turgenieff and Dostoievsky, and, to come nearer home, for such men as E. W. Howe, author of The Story of a Country Town. And on the whole, an essayist of an empty and kittenish variety, he has still managed to be mildly entertaining, and to develop a style that often shows the pungent charm of the unexpected.

Americans always judge their authors, not as artists, but as men. Edgar Allan Poe, I daresay, will never live down the fact that he was a periodical drunkard. Mark Twain, the incomparable artist, will probably never shake off Mark Twain, the after-dinner comedian, the flaunter of white dress clothes, the public character, the national wag. As for Dr. Howells, he gains rather than loses by this confusion of values, for he is a highly respectable gentleman, a sitter on solemn committees, an intimate of college presidents and reformers, a man vouched for by both the *Atlantic Monthly* and the *Ladies' Home Journal,* and the result is his general acceptance as a member of the literary peerage, and of the rank of earl at least. For twenty years past his successive books have not been criticised, not even adequately reviewed; they have been merely hymned and fawned over. The dean of American letters in point of years, and in point of published quantity, and in point of public prominence and influence, he has been gradually enveloped in a web of superstitious reverence, and it grates harshly to hear his actual achievement discussed in cold blood.

Nevertheless, all this merited respect for an industrious and inoffensive man is bound, soon or late, to yield to a critical examination of the artist within, and that examination, I fear, will have its bitter moments for those who naïfly accept the current Howells legend. It will show, without doubt, a first-rate journeyman, a contriver of pretty things, a clever stylist—but it will also show a long row of uninspired and hollow books, with no more ideas in them than so many volumes of the *New Republic,* and no more deep and contagious feeling than so many reports of autopsies, and no more glow and gusto than so many tables of bond prices. The profound dread and agony of life, the surge of passion and aspiration, the grand crash and glitter of things, the tragedy that runs eternally under the surface—all this the critic of the future will seek in vain in Dr. Howells' urbane and shallow volumes. And seeking it in vain, he will probably dismiss all of them together with fewer words than he gives to *Huckleberry Finn . . .*

Intrinsically, *The Leatherwood God* is little more than a stale anecdote, and the dressing that Dr. Howells gives it does not lift it very far above this anecdotal quality. The central character, one Dylks, is a backwoods evangelist who acquires a belief in his own buncombe, and ends by announcing that he is God. The job before the author was obviously that of tracing the psychological steps whereby this mountebank proceeds to that conclusion; the fact, indeed, is recognized in the canned review, which says that the book is "a study of American religious psychology," and by the fair critic of the New York *Times,* who praises it as "a remarkable psychological study."[6] But an inspection of the text shows that no such study is really in it. Dr. Howells does not *show* how Dylks came to believe himself God; he merely *says* that he did so. The whole discussion of the process, indeed, is confined to two pages—172 and 173—and it is quite infantile in its inade-quacy. Nor do we get anything approaching a revealing look into the heads of the other converts—the saleratus-sodden, hell-crazy, half-witted Methodists and Baptists of a remote Ohio settle-ment of seventy or eighty years ago. All we have is the casual statement that they are converted, and begin to offer Dylks their howls of devotion. And when, in the end, they go back to their original bosh, dethroning Dylks overnight and restoring the gaseous vertebrate[7] of Calvin and Wes-ley—when this contrary process is recorded, it is accompanied by no more illumination. In brief, the story is not a study at all, but simply a story—as I have said, an anecdote. Its characters reveal only what a passing glance would reveal; its dialogue is tedious; its well-made sub-plot is pointless; it skims the skin. There is not even the charm of good writing. Dr. Howells forgot his style as he forgot his psychology. Any fifth-rate novelist might have put the thing together as well; there are dozens of American novelists who would have done it far better. . . . I surely hope I have been polite.

But what an invitation is in the subject! What a great novel is there! The United States, from the earliest times, has swarmed with just such jit-ney messiahs as Dylks—some of them even more self-deluded than he was, some of them plain rogues. Joseph Smith, Schlatter, Mary Baker G. Eddy, John Alexander Dowie, the prophets of the Shakers, the Holy Rollers, the Holy Ghost and Us maniacs, the Seventh Day Adventists, the various Mennonites, the nigger Methodists—the list is a long and juicy one.[8] The spectacle of a Billy Sunday assaulting Pittsburgh, Philadelphia, Baltimore, Kansas City and Boston is not new; there have been periodical outbreaks of this same religious savagery ever since the Great Awakening of 1734, and before that time the colonies were full of heretic-hunters, and the politics of some of them was chiefly a combat between theologians. To be an American, indeed, means to carry a depressing cargo of religious balderdash; the great-grandfathers of two-thirds of us thought that hell was yawning for them, and were willing to believe anything in order to escape. It is thus always easy to get a hearing for theological ideas in the United States; they enter into our very laws and customs, and are heard with a gravity that it would be hard to match anywhere else in Christendom. Democracy, Puritanism, Philistinism—they are sisters under their skins—

nay, they are one and the same. And yet how little the latter-day Puritan appears in our literature—how seldom he has been studied objectively, and his quirks platted. A penetrating and admirable small sketch appears in a book I have already mentioned: E. W. Howe's *The Story of a Country Town*. But Howe had other fish to fry; he slapped in his Methodist hound of heaven brilliantly, and then passed on to melodrama and the pains of young love. I advocate a novel by Dreiser, to be called *The Puritan*—a full-length study, in all his relentless meticulousness, of the sort of fellow who contributes money to Billy Sunday funds, and believes that all will go to hell who are not purged by total immersion in water, and opposes Sunday baseball and moving-pictures, and whoops for prohibition, and delights in vice crusades, and has, perchance, an eye for a shapely leg. In New York this gladiator of the gospels tends to disappear; save when some new Parkhurst or Comstock heats up his fires, he is seldom heard of. But in the hinterland he rages so steadily that he may be almost accepted as the normal American type. And there is an endless supply of mad mullahs, all divinely inspired and impassioned, to keep him snorting. Few of them, in these later days, actually claim to be God, but all of them claim to be on intimate and confidential terms with Him, and all of them launch thunderbolts of anathema on every man who ventures to hoot at their revelations. ["Sufferings among Books," *SS* 51, no. 1 (January 1917): 266–68]

Jack London

John Barleycorn (1913)

John Barleycorn, by Jack London, is marked by the two qualities which give Mr. London a peculiar distinction: extraordinarily brilliant writing and extraordinarily jejune and fallacious thinking. The book is a frank confession of personal combats with old John (not uncontaminated by justifiable boasting!), and its gradual *crescendo* leads to a prohibition stump speech at the end. The prime cause of the liquor evil, says London, is the deadly saloon, that private office of the devil, with its alluring warmth, its inviting red lights, its large, shiny spittoons, its promise of good company and *gemüthlichkeit*. Not one man in a hundred thousand is born with a thirst for alcohol. To the great majority it is distasteful at the start, even more so than tobacco. The neophyte swallows it merely because he wants to be sociable, because all the men he knows and likes are swallowers, because their swallowing is done amid scenes of ease and glitter, and to the tune of automatic pianos and persiflage. *Ergo*, the way to stop the swallowing is to shut up the saloon. Abolish the seductive *gemüthlichkeit* and you have abolished the one genuine temptation to wrestle with John. . . . A fine theory, to be sure, and one voiced full oft by loud wizards of the Chautauquas, but alas, what holes are in it! *Imprimis*, how are you going to abolish the saloon? The majority of sinners want it; the majority of sinners get what they want. The pious have been abolishing the saloon in Maine for sixty years, but it still flourishes amazingly as the blind pig. And elsewhere, too, it has resisted all the celestial artillery, from simple anathemas to federal injunctions. As Mr. London himself admits, it serves a human need, it satisfies a human appetite. And before it may go, "some other institution will have to obtain, some other congregating place of men where strange men and stranger men may get in touch, and meet and know." Well, what is that "other institution" to be? Who has invented it? Where is it being tried? . . . To these questions, the author of *John Barleycorn* has no answers, and so his fine structure of argument has sandy soil beneath it. But how beautifully he writes! How his sentences hiss and sing! What an ear he has for nervous, vibrant, bouncing English! ["Marie Corelli's Sparring Partner," SS 41, no. 3 (November 1913): 160]

The Strength of the Strong (1914)

In the fiction that has reached me since our last meeting I can find little that is worth extensive notice. The best of it, perhaps, is to be found in Jack London's book of short stories, *The Strength of the Strong*. For London's literary talents I have the very highest admiration: he is one of the few novelists now at large among us who actually know how to write. But he has an unhappy habit of introducing a didactic purpose into his compositions, and nine times out of ten it spoils them out of hand, for the things he believes in are chiefly foolish things—*e.g.*, Socialism and Prohibition—and his manner of arguing for them is extraordinarily inept and tedious. In the present volume, five of the seven stories are more or less contaminated by this fatuous endeavor to be instructive and uplifting. But the two that re-

main, "The Sea Farmer" and "Samuel," more than make up for the bore-
dom thus inflicted. Each of them presents a thoughtful and penetrating
study of a simple soul in conflict with inscrutable destiny, and in each
there is the sound work of a first-rate artist. The first of the two, in particular, reveals a profound sincerity and poignancy. London is here experimenting with the method and materials of Joseph Conrad, and with a very
near approach to complete success. His Captain MacElrath might well
claim entry into the company of Conrad's immortal merchant skippers.
He is of the clan of Captain Allistoun, of the *Narcissus*, and Captain
MacWhirr, of the *Nan-Shan*. ["A Review of Reviewers," SS 44, no. 2 (October 1914): 160]

The Star Rover (1915)

The Star Rover, by Jack London, proves anew what I have often maintained in this place, to wit, that London is probably the most competent
literary workman, the soundest and cleverest technician, now at work
among us. His actual stories of late years have tended toward a feeble mar-
velousness and silliness (it is so of this one), but the manner in which they
are written is always excellent and sometimes superb. Not only does he
know how to devise and manage a fable; he also has a delicate taste in
words, and seldom makes a tactical mistake in their use. Out of all this
comes the charm, the plausibility, the address of the man, which is to say,
his success. No current novelist writing in English, save perhaps H. G.
Wells, comes closer to a mastery of the trade. . . . Style, of course, is the
man. London writes pleasingly, not only because he is skilful, but also, and
perhaps chiefly, because he must be a man of hearty and agreeable personality. ["Partly about Books," SS 48, no. 1 (January 1916): 309]

Abraham Cahan

The Rise of David Levinsky (1917)

In March, weeping here, I lamented the badness of the current native
novel, and brought up various specimens of far better stuff from beyond
the seas. This month I might loose the same sobs again. In such fictions as
are offered by Mrs. Atherton, Gouverneur Morris, Leroy Scott, Zane Grey,

James Oliver Curwood and the rest of the corn-fed genuises, I can find only a pale and preposterous silliness—the sort of piffle that irritates and depresses. But in the works of two foreign gentlemen, the one a Russian Jew and the other an Englishman, I discover the precise qualities that are missing from the homemade books, to wit, the qualities of clear structure, of penetrating characterization, of unflagging plausibility, and of sound style. The first of these invaders is *The Rise of David Levinsky.* [. . .]

The case of Cahan is really quite astonishing. Here is a man born in Lithuania, educated there, and come to manhood there. He had reached the age of 22 before he immigrated to America; during all his youth it is doubtful that he ever saw half a dozen Americans or heard ten connected sentences in English. Moreover, he has spent his days and nights, since his arrival, among Yiddish and Russian speaking people. He is a leader among the East Side Jews; he uses Yiddish in his daily business; he is the editor of a large Yiddish newspaper; he writes Yiddish every hour of the day. Nevertheless, he has here produced a novel of 530 closely-printed pages in absolutely perfect English. Not once, in reading it, have I tripped upon an inept phrase; not once have I detected the slightest note of foreignness. It seems to me that this is a feat of the first magnitude, even forgetting the intrinsic merits of the book. Among all the editors of English newspapers in New York there is not one who could have done the thing better. Among all the native novelists of the country I can't think of more than six. Moreover, it is not merely correct English; it is nearly always musical English, and sometimes it is highly felicitous English. Good phrases are in it; the right word is in the right place; there is very little use of those worn-out rubber-stamps which show in nine-tenths of our fiction. Altogether, I marvel at the miracle, and give it a dutiful cheer. If this is the sort of thing that the East Side can produce, then Indiana, in self-defense, had better start an anti-Semitic movement at once.

In content, *The Rise of David Levinsky* is very simple, as sound novels always are. It offers no intrigue, no mystery, no plot. It argues nothing and professes to teach nothing. All it does is to set before us, against a background of moving actuality, the life story of a somewhat exceptional, but by no means heroic or transcendental Russian Jew. Born in poverty, he struggles through a youth full of hardship but probably not unhappy, is dedicated by his pious mother to a learned life, puts in five or six years poll-parroting and dissecting the fossilized platitudes of the Talmud, is driven to America by poverty, sheds his piety and his spit-locks, becomes a peddler, learns garment-working, starts a shop of his own on a shoe-string, fights his way to security by devious devices, makes a lot of money, wars upon the unions, fades into a lonely middle age—and pauses by the way to write his story. A man above the general, but still a man always in contact with the general. The actual East Side is swarming about him; he never gets far from his own people; they are quite as much a part of the picture as he is himself. It is a picture that seems to me to be extraordinarily incisive and brilliant. There is not a single blot of improbability upon it. If any more vivid and persuasive presentation of the immigrant's hopes, fortunes and processes of mind has ever been made, then it has surely never reached me. All other novels upon the same theme fall short, in one way or another, of this one.

The *milieu*, of course, is not novel. Montague Glass, in his tales of Potash and Perlmutter, has got it into books, and what is more, he has done the business with high skill. In those tales, indeed, there is some of the best writing on view in America for a dozen years; they are well imagined and often superbly worked out; it was a blue day when Glass stopped writing stories and took to manufacturing farces for Forty-second street. But his comedies, after all, are seldom anything but comedies. They are concerned, not with the deeper springs and processes of character, but with the mere bubblings and oddities of character; they hold to the genially superficial note which belongs properly to the comic. Cahan, without missing any of the surface grotesquerie—some of his humorous scenes are quite as good as Glass'—gets further down. What he is trying to accomplish is not simply to show us what a typical crowd of Russian Jews say and do, but also to show us how they arrive at such notions and acts—in other words, to explain them, and make them coherent and real. It seems to me that he has done this with great success. Not only his Levinsky, but also all the rest of his people, down to the least of them, are genuine human beings. They may be from life, or they may be wholly imaginary, but there is never the slightest stiffness of the dummy in them, they are never mere characters in an idle tale, they are never pulled and hauled about like the mannikins in an ordinary novel.

Technically, the story is naturalistic in manner. That is to say, it avoids moralizing and idealization, and presents its people and their transactions with some show of literalness. The element of sex, which must needs enter into a naturalistic study of a normal man, is not overlooked. We have a long series of sex episodes, some of them romantic and some of them rather hoggish; all are described. But in this description Mr. Cahan quite avoids the meticulous nastiness that is so often the undoing of the naturalistic novelist. He says what he has to say with sufficient clarity, and then he passes on; there is no lingering gloating over details; one finds absolutely nothing in the book to get it beneath finishing-school pillows, or into the public manifestos of such swine as the Comstocks are. Here, as elsewhere, he shows the sound taste and discretion of a man of culture. He neither views his world like a yokel at a peep-show nor like a fat woman snuffling over a moral moving-picture, but like a civilized adult, masculine, tolerant and above all facile emotion.

All this, of course, is merely saying that much of the merit of the novel lies in the novelist. The connection is bound to be close and obvious. The primary trouble with a good deal of our native fiction is that it is written by cads, male and female—believers in the uplift, remediers of abuses, cheap sensation-mongers, sobbers and snivelers, moralists, pornographers, stupid clodpolls, admirers of the contemptible, childish romantics, gigglers, posturers—in brief, the sort of ignobles it would be embarrassing to meet at dinner. When one encounters an American novelist who thinks and writes, so to speak, like a gentleman, there is a refreshing novelty in the experience. Henry James did it. Mrs. Watts does it. Cabell does it. Hergesheimer does it. But not many others. The rest, in the main, are shoddy souls. . . . That a recruit for the minority should come out of the despised East Side, elbowing his way through a mob of peddlers and buttonhole workers—this, surely, is a jest most savoury and most foul. ["The Stream of Fiction," SS 55, no. 1 (May 1918): 138–40]

Ring Lardner

How to Write Short Stories (1924)

Some time ago a young college professor brought out a "critical" edition of *Sam Slick*, by Judge Thomas C. Haliburton, eighty-seven years after its first publication.[9] It turned out to be quite unreadable—a dreadful series of archaic jocosities about varieties of *Homo americanus* long perished and forgotten, in a dialect now intelligible only to paleophilologists. Sometimes I have a fear that the same fate awaits Ring Lardner. The professors of his own day, of course, are quite unaware of him, save perhaps as a low zany to be enjoyed behind the door. They should no more venture to whoop him up publicly and officially than their predecessors of 1880 would have ventured to whoop up Mark Twain, or their remoter predecessors of 1837 would have dared to say anything for Haliburton. In such matters the academic mind, being chiefly animated by a fear of sneers, works very slowly. So slowly, indeed, does it work that it usually works too late. By the time Mark Twain got into the text-books for sophomores, two-thirds of his compositions, as the Young Intellectuals say, had already begun to date; by the time Haliburton was served up as a sandwich between introduction and notes he was already dead. As I say, I suspect sadly that Lardner is doomed to go the same route. His stories, it seems to me, are superbly adroit and amusing; no other contemporary American, sober or gay, writes better. But I doubt that they last: our grandchildren will wonder what they are about. It is not only, or even mainly, that the dialect that fills them will pass, though that fact is obviously a serious handicap in itself. It is principally that the people they depict will pass—that Lardner's incomparable baseball players, pugs, song-writers, Elks, Rotarians and golf caddies are flitting figures of a transient civilization—that they will be almost as puzzling and soporific, in the year 2000, as Haliburton's Yankee clock peddler is to-day.

The fact—if I may assume it to be a fact—is certainly not to be set against Lardner's account; on the contrary, it is, in its way, highly complimentary to him. For he has deliberately applied himself, not to the anatomizing of the general human soul, but to the meticulous histological study of a few salient individuals of his time and nation, and he has done it with such subtle and penetrating skill that one must belong to his time and nation to follow him. I doubt that anyone who is not familiar with professional ball players, intimately and at first hand, will ever comprehend the full merit of the amazing sketches in *You Know Me, Al*; I doubt that anyone who has not given close and deliberate attention to the American vulgate will ever realize how magnificently Lardner handles it. He has had more imitators, I suppose, than any other living American writer, but has he any actual rivals? If so, I have yet to hear of them. They all try to write the vulgar speech as adeptly and as amusingly as he writes it, and they all fall short of him; the next best is miles and miles behind him. And they are all equally inferior in observation, in sense of character, in shrewdness and insight. His studies, to be sure, are never very profound; he makes no attempt to get at the primary springs of passion and motive; all his people share the same amiable stupidity, the same transparent vanity, the same shallow inconsequentiality; they are all human Fords, and absolutely alike at bottom. But if he thus confines himself to the surface, it yet remains a fact that his investigations on that surface are extraordinarily alert, ingenious and brilliant—that the character he finally sets before us, however roughly articulated as to bones, is so astoundingly realistic as to hide that the effect is indistinguishable from that of life itself. The old man in "The Golden Honeymoon" is not merely well done; he is perfect. And so is the girl in "Some Like Them Cold." And so, even, is the idiotic Frank X. Farrell in "Alibi Ike"—an extravagant grotesque and yet quite real from glabella to calcaneus.

The present collection has a buffoonish preface on the art of writing short stories—a devastating *reductio ad absurdum* of the sort of bilge ladled out annually by Prof. Dr. Blanche Colton Williams and other such self-constituted experts.[10] Lardner actually knows more about the management of the short story than nine-tenths of its most eminent practitioners. His stories are always built very carefully, and yet they always seem to be wholly spontaneous, and even formless. He has grasped the primary fact that no conceivable ingenuity can save a story that fails to show a recognizable and interesting character; he knows that a good character sketch is always a good story, no matter what its structure. He gets less critical attention than he ought to get, mainly, I believe, because his people are all lowly ignoramuses, presented without any sociological eye rolling. The reviewers of books, with few exceptions, seem to be easily impressed by lofty and fashionable pretensions. They praise F. Scott Fitzgerald's stories of country club flappers eloquently, and overlook his other stories, some of which are much better. They can't rid themselves of the superstition that Edith Wharton, whose people have butlers, is a better novelist than Willa Cather, whose people, in the main, dine in their kitchens. They linger under the spell of Henry James, whose most lowly character, at all events in his later years, was at least an Englishman, and hence superior. Lardner, so to speak, hits these critics below the belt. He not only fills his stories with people who read the New York *Evening Journal*, say "Shake hands with my friend," and wear diamond rings; he also shows them having a good time in the world, and quite devoid of inferiority complexes. They amuse him intensely, but he does not pity them. A fatal error! The moron has a place in fiction, as in life, but he is not to be treated too easily and casually. It must be shown that he suffers tragically because he cannot abandon the plow to write poetry, or the sample-case to study for opera. Lardner is more realistic. If his typical hero has a secret sorrow it is that he is too old to take up osteopathy and too much in dread of his wife to venture into bootlegging.

On the slip-cover of *How to Write Short Stories* I find the following gem: "One can say of Ring Lardner what can be said of few writers, that he never wrote an insincere word." I smack my lips over this singular blurb: can it be that the Scribners are trying to make good Ring respectable? If so, the effort will fail. The professors will shy at him until he is dead at least fifty years. He is doomed to stay outside where the gang is. ["The Library," *AM* 2, no. 3 (July 1924): 376–77 ("Ring W. Lardner")]

The Love Nest and Other Stories (1926)

I commend this volume to those critics who have fallen into the habit of treating Mr. Lardner as a mere harmless clown, comparable to Kin Hubbard and Bugs Baer.[11] Let them give a diligent and prayerful reading to the whole book, but especially to the sketches called "Haircut," "Zone of Quiet" and "Rhythm." What they will find is far more than clowning, harmless or otherwise. What they will find is satire of the most acid and appalling sort—satire wholly removed, like Swift's before it, from the least weakness of amiability, or even pity. That taste of bitterness has been in all of Lardner's work since his beginnings. His earliest sketches of baseball-players went far beyond simple buffoonery. True enough, he delighted in his creatures as comedians, but it was also as plain as day that he was filled with a vast contempt for them as men. One could almost discern a moral purpose in him. Under the guise of entertaining them, he seemed to be eager to show the American people what dreadful swine they applauded and venerated. His Al Keefe is not only a jackass, but also a transparent and disgusting scoundrel. And the rest are of the same stripe. I can recall no character in the Lardner gallery, early or late, male or female, old or young, who is not loathsome.

But in *The Love Nest* he goes further than ever before. His programme, in brief, is to take familiar personages, usually regarded with tolerant smiles, and to show the viciousness under their superficial imbecility. One, for example, is a movie gal married to a magnate of the films. On the surface she seems to be nothing but a noodle, but underneath there is simply a sewer: the woman is such a pig that she makes one shudder. Again, he investigates another familiar type: the village practical joker. The fellow has been laughed at since the days of Aristophanes. Well, here is a realistic examination of his dung-hill humor, and of its effects upon decent people. A third figure is a successful theatrical manager: he turns out to have the professional competence of a chiropractor and the honor of a Prohibition agent. A fourth is a writer of popular songs: stealing other men's ideas has become so fixed a habit with him that he comes to believe that he has an actual right to them. A fourth is a trained nurse—but I spare you this dreadful nurse. The rest are bores of the homicidal type. One gets the effect, communing with the whole gang, of visiting a museum of anatomy. They are as shocking as what one encounters there—but in every detail they are as unmistakably real.

Lardner conceals his savagery, of course, beneath the grotesque humor for which he is celebrated. It does not flag. No man writing among us has greater skill at the more extravagant variety of jocosity. He sees startling and revelatory likeness between immensely disparate things, and he is full of pawky observations and bizarre comments. Two baseball-players are palavering, and one of them, Young Jake, is boasting of his conquests during Spring practise below the Potomac. "Down South ain't here!" replies the other. "Those dames in some of those swamps, they lose their head when they see a man with shoes on!" The two proceed to the discussion of a third moron, guilty of some obscure tort. "Why," inquires Young Jake, "didn't you break his nose or bust him in the chin?" "His nose was already broke," replies the other, "and he didn't have no chin." Such wheezes seem easy to devise. Broadway diverts itself by manufacturing them. They constitute the substance of half the town shows. But in those made by Lardner there is something far more than mere facile humor: they are all rigidly in character, and they illuminate that character. Few American novelists, great or small, have character more firmly in hand. Lardner does not see situations; he sees people. And what people! They are all as revolting as so many Methodist evangelists, and they are all as thoroughly American. His portrait gallery is as extensive as Sinclair Lewis,' and even the least of his portraits is brilliantly done.

But comparisons, in the case of Lardner, are bound to be futile. He is trying to do something that no other current fictioneer has tried to do. Without wasting any wind upon statements of highfalutin æsthetic or ethical purpose, he is trying to get the low-down Americano between covers. ["The Library," AM 8, no. 2 (June 1926): 254–55 ("A Humorist Shows His Teeth")]

Lose with a Smile (1933)

Writing in this place in July, 1924, I permitted myself to predict that it would be a long while before the professors of literature would become aware of Ring Lardner—indeed, I ventured to say that they would probably not discover him and begin to titter over him until years after he had got to the electric chair. That prophecy has now gathered a considerable age, as such things go, and is become mellow and even mossy. Lardner goes on publishing his incomparable studies of the low-down American, and the professors continue to look straight through him, just as they looked through Mark Twain in 1900 and Walt Whitman in 1875. A few critics outside the academic breastworks, notably Clifton Fadiman,[12] have begun to write about him appreciatively, but not, so far as I know, a single debaucher of youth. He remains, by the classroom standard, a mere popular entertainer, clowning for the club-car and the locker-room in the *Saturday Evening Post*. But he is really very much more than that, and in some remote age, no doubt, a pedagogue rooting in the past will unearth him and be enchanted by him, as William Lyon Phelps unearthed and was enchanted by Mark Twain.

What are the hallmarks of a competent writer of fiction? By what attributes do we estimate and esteem him? The first, it seems to me, is that he should be immensely interested in human beings, and have an eye sharp enough to see into them, and a hand clever enough to draw them as they are. The second is that he should be able to set them in imaginary situations which display the contents of their psyches effectively, and so carry his reader swiftly and pleasantly from point to point of what is called a good story. And the third is that he should say something about the people he deals with, either explicitly or implicitly, that is apposite and revelatory —in brief, that he should play upon them with the hose of a plausible and sufficiently novel and amusing metaphysic. All of these kinds of skill you will find in every really first-rate novelist. They are what make him what he is.

In Lardner, it seems to me, they are all conspicuous. No writer in our history has ever done livelier or more life-like portraits of the nether American. There can never be any doubt in a rational mind that his people are real. There is, indeed, an overwhelming reality in every detail of their clumsy and brutal behavior, in every tremor of their shabby souls, even in every grunt of their half-simian speech. Observing these dismal pugs, song writers, movie wenches, radio crooners and baseball players as they shuffle across the stage, it is quite impossible to doubt them. Never for an instant do they do or say anything that is out of character. Nor is there ever anything improbable in the tricks that fate plays upon them. If accurate character-drawing and adept plot-making were the whole of imaginative writing, then it would be difficult to think of even a pedagogue denying Lardner's high place in the trade.

What makes him suspect, of course, is the nature of his philosophy. He offends by denying the doctrine that the purpose of literature is to spread sweetness and light. He seems to be wholly innocent of any aim to make the world a better place to live in, whether for pedagogues or for the rest of us. What interests him is not human aspiration, but only human frailty, and his taste inclines him to examine it in some of its most sordid and discomforting forms. There is not the slightest reason for saying that he actually admires his wretched cowards and scoundrels; on the contrary, it must be plain that his contempt for them amounts almost to detestation. But certainly they interest him enormously—certainly he is far more interested in them than he is in more seemly folk. So he is damned for not keeping better company, and under cover of that virtuous damnation his extraordinary skill is overlooked.

Sinclair Lewis, after *Elmer Gantry*, suffered from the same stupidity. He had shocked American prudery by showing that a man of God could be also a rogue, and he was belabored for it violently and dishonestly. Indeed, until the Nobel Prize forced a certain respectability upon him and the sentimentality of *Ann Vickers* proved that his heart, after all, was in the right place, there was a general tendency to dismiss him as one who had degraded the inspiring art of fiction to the uses of atheistic propaganda. Lardner, unsuccored by the Swedes and sticking to his guns, is not likely to enjoy any such moral rehabilitation. He will be avoided by the champions of literary delicacy until he is no longer a menace to idealism, and then they will try to convert him into something that he is not, as they have long since converted Swift, Smollett and Sterne. But meanwhile he bangs on in his own way, choosing his own marks and his own weapon. He writes little, but most of that little, within its limits, is perfect.

There are no heroes in *Lose with a Smile*. The baseball player who is its principal figure is a mephitic shape, and his girl is scarcely better. They are far too elemental to come within the orbit of Freudism. In their psychology there is no maze of complexes; they are simply souls whose only hope and aspiration is to scratch along. Nor does Lardner try to read anything into them that is not there. He takes them as they are, and lets them tell their own story. It is vastly amusing, but there is a great deal more in it than a series of laughs. ["The Library," *AM* 39, no. 2 (June 1933): 254–55 ("Pongo Americanus")]

Ellen Glasgow

They Stooped to Folly (1929)

The South, politically, is in almost as sad a state as it was in the days of Reconstruction. Here and there, to be sure, a statesman of a certain elemental dignity hangs on, but almost always it will be found, on examining him closely, that his ears have been cut off, his gluteus maximus well paddled, and his insides filled with BB shot. Such mutilated survivors of a gentler day cannot last much longer; they are going out as Methodism comes in. In a few years, I predict formally, Pat Harrison of Mississippi will find himself, relatively speaking, a publicist of lofty talents and sterling rectitude, no doubt to his own unaffected astonishment.[13] For the morons are in the saddle down in that hot, lush, charming country, and they prepare to ride to Hell and back. The catastrophe that shamed and staggered the gentlemen of Virginia last November will be repeated often, and on a larger and larger scale. In more than one State it is already impossible for a self-respecting man to get his nose into politics: the business of statecraft becomes a monopoly of pliant Jenkinses, with cotton-mill sweaters leading them by the nose and roaring ambassadors of Christ helping them with kicks *a posteriori*. Is Bishop Cannon destined to be crowned Emperor of the Confederacy?[14] I doubt it, but only because too much decency lingers in him—a legacy of the days when, at ordination, he swore that he "groaned after perfection," and was as yet unseduced by games of chance. He will be upset soon or late by a greater and worse, combining all the gifts of Jonathan Edwards, Frank Hague, Anthony Comstock, Cole Blease, Mabel Walker Willebrandt, Wayne B. Wheeler and Al Capone.[15] I look for this marvel confidently, and have grabbed a good seat in the gallery. It will be the greatest show since the Massacre of St. Bartholomew's.

Meanwhile, the intellectuals of the South take it out in satire, the immemorial refuge of the skeptic who has abandoned hope. It is a good sign, for the thing that the satire displaces is sentimentality, for years the dominant Southern curse. Even so recently as twenty years ago it was hard to imagine a Southerner (not obviously insane) poking fun at the South, but now, under the tutelage of Miss Ellen Glasgow and James Branch Cabell, they are all doing it, and some of the imbecilities that they expose, it must be confessed, are really most amusing. In *They Stooped to Folly* Miss Glasgow herself shows how neatly and effectively the thing may be done. Her theme is nothing less than the Southern attitude toward fornication— certainly a ticklish enough subject, even to-day; in the old days the barest mention of it would have covered the James river with blue flames. The action swirls around the bewildered soul of Mr. Virginius Curle Little-page, a human bridge between the old Virginia and the new. Brought up during the Civil War *Katzenjammer,* with the Victorian domestic ethic in full blast about him, he saw his Aunt Agatha, for a trivial slip, exiled to the third floor back, and there doomed to drag out her years in sombre atonement. The next generation, his own, took a bold step toward antinomianism. The voluptuous Amy Paget, caught in indiscretion, was incarcerated in no such hoosegow. To the contrary, she went to Paris, acquired there the whitewash of a husband, buried him in Père Lachaise, and then came back to flaunt her sins and tempt poor Virginius himself. It is not Amy, however, who gives him the most painful cause to think, but his young stenographer, Milly Burden. She represents the new generation, wholly emancipated and completely appalling. She neither falls on the field, like Aunt Agatha, nor runs away, like Amy. Instead, she stands her ground, admits everything shamelessly, and defies anyone to do anything about it.

The fable, in its essence, is not Virginian; it might be laid in any State of this imperial realm, North, East, West or South. But Miss Glasgow is no mere story-teller. Her merit lies precisely in her skill at giving her tale a local investiture and a local significance. Her Virginius Littlepage is not simply an American staggered by a more or less familiar situation; he is a Virginian utterly demoralized and undone by a situation that, in the Virginia now dying so stertorously, remains unimaginable to a man of the right instincts. What makes the comedy is his effort to dispose of it in the traditional Southern manner—by encasing it in humane assumptions, by refusing to regard its more inconvenient facts, by waving it away with gallant and poetic gestures. The device used to work magnificently, but no more. We are in a new world. The Aunt Agathas of to-day, even in Virginia, refuse to climb the obliterating third-floor stair. They remain in the drawing-room, discussing the business as if it were a public question. Worse, they get a great deal of plausibility in what they say: it becomes increasingly difficult to think of effective answers to them. Thus poor Virginius swoons out of the picture, shocked and gasping. The human race, in its reproductive aspect, has become unintelligible to him. He has begun to distrust all women. He has even begun to fear for himself.

Miss Glasgow writes very skillfully. She knows how to manage situations and she has an eye for the trivialities which differentiate one man or woman from another. Her humor is not robust, but it is sly and never-failing. If she has a salient defect, it is that she sometimes yields a bit too easily to the lure of pretty phrases. Her dialogue could be a great deal more realistic than it is; only too often her characters simply make speeches to one another. They are usually amusing speeches, but that fact doesn't dispose of their stiffness. Rather too much of the story, it seems to me, is devoted to Milly and her Greenwichy rebellion. It is too typical of the age to need so much exposition. I'd like to have heard more about the discreet peccadilloes of Mrs. Dalrymple, *née* Paget, and a great deal more about the disaster of Aunt Agatha. In Aunt Agatha, indeed, there is plainly a whole book. It would be instructive to find out precisely how she got into her forlorn third-floor back, and what went on in her head during her long years of expiation there. That story would be worth the telling. ["The Library," AM 18, no. 2 (October 1929): 251–52 ("Two Southern Novels")]

Works (Old Dominion Edition) (1933)

Some time ago, in the eminent Nation, Miss Glasgow printed an article under the title of "What I Believe."[16] It might have served admirably as a general preface to the present edition of her novels, for it set forth plainly the origins and scope of the amiable skepticism that is at the bottom of all of them. That skepticism came in the first place out of the circumstances of what must have been an extremely lonely and unhappy childhood.

Here was a little girl of an almost morbidly sensitive and imaginative sort, set down in a Virginia that had been reduced by the fortunes of war to a kind of aching chaos, socially, politically and economically, and was try-ing desperately to fashion a new social order out of the black stumps and smouldering brands of the old. The easy way, obviously, was to seize upon a few simple principles, a set of bold and easy patterns, and give them, by a sort of acclamation, tlte authority of Sinai. But many of them, alas, would not work, and not a few of them were plainly false, so what issued out of the struggle was no more than a mass of gaudy artificialities, com-forting to the simple but immensely unpleasant to the intelligent. Among the intelligent was the little Glasgow girl, a decorous pigtail down her back. She revolted against the blather, but had no philosophy to meet it. "I excelled only in imaginary adventures. . . . I saw painful sights. . . . The tragedy of life and the pathos which is worse than tragedy worked their way into my nerves."

Escape came at the hands of a teacher encountered in Richmond — a sort of miraculous accident. He recalls forcibly the bearded youth who, at the same time, was arousing and inflaming young Frank Harris in faraway Kansas. Dead at twenty-six, he yet managed in his short years to cover a vast area of reading, and, what is more important, a vast area of genuine thinking, centering on what was then called political economy, but run-ning up hill and down dale in all directions. Miss Glasgow herself was but sixteen when she encountered this extraordinary pedagogue, but she was ripe for him, and when he presently passed out of her life and his own he left her with something closely resembling a philosophy. It is with her yet, and every one of her long series of books is informed by it. It is a kind of skepticism that is pungent without being harsh; at least two-thirds of it is simple tolerance. "I believe that the quality of belief is more important than the quantity, that the world could do very well with fewer and better beliefs, and that a reasonable doubt is the safety-valve of civilization."

One may applaud this platform without forgetting how seditious it must have seemed in the Virginia of thirty years ago. But Miss Glasgow, having once mounted it, did not budge an inch. Some day the history of her novels in her home-town must be written. They began as scandals of high voltage, and it was years before Richmond was ready to admit that there was anything in them save a violent enmity to the true, the good and the beautiful. As the news gradually oozed over the Potomac that they were regarded with high politeness in the North there was some reconsideration of this position, but it was not actually abandoned until comparatively recent years. To this day, indeed, Virginia is a bit uneasy about its most distinguished living daughter, and even her appearance in all the solemn panoply of Collected Works will probably leave her something of a suspicious character. For skepticism, save in a few walled towns, of which Richmond is surely not one, is still a kind of wickedness in the South. The thing most esteemed down there, whether by the hidalgos who weep for the lost Golden Age or by the peasants who sweat and pant for the New Jerusalem, is the will to believe.

Frankly, I do not blame the Virginians for stopping cautiously short of taking Miss Glasgow to their arms, and covering her with proud kisses. For the plain fact is that the whole canon of her works is little more or less than a magnificent *reductio ad absurdum* of their traditional metaphysic. Thrown among them, and essentially of them despite her struggle against the bond, she has had at them at close range, and only too many of her shots have hit them in almost pathologically tender places. In her gallery all of the salient figures of the Virginia zoölogy stalk about under glaring lights, and when she has done with them there is little left to know about them—and not too much that is made known is reassuring. She has, in brief, set herself the task of depicting a civilization in its last gasps, and though her people have their share of universality they are still intrinsically Virginians, and hardly imaginable outside their spooky rose-gardens and musty parlors. They remain so even when the spirit of progress seizes them, and they try to take on the ways and habits of mind of the outside world. Surely the polyandrous Edmonia Bredalbane, in *The Romantic Comedians*, seems, at first glance, to be anything but provincial. But that is only at first glance. Soon it appears that she is Virginian in every corpuscle, despite all her far rides on her witch's broomstick. One parts from her quite sure that this witch, precisely, could not have happened anywhere else on earth. ["The Library," *AM* 39, no. 4 (August 1933): 504–6 ("A Southern Skeptic")]

Trade Goods

4

O. Henry

Roads of Destiny (1909)

O. Henry (Sidney Porter), author of *Roads of Destiny*, is an insoluble riddle. I give him up. Either he is the best story-teller in the world to-day, or the worst. Sometimes I think he is the one and sometimes I am convinced that he is the other. Maybe he is both.

And why the best? Because no other man now living equals him in the invention of preposterous intrigues and the imagining of fantastic characters. He can borrow an idea from Stevenson—as in the title story of the present book—and give it so many novel and outlandish twists that it becomes absolutely new. He can construct a farce plot that would have sent Offenbach flying to his music paper, as in "Next to Reading Matter"; and he can bring back again, with all its sentimental melodrama, the Golden West of Bret Harte, as in "Friends in San Rosario." Always his stories have action in them—action and "an air." They are full of queer ambuscades and surprises. The end is never visible at the beginning.

And why, being so marvelously ingenious and resourceful, is Mr. Porter also so bad an artist? Chiefly, because his fancy is a bucking broncho without a rider. He has no conception of the value of restraint. He lays on his effects with a shovel. As he writes, innumerable comic ideas occur to him—bizarre phrases, impossible slang, ridiculous collocations—and he slaps them in at once. If they fit, well and good; if not, he uses them all the same. The result is that his characters all speak the same tongue. At the beginning of a story, now and then, he manages to keep them differentiated, but before long they are all spouting Porterese.

Again, this same exuberance leads to a painful piling up of snickers. In "The Discounters of Money," for example, a capital story is spoiled by too much smartness. There are twenty wheezes to a page. Instead of helping on the tale, they make it bewildering and unreal. You grow interested in a character study—and the author asks you to halt at every third line and marvel at some banal wit from Broadway.

But it is an ungrateful task to point out defects in a writer so amusing as Mr. Porter. At his worst, true enough, he is very, very bad, but at his best he is irresistible. Some day, let us hope, he will acquire resolution enough to stick to the letter of his text, no matter how great the temptation to fly off into literary roulades. Meanwhile, it might benefit him to give a month or two of hard study to a book called *In Babel*, by George Ade—a book containing some of the best comedies in the English language. ["The Best Novels of the Year," *SS* 28, no. 3 (July 1909): 156–57]

Will Levington Comfort

Fate Knocks at the Door (1912)

Brief but spicy note from an estimable (and, I hope, not altogether uncomely) lady in Oswego, New York:

> Don't write so much about yourself. Stick to the books and you will give better value for the money. *Verbum non amplius addam.*

The point is well taken, and I accordingly address myself to the books, which happen, this month, to be all of fiction, and chiefly bad. For example, *Fate Knocks at the Door*, by Will Levington Comfort, a shining example of that occult windiness which passes, in these days of soul searching and the

New Thought, for profundity. By the simple device of printing them with
capital letters, Mr. Comfort changes quite ordinary words into symbols of
lofty and ineffable things. On one page I find Voices, Pits of Trade, Woman,
the Great Light, the Big Deep and the Twentieth Century Lie. On another
are Mystic Motherhood, the Third Lustrous Dimension and the Rising
Road of Man. It appears quickly that Woman is a creature far superior to
woman. The latter is a shameless baggage, a beggar of kisses, a fibber of fibs,
a partner in unutterable naughtinesses, a hussy. The former, on the contrary,
is a Holy Spirit, the Transcendental Soul Essence, the Sempiternal Mother,
the Way Uphill. Thus Andrew Bedient, the spouting hero:

> I believe in the natural greatness of Woman; that through the
> spirit of Woman are born sons of strength; that only through the
> potential greatness of Woman comes the militant greatness of
> man.
>   I believe Mothering is the loveliest of the Arts; that great moth-
> ers are handmaidens of the Spirit, to whom are intrusted God's
> avatars; that no prophet is greater than his mother.
>   I believe when humanity arises to Spiritual evolution (as it
> once evolved through Flesh, and is now evolving through Mind)
> Woman will assume the ethical guiding of the race.
>   I believe that the Holy Spirit of the Trinity is Mystic Mother-
> hood, and the source of the divine principle is Woman; that
> prophets are the union of this divine principle and the higher man-
> hood; that they are beyond the attractions of women of flesh, be-
> cause unto their manhood has been added Mystic Motherhood.
>   . . .
>   I believe that the way to Godhood is the Rising Road of Man.
>   I believe that, as the human mother brings a child to her hus-
> band, the father—so Mystic Motherhood, the Holy Spirit, is bring-
> ing the world to God, the Father.

The capitals are Andrew's—or Mr. Comfort's. I merely transcribe and
perspire. This Andrew, it appears, is a sea cook who has been mellowed
and transfigured by exhaustive study of the Bhagavad Gita, one of the
sacred nonsense books of the Brahmans. He doesn't know who his father
was, and he remembers his mother only as one dying in a strange city.

When she finally passed away he took to the high seas and mastered marine cookery. Thus for many years up and down the world. Then he went ashore at Manila and became chef to an army packtrain. Then he proceeded to China, to Japan. Then to India, where he entered the forestry service and plodded the Himalayan heights, always with the Bhagavad Gita under his arm. At some time or other, during his years of culinary seafaring, he saved the life of a Yankee ship captain, and that captain, later dying, left him untold millions in South America. But it is long after all this is past that we have chiefly to do with him. He is now a young Monte Cristo at large in New York, a Monte Cristo worshiped and gurgled over by a crowd of mushy old maids, a hero of Uneeda biscuit parties in Godforsaken studios, the madness and despair of mellowing virgins.

But it is not Andrew's wealth that inflames these old girls, nor even his manly beauty, but rather his revolutionary and astounding sapience, his great gift for solemn and incomprehensible utterance, his skill as a metaphysician. They hang upon his every word. His rhetoric makes their heads swim. Once he gets fully under way, they almost swoon. Well, all I ask is that you get the book and examine this precious "philosophy" of his for yourself. If you can find anything in it save a new variation upon the inevitable New Thought rumble-bumble, a vague and chlorotic hostility to the healthy joys and instincts of the flesh, a sentimental denial of the fundamental realities of life, a romantic and muddle-headed woman worship, then I offer you my affectionate regards and envy you your superior penetration. And the girls themselves! Alas, what pathetic neck stretching toward tinsel stars! What eager hearing of the soulful, gassy stuff! One of them has red hair and "wine dark eyes, now cryptic black, now suffused with red glows like the night sky above a prairie fire." Another is "tall and lovely in a tragic, flowerlike way" and performs upon the violoncello. A third is "a tanned woman rather variously weathered," who writes stupefying epigrams about Whitman and Nietzsche—making the latter's name Nietschze, of course! A fourth is the Gray One—O mystic appellation! A fifth—but enough! You get the picture. You can imagine how Andrew's sagacity staggers these poor dears. You can see them fighting for him, each against all, with sharp, psychical excaliburs.

And I have no doubt that thousands of other women, reading this chronicle of his portentous sayings and doings, will be charmed as much, if not more. Mysticism is now in fashion in these States. Such things as Karma, the Ineffable Essence and the *Zeitgeist* become familiar fauna, chained up in the cage of every woman's club. Thousands of American women know far more about the Subconscious than they know about plain sewing. The idea that Mind is altogether superior to Body and that Spirit is the boss of both—this idea runs through the country like a pestilence. Physiology has been formally repealed and repudiated: its laws are all lies. Naturally enough, all this Advanced Thinking is reflected in a rising literature. Books upon the New Thought pour from the presses in copious streams, and among them works of sublimal fiction begin to appear. No doubt the old-fashioned fleshly novel, with its seductions and obstetrics, will have hard sledding to-morrow. In place of it there will be the New Thought novel, in which hero and heroine will seek each other out, not for the vulgar purpose of spooning in the dark, but for the lofty purpose of Uplifting the Race. Kissing is already unsanitary; in a few years, I suppose, it will be downright sacrilegious, a crime against some obscure avatar or other, a business libidinous and accursed. It will be worth a man's life to chuck his wife under the chin.

Meanwhile, let it be said for Mr. Comfort that he shows a considerable facility in composition, at least in his more earthly moments. When he is describing something physical his descriptions are sometimes very vivid. This you will note especially in the earlier chapters of his book, wherein he deals with Andrew's carnalities on land and sea. He has a taste for the gypsy phrase; one senses a genuine artist in him. But in his more soulful passages, when he goes sky-hooting into the interstellar spaces of Mystic Motherhood, he tends to adopt the common jargon of all New Thoughters. An inevitable decay. Style, after all, is inseparable from content, however the stylists may seek to make it appear not so. The sting and sweetness of words are in the concepts behind them. No man will ever write nonsense as magnificently as Huxley wrote sense. The New Thought will never produce a Pater. ["Novels Bad, Half-Bad and Very Bad," SS 38, no. 3 (November 1912): 153–55]

Marjorie Benton Cooke

Bambi (1914)

Midway between the tales of persecution and passion that address themselves frankly to servant girls, country schoolteachers and the public stenographers in commercial hotels and those works of popular romance which yet hang hazardously, as it were, upon the far-flung yardarms of beautiful letters—midway, as I say, between these wholly atrocious and quasi-respectable evangels of amour and derring-do, there floats a literature vast, gaudy and rich in usufructs, which outrages all sense and probability without descending to actual vulgarity and buffoonery, and so manages to impinge agreeably upon that vast and money-in-pocket public which takes instinctively a safe, middle course in all things, preferring Sousa's band to either a street piano or the Boston Symphony Orchestra, and the New York *Times* to either the *Evening Journal* or the *Evening Post*, and Mr. Woodrow Wilson to either Debs or Mellon, and dinner at six o'clock to either dinner at noon or dinner at eight-thirty, and three children (two boys and a girl) to either the lone heir of Fifth Avenue or the all-the-traffic-can-bear hatching of the Ghetto, and honest malt liquor to either Croton water or champagne, and Rosa Bonheur's "The Horse Fair" to either Corot's "Danse de Nymphes" or a "Portrait of a Lady" from the *Police Gazette*, and fried chicken to either liver or terrapin, and a once-a-week religion to either religion every day or no religion at all, and the Odd Fellows to either the Trappists or the Black Hand, and a fairly pretty girl who can cook fairly well to either a prettier girl who can't cook a stroke or a good cook who sours the milk.

To make an end, the public I refer to is that huge body of honest and right-thinking folk which constitutes the heart, lungs and bowels of this great republic—that sturdy multitude which believes in newspapers, equinoctial storms, trust-busting, the Declaration of Independence, teleology, the direct primary, the uplift, trial by jury, monogamy, the Weather Bureau, Congress and the moral order of the world—that innumerable caravan of middling, dollar-grubbing, lodge-joining, quack-ridden folk which the Socialists sneer at loftily as the *bourgeoisie*, and politicians slobber over as the bulwark of our liberties. And, by the same token, the meridional, intermediate literature that I speak of is that literature without end which lifts its dizzy pyramids from the book-counters in the department stores, and from which, ever and anon, there emerges that prize of great price, the best-seller. The essence of this literature is sentiment, and the essence of that sentiment is hope. Its aim is to fill the breast with soothing and optimistic emotions—to make the fat woman forget that she is fat, to purge the tired business man of his bile, to convince the flapper that Douglas Fairbanks may yet learn to love her, to prove that this dreary old world, as botched and bad as it is, might yet be a darn sight worse.

I offer *The Rosary, Soldiers of Fortune, Laddie, The Helmet of Navarre, Little Lord Fauntleroy, Freckles, Eben Holden* and *V. V.'s Eyes*[1] as specimens, and so pass on to the latest example, to wit, *Bambi*, by Marjorie Benton Cooke. By the time this reaches you, I have no doubt, *Bambi* will be all the rage in your vicinage. You will be hearing about it on all sides. You will see allusions to it in your evening paper. You will observe it on the desk of your stenographer. Your wife (if you belong to the gnarled and persecuted sex) will be urging you to read it and mark it well. You yourself (if you are fair and have the price) will be wearing a Bambi petticoat or a Bambi collar or a pair of Bambi stockings or a Bambi something-more-intimate-still. Such, alas, is the course that best-sellers run! They permeate and poison the atmosphere of the whole land. It is impossible to get away from them. They invade the most secure retreats, even the very jails and almshouses. Serving thirty days myself, under the Sherman Act, during the late rage for *The Salamander*,[2] I had it thrust upon me by the rector of the bastile, and had to read it to get rid of him.

Wherefore in sympathy, as it were, I have ploughed through *Bambi* in time to tell you what it is about before you have to read it yourself, thus hoping to save you from the dangers of too much joy. It is a tale, as you may suspect, of young love, and the heroine is a brilliant young lady named Miss Francesca Parkhurst, the daughter of Professor James Parkhurst, Ph.D., the eminent but somewhat balmy mathematician. Professor Parkhurst, as Bambi herself says, knows more about mathematics than the man who invented them, but outside the domain of figures his gigantic intellect refuses to function. Thus he always forgets to go to his lecture-room unless Bambi heads him in the right direction at the right hour, and if it were not for her careful inspection of his make-up, he would often set off with his detachable cuffs upon his ankles instead of upon his wrists, and the skirts of his shirt outside instead of inside his pantaloons. In a word, this Professor Parkhurst is the standard college professor of the best-sellers—the genial jackass we know and love of old. The college professor of the stern, cold world, perhaps, is a far different creature: I once knew one, in fact, who played the races and was a first-rate amateur bartender, and there is record of another who went into politics and clawed his way to every high office. But in romance, of course, no such heretics are allowed. The college professor of prose fiction is always an absentminded old boob, who is forever stumbling over his own feet, and he always has a pretty daughter to swab up his waistcoat after he has dined, and to chase away the *ganovim* who are trying to rob him, and to fill his house with an air of innocent and youthful gayety.

Naturally enough, this Professor Parkhurst of our present inquest is not at all surprised when sweet Bambi tells him that she has decided to marry young Jarvis Jocelyn, the rising uplifter, nor even when she tells him that Jarvis knows nothing about it, nor even when she kidnaps Jarvis while he is in a state of coma and sends for a preacher and marries him on the spot, nor even when she puts him to bed *a capella* on the third floor of the house, and devotes her honeymoon to gathering up and sorting out the flying pages of the Great Drama that he is writing. College professors of the standard model do not shy at such doings. Like babies in arms, they see the world only as a series of indistinct shadows. It would not have made much impression upon Professor Parkhurst had Bambi invited the ash-man to dinner or flavored the soup with witch-hazel or come to the meal herself in a bathing-suit. And so it makes very little impression upon him when she shanghais Jarvis and internes the poor fellow in the garret and kicks up a scandal that shakes the whole town. He is dimly conscious that something is going on, just as an infant is dimly conscious that it is light at times and dark at times, but further than that he recks and wots not.

Well, well, we must be getting on! What does Bambi do next? Next she grabs a pencil and a pad of paper and dashes off a short story of her own, with herself, Jarvis and the professor as its characters. Then she tires of it and puts it away. Then, one day, she picks up a New York magazine containing an offer of $500 cash for the best short story submitted in competition. Then she gets out her story, has it typewritten and sends it in. Then—what! have you guessed it? Clever you are, indeed! Yes, even so: then she wins the prize. And then, tucking Jarvis under her arm, she goes to New York and tries to sell the Great Drama. And then she spends a week of sitting in the anterooms of the theatrical managers. And then, her story being published under a *nom de plume*, she finds herself an anonymous celebrity and is hospitably received by the genial Bob Davis, editor of *Munsey's*.³ And then another and much slimmer magazine editor—no doubt G. J. Nathan, thinly disguised—falls in love with her and gives her many valuable pointers. And then Charles Frohman proposes to have her story dramatized, and she lures him into offering Jarvis the job, and then pitches in and helps to perform it. And then the play makes a tremendous hit on Broadway, and she confesses the whole plot, and Jarvis falls desperately in love with her, and we part from them in each other's arms.

A sweet, sweet story. A string of gum-drops. A sugar-teat beyond compare. Of such great probabilities, of such searching reports of human motive and act, the best-seller is all compact. If you have a heart, if you can feel and understand, if your cheers for the true, the good and the beautiful are truly sincere, then this one will squeeze a tear from your leaden eye and send it cascading down your nose. And if, on the contrary, you are one of those cheap barroom cynics who think it is smart to make game of honest sentiment and pure art, then it will give you the loud, coarse guffaw that you crave. But do not laugh too much, dear friend, however hard your heart, however tough your hide. The mission of such things as *Bambi* is, after all, no mean one. Remember the fat woman—how it will make her forget that she is fat. Remember the tired business man—how it will lift him out of his wallow and fill him with a noble enthusiasm for virtue and its rewards. Remember the flapper—how it will thrill her to the very soles of her feet and people her dreams with visions of gallant knights and lighten that doom which makes her actual beau a baseball fan and corrupts him with a loathing for literature and gives him large, hairy hands and a *flair* for burlesque shows and freckles on his neck. ["Mush for the Multitude," *SS* 44, no. 4 (December 1914): 304–6]

Winston Churchill

A Far Country (1915)

Winston Churchill's latest and thickest confection, *A Far Country*, at once challenges comparison with Theodore Dreiser's *The Titan*, for both deal with the conflict between the Uplift and the Invisible Government in

These States, and in each the central figure is a gentleman who serves the
latter with skill and daring, and who grows rich by the business. But there
the similarity ends, and thereafter all the odds are in favor of *The Titan*. It
is only, indeed, by reading the Churchill book that one attains, retrospec-
tively, to the true measure of the Dreiser book. Churchill, of course, knows
how to write, and, what is more, he has a first-hand knowledge of the conflict he is here writing of. But when all is said, how superficial his facility,
how cocksure and platitudinous his philosophy, how polite and trivial his
drama, how puny and unconvincing his Hugh Paget beside the sweating,
mole-like meticulousness, the remote and cautious detachment, the stupendous play of blind forces, the sinister and gargantuan Frank Cowperwood of Dreiser! It is the difference between a fairy tale and an epic,
Moszkowski and Brahms, the First Symphony and the Ninth. Churchill is
content to skim the surface of things; he really tells us precious little, for all
his 509 pages, about the inner workings of the System he is exposing; in
truth, he really tells us very little about Paget, his hero, for the man's fundamental concepts and motives remain tantalizingly vague at the end. But
Dreiser, in his crude, blundering way, plows down to the very bottom of
things. He reduces the combat, like John Galsworthy in *Strife*, to its elementals; he makes it thrilling and intelligible by blowing away its smoke.
And as for Cowperwood, he puts into that Colossus the very breath and
bloom of life.

The relative failure of Mr. Churchill, I take it, is due chiefly to the
wholly illogical, and hence more or less incredible, *volte-face* that he im-
poses upon his hero at the end. I have no doubt that there are corporation
lawyers who have succumbed to early piety and gone over to the Uplift,
just as there are possibly French lieutenants who have succumbed to
Pilsener and *Schwartenmagen* and gone over to the Germans, but it is
surely as absurd to depict the Money Power through the eyes of the one as
it would be to depict the French Army through the eyes of the other. And
having thus erred capitally in the plan of his story, Mr. Churchill proceeds
to err in its execution by ascribing Paget's conversion to influences which
so sharp-witted and strong-willed a man would obviously resist as a primary
condition of his strength and sagacity. One cannot be a realist to-day and a
sentimentalist to-morrow. If what we hear of Paget's resolution and resourcefulness in the first 300 pages is true, then his ready yielding to

puerile moralizing in the pages that remain becomes incomprehensible. And if we accept the weak, watery Paget of these last pages as the true Paget, then it is impossible to believe in the prodigies of ingenuity and daring that we see him performing in the earlier pages. In brief, the man before us fails to hang together. Desiring belief in his hero, Mr. Churchill should have either committed him less firmly to the devil at the start or left him more resistant to the archangels at the finish.

But the book's weakness as a work of art is of less importance, after all, than its light-headedness as a social document. When I say that any of the traveling uplifters who now infest the country might have supplied its point of view, I say enough, I hope, to show its lack of value as a serious criticism of American civilization. If this point of view is the product of Mr. Churchill's adventures into politics in New Hampshire, then those adventures did not carry him very far upon the journey to first causes. His attitude to practical politics is almost identical with that of the horrified newspaper reader, the believer in muckrakers, the amateur reformer. He sees on the one side a small group of soulless and relentless despots, bent upon bringing all power and wealth into their own hands, and he sees on the other side a vast host of patient, hard-driven, helpless slaves, robbed of their birthright by cruel trickery and extortion. The way out, if I understand him rightly, lies in the "awakening" of the former to a sense of their responsibility, a revival of the ideal of service, an abandonment of the philosophy of enlightened self-interest—an idea previously set forth, by the way, in *The Inside of the Cup*. The people are unable to lead themselves out of the wilderness, and produce too few leaders of their own stock to manage so huge and perilous an exodus. There must be, then, a stooping down from above, a renaissance of brotherhood, the revival of a more genuine democracy.

A sweet vision! A laudable plan! But in so far as it has been tested in practise, it has revealed, alas! certain fundamental defects, and the chief of those defects lies in the perversity of its beneficiaries. Even the most altruistic of the new social servants, before he may accomplish any service of ponderable value, must first get the cooperation, or at all events the consent, of the folks he would serve—and experience shows that those folks, when they have a free choice between one who is actually intelligent and honest enough to serve them usefully and one who is merely a self-seeker masquerading in a servant's apron and towel, almost invariably spit into the eye of the former and take the latter to their bosoms. In other words, the common people, with sure instinct, choose the one whose motives and habits of mind most nearly approximate their own—*i.e.*, the one who is most the quack, the ignoramus, the eager *jaeger* of the dollar. If the deliverers of the republic could be selected by some impartial and benevolent despot, then there would be a chance of achieving the delivery in a shipshape and fiduciary manner. But inasmuch as they have to be selected by the mob, which is admittedly so stupid that it doesn't even know what is the matter with it, to say nothing of the prudent process of cure, it follows that the enterprise is full of snares and ambuscades, and that its accomplishment will call for brains of a vastly greater horse-power than any now on tap among us.

And the conclusion that we thus reach, as it were, in the chair, and by the austere devices of the science of logic, is amply borne out by the experience piling up on all sides. No business currently resorted to by gentlemen who crave the rewards and excitement of power is more prosperous than the business of saving the dear people from their wrongs and woes unspeakable, the business of the Uplift. The exclusive concern, a few years ago, of clergymen, retired merchant princes, pious old women and other such ineffective dilettanti, it now engages the talents of an increasing army of sharp professionals, each of them bent upon marketing a more attractive bauble than the others and upon wringing from the marketing a more satisfying usufruct. The result, on the one hand, is the wholesale bedazzlement of the plain people, and on the other hand, the wholesale gouging of the plain people. And on the third hand, so to speak, it is the swift downfall of the few honest men who venture to enter the arena—of the few men actually competent to instruct and serve. What would be the fate, let us ask, of a Justice of the Supreme Court of the United States who stepped down from his bench to advise the people regarding the solution of the complex and exasperating liquor problem? What would happen to him if he essayed to pit his knowledge of legal processes and limitations, his practical experience of life, his habit of judicial impartiality against the ecstatic whooping of the trained rabble-rousers of the Anti-Saloon League? What would be the majority against him south of the Potomac—or north of the Potomac? How long would he last, once the gentlemen whose graft he was destroying got their Busy Berthas of invective, of innuendo, of appeals to emotion, ignorance, hatred, into action against him?

No man with any practical experience of American politics will hesitate in giving the answer. He sees before him too many melancholy and horrible examples of the malignant perversity of the populace, of its almost invariable error in judging men, of its endless weakness for the brummagem. The ideal of service, set up to conquer the old ideal of intelligent self-interest, has in a few short years been conquered and engulfed by it. The most successful uplifter of to-day, the one with the largest following and hence the largest power for either good or evil, is precisely the one who practises uplifting as a means of eager self-seeking—the machine politician turned reformer, the itinerant moral evangelist, the slick merchant of new cures for all the sorrows of the world. Mr. Churchill, in his story, shows us something of the effect of the new notions upon the United States Senate—that favorite butt of all the peruna-mongers.4 Well, let us examine the Senate. Have the changes there made for the national security, the common weal? The old leaders have departed, taking with them their hunkerousness, their reverence for property, their distrust of mob rule—let us add it frankly: their subservience to wealth and power. But what have we in their places? Honest, intelligent, self-sacrificing, patriotic men? Hardly. What we have is a camorra of the most impudent and dunderheaded quacks that ever gathered under one roof—an obscene collection of tin-pot Savonarolas and bogus Messiahs, each trying to engage and enchant the people with *his* merchandise, *his* sovereign remedy—a crowd of Munyons and male Lydia Pinkhams5 whom it would be a gross flattery to call earnest, and sheer lunacy to call intelligent. If you doubt it, go ask any old-time Washington newspaper correspondent. He will tell you that there are not twenty men in the Senate to-day who put the public good above their private political advantage, and not ten whose discussion of public problems on the floor rises above the empty windjamming of an elocutionist in a Chautauqua.

Yet practically all of these men, as I say, are recognized uplifters. Practically all of them were washed into office by the wave of the new madness. They are not the agents and attorneys of the Money Power, the Interests, the Invisible Government, as their predecessors of fifteen years ago were; they are the products of the direct primary, the rule of the people, the New

Freedom. Each was chosen, consciously and deliberately, to help rescue the people from the old oligarchy; each wears at his belt the scalp of one of the old oligarchs. But what is the bunch worth? Not a continental damn. The people, having their free choice of gentlemen sworn to their service, picked out in almost every case the one least fitted to serve them prudently, faithfully and effectively. Called to discharge their supreme duty as citizens, they yielded, as always, to their immemorial hatred of the superior man, and so selected petty men to do their work for them. This immemorial hatred turns the whole theory of service into something hollow and vain. Such a man as Paget could not hope to accomplish anything for the people, save he stooped to a pretense of accepting their own delusions. They would distrust him more, being on their side, than ever they distrusted him when he was against them. Pitted against a rival rescuer to their taste—*i.e.*, one spouting imbecilities and pledged to impossibilities—he would be exposed inevitably to humiliation and defeat.

The answer that the optimists make to all this is that, despite its obvious and admitted failures, the Uplift still makes for a better day—that, even though there has been a good deal of slipping back, there has still been, of late, a very appreciable going ahead. Here, I am convinced, optimism falls into one of its characteristic errors. That is to say, it makes so much of the little that has been gained that it is blind to the much that has been lost. The truth is that there is a vast exaggeration of the value of the changes that have taken place, just as there was a vast exaggeration of the evils they have abolished. Too much confidence has taken the place of too much suspicion. The common people, even in the worst times of their exploitation, were probably quite as well off as they are to-day, with their fate largely in their own hands and a horde of mountebanks preying upon their credulity, their lack of sound vision and their easy emotionalism. What has Georgia gained by going dry? What has Oregon gained by scotching a legislature of a few score ignorant and vulnerable men and setting up a legislature of even more ignorant and vulnerable thousands? Is Colorado, with woman suffrage, a more civilized state than Indiana, without it? What is the net value, to sound and orderly government, of the twenty years of Bryanism? What has it profited the republic to turn such men as Hale and Aldrich out of the Senate and such men as Work and Kenyon in?[6] Is the average "reform" boss, say in Virginia or Pennsylvania, a safer leader or a decenter man than the machine boss he has displaced? Is the Anti-Saloon League, taking one day's work with another, an influence for cleaner politics, for better thought of the ultimate public welfare, for the selection of more clear-headed and honorable lawmakers, than the Pennsylvania Railroad?

I doubt it, Messieurs. And doubting it, I arrive at a low, sniffish opinion of the whole rumble-bumble of the Uplift. It has failed in all directions. It has failed no less in its dealing with such vexatious social problems as prostitution than in its dealing with such capital political problems as taxation. No business is so badly run as the public business. No other "experts," not even the alienists who glower at one another in murder trials, are such arrant frauds as the "experts" who arise on all sides to tell the people how this or that department of it should be conducted. The reason is not far to seek. It lies, as I have said, in the fact that these "experts" are judged and selected, not by their actual competency, but by their capacity for producing an illusion of competency in the minds of the people — in other words, by their capacity for convincing persons who are admittedly incompetent to judge. In this enterprise, it goes without saying, the quack has all the advantages, for so long as he makes his doctrine charming it is immaterial whether he also makes it true. The honest man cannot hope to compete with him. On the one hand, this honest man can never promise half so much, for the more he actually knows of the problem he discusses, the more he must be impressed by the limitations set upon all human knowledge. And on the other hand, he cannot hope to offer his hearers much enchantment, for the truth is seldom, if ever, charming. Thus the quack prospers like a hog in a cornfield, and the grunt of his satisfaction is heard in the land. And thus we shall be quack-ridden and folly-ridden until mobocracy comes to its unescapable *débâcle*, and the common people are relieved of their present oppressive duty of deciding what is wrong with their tummies, and what doctor is safest for them to consult, and which of his pills is most apt to cure them.

Here I have filled pages with a solemn treatise upon austere and ineffable subjects — and quite forgotten Mr. Churchill's novel! But, after all, I have really had it in mind the whole time, for it, too, deals grandly with those subjects, and if their discussion be taken out of it not much will remain. It is, in fact, much less a work of the imagination than a piece of pamphleteering, and if it fails as the latter it fails even more certainly as the former. The story that Mr. Churchill tells is not only incoherent and un-convincing; it is also quite uninteresting. It is heavy with small details, but they are details that burden the reader without either enlightening him or diverting him. Page follows page and chapter follows chapter, finely printed, laborious and meticulous, but at the end one sees Hugh Paget only dimly. What are his vices? What is his notion of beauty? What is his view of women, the sex war? Who are his heroes at forty-five? Reading the book from end to end, I get no satisfactory answers to these questions. Paget passes through it like a shadow, one never sees clearly into his soul, one never comes to actual grips with him. Nor is there any charm in its writing to mask this fundamental lack. Mr. Churchill's style is the nega-tion of style. He writes correct English, and that is all. Like his hero, he seems to be deficient in the æsthetic sense. His view of life and its won-drous mystery is the ethical, the Puritan view. He is far too good an Amer-ican to be an artist. ["The Sawdust Trail," SS 46, no. 4 (August 1915): 150–54]

Mary MacLane

I, Mary MacLane (1917)

I arise from *I, Mary MacLane* with the one thought: what a ghastly thing it must be to be a Puritan, and fear God, and envy the wicked, and flee from carnal joys! The truth about the Butte Bashkirtseff[7] comes out at last, and it is simple and pathetic. When, at nineteen, she shocked the Sunday-schools with *The Story of Mary MacLane*, it was still left obscure; the monkey-shines of her flapperhood, so to speak, distracted attention from it and concealed it. But now, at thirty-five (she herself says "thirty or so"), it emerges crystal-clear; she has learned how to describe her malady accurately, though she still wonders what it is. And that malady? That truth? Simply that a Scotch Presbyterian with a soaring soul is as cruelly beset as a wolf with fleas, a zebra with the botts. Let a spark of the divine fire spring to life in that arid corpse, and it must fight its way to flame through a drum fire of wet sponges. A humming bird immersed in *Kartof-felsuppe*. Walter Pater writing for the *London Daily Mail*. Lucullus traveling steerage . . . A Puritan wooed and tortured by the lewd leers of beauty. Mary MacLane in a moral republic, in a Presbyterian diocese, in Butte . . .

I hope my figures of speech are not too abstruse. What I mean to say is simply this: that the secret of Mary MacLane is simply this: that the origin of all her inchoate naughtiness is simply this: that she is a Puritan who has heard the call of joy and is struggling against it damnably. Remember so much, and the whole of her wistful heresy becomes intelligible. On the one hand the loveliness of the world enchants her; on the other hand the fires of hell warn her. This tortuous conflict accounts for her whole bag of tricks; her timorous flirtations with the devil, her occasional outbreaks of finishing-school rebellion, her hurried protestations of virginity, above all her incurable Philistinism. One need not be told that she admires Major General Roosevelt and Mrs. Atherton, that she wallows in the poetry of Keats. One knows quite as well that her phonograph plays the "Peer Gynt" suite, and that she is charmed by the syllogisms of G. K. Chesterton. She is, in brief, an absolutely typical American of the transition stage between Christian Endeavor and civilization. There is in her a definite poison of ideas, an æsthetic impulse that will not down—but every time she yields to it she is halted and plucked back by qualms and doubts, by the dominant superstitions of her race and time, by the dead hand of her kirk-crazy Scotch forebears.

It is precisely this grisly touch upon her shoulder that stimulates her to those naif explosions of scandalous confidence which make her what she is. If there were no sepulchral voice in her ear, warning her that it is the mark of a hussy to be kissed by a man with "iron-gray hair, a brow like Apollo and a jowl like Bill Sykes" she would not confess it and boast of it, as she does on page 121 of her new tome. If it were not a Presbyterian axiom that a lady who says "damn" is fit only to join the white slaves, she would not pen a defiant Damniad, as she does on pages 108, 109 and 110. And if it were not held universal in Butte that sex passion is the exclusive infirmity of the male, she would not blab out in meeting that—but here I get into forbidden waters and had better refer you to page 209. It is not the godless voluptuary who patronizes leg-shows and the cabaret; it is the Methodist deacon with unaccustomed vine-leaves in his hair. It is not genuine artists, serving beauty reverently and proudly, who herd in Greenwich Village and bawl for art; it is precisely a mob of Middle Western Baptists to whom the very idea of art is still novel, and intoxicating, and more than a little bawdy. And to make an end, it is not cocottes who read the highly-spiced magazines which now burden all the book-stalls; it is sedentary married women who, while faithful to their laborious husbands in the flesh, yet allow their imaginations to play furtively upon the charms of theoretical intrigues with such pretty fellows as Francis X. Bushman, Enrico Caruso, George Jean Nathan and Vincent Astor.[8]

An understanding of this plain fact not only explains the MacLane and her gingery carnalities of the chair; it also explains the better part of latter-day American literature. That literature is the self-expression of a people who have got only half way up the ladder leading from moral slavery to intellectual freedom. At every step there is a warning tug, a protest from below. Sometimes the climber docilely drops back; sometimes he emits a petulant defiance and reaches boldly for the next round. It is this occasional defiance which accounts for the periodical efflorescence of mere schoolboy naughtiness in the midst of all our oleaginous virtue—for the shouldering out of the *Ladies' Home Journal* by magazines of adultery all compact—for the provocative baring of calf and scapula by women who regard it as immoral to take Benedictine with their coffee—for the peopling of Greenwich Village by oafs who think it a devilish adventure to victual in cellars, and read Krafft-Ebing, and stare at the diabetic and corset-scarred nakedness of decadent cloak-models.

I have said that the climber is but half way up the ladder. I wish I could add that he is moving ahead, but the truth is that he is probably quite stationary. We have our spasms of revolt, our flarings up of peekaboo waists, free love and "art," but a mighty backwash of piety fetches each and every one of them soon or late. A mongrel and inferior people, incapable of any spiritual aspiration above that of second-rate colonials, who seek refuge inevitably in the one sort of superiority that the lower castes of men can authentically boast, to wit, superiority in docility, in credulity, in resignation, in morals. We are the most moral race in the world; there is not another that we do not look down upon in that department; our confessed aim and destiny as a nation is to inoculate them all with our incomparable rectitude. In the last analysis, all ideas are judged among us by moral standards; moral values are our only permanent tests of worth, whether in the arts, in politics, in philosophy or in life itself. Even the instincts of man, so intrinsically immoral, so innocent, are fitted with moral false-faces. That bedevilment by sex ideas which punishes continence, so abhorrent to nature, is converted into a moral frenzy, pathological in the end. The impulse to cavort and kick up one's legs, so healthy, so universal, is hedged in by incomprehensible taboos; it becomes stealthy, dirty, degrading. The desire to create and linger over beauty, the sign and touchstone of man's rise above the brute, is held down by doubts and hesitations; when it breaks through it must do so by orgy and explosion, half ludicrous and half pathetic. Our function, we choose to believe, is to teach and inspire the world. We are wrong. Our function is to amuse the world. We are the Bryan, the Billy Sunday among the nations . . .

As for the MacLane, to return to her upon her Montana Alp, she is typical in her character as philosopher, but assertively untypical in her character as artist. The thing that is the matter with her is the thing that is the matter with all the literati of the current (and so vain!) revolution; her point of difference lies in her vastly greater skill at revealing her symptoms. She is, in fact, a highly competent performer with the stylus—so competent that she manages to conceal her competency almost completely. On the surface her book is all schoolgirl naughtiness and innocent prattling; beneath there is a laborious artificiality which must needs evoke professional commendation. One fancies her painfully concocting her phrases, testing her effects, planting her bombs for the boobs. I do not hesitate to say that I admire the lady, let the chips fall where they may. She is one of the few damsels of letters in this republic of the moral and damned who actually knows how to write English, the other being Lilith Benda. She senses the infinite resilience, the drunken exuberance, the magnificent power and delicacy of the language. She knows words; she has the style . . . But Mary MacLane the stylist is not the Mary MacLane who sells so copiously in the department stores and is touted in the newspapers. Nor is that best-selling, eyebrow-lifting Mary quite the moral American I have descanted upon, the Presbyterian stripped. Nay, the Mary whose works hide under boarding-school pillows is no more than a humble shocker, an American Glyn, a lady Chambers. That Mary of the vulgar adoration, I hope and believe, does not actually exist in Butte. The real Mary, at bottom, is a genuine artist, and there must be in her something of the artist's fine earnestness and self-respect. Her followers must needs disgust her; she must needs laugh at the Philistines who are even further down the ladder than she is herself . . . Oh, the irony of it! To feel the thrill of words, to be lured and caressed by beauty—and to be doomed to play *agent provocatrice* to moony flappers and lascivious fat women! . . . I almost hope I am wrong. ["The Cult of Dunsany," *SS* 52, no. 3 (July 1917): 139–42]

E. M. Hull

The Sheik (1921)

I think of all the great and good men who labor so homerically, week in and week out, to lift up the art of letters and establish a sound literary taste in America—the assiduous Canby at work all night down there in his Vesey Street cage, with young Benét passing him the instruments; Hackett sweating and puffing in the blast-furnaces of the *New Republic*, down near the docks; Van Wyck Brooks wearing out his soul and his gizzard in the literary rolling-mills of the *Freeman*; Van Doren, still at it long after midnight, calling piteously upon God in the den of the *Nation*; Phelps making his cultural rattan whistle through the air at New Haven; Jones and Hansen (not to forget Fanny Butcher) wrestling with the chelonian numskullery of Chicago; Firkins fighting jazz in the *Profiteers' Review*; Lawrence Gilman bawling for all the bozarts in the *North American*; Paul Elmer More moaning unceasingly under the campus pump; De Casseres vivisecting Philistines in *Judge*; Thayer and company eternally at it in the *Dial*; the fair Anderson fighting both Comstockery and Christian Endeavor in the *Little Review*; Sherman pouring out his life-blood for a 100% American æsthetic in Urbana, Ill.; Broun chasing the cheese-mongers and tripe-sellers in the *Tribune*; La Dawson flourishing her fearsome hatpin in the *Globe*; Finger trying to civilize Arkansas in *All's Well*; the New Southerners slitting the throats of Timrod, Coogler and Thomas Nelson Page in the *Double-Dealer* and the *Reviewer*; a vast multitude of other Taines and Benedetto Croces, great and small, furiously expounding the pure and uplifting gospel, the evangel that will save us, in a host of miscellaneous and far-flung gazettes: the *Atlantic Monthly*, *Vogue*, the Boston *Evening Transcript*, the Detroit *Journal*, the Baltimore *Evening Sunpaper*, the *Bookman*, the *Liberator*, the Peoria *Tageblatt*, the Los Angeles *Times*, the New York

Call, the Gopher Prairie *Tribune*. I add a few names of the living and dead: Louis Untermeyer, Huneker, Harriet Monroe, Braithwaite, Percival Pollard, Brander Matthews, Burton Rascoe, Ernest A. Boyd, John Macy, Randolph Bourne, Harold Stearns, Brownell, Spingarn, Boynton. I add myself: for thirteen consecutive years in eruption in this place, and unfalteringly consecrated to the true, the good, and the beautiful.

And with what result? What great usufruct, imperishably utile to our *Kultur*, has come out of all that agony? Simply this: that the best-selling book in the United States, for at least six weeks past, has been a preposterous piece of rubbish called *The Sheik*, by E. M. Hull—a novel so imbecile that, put beside it, even the worst stuff of Harold Bell Wright is literature!

Of the literary manner of this endemic work I choose a specimen from page one. The scene is the verandah of the Biskra Hotel, at Biskra in Algeria. The time is after dinner. Lady Conway *loquitur*:

> I thoroughly disapprove of the expedition of which this dance is the inauguration. I consider that even by contemplating such a tour alone in the desert with no chaperon or attendant of her own sex, with only native camel drivers and servants, Diana Mayo is behaving with a recklessness and impropriety that is calculated to cast a slur not only on her own reputation, but also on the prestige of her country. . . . No opportunity is slight enough for our continental neighbors to cast stones, and this opportunity is very far from being slight. It is the maddest piece of unprincipled folly I have ever heard of.

The style, in brief, of the Right Hon. Arthur James Balfour lying sonorously to the House of Commons: even the terminal preposition is there. The style of the *Times* on Belgian atrocities ten years ago, German atrocities six years ago, Irish atrocities to-day, and American atrocities to-morrow. But Diana is unmoved by the polysyllables. Not even the expostulations of her brother, Sir Aubrey Mayo, in the manner of an American actor imitating an English actor, can shake her from her wild purpose. Of Sir Aubrey, indeed, she has a generally low opinion, for he is planning to go to America to hunt a wife, and to her all Americans are muffs. "When God made me," she says frankly, "He omitted to give me a heart. I have never loved anyone in my life. My brother and I have tolerated each other, but there has never been any affection between us." Ah, Diana, how you slander God! In a few short weeks you will be—But I anticipate. . . .

Well, next day Diana starts out on her journey. Sir Aubrey, with his excellent valet, Stephen, goes with her for a few versts to stay the gossips, but then he turns back, and she is alone—alone, that is, save for her guide, Mustafa Ali. This Mustafa Ali seems to be a respectable man, but on the second day he begins to show the cloven hoof. Diana wants to camp at a certain small oasis; she is tired of riding and the pigeons in the trees coo seductively; moreover, it is near sundown. But Mustafa Ali professes to be afraid; the place, he says, is full of evil spirits. Very well, they will ride on. But not at the slow pace of the main caravan. Mustafa Ali and she have fleet Arab steeds. Forward! . . . No doubt you suspect what follows. You are right. The brigands are on them in half an hour, Mustafa Ali pretends to be wounded in the first clash—and presently Diana is looking into "the handsomest and cruellest face that she has ever seen." In the face are two "fierce burning eyes." They "sweep" her until she feels that "the boyish clothes that cover her slender limbs are stripped from her, leaving the beautiful white body bare under his passionate stare." "Who are you?" she gasps hoarsely. "I am the Sheik Ahmed Ben Hassan," answers the scoundrel. "Why have you brought me here?" she demands. "Why have I brought you here?" he replies in excellent French. "*Bon Dieu!* Are you not woman enough to know?"

And so to the villain's tent. His Awful Purpose is now plain to poor Diana, and she wishes heartily that she had listened to Lady Conway and stayed in Biskra. I quote the text (English edition, p. 50):

> The flaming light of desire burning in his eyes turned her sick and faint. . . . She writhed in his arms as he crushed her to him in a sudden access of possessive passion. His head bent slowly down to her, his eyes burned deeper, and, held immovable, she endured the first kiss she had ever received. And the touch of his scorching lips, the clasp of his arms, the close union with his warm, strong body robbed her of all strength, of all power of resistance.

But not yet! The scene must be labored a bit, and suitably gilded. He carries her into an adjoining room—his tent, it appears, is almost as large as an apartment-house—and lays her on soft cushions. "Do not make me wait too long," he whispers, and departs to still another room. Then a long page of refined agony. She shivers, trembles, looses a "bitter cry," shudders, clenches her fists frantically, comes to "a complete moral collapse." Then, stealthily, the *Schuft* returns. His eyes are fierce; his stern mouth parts in a cruel smile; in a slow voice, half angry and half amused, he says: "Must I be valet as well as lover?"

The rest I pass over lightly, though in it there is the psychological nub, the bait for women's clubs, the finishing-school-dormitory kernel, of the whole book. For thirty-one days Diana raves and suffers. It is, indeed, a fate to wring the heart; even a Wall Street stockbroker would deprecate it. And then, suddenly, she falls in love with her captor! Yes, violently, madly in love. The discovery appalls her. Is it really possible? Aye, it happens. And when another brigand steals her, and the first one brilliantly rescues her, and is sorely wounded, she falls on her knees at his side. "You won't send me away?" she whispers pleadingly, like a terrified child. "Never!" he replies in good English. "You know the worst of me; you will have a devil for a husband." Enter the estimable rector of the parish—the mullah, or dervish, or whatever it is that the Moslems call him. "I am not afraid," she murmurs ecstatically. "I am not afraid of anything with your arms around me, my desert lover! Ahmed! Monseigneur!" Appendix: it turns out, of course, that he is not an Arab at all, but a 100% Englishman, though his mother was a Spaniard. His father, in fact, is the Earl of Glencaryll. More, the old gentleman has a high blood pressure, and is failing. A year more of this gypsying in the desert, and, barring acts of God and the public enemy, Diana will be Countess of Glencaryll, and all the Americanos she despises will be kissing her hand.

Go buy the book and read it carefully. It is drivel, of course, but it is also a social document of the first importance. After fifty years of frenzied effort by the Comstocks to prevent the presentation of "impure thoughts" to "the minds of persons that are susceptible to impure thoughts," after all that long and furious campaign of extermination against everything likely to "arouse a libidinous passion in the mind of a modest woman" (I quote literally from U.S. vs Moore, 129 Fed., 160–1, 1904), after the heroic assaults upon *Jurgen, The "Genius," Madame Bovary, Mlle de Maupin* and dozens of other honest and dignified books, this is the sort of garbage that is preferred above all other literature by the women of the United States!

This is the net product of government by utter damned fools. ["Notes on Books," SS 66, no. 2 (October 1921): 138–40]

Gertrude Atherton

Black Oxen (1923)

Connoisseurs of the Ku Klux, American Legion or Daughters of the Revolution movement in American criticism will recall with agreeable sentiments an article by Mrs. Gertrude Atherton, the estimable 100% novelist, entitled "The Alpine School of Fiction" and published in the instructive *Bookman* for March, 1922. The thesis of this monograph was that American fiction is going to pot because our current novelists, neglecting the dolichocephalic Nordic blonds who constitute the cream of our population, and of every truly Christian population, are devoting themselves almost wholly to depicting the ideals and agonies of the inferior herd. "In the large and increasing number of midwestern novels that have achieved so remarkable a notoriety," said Mrs. Atherton, "every character is a round-headed, brachycephalic Alpine." With what result? With the result that the degraded defects and delusions of these *Chandala* have spread upward to the higher strata, and American society is "losing its class pride, its aristocratic standard." Even those novelists who "may be of the best American stock . . . have been democratized and debased by their round-head environment."

I need not say, I hope, that these sentiments filled me with a certain elevated satisfaction. I am, as my customers are probably by this time aware, one who holds the basic democratic doctrine in considerable suspicion, and no admirer, surely, of concrete democrats. What is less widely advertised, perhaps, is the fact that I am personally a Nordic blond of the purest Teutoburger Wald or greyhound type, dolichocephalic, azure-eyed and without hair on my arms or legs. My cephalic index, as determined by the experts of the Department of Justice, is 72.3. I am entirely devoid of Alpine and Mediterranean blood, and, though a Southerner, of African blood. The last man who called me a Jew had to pay $8,000 into court to get rid of my solicitor. Thus the theory of La Atherton gave me great delight—though some of her deductions from it, I confess, somewhat shook me. For example, her apparent notion that the Southern crackers, *i.e.*, the low-caste whites who now run the South, are not Nordic blonds; they are actually the purest Nordic blonds, forgetting my own case for the moment, in America. Again, her failure to distinguish clearly between Alpines and Mediterraneans, two very distinct stocks. Yet again, her rather naïve acceptance of the anthropology of Prof. Madison Grant, a *savant* whose study of crania has always seemed to me to have some flavor of osteopathy, or even chiropractic, in it.⁹ Nevertheless, I was a good deal flattered by her general doctrine, and caused copies of her article to be sent privately to all of the principal Middle Western novelists, including Dreiser, Ben Hecht, Anderson, Miss Cather and Harold Bell Wright. . . .

Ah, that she had let well enough alone, content with this one brilliant and caressing venture into Sulgrave Foundation anthropology! But alas, alas, they never do! When Prof. Dr. Brander Matthews, his *Mayflower* blood boiling in his arteries, composed his patriotic treatise upon Prof. Dr. Ludwig Lewisohn, proving beyond the peradventure of a doubt that Ludwig, being a low *Schnorrer* from the ghetto of Berlin, could not possibly get his teeth into American ideals, what did he do with the manuscript? Did he send it to the Iowa *Légionnaire*, the Boston *Transcript*, the *Congressional Record*, or some other such great organ of the Anglo-Saxon *Kultur*? Nay, he sent it to Mr. Ochs, an honest Jewish man, editor of the New York *Times*, and in the pages of that able *Tageblatt* for Potash and Perlmutter it got into type, greatly, I daresay, to their astonishment.¹⁰ Consider, again, the case of Prof. Dr. Sherman *de l'Académie Américaine*, that daring and gallant exponent of 200 proof Americanism. Sweating stupendously to read Theodore Dreiser and Carl Sandburg out of the national letters on Mendelian grounds, he also inadvertently read out Walt Whitman, who was partly Dutch, and Bret Harte, who was half Jew. Once more, there is Prof. Dr. Leonard Doughty,¹¹ of the University of Texas, Grand Cyclops of the Sassenachs in the Confederacy. First denouncing all the viable authors of the Republic as "a horde of chancre-laden rats," and laying down the harsh axiom that not one of them "is a member of the white Northern race," he then fell into the incredible *faux pas* of choosing, as his horrible and only example, James Branch Cabell, an Anglo-Saxon of no less than 256 impeccable quarterings, and a Southerner so unequivocally white

that beside him even an albino Texan appears like the late Bert Williams.¹²
Mrs. Atherton, I regret to say, yielded to a similar and perhaps even worse
excess. Not content with doing critical execution upon all the other novelists of America for filling their books with brachycephalic Alpines, she
sat herself down and undertook to show them, by example as well as by
precept, how to make a novel of dolichocephalic Nordic blonds . . . This
ambitious work now engages us.

I shall not bore you with a long recounting of the central intrigue, for
it has been discussed at length in the newspapers, and is no doubt familiar
to you already, at least in its outlines. A lady calling herself the Countess
Josef Zattiany suddenly appears in New York and is at once the rage. Her
beauty is of a rare and blooming sort; not to put too fine a point upon it,
she is an aphrodisiac of the most devastating sort, and one glance at her is
almost fatal. So powerful, indeed, is her appeal that even Lee Clavering, a
superb example of the dolichocephalic Nordic and a man hitherto almost
anæsthetic to women, instantly falls for her, as the saying is, and proposes
to marry her without delay. This Clavering is not only extremely handsome, but a familiar figure in the most delicate and forbidding circles of
the New York *noblesse* and a great literary artist to boot. His daily column
of sardonic, world-weary comment in one of the intellectual daily papers
of the town, for writing which he is paid $15,000 a year, is the last thing in
American criticism. If he praises a play, the ticket speculators rush to the
nearest synagogue to give thanks to Jahveh; if he sniffs at a book, the author
takes the first train back to Muscatine, Iowa; if he gets up in the middle of
a prize-fight and stalks out with sneers, the manager shoots both pugs, and
departs himself for Arabia to hide his shame and the gate receipts. Clavering is the male de Rambouillet of a private society of *illuminati*, the Sophisticates, which includes all the most brilliant minds of the nation, and
at its daily meetings at a hotel in 44th street there is such talk as has not
been heard on earth since the days of the Twelve Apostles. In brief, a sort
of combination of Christopher Morley, Heywood Broun, Franklin P.
Adams and Johnny Weaver, with overtones of Charles Hanson Towne,
Frank Crowninshield, Nicholas Murray Butler and Mrs. Atherton her-
self.¹³ Nevertheless, this extremely wise guy tumbles head over heels in
love with the Countess Josef Zattiany. Thirty-six hours after he meets her

he is following her about like a stockbroker trailing one of the colored girls in "Shuffle Along."

Unluckily, whispers are heard—at first only in the most exclusive circles. Who, in a word, is this so-called Countess Josef Zattiany? The question is debated in boudoirs and in clubs, to all of which, of course, Clavering has access. Everyone remembers a beauty of the last generation, Mary Ogden by name, who married one Zattiany, an Hungarian nabob, and disappeared into the wilds of Herzegovina. But this Mary, by now, would be at least 57 years old, and no one has heard of her for years: the Countess Zattiany on exhibition looks to be no more than 27. A daughter, perhaps? At once the records show that the original Countess Zattiany had no daughter in lawful wedlock. Well, then, perhaps, a surreptitious, extra-legal daughter? The theory is not implausible. Mary Ogden, once she got to Hungary, is known to have been a gay one. Hungary, moreover, is an immoral country, and full of loose Austrian barons and gypsy violinists. Clavering himself seems to incline to this explanation. It shocks him a bit, I daresay, for his Nordic blond prejudices are against profligacy, but he quickly decides to see it through. Legitimate or illegitimate, he will marry this gorgeous creature, and so cover her dubiousness with the cloak of his own genealogical impeccability and literary puissance.

Then comes the thunderbolt. Cornered by this great love, the Countess knocks him cold with the news that she is actually the Countess, *i.e.*, the original Mary Ogden. What! Even so. The story she tells is genuinely startling—a mixture of Pinero, Ibsen's *Ghosts*, the *Dial* and the magazine section of the New York *Sunday American*. Her life in Mitteleuropa was one of incessant and often hectic loves—years of wild and exhausting passion. Then came the war, and with it the new exhaustion of the hospitals. She emerged a wreck—a woman of 55, but looking fully 130. . . . Well, let us cut it short. She went to the professor in Vienna, took his x-rays "on the portion of the body covering the ovaries" and was restored to youth in six months. Now she has the shrewd and fertile mind, the serpentine and gaudy sophistication of a woman of 75 or 80, and the resilient, beautiful body of a woman of, say 27. . . . Clavering is for calling up the rector at once, but she stays him. Such an alliance, after all, would be against nature, and perhaps even *contra bonos mores*. So she gives him the gate, and marries an old lover, Count Hohenhauer, who fortunately turns up toward the end of the third act. Clavering, with great dignity, bids her good-bye, at the same time wishing her well.

Such are the main outlines of this dolichocephalic tale. It gives me, I confess, a certain uneasiness. Obviously, the corruption of the Nordic blonds by the Alpine brachycephalates has gone a great deal further than I ever suspected; it has, indeed, apparently gone so far that the Nordics are now even worse than the *Chandala* who have dragged them down. Mary Ogden is as blond as John Farrar, editor of the *Bookman,* but nevertheless it is impossible to escape the fact that she is, in essence, a loose woman; in fact, she boasts openly that she has had a whole herd of lovers, and even admits shamelessly that she is glad of it, and hints that she went to the professor in order to take on some more. As for Lee Clavering, though he is depicted as a New York *Junker* and the very *Sheik ul Islam* of the Nordic *literati*, it must be confessed regretfully that he never shows the slightest sign, either in his purely literary conversation or in his social persiflage, of being much above the general intellectual level of a cockroach. Mrs. Atherton admits us to several of the most intimate soirées of the Sophisticates. Their notion of aristocratic relaxation seems to be to play charades, hold spelling bees, pinch arms and drink cocktails at 10 P.M. — the precise sports, as everyone knows, that entertain the brachycephalic hinds of the Pennsylvania mining regions. The first time that I found Clavering drinking cocktails *after* dinner I thought I must have fallen upon a misprint. But in the next chapter he was doing it again. True enough, Clavering is not an absolutely unchallengeable Nordic; he belongs, in fact, to the "black Claverings," and in him the purity of his anthropological inheritance from "the Bretwaldas, overlords of Britain," is contaminated by a "resurgence of the ancient Briton." But surely old Mr. Dinwiddie, his uncle, is a pure Nordic, and yet even Dinwiddie drinks cocktails after the liqueurs.

Worse, many of the minor characters of the story display an almost inconceivable indecency — more gross and lamentable, in fact, than that of Prof. Dr. Doughty's "chancre-laden rats." I point to two examples, the one being Mr. James Oglethorpe, one of the most blond and Nordic members of the New York *haut ton,* and the other being Miss Agnes Trevor, a maiden lady of the highest social eminence. Mr. Oglethorpe's daughter,

Janet, is in love with Clavering, and proceeds against him with all the furious concupiscence of a dolichocephalic servant girl pursuing an ash-
man. One might fancy that Mr. Oglethorpe would be somewhat nettled by
this, but he actually takes it very calmly. "Where girls used to be merely romantic," he says to Clavering, "she's romantic . . . plus sex-instinct ram-
pant. At least that's the way I size 'em up, and it's logic. There's no virginity
of mind left, mauled as they must be and half-stewed all the time, and
they're wild to get rid of the other. But they're too young yet to be promis-
cuous . . . and they want to fall in love and get him quick." Clavering, alas,
is not gentleman enough to sacrifice himself; even when Janet breaks into
his chambers he resists her. The case of Miss Trevor is yet more appalling;
I hesitate, in truth, to report her conversation with Mme. Zattiany. The
essence of it is that she has a fearful case of Freudian suppressions, and is
eager to get rid of them at any cost. "I could have killed every man I've
met," she yells, out of "the dark vortex of her secret past," "for asking nothing of *me*. It seems to me that I've thought of nothing else for twenty years
. . . I wonder I haven't gone mad. Some of us old maids do go mad. And
no one knew until they raved what was the matter with them. When Hannah de Lacey lost her mind three years ago I heard one of the doctors tell
Peter Vane that her talk was the most libidinous he had ever listened to."
Mme. Zattiany, unluckily, can't help her. A woman of the widest imaginable amorous experience herself—"I am not going to tell you how many
lovers I have had," she says to Clavering when he asks her to marry him—
, she is yet unable, it appears, to snare one for her poor friend. . . .

   Black Oxen is the name of this earnest and astounding book. It runs to
346 pages of small print, and has been greatly praised by distinguished
critics, including most of those mentioned in it. It has, as the first effort to
break through the brachycephalic miasma which now enshrouds the national letters, a certain historical importance, and no doubt it will be put
to effective use by patriotic professors of literature in the universities. As a
Nordic blond, I am naturally eager to give it all the help I can. I do so
herewith, and very cheerfully. It is better, in spots, than the novels of
Harold Bell Wright; it is fully as good, in more than one place, as the
works of Robert W. Chambers. But I'd be a thumping liar, and, what is
more, a very transparent one, if I did not warn you that, in many ways, the

brachycephaic work of Miss Willa Cather, and particularly her *My Antonia*, is appreciably superior. ["Nordic Blond Art," *SS* 71, no. 1 (May 1923): 138–41]

Thomas Dixon, Jr.

The Love Complex (1925)

This is the story of Donna Sherwood, a designer of cretonnes and print cloths, employed by "a large manufacturer at a salary of $7,000 a year," and of her mad, sub-diaphragmmic love for Leopold Banning. When we first encounter her she has not yet met Banning, and so his dreadful inflammation of her hormones is still in the future. At this time she is respectably engaged to Dr. Alan Holt, a young medical man, and Holt is torn between his desire to marry her and his yearning to complete his investigation of "the new gland of the Unconscious Nervous System." This gland, it appears, has eluded all previous anatomists. It is both a gland and "a new nerve center," and has extraordinary powers and properties. It is "like the coil of a radio receiver," and "under the influence of acute worry it may pour into the blood a poison so deadly that life itself could be threatened." For two long years Holt searches for it, and meanwhile Donna waits for him. Finally, he finds it, and is famous overnight. The massed scientists of the world join in hailing him. He is called to a lectureship on the Sympathetic Nervous System at the Polyclinic. He is elected an associate of the Rockefeller Institute, at $5,000 a year. At once he rushes to Donna's house in Gramercy Park and proposes that they go through the legal formalities instantly. "Our combined salaries," he says, "will be $12,000 a year. Going some for two youngsters under thirty—eh, what?" But Donna stays him. "Marriage," she says, "is too solemn a thing for such haste. To me it is a divine sacrament, whether the ceremony is performed by a priest or a magistrate. It's for eternity. I want an old-fashioned wedding somewhere in a little church with those who love us standing near."

"But, dearest!"

"I waited for you two years, didn't I?"

"Sure—"

"You can wait a few weeks for me, can't you?"

The delay, alas, is fatal. It is the cause of all the criminal and physiological phenomena that follow. Before Holt can answer Donna's logic a pistol shot is heard, there is a shuffling sound on the sidewalk, and on looking out they see a man stagger and fall. They drag him in and deposit him on a couch, and Holt quickly examines him. There is a bullet wound behind the left shoulder blade. Holt rushes off to get his surgical instruments, and Donna proceeds to make the stranger comfortable. At once she is conscious of a sinister fascination. She feels herself drawn toward the wounded man "by an inner resistless force." The impulse "to touch his flesh" becomes "an obsession." The more she resists it, the more violent it becomes. Presently she is frankly pawing him. He wakes, gasps "What on earth's the matter with me?," pulls himself together, gets up, and then insists upon leaving at once. Donna protests that he must wait until the doctor returns, but he waves her away. At the door he turns politely and says, "I'd like to come back in a few days and thank you again for your kindness—if I may."

"Please do—yes," replied Donna.

"Thank you," says the stranger.

If you have any acquaintance with modern psychology you can guess what follows. Poor Donna is instantly beset by every known complex, and by all the hormones and glands so far discovered. Her mind becomes a seething cauldron of libidos. The stranger—who is the Banning aforesaid—looks like her late father; she is thus at the mercy of the Oedipus complex. He radiates the foul sexual magnetism of a movie actor or fashionable rector. He has slick city ways and an oily tongue. His touch is a thrill; his kiss is a mule-kick. He is mysterious and romantic—a war hero, and now engaged, as he says, in tracking down Bolsheviki for Uncle Sam. Donna scarcely resists. In a few days we find her in an automobile making 55 miles an hour, with Banning at the wheel. They are on their way to Kingston, N.Y., to be married. Ahead lies a lonely camp in the Catskills. There they are to spend their honeymoon.

Holt, of course, does not let her go without a struggle. He not only loves her vastly; he is also a scientific man, and can thus understand what has happened to her. He tries to save her by enlightening her. "Your interest in this man," he explains, "is one of the simplest illusions of the Unconscious Mind, produced by your father's image. Your father was the first man in both your conscious and unconscious life. You idealize him. You

meet a man who suggests his personality, and because you loved your father, imagine that you love him. The greatest tragedies of married life are
based upon such mistakes." But Donna merely sneers a "Thank you," and
Holt is forced to take another tack. He investigates Banning, finds that he
is a celebrated criminal, and brings forth the damning evidence. But
Donna remains unmoved. Holt is thus reduced to employing Strong Stuff.
"Your sudden obsession," he exclaims, "has nothing to do with love." "With
what then?" demands Donna. "With the flesh and the flesh alone—!" The
idea staggers her, but she rises quickly. "It was love at first sight," she argues. "There is no such thing," replies Holt, "as love at first sight. Strip the
dime novel romance from the thing and it stands naked. A mere sex
impulse, fierce, savage, blind—beast calling to beast!" But can science
contend with the glands? It cannot. Donna hastens to her undoing. At
Kingston she and Banning are married. Far up in the Catskills, in a lonely
camp run by bootleggers, is the scene of the profound scientific events that
follow.

The psychological currents in this part are not quite clear, for in addi-
tion to all the familiar glands the new gland but lately discovered by Holt
seems to be working. Worse, Holt does not give up, but follows Donna and
Banning into the wilds, and there renews his arguments. There follows a
complex and gigantic conflict. Banning, inflamed by moonshine, prepares
to start the honeymoon forthwith. Holt, present without Banning's knowledge, sneaks into the loft of the camp, and takes a heavy dose of bromides.
And Donna? Poor Donna is torn to tatters—at first merely emotionally,
and then physically. She begins to suspect that her husband, after all, must
be a criminal—that Holt is right about him. She accuses him. He confesses; nay, boasts. The war, it appears, made a cynic of him; he is now an
enemy to society and specializes ironically in the stealing of Liberty
Bonds; one year more, and he will have $500,000 worth. Suddenly Donna
is filled with loathing. His cynicism quenches the conflagration within
her. Her glands freeze. "You are not the only man who went to war," she
exclaims scornfully. "Thousands of others passed through the same fiery
ordeal and came out of its furnace pure gold. . . . I've listened to your
tirade, not because I believed you, but because you asked it. Your cheap
philosophy doesn't hide your lack of character!"

The hot words make Banning furious, and he comes to a sinister decision. The woman is his and he will have her. "You're my wife," he thunders. "I didn't invent marriage. . . . You're my woman—mine for life—you said it, didn't you? . . . It's bedtime for you—I'll join you when I've had a couple of drinks." Her body "grows rigid." "I'm not going—" she begins. Banning cuts her off. "Oh, yes you are. Somebody's got to be boss in every house." She lifts her head defiantly. "I suppose so," she says, "and for that reason I've made up my mind to die before I submit to you!" What follows I summarize briefly. Banning is "an expert boxer"; he gives her a crack on the chin, and she takes the count. When she revives she grabs a stool, and smashes it over his head. He grips her by the throat; he pinions her arms; she hurls him across the room. Suddenly her groping hands encounter the cold steel of a breech-loading gun on the wall—the bootleggers' defender against Prohibition agents. She aims it at Banning; he seizes it and grapples with her. She is hurled across the room and hits the fireplace with her shoulder. And then Banning begins to "play his trump card." He grabs her by the legs and hauls off her shoes and stockings. When her bare feet touch the cold floor she feels "a surge of anger and dawning panic." Banning keeps on. He pulls off her waist, her skirt, her underwear. She stands naked before him, but "without shame, without fear" and holding his gaze "in a steady stare of hate." She disdains to yell for Holt. He is snoring upstairs, full of the bromides before-mentioned.

The end is less scientific and instructive. Though she is now stark naked, Donna nevertheless eludes Banning. He returns to his guzzling with the bootleggers—who have been conveniently waiting in the barn during the combat—and is presently very drunk. When he recovers it is found that he has a fatal knife wound in the chest. Holt, recovering from the bromides and coming downstairs, accuses Donna of inflicting it. Donna accuses Holt. They argue violently, but neither can convince the other. Holt then prepares to operate to save Banning's life, but the patient dies on the table. Suddenly and unexpectedly, the chief bootlegger's wife confesses that it was she who stalked him. There is uneasy talk about calling the police, but the murderess puts an end to it by jumping off a cliff 400 feet high. "If you'll take me back," says Donna, "I'm going to be a very humble girl." Holt opens his arms. The glands of all present are restored to normalcy.

I commend this lush and thoughtful work to all students of American

Kultur. The author belongs to the new scientific school of novelists founded by Mrs. Gertrude Atherton. He is not only privy to every novelty of the laboratories; he marches a step ahead of the actual scientific men, most of whom lack imagination. In his very first chapter, for example, are two marvels that official science is not yet aware of—a man who suffers from tuberculosis of the spine for years and yet manages to keep it secret, and a doctor who dies of a malignant disease "contracted from a patient." But more important than his scientific attainments is the fact that Dr. Dixon is a Baptist clergyman. The Baptists are not commonly regarded as artists. One hears of them chiefly as engaged in non-æsthetic or anti-æsthetic enterprises—ducking one another in horse-ponds, scaring the dark-eys at revivals, acting as stool-pigeons for Prohibition agents, denouncing the theatre and the dance, marching with the Klan. But here is one who has felt the sweet kiss of beauty; here is a Baptist who can dream. ["The Library," *AM* 6, no. 1 (September 1925): 122–24 ("A Reverend Novelist")]

Some Thoughts on
Literary Criticism

5

Chapter

The curse of criticism in America, and of literature with it, is the infernal babbling of the third-
rate college professor, which is to say, of the
overgrown sophomore. I am not one, of course, to deny
the usefulness of the learned Ph.D. in the palace of
beautiful letters, or, at all events, in the ante-chambers
thereof. He, too, is one of God's creatures, and he has
his high utilities. It is his business, *imprimis*, to ground
unwilling schoolboys in the rudiments of knowledge
and taste, that they may comprehend the superiority
of Ralph Waldo Emerson to Old Cap Collier, and
know wherein the poems of Crabbe transcend *Only a
Boy*.[1] It is his business, *secondamente*, to do the shovel
and broom work of literary exploration—to count up
the weak and strong endings in *Paradise Lost*, to guess
at the meaning of the typographical errors in Shakespeare, to bowdlerize Hannah More for sucklings, to
establish the date of *Tamburlaine*, to prove that Edgar
Allan Poe was a teetotaler and a Presbyterian, to list all
the differences between F_1 and F_2, to edit high school
editions of *Tales of a Traveler*, *Die Jungfrau von Orleans*

and *La Mort de Pompée*. But it is *not* his business to sit in judgment upon the literature that is in being, for that job requires, above all things, an eager intellectual curiosity, a quick hospitality to ideas, a delight in novelty and heresy—and these are the very qualities which, if he had them, would get a professor cashiered in ten days. He is hired by the God-fearing and excessively solvent old gentlemen who sit on college boards, not to go scouting for what is new in the world, but to concentrate his mind upon the defense of what is old and safe. It is not his job to inflame his pupils to the pursuit and testing of ideas, but to make them accept docilely the ideas that have been approved as harmless, and his security and eminence in the academic grove run in direct proportion to his fidelity to that programme. If you want to know what happens to a professor who departs from it in the field of social theory, examine the life, crimes, trial, condemnation and execution of the late Scott Nearing, B.S., B.O., Ph.D.[2] And if you want to measure the extent of the pressure in the field of the arts, think of what would have happened to a Princeton instructor who pronounced Walt Whitman a great artist in 1867.

It is the curse of American criticism, as I have hinted, that our rev. professors do not stick to their last—that they are forever poaching upon the preserve of criticism proper, and that a large body of public opinion follows them in their gyrations there. Fool that I am, I once welcomed that extension of function, and even mistook it idiotically for a proof that the professors were growing intelligent. I now know better, and recant without reservation. This roving of the birchmen has been, almost invariably, a damage and a nuisance. It has set up and fortified the formulæ of the college pump in the precise field where all formulæ are most dubious and most dangerous. It has created a caste of class-room big-wigs whose ponderous stupidity and mania for senseless labelling have corrupted the taste of two-thirds of our people. And it has worked steadily, maliciously and lamentably against the recognition of every new writer who has had anything sound and original to contribute to the national letters, from Poe to Whitman, from Whitman to Mark Twain, and from Mark Twain to Dreiser, George Ade and Montague Glass, and in favor of every platitudinizing old woman who has offered tripe in the market-place, from John Greenleaf Whittier to George E. Woodberry, the New England spinsters and Henry van Dyke.

If this reign of mush-heads went unchallenged it would bring complete disaster; we would have no literature at all, but only a manufacture of books. Fortunately, it is not. Challengers arise on all sides, or at least on a side or two, emitting red fireworks from their nostrils. Watchmen cry "*Halt! Wer da?*" Better still, seductive barkers invite to livelier and better shows. And none more eloquently, none with greater caress and plausibility, than James Huneker. Who shall ever estimate the value of this Huneker to the arts in America? Who shall figure out what the pedagogues might have done for us had he never broken into their solemn vespers? He has been, for nearly thirty years, the chief of all our æsthetic explorers. He has been our introducer of intellectual ambassadors. He has ranged, at home and abroad, the free field of ideas, and brought back all he could find that was valid, and stimulating, and significant. And always, to the lugubrious branding and ticketing of one school of professors and the puerile moralizing of the other, he has opposed the fluent and resilient criteria of a genuine culture, and the spacious tolerance of a civilized man.

Such a critic, it seems to me, is a definite national possession, a mammal to be valued. He is worth, not only a whole herd of Harvard poets and essayists, but the whole of Harvard. It is not that he has played fugleman to this or that exotic revolutionist, or held out a hand to this or that neophyte of the soil; it is that he has taken away from æsthetic experience its smack of schoolmastering and "improvement" and turned it into a kindling and even gay adventure. Time and again I go to his books to get rid of my cobwebs—particularly after arising from such a terrible piece of punditry as the *Standards* of W. C. Brownell. There, indeed, is eternal recuperation for the reader and reviewer—a Pierian spring that not only flows, but bubbles. There the thing is made joyous, and hence once more engrossing and important. It is just this faculty which sets off Huneker from all the rest: he can, without apparent effort, achieve that magic re-creation for which the learned Dr. Spingarn, echoing Goethe, Carlyle and Benedetto Croce, so pathetically bawls. He is himself an artist, and so he is at home among artists, and is able to understand what they are trying to do, and to sympathize with them in their pains and hesitations, and to make them interesting to the rest of us. ["Critics Wild and Tame," SS 53, no. 4 (December 1917): 138–39]

Percival Pollard

Their Day in Court (1909)

Let us now thank the gods for a literary critic with something to say and the good will to say it in a loud voice—a critic who has thought things out for himself, to five places of decimals, and evolved plain definitions of good and bad—a critic without reverence or respectability, but with a hard fist and steam behind his wallop! Such a rare immoralist is Percival Pollard, whose book of praise and blame, *Their Day in Court*, has kept me chuckling for a week. In many matters I fail to follow Mr. Pollard. When he maintains, for example, that Ambrose Bierce is a genius of the first water, I am tempted to howl. And when, in a book plainly designed to be comprehensive, he fails to mention H. G. Wells, Frank Norris, Joseph Conrad, *In Babel, Sister Carrie* or *Dragon's Blood*, I wonder. And when, finally, he excepts *Three Weeks* from his anathemas, as a work "too fine in its art to be critically reviled," I swoon away completely. But these stray faults do not contaminate the rich, full flavor of the book. It is to the customary scrapple as blood is to ditch water, or quinine to molasses taffy. In a country, indeed, which regards Hamilton Wright Mabie as a serious critic and James Whitcomb Riley as a great poet, a man of Mr. Pollard's assertive masculinity stands forth like a truth seeker in the Baptist college of cardinals.

The charge of effeminacy seems to lie at the bottom of his sweeping indictment of current American letters, and that charge, I am convinced, is well founded. Nine-tenths of our readers of books are women, and nine-tenths of our women get their literary standards from the *Ladies' Home Journal*. As a result, their literary deities are Hopkinson Smith, Mary E. Wilkins, Dr. Henry van Dyke and Mrs. Burton Harrison. So far we have come only upon harmless virtue. But harmless virtue, even when indubitably kosher, sometimes palls, and the great human yearning to be devilish—that universal impulse toward the forbidden which prompts even innocent old ladies, who would perish of blushes over Boccaccio, to indulge in tedious tournaments of obstetrical anecdote—that yearning or impulse asserts itself. Thus we arrive at *The Yoke, Sir Richard Calmady, The Awakening* and other such putrid stuff, beloved of high school girls and discussed in hoarse whispers by the woman's clubs.[3]

In this way feminine prudery and eroticism produce two classes of books, the one made up of incredible love making in the open air, and the other made up of indecent love making on the hearth rug. The books of the first sort pour forth in immense quantities, for not even a servant girl would be silly enough to read one of them twice; but those of the second sort need not be produced so copiously, for every one of them is read to pieces. For novels that deal seriously with life as it is actually lived by human beings, putting love making in its proper place—which is to say, far down the scale, above eating, perhaps, but well below dying—there is no profitable audience in our fair republic. That field, indeed, is entirely forbidden to the author. If he would see his portrait in the "literary section" and know the taste of truffles, he must keep out.

Mr. Pollard puts half of the blame for all this upon the American critics, but that attempt to be just merely complicates his task without helping it, for a majority of all the professional critics in America are women, and many of the men in the minority are tenors. It is quite the rule in newspaper offices for women to write the book reviews, and even the literary monthlies seem to prefer them. That these fair critics are often well educated, as education goes, and almost always honest I freely grant, but the fact that they are women remains insistent, and that fact must inevitably color their judgments. If they are "ladies," they must necessarily start out with the firm conviction that old Frankie Rabelais was a vile and clumsy fellow, without true wit; that Machiavelli was a bad philosopher and Congreve no gentleman; that *Studies in the Psychology of Sex* is a nasty book and *The Secret Agent* a dull one.[4] Such convictions are essential to the "lady," but they are very dangerous, I believe, to the critic. Once embraced, they lead with certainty to the theory that Robert W. Chambers is a master of his art and Dr. Elwood Worcester a deep thinker.

It is against all such notions of literature that Mr. Pollard wages his holy war. He argues for the truth in letters—not for groveling, flea hunting naturalism, but for that larger truth seeking which essays to study the anatomy of human impulse and to depict with understanding the eternal struggle between man's will and his destiny. He gives praise where it is due, and he calls names when they are deserved. There is a hearty honesty about him, an evident desire to do justice at all costs, a will to acknowledge merit and denounce sham. He follows no man in his judgments, and he apes no man in his writing. There is individuality in his style. He knows how to set forth his ideas in English that has character. If you read his thick book you will probably damn him now and then, as I have done, but you will never fall asleep over it. ["Books to Read and Books to Avoid," *SS* 30, no. 2 (February 1910): 157–58]

Leon Kellner

American Literature (1915)

It remained for a pundit of German name, Polish nationality and Jewish race to write the clearest and most sagacious critical history of American literature that has ever charmed these old eyes—to wit, for Dr. phil. Leon Kellner (*Anglais*, waiter, bartender), professor of English philology in the Franz-Josef University of Czernowitz. Czernowitz is the capital of Bukowina, the Austrian jumping-off place: cross its border and you are in Russia. During the present lamentable war, which no one deplores more than I do, it has been tossed like a ball between Slav and Teuton, and the learned professor, I daresay, has had to do some lively jumping, for the Slavs are suspicious of Jews with German names and the Teutons take a bilious view of Poles who teach English. But whatever his troubles he can at least console himself with the knowledge that his *Geschichte der Nordamenkanischen Literatur* is a very penetrating and excellent little book, and that Miss Julia Franklin has put it into good English, and that Gustav Pollak has written a useful preface to it, and that the newspaper critics, estimating it by its bulk, will probably give it as much as ten lines of notice.

This Professor Kellner, remember, did his work at long distance, and, as it were, by wireless. He has never been in the United States; he doesn't know what it means to read the New York *Times Review of Books*; he has never heard (at least he doesn't mention it) of Harold Bell Wright, Henry van Dyke, Richard Harding Davis and Gene Stratton Porter; he would probably mistake a best-seller, in its gaudy slip-cover, for a box of cheap chocolates or a can of Russian tea. And yet, for all this lack of the usual training of critics, and for all the difficulties of writing about a literature (such as it is) in a different and hostile language, he has managed to put together a treatise that is truly remarkable for its clarity and coherence and for the independence and justness of its judgments. How easily he sweeps away the accumulated cant and academic fustian of years, and tells the truth in a few sentences! For example, in dealing with Emerson. With one stroke the gas is let out of the windy and muddled "philosopher"; with another stroke the "poet" is sent packing; the figure that emerges is the genuinely brilliant aphorist, the incomparable psychologist of *English Traits*, the defiant egoist, the amazingly curious and interesting man. The bugaboo of schoolboys, the victim of college professors, the god of New Thoughters disappears; one discovers that, after all, this Emerson was a literary artist, and hence vastly more respectable than the brummagem Messiah his obfuscators have sought to make him.

So in other directions: Kellner shows that he has really given hard study to the men and women he writes about, and that he has studied them and thought about them to some purpose. You will search in vain for the rubber-stamp formulæ of the textbooks. When he deals with J. Fenimore Cooper, for example, he pollparrots neither the ignorant adulation of the critics of the old school nor the equally ignorant iconoclasm of those younger pedants who would deny Cooper all merit whatever. On the contrary, he shows both what is sound and praiseworthy in the man and what is shoddy and ridiculous—his alert pictorial sense, his love and understanding of nature and his faculty of meticulous observation on the one hand, and his lack of imagination, his defective feeling for character and his almost total absence of humor on the other. Whitman is treated in the same manner. Instead of taking up the cudgels either for or against him, submerging the words-drunk rhapsodist in the feeble prophet and platitudinarian, he devotes a few illuminating pages to Whitman's actual poetry, showing what is honest and worthy in it and what is merely pot-house ranting. His decision, on the whole, is one of skepticism. He admits the sensuous charm, the emotional appeal of some of those flamboyant dithyrambs, but he is not blind to their general poverty of content nor to their not infrequent descent to hollow jingling. Whitman's influence in America has been very slight; his only admitted followers to-day are jokes. Even in France and Germany his ripples subside. Max Dauthendey, in *Die geflügelte Erde*, has gnawed his whitening bones, and such professional revolutionists as Johannes Schlaf and Paul Remer have credited him with æsthetic subtleties of which he was entirely innocent, and no doubt incapable; but in the main he has been forgotten. Swinburne, admiring him, nevertheless met and floored him.[5]

For one thing, however, Whitman deserves to be remembered, and that is for the fact that he was the only American writer of his day who stood firmly against Puritanism and yielded not his neck to the pussy-foots of the pulpit and the academic grove. But even in this direction he accomplished very little, for as soon as he was gone the fog of Puritanism closed in again, and to-day it permeates all departments of our literature. Moral ideas completely engulf and obliterate æsthetic ideas. A novel or a poem is judged among us, not by its dignity of conception, its artistic honesty, its perfection of workmanship, but almost wholly by its orthodoxy of content, its platitudinousness, its value for pointing a moral. A digest of the reviews of such a book as *Sister Carrie* or *The Titan* would make astounding reading for a Continental European. Not only our newspaper reviewers, but also most of our more serious critics, seem quite unable to estimate a piece of writing as a piece of writing; they are forever dragging in irrelevant gabble as to whether this or that character in it is respectable, or this or that situation edifying. Fully nine-tenths of the notices of *The Titan*, without question the best American novel of its year, were devoted chiefly to denunciations of the morals of Frank Cowperwood, its principal personage. That the man was superbly imagined and magnificently depicted, that he stood out from the book in all the colors of life, that his creation was an artistic achievement of a very high order—these facts seem to have made no impression upon the reviewers whatever. They were Puritans writing for Puritans and all they could see in Cowperwood was an anti-Puritan. It will remain for Europeans to discover the true merit of *The Titan*, as it remained for Europeans to discover the merit of *Sister Carrie*.

This moral obsession is the thing that strikes Dr. Kellner most forcibly as he surveys the field of American letters. He sees the cold hand of Puritanism, not only in our grand literature, but also in our more ephemeral writing, in our minor poetry, even in our humor. The Puritan's unmatchable intolerance of opposition, his notion that his own narrow views are impeccable and unimprovable, his savage cruelty of attack, his delight in persecution—these things have profoundly hampered all free thinking in the United States, and particularly that form of it which delights in playing with ideas for the mere game's sake. On the other hand, the writer who would deal seriously with the great problems of life has been restrained by laws which would have doomed a Balzac to a permanent residence in jail, and on the other hand the writer who would proceed against the reigning superstitions by mockery has been throttled by taboos even more stringent. For all our professed delight in and capacity for jocosity, we have produced but one genuine wit—*i.e.*, Ambrose Bierce—and he remains almost unknown to-day. Our great humorists, including even Mark Twain, have not tilted at the stupidities of the Puritan majority, but at the evidences of lessening stupidity in the anti-Puritan minority. That is to say, they have always played the Philistine, which is but another name for the Puritan.

Mark Twain was a great artist, but his nationality hung around his neck like a millstone. So long as he confined himself to the sympathetic portrayal of American people and American scenes, laughing gently and caressing while he laughed—for example, in *Huckleberry Finn*—he produced work that will live long after the artificialities of the Boston Brahmins are forgotten. But the moment he came into conflict, as an American, with the ideas and ideals of other peoples, the moment he essayed to convert his humor into something sharp and destructive, that moment he became merely silly and the joke was on him. One plows through *The Innocents Abroad* and through parts of *A Tramp Abroad* with something akin to amazement. Is such coarse and ignorant clowning to be accepted as humor? Is it really the mark of a smart fellow to laugh at *Lohengrin?* Is Titian's chromo of Moses in the bullrushes really the best picture in Europe? Is there nothing in Catholicism save petty grafting, monastic scandals and the worship of the knuckles and shin-bones of dubious saints? May not one, disbelieving in it, still be profoundly moved by its dazzling history, the lingering monuments of its old power, the charm of its prodigal and melancholy beauty? In the presence of the unaccustomed, Mark Twain the artist was obliterated by Mark Twain the American: all he could see in it was strangeness, and all he could see in strangeness was hostility. There are chapters in *Huckleberry Finn* in which he stands side by side with Cervantes and Molière; there are chapters in *The Innocents Abroad* in which he is indistinguishable from Mutt and Jeff. Had he been born in France (the country of his chief abomination!) instead of in a Puritan village of the United States, he would have conquered the world. But try as he would, being what he was, he could not get rid of the Puritan smugness, the Puritan distrust of ideas, the Puritan incapacity for seeing beauty as a thing in itself, entirely distinct from and beyond all mere morality.

Most of our native critics, being Puritans themselves—consider, for example, the prim virgins, male and female, of the *Dial*, the *Nation*, the New York *Times!*—are quite anæsthetic to the rank Puritan flavor of our national literature, such as it is. But to Dr. Kellner, with his Continental training, it is always distinctly perceptible, and so he is constantly referring to it, though he by no means denounces it. He senses it, not only in the harsh Calvinistic fables of Hawthorne and the pious gurglings of Longfellow, but also in the poetry of Bryant, the tea-party niceness of Howells, the "maiden-like reserve" of James Lane Allen, and even in the work of Joel Chandler Harris. What? A Southern Puritan! Well, why not? There is nothing but empty nonsense in the common superstition that Puritanism is exclusively a Northern, a New England, madness. Berkeley, the last of the Cavaliers, was kicked out of power in Virginia so long ago as 1650. Lord Baltimore, the Proprietor of Maryland, was brought to terms by the Puritans of the Severn in 1657. The Scotch Covenanter, the most poisonous of all Puritans, flourished in the Carolinas from the start, and in 1698, or thereabout, he was reinforced from New England. In 1757 a band of Puritans invaded what is now Georgia—and Georgia has been a Puritan paradise ever since. Even while the early (and half-mythical) Cavaliers were still in control of these Southern plantations, they clung to the sea-coast. The population that moved down the chain of the Appalachians in the eighteenth century, and then swept over them into the Mississippi valley, was composed almost entirely of Puritans—chiefly of adventurers from New England, kirk-crazy Scotch, and that singular folk, the so-called Scotch-Irish. "In the South to-day," says John Fiske, "there is more Puritanism surviving than in New England." If you doubt it, turn to prohibition and the lynching-bee (the descendant of the old Puritan sport of witch-burning), or run your eye over any newspaper published South of the Potomac. In that whole region, an area three times as large as either France or Germany, there is not a single symphony orchestra, nor a single picture worth looking at, nor a single public building or monument of the first rank, nor a single factory devoted to the making of beautiful things, nor a single poet, novelist, historian, musician, painter or sculptor whose

reputation extends beyond his own country. Between the Mason and
Dixon line and the Gulf of Mexico there is but one opera-house, and that
one was built by a Frenchman, and is now, I believe, closed. The only domestic art this huge and opulent empire knows is in the hands of Mexican
greasers. Verily, Puritanism hath made a fine job of the South!

But Dr. Kellner's little volume, of course, is not a history of Puritanism; what concerns him is merely the literature of Puritanism, the literature of a people among whom the hatred of beauty takes on the
virulence of a religious frenzy. Naturally enough, he finds it dismal and
dour. There is nothing in it to awaken the enthusiasm of a civilized European; at its best it is always intensely timid and self-conscious; one finds
nothing in it comparable to the gorgeous flowering of a Shakespeare, a
Molière, a Goethe, a Turgenieff. It has not even produced a Synge, a
Thackeray, an Anatole France, a Björnson, a Strindberg, a Hauptmann. Its
one undoubted artist, Edgar Allan Poe, spent half his life trying to prove to
his countrymen that his art was not really an art at all—that it was merely
a clever trick, and hence not unworthy of a God-fearing man. But for all
this fear of beauty, Dr. Kellner still finds a lot in American literature to interest him, and he writes of it understandingly and sympathetically. His
book, indeed, is extremely urbane: he tells the bitter truth, but he does not
put it in the form of denunciation. He is full of hope, one believes, that a
better day is coming, that the inherent falsity of Puritanism must one day
bring about its collapse, that the artist among us must come into his own.
I commend his *American Literature* to your kind notice. ["The Literature
of a Moral Republic," *SS* 47, no. 2 (October 1915): 150–53]

Wilson and Helen Follett

Some Modern Novelists (1918)

Mr. and Mrs. Wilson Follett open their book on *Some Modern Novelists* with blushful apologies. This is really no time, they say, to be lingering
over the flesh-pots of the bozart. There is, indeed, something subtly indecent about a man "trying irresponsibly to enjoy the fine fruits of his heritage of race, language, and tradition, just when the whole tree that bore
those fruits is all but uprooted." A lofty sentiment, but after all a mere sentiment—in fine, empty cant, a notion as hollow as a jug. On the one hand,

it vastly overestimates the effects of war, and particularly of modern war, upon the general flow of human progress, and on the other hand it overlooks the elemental fact that the chief aim of art is to afford us a means of escape from life, and that such an escape is never more desirable than when life is most hazardous and unpleasant. This thirst for comforting illusion is actually carried over into war itself. The human mind gropes instinctively for romance and beauty in the harshest business imaginable. War is made lyrical, ecstatic, transcendental; its aims become messianic; its very methods take on a lovely glamour. And when some Henri Barbusse, or Bernhardi, or Lieut. Latzko[6] comes along and describes it realistically, he is either denounced out of hand as a scoundrel, or read furtively and with a sense of sin, as schoolgirls read *Three Weeks* and Ibsen.

Nor is there the slightest sign that the present war, vast as it is, will "uproot" anyone's "heritage of race, language and tradition"; on the contrary, it will probably greatly augment the value of that heritage to all men. Nor will its gigantic distraction, its despotic flooding of the mind, paralyze all æsthetic feeling and effort, save perhaps temporarily; on the contrary, the rebound from it will stimulate all the arts and make men turn to them as never before, for their chief use, as I have said, is to rescue all of us from the unbearable contemplation of an intolerable world. Poetry is not the pursuit of truth; poetry is the emotional evasion of truth. Its practise is a form of benign idiocy—sometimes sublime, often very caressing, but always anti-fact, illusion-born. So with music. It is an attempt to organize what in nature is chaotic. Its fundamental achievement is orderly rhythm, and the thirst for that rhythm, among persons beset endlessly by the strident and disorderly aural sensations of civilization, often amounts to a downright frenzy, as the success of our American popular music shows. I spent the third day of last July composing an article for these refined pages. My neighbors are fecund and patriotic; their children, in anticipation of the national holiday, devoted the day to setting off firecrackers. The din, after a while, stopped my work, and I fell to wandering about the house. In a few moments I found myself at the piano, laboriously performing a Mozart sonata. Why? I hadn't touched that piano for ten days. Especially, why Mozart? I hadn't so much as glanced at his sonatas for three months. The problem puzzled me, but soon the solution became clear enough.

My sudden desire for music was a quite natural reaction from the unor-
ganized noises around me. I sought a typical escape in the arts from the
harshness of reality. And my unconscious choice of Mozart was as sound
as unconscious choices always are, for it is in Mozart that music is most
perfect and crystal-clear, and so most superior to the abominable cacophony of the actual world. It is by precisely the same process, though usually
less obviously, that all of us are led to the arts. The man who uses them and
esteems them most, the man of noticeably æsthetic inclinations, is simply
the man who is most out of conceit with the life of his race and time. It is
not without reason that the artist, at all times and everywhere, has been regarded as malcontent and anti-social by the average respectable citizen.
And it is not without reason that the respectable citizen, placidly content
with the existing order, has been regarded as a numskull by the artist.

That war petrifies the concrete artist is a notion as false as the notion
that it paralyzes the arts. It may interrupt, true enough, his expression; it
may even destroy him. But if he gets out alive he gets out with his withers
unwrung, and his rebellion against reality anything but diminished. The
United States, since 1776, has produced three artists of the first consideration in the department of letters: Edgar Allan Poe, Walt Whitman and
Samuel L. Clemens. Poe died in 1849, but both Whitman and Clemens
lived through the colossal upheaval of the Civil War. That war tore up the
United States infinitely more than the present war will tear it up, and both
men saw the business at close hand, and, as citizens, were profoundly affected by it. Yet its net effect upon them, as artists, was almost nil. If Whitman was influenced at all, it was to his advantage: his experience made a
better poet of him, a more resolute artist. As for Clemens, I defy any one to
show that those four years of ferocious strife influenced him so much as
any ordinary man would be influenced by going bankrupt, or learning
Greek, or marrying a red-haired wife. And don't, mon chair, forget Ludwig
van Beethoven! The infernal uproar of the Napoleonic wars, raging in his
very dooryard, menacing him personally, left him absolutely unmoved as
an artist. Even in the C minor symphony there is no more actual war than
in Schubert's C major. He dedicated it to Bonaparte as an afterthought,
and then launched it *against* Bonaparte as a second afterthought.[7] And all
the while, with armies marching upon Vienna and cannon thundering

in the suburbs, Schubert was diligently cramming thoroughbass at the Convikt under Ruzicka, and preparing himself to write the most ravishing tunes in the world—and all of them as bare of war and the frenzies and neuroses of war as so many hymns by a choir of nuns.

I expose this sentimentality *inter arma* of Dr. Follett at such length because it crops up on all sides just now, and because it sends echoes through the whole of his book. That book has very noticeable merits. It shows an independent thinking out of many of the current problems of literary criticism. It avoids the more idiotic blather of the campus-pump critics, though it yields senselessly to their mania for pigeon-holing. It is discreet in its selections. It presents very acute studies of Arnold Bennett, Henry James and Joseph Conrad. It is urbane in manner. It is well-written. But in it, from end to end, there appears a critic who, with the best intentions in the world, is not yet fully emancipated from the puerile doctrines of the class-room, manufactured for the half-mature by the half-intelligent —a critic who, in the midst of his æsthetic valuations, falls back constantly upon extrinsic and irrelevant values—in particular, upon moral values, notions of what is nice, the criteria of the pedagogic snuffler. The weakness, in the case of Thomas Hardy, leads him to absurdity. In the case of Dreiser, it leads him almost to imbecility. It leaves a blemish upon an otherwise penetrating and instructive book. Let us repair to our respective houses of worship and make petition to God that it does not lie upon the author's next one. Of the young critics that emerge from the ether of the schools, this Follett (I assume, following the legal maxim, that what his wife does in his presence she does by his order) is the most attractive. He has a future ahead of him, if only he manages to forget that the first aim of a novel worth reading is not to teach something, but to interpret something—that its worth lies, not in the sweetness of its doctrine, but in the brilliance with which that doctrine is applied. ["Rattling the Subconscious," SS 56, no. 1 (September 1918): 140–42]

Paul Elmer More

A New England Group and Others (1921)

Paul Elmer More's *A New England Group* offers simply one more solemn statement—the eleventh in the order of the Shelburne Essays—of his familiar ideas. More is the Bourbon of criticism in These States: he never learns anything and he never forgets anything. Let hell bubble and Rome howl: he sticks to his guns. What occupies him primarily is a war that was fought to a finish, with both sides fearfully beaten, fully a century ago, to wit, the historic war between the classicists and the romantics. His side is that of the classicists (which he constantly identifies with that of the New England blue-noses), and to the business of supporting it he brings a learning fit for a German professor and a diligence beyond compare. The new roaring that goes on in the world of letters does not reach his ears; he knows nothing about all the wild movements of the moment, and cares less. So far as his books offer any evidence, he has never heard of Dreiser and the Dreiser following, or of Amy Lowell and her janissaries, or of George Bernard Shaw, or of any of the new novelists in England, or even of Joseph Conrad, Thomas Hardy or George Moore, or even, God help us all, of Ibsen. The only living authors mentioned in his index are Arthur Symons, W. B. Yeats, Henry Holt, Viscount Morley and Ernest Poole. The Goths and the Huns are at the gate, but More is deaf to them. High above the gory battlements whereon the artists of forty schools fight, slay and devour one another, he sits in an ivory tower reinforced with steel and concrete, and there shut off from the world he piles up his monumental proofs that there is "peril in following the electric thrill of freer feeling" and that what man needs most is order, restraint, discipline, the goose-step. There is no boyish curiosity in him, no sneaking desire to go out and take a hand in the current row, no lust for mere combat. His method is wholly judicial, scientific, *ex parte*. Year after year he goes on reiterating the faith that is in him, seldom so much as changing a word.

So much for his principles. In detail, of course, he occasionally ventures upon a novelty. This time it takes the form of a strange politeness to the late Friedrich Wilhelm Nietzsche, the scoundrel who plotted the Great War twenty-five years ago, and then launched it suddenly fourteen years after his own death, to the colossal surprise of the French War Office and the British Admiralty, neither of which suspected that anything of the sort was afoot. Ten years ago More had many harsh things to say about Nietzsche, in whom he discerned a lingering romantic, by Wagner out of the Chopin waltzes; now he salutes and almost embraces the brute. Well, perhaps it is not so astonishing, after all. Wasn't it Nietzsche who said "Be hard!"? And isn't this, at bottom, the substance of the Morean æsthetic? More, I suspect, misunderstood Nietzsche in those first days (as, indeed, I presumed to tell him at the time); now he knows better. At all events, he gives the Prussian Antichrist a very courtly bow, and even forgets to blame him for causing the war, to the surprise, as I have said, of the French War Office and the British Admiralty, not to mention the Russian Foreign Office. . . . Even stranger than this new flirtation with Nietzsche is a long (and, I regret to report, rather flabby) chapter on the adventures of the venerable Henry Holt among ghosts. Here, of course, More is a bit cautious. "No doubt," he says, "there has been a vast amount of deliberate deception in the table-turning and other so-called mediumistic phenomena." Nevertheless, the combined effect of so much evidence, even though it be dubious in severalty, is powerful, and there remains "a residue of facts which cannot be accounted for by the ordinary faculties." But even so, the strangeness is not wholly strange. Didn't Jonathan Edwards believe in witches, and wasn't he "the greatest theologian and philosopher yet produced in this country"? Assuming that man has an immortal soul—a gaseous part that resists both the metabolism of the worm and the hot coals of the crematory—, isn't it reasonable to assume further that this soul may occasionally long to tread its old paths on the earth, and that, so longing, it may make the attempt? The first assumption is certainly one that no defender of the New England enlightenment can reject. Jonathan Edwards not only believed in witches; he also believed in souls, and in spooks to boot. Thus it is not surprising to find More disinclined to flout the last-named. He warns Mr. Holt to be careful and upbraids him for certain romantic generalizations, but is quite willing to allow a high dignity to his quest.

This More is a man who always entertains me. I couldn't imagine a man whose ideas stood at great variance with the prejudices and superstitions that I personally cherish, but I always forget his specific notions in admiring the pertinacity with which he holds and maintains them. The vacillating type of man, believing one thing this year and the contrary next year, and always ready to be converted back and forth—this fellow I dislike intensely. I dislike him most when he flops suddenly to my side, and so embarrasses me with a fiery enthusiasm for ideas that I always mix with doubts. More will never flop. With his last gasp he will cry out against "the electric thrill of freer feeling" and declare anew his immovable belief in a moral order of the world. ["Books about Books," *SS* 65, no. 2 (June 1921): 142–43]

Stuart P. Sherman

Americans (1922)

Just what ails Prof. Dr. Sherman is rather difficult to determine. During the war it was easy to recognize him as a patriot driven to a desperate and heroic resistance by the Kaiser's plot to destroy Christianity, conquer Europe and enslave the United States. Like many another brave pedagogue of the time he was moved by this threat to throw down his rattan and mount the stump. The historian will find an eloquent record of his sweatings for democracy in one of the publications of the Creel Press Bureau, by title, *American and Allied Ideals.* This brochure, which was distributed to the conscripts of the Republic before the battle of Chateau-Thierry, to heat up their blood, is now somewhat rare, but fortunately it is not copyrighted, and so I may reprint it later on, with a gloss. But all that, as I say, was in war-time, and Sherman followed a large and clearly visible star. Now, however, with the ideals of the Allies in a somewhat indifferent state of repair, it is hard to make out precisely what he is in favor of, and what he is against. On the one hand he lays down the Ku Klux doctrine that no American who is not 100% Anglo-Saxon can ever hope to write anything worth reading and on the other hand he praises the late Andrew Carnegie, who was no more an Anglo-Saxon than Abraham Cahan is, and reads a severe lesson to Paul Elmer More, who is the very archetype of the species. The truth about Dr. Sherman, I fear, is not to be sought in logical and evidential directions. It lies deeper, to wit, among the emotions, or, as Prof. Dr. Freud would say, in the unconscious. What afflicts him, no doubt, is what afflicts many another Americano of his peculiar traditions and limitations: the uneasy feeling that something is slipping from under him. The new literature of the Republic, both in prose and in verse, tends more and more to be written by fellows bearing such ghastly names as Ginsberg, Gohlinghorst, Casey, Mitnick and Massaccio. To put down these barbarians by purely critical means becomes increasingly difficult, for the scoundrels begin to practise criticism themselves, and some of them show

a lamentable pugnacity. Well, then, let us put them down by force. Call
out the American Legion! Telephone the nearest Imperial Wizard! Set the
band to playing "The Star-Spangled Banner"!

Such impulses, I venture to say, are at the bottom of the learned pedagogue's frequent public exhibitions of anguish. He longs secretly, I suspect, for the gone but happy days of the Creel Press Bureau, when the easy
way to get rid of a poet who wrote against the Anglican Holy Ghost was to
allege that his grandfather was a Bavarian. That scheme is no longer effective, and so it has to be changed. But Dr. Sherman, as yet, has not devised any effective substitute, and in consequence his writings show the
uncertainty and inconsistency that I have mentioned.

Two courses lie before him, if he would avoid exhausting himself by
chasing his own tail. On the one hand, he may join the Ku Klux openly,
and perhaps become its Literary Grand Cyclops or Imperial Kritik. On the
other hand, he may undertake a conquest by peaceful penetration, as he
has already attempted, indeed, in the cases of Sinclair Lewis (a Hun at
heart) and Dr. Ludwig Lewisohn. But neither device, I fear, will really
achieve much for the sacred cause of the Anglo-Saxon. If he adopts the
second, that cause will be swallowed up. And if he adopts the first, he will
simply get himself laughed at for his pains. For what distinguishes the
American Goths, Wops and Kikes above all other barbarians, as Dr. Sherman himself accurately argues, is their defective respect for the purely spiritual inheritance of their Anglo-Saxon compatriots. On the material side
they are less contumacious. They respect and even venerate the American
bathroom; they esteem the ease with which money may be cadged in
America; they admire the professional efficiency of bootleggers. But they
regard James Russell Lowell, alas, with much lack of reverence; they snore
over Irving and Cooper; they find Emerson too often windy and the rest
too often bores. Ignorance? I doubt it. Certainly the gems of the Yanko-
Saxon heritage have been on display enough during the past eight years for
all literate men to be aware of them. But awareness is not always translated
into admiration; sometimes it may be translated into snickers.

But I forget Dr. Sherman's book, which starts off by charging that I am
the Grand Cyclops of a vast horde of extremely toothsome but unhappily
antinomian young gals from the foreign missions and mail order belt, descending upon New York in perfumed swarms to hear me defame

Jonathan Edwards, the *Stammvater* of Billy Sunday and Paul Elmer More. Ah, that it were true—but the facts are the facts! No such sweet ones ever appear; I have yet to see a single ankle of the kind the professor so lasciviously describes; all the actual arrivals are overweight and of a certain age. But to proceed. From this Freudian nonsense the learned critic goes on to sober, correct papers on Franklin, Emerson, Hawthorne and Joaquin Miller, to somewhat waspish notes on Carl Sandburg and Roosevelt, to delirious dithyrambs on Andrew Carnegie, and to a final essay on Dr. More, before alluded to. A respectable book, and mainly quite safe and sound in doctrine. But I doubt that it accomplishes its patriotic purpose. The members of what the professor calls "the Loyal Independent Order of United Hiberno-German-Anti-English Americans," having faced the Department of Justice in its palmy days, are not likely to be shaken by pedagogical denunciations now. Moreover, if a thirst for the golden elixirs of Sassenach snivelization ever seizes them, they are very apt to seek satisfaction for it, not at an Iowa silo but at the *Urquell* in the Motherland. ["Adventures among Books," SS 70, no. 3 (March 1923): 142–43]

T. S. Eliot

For Lancelot Andrewes (1929)

In this little volume Mr. Eliot lets a pale and chromovitreous but none the less searching light into the pseudo-Humanism which now enchants so many young American college professors, with Professor Irving Babbitt serving as its Bishop Cannon, Dr. Paul Elmer More as its Mrs. Willebrandt, and the late Stuart P. Sherman as its martyred Wayne B. Wheeler. What is revealed, of course, is what everyone unaffected by the movement knew was there all the while, namely, a somewhat sickly and shame-faced Christian mysticism. The Humanist of the current model, at his best, is what Mr. Eliot seems to be himself: a natural Catholic who finds it impossible to swallow a church ruled by an Italian paleographer and so compromises on one ruled (at least transiently) by a Scotch labor agitator. At his worst, he is what Dr. Sherman was: a rustic Methodist somewhat flustered by what passes for learning among us, but still unable to throw off the feeling that all city men are sinful and will go to Hell. At one place, with sly humor, Mr. Eliot compares Professor Babbitt to Socrates. "How far

Socrates believed," he says, "and whether his legendary request of the sacrifice of a cock was merely gentlemanly behavior or even irony, we cannot tell; but the equivalent would be Professor Babbitt receiving extreme unction, and that I cannot at present conceive." This, plainly enough, is a figure of speech: its name, unless I forget my schoolbooks, is antiphrasis. I herewith predict formally that Dr. Babbitt, when his time comes, will heave his Phi Beta Kappa key out of the window and demand the holy oils—that is, if the clergy of the Presbyterian rite administer them. For he is not only a Christian, his protestations to the contrary notwithstanding; he is also a Calvinist, though he may not know it. So are all the other hortatory pedagogues, including Dr. Robert A. Millikan, the reconciler of Einstein and the International Sunday-school Lessons.[8] To call such denizens of the catacombs Humanists is as absurd as it would be to call Mr. Chief Justice Taft a Liberal.

Mr. Eliot began life as one of Professor Babbitt's disciples, but hard study at the British Museum convinced him that the current Humanism was full of buncombe. His present point of view, he says, "may be described as classicist in literature, royalist in politics, and Anglo-Catholic in religion." Parts of this, as he himself confesses, are vague and savor of claptrap; it is hard, for example, to think of the author of *The Waste Land* as a genuine classicist. But on the religious side there is no reason to doubt the author's seriousness. He proves it by exhuming various sacerdotal obscurities from oblivion, and arguing gravely that they were profound thinkers—nay, even gifted stylists. The enterprise is not new; I have heard Christian Scientists maintain that even Mrs. Eddy was a sound writer. Bur Mr. Eliot carries it off with more than the usual grace, for he writes very effectively himself, and is full of that odd and useless learning which gives an air of persuasiveness to otherwise bald and unconvincing disputation. For one, I remain unconvinced that either Bishop Andrewes or his brother Bramhall could write, but I confess that reading about them was pleasant, and did me no harm.

It is, however, when he discusses religion *per se* that Mr. Eliot is at his best. The failure of the so-called Humanists to get rid of it plainly delights him, as his exposure of that failure must delight the more malicious sort of reader. The moment they begin to lay down their cocksure rules as to what is virtuous and what is not, they find themselves, willy nilly, toying with a concept of the will of God, and the moment they admit that concept to their exhortations and objurgations "then some doctrine of Grace must be admitted too." The rest is a primrose path, and at the end lies a state church—maybe not the political Methodism which now afflicts the United States, but nevertheless a church. Some of the Humanists peer longingly through the area windows of Rome; others, like Mr. Eliot himself, succumb to the imperial pomps of the Anglican communion; yet others, such as Dr. Millikan, bring all their compromises to a head by embracing the arch-compromise of Unitarianism. As for Professor Babbitt, "his Humanism is, . . . to my mind, alarmingly like the very Liberal Protestant theology of the Nineteenth Century; it is, in fact, a product—a by-product—of Protestant theology in its last agonies." I can imagine no definition of the movement which would define it more precisely. ["The Library," AM 18, no. 1 (September 1929): 123–24 ("The New Humanism")]

Margaret Anderson

My Thirty Years' War (1930)

Miss Anderson was the founder and editor of the *Little Review*, and for ten years reigned as the undisputed queen and prima donna of Greenwich Village, first in its crude, corn-fed days in Chicago, then when it was transported to New York, and then when it sought a last asylum in the Café Dôme, on the left bank of the Seine. She says that the movement was already aged and dying in New York when she got there, but that is overmodest, for the really palmy days came after she landed. The best that her predecessor, the sainted Guido Bruno, ever accomplished was to have himself written up humorously in the Sunday magazine sections, but after the *Little Review* arrived in town the Four-Square Gospel of Emancipation became first-page stuff, and there was such a roar of combat with the Comstocks that no one could escape it. In the end La Anderson achieved the triumph of being fined in General Sessions for printing parts of James Joyce's *Ulysses*, the while John Quinn belabored the three learned justices in his best Donnybrook manner, the whole neighborhood was fogged by the smoke of flashlights, and the redoubtable John S. Sumner, overcome by the pulchritude of the prisoner at the bar, lost all his Methodist fury and came close to shedding tears.[9] It was a grand day for the Village, but its heroic queen lived to regret that she had not made it perfect by keeping her $100 fine and going to jail. Once among the lizards and scorpions, she would have been on the way to immortality. As it is, she threatens to be forgotten.

She issued, it appears, out of the rising town of Columbus, Ind., the seat of "extensive manufactures of pulleys, tanned leather, threshing and sawmill machinery, tools, transmission gears, gasoline engines, flour, furniture, etc.," and imbibed the elements of culture at Western College, a well-policed Presbyterian institution at Oxford, Ohio, a village forty miles north of Cincinnati. Her mother was a Christian Scientist of the missionary variety, who often kept her up half the night arguing the Eddyan revelation; her father was a business man who lost his mind and soon afterward died. The magazines read in the household were the *Ladies' Home Journal* and *Good Housekeeping*. In the latter there was a department of advice to young girls, conducted by a metaphysician named Clara E. Laughlin, author of *Stories of Authors' Loves, Reminiscences of James Whitcomb Riley* and *So You're Going to Paris?* Young Margaret, revolting against the bellicose theology of her mamma, took refuge in Dr. Laughlin's wisdom, and one day wrote to her, asking "how a perfectly nice but revolting girl could leave home." The first result was a visit to the sage in Chicago, properly chaperoned by Papa Anderson. The end result, after certain painful domestic scenes and a job reviewing books for the highly respectable Chicago *Evening Post*, was the *Little Review*.

At the start, it appears, the editor was not quite sure what it was about. It had, indeed, a political rather than a literary character, and its first enterprise was to whoop up the ideas of Emma Goldman. At that time young Margaret knew very few authors, and was apparently unaware that the whole art of writing was about to be reformed. Who made her privy to the new arcanum she doesn't say, but there is reason to suspect the sardonic Ben Hecht, then in practice in Chicago as hanging reporter for the *Daily News*. At all events, the *Little Review* soon began to bristle with saucy reviews and antinomian short stories, many of the latter from Ben's red-hot pen, and presently all the more advanced literary boys and girls along Lake Michigan were writing for it, and it began to attract notice. But it never really got its gait until Ezra Pound took a hand in it, and the author met Miss Jane Heap.

This Miss Jane Heap came out of the Northwest, and was of Norwegian stock. The Norwegians, in general, are the most respectable nation in
the world; they are, indeed, the only great people whose chief poet wore a
high silk hat and had his shoes shined every day. But Miss Heap had revolted against the decent Lutheranism of her ancestors, and when she arrived in Chicago she was arrayed in mannish clothes, smoked cigarettes,
and was ready and eager to pull the world's vibrissæ. Her specialty was æs-
thetics, and upon it she would discourse at immense length, sometimes all
night. Young Margaret from Columbus, Ind., got mashed on her at once,
and listened to her endlessly. It was, indeed, a genuine schoolgirl crush,
but, unlike most other such crushes, it lasted a long while. First in
Chicago and then in New York they would sit for hours and hours, Jane expounding the nature of beauty and the problem of the artist, and Margaret
listening open-mouthed. Margaret begged Jane to write down what she
was saying that it might be embalmed in the *Little Review*, but lazy Jane
made excuses. Finally, in New York, she was induced to tackle the job.
Here is a part of the result:

> When I was a little child I lived in a great asylum for the insane. . . .
> The others knew nothing about anything, or knew only uninterest-
> ing facts. From the insane I could get everything. They knew
> everything about nothing and were my authority; but beyond that
> there was silence. Who had made the pictures, the books and the
> music in the world? And how had they made them? And how
> could you tell the makers from just people? Did they have a light
> around their heads? Were there any of them in the world now? And
> would I ever see one? . . . Then a name came across the world, with
> a new radiance—Mary Garden.[10]

This subtle and searching stuff, printed in the *Little Review*, greatly
pleased its customers, but they were not numerous enough to make the
venture pay, and Margaret and Jane had a hard time squaring the printer.
Now and then Jane received a check from her oafish Norsk relatives, but
apparently it was not often; in the main the two friends had to depend
upon chance windfalls. Once they thought they had Otto H. Kahn[11] lined
up as their angel, but after some pretty speeches he retreated to Wall Street

and spent his money otherwise. For three days there was nothing to eat but potatoes. But all day and most of the night, whether on potatoes or on caviare, Jane talked on and on, and all day and most of the night Margaret listened. Alas, that so little of this wisdom ever got upon paper!

It was not Jane, however, but Ezra Pound who really put the *Little Review* on its legs. Lurking melancholiously in Europe, nursing a long series of just grievances against the Republic, he yet yearned for some comfortable medium of expression on this side. The *Little Review* seemed made precisely for his purpose, and so he quickly appointed himself its foreign editor, and proceeded to pay the rent for the space his own fiery compositions occupied by sending in hot stuff by other authors, all of them resident in Europe. It was thus that the magazine acquired Wyndham Lewis's *Tarr*, which brought it into its first brush with the wowsers, and it was thus that it acquired *Ulysses*. La Anderson describes eloquently the thrills that ran over her when the latter came in. Here is the passage that principally fetched her:

> Inelectable modality of the visible: at least that if no more, though through my eyes, Signatures of all things I am here to read, seaspawn and seawrack, the nearing tide. . . .

"This," she exclaimed, "is the most beautiful thing we'll ever have!" Maybe that judgment was excessive: she was later to print both William Carlos Williams and Elsa von Freytag-Loringhoven. Nevertheless, *Ulysses* was indubitably good copy, and in a little while the *Little Review* was selling like *True Stories*, and the editor was as much a museum piece in New York as Flo Ziegfeld or Rabbi Stephen S. Wise. And then, having saved literature and become eminent, she suddenly tired of the struggle, and moved to the Left Bank, and there the *Little Review* has since joined the *Dial* and *Godey's Lady's Book* in the Valhalla of magazines that were but are not. Troubles pursued the editor to the end. Whenever an extra incandescent number was issued the Postoffice threw it out of the mails; thus the inflow of *mazuma* was irregular, and the printer often went without his honorarium, as the contributors, indeed, did at all times. Worse, there were uproars among those contributors, due to jealousy and worse. Once the Baroness von Freytag-Loringhoven fell in love with Dr. Williams, and pursued him into his Jersey fastnesses, where he was known as a respectable family doctor. When he spurned her she sat sentinel in his automobile while he brought squalling Jerseymen into the world. When he chased her out she shaved her head and dyed her scalp vermilion. Altogether, it was a hard job managing such geniuses, and Miss Margaret breathed a loud sigh of relief when her ship got to Havre and she entered Mlle Georgette Leblanc's swell automobile for the trip to Paris.

Her book is naïve stuff, and immensely amusing. The tone throughout is that of a gurgling schoolgirl. The author seems never to be clear in her own mind about the purpose of the *Little Review*, and her reports of the endless dogmas and theories of the Socratic Heap are magnificently obscure. Nevertheless, the magazine was diverting in its day, and probably did some good. It opened the way for more than one young writer who would have had hard sledding otherwise, it gave space to a large number of exhilarating mountebanks, and it helped to scare the young college professors of the land into the camp of the Humanists. The day will come when a file of it will bring a stiff price. ["The Library," AM 20, no. 3 (July 1930): 379–81 ("Schwärmerei")]

✒ Notes

Introduction

1. Mencken, *My Life as Author and Editor*, ed. Jonathan Yardley (New York: Knopf, 1993), p. 10.

2. "A Road Map of the New Books," *SS* 27, no. 1 (January 1909): 153.

3. E. M. Hull is a British author, but HLM's review of her best-selling novel, *The Sheik* (1921), so perfectly encapsulates his views of the best-seller as a literary and cultural phenomenon that I have felt it worthy of inclusion in this compilation.

4. *My Life as Author and Editor*, p. 329.

5. Vincent Fitzpatrick, *H. L. Mencken* (New York: Continuum, 1989), p. 37.

6. "Hark, Hark, the Lark!" *SS* 55, no. 2 (June 1918): 143.

Chapter 1
The Travails of a Book Reviewer

1. In fact, HLM took brief notice only of his first volume, *Ventures into Verse* (1903), in *SS*, February 1917, of the collaborative work *Europe after 8.15* (1914; written with George Jean Nathan and Willard Huntington Wright) in *SS*, October 1914, and of *A Book of Prefaces* (1917) in *SS*, January 1918.

2. *Floradora* (1899) is a British musical comedy (book by Owen Hall, lyrics by E. Byrd Jones and Paul Rubens, music by Leslie Stuart) that opened in New York on 12 November 1900 and ran for 549 performances (1900–1902); it was revived in 1905 and 1920. Contrary to HLM's assertion, the show was not running on Broadway in 1908.

3. The reference is to the hand-printed limited editions prepared by Elbert Hubbard's Roycroft Press.

4. A forgery (a facsimile of the first edition) of William Makepeace Thackeray's *The Second Funeral of Napoleon* (1841) was issued either in Chicago or in Philadephia around 1896.

5. The New York Society for the Suppression of Vice threatened to take action against Dreiser's *The "Genius"* (1915), with the result that the publisher withdrew the book from sale less than a year after publication. HLM countered by leading a campaign to collect signatures from leading literary figures defending Dreiser.

6. *What a Girl of 45 Should Know* is a parody of a series of sex manuals—e.g., *What a Young Boy Ought to Know* (1897), *What a Young Husband Ought to Know* (1897), etc.—written by Sylvanus Stall (1847–1915), a Baltimore clergyman with whom HLM was acquainted. The passage from 2 Samuel relates to the affair of David and Bathsheba.

7. HLM reviewed all but one of these works in *SS*: Sudermann (February 1912); France (January 1915); Dunsany (July 1917); Dreiser (August 1914); Wells (February 1910); Wharton (December 1911); Beerbohm (July 1912); Conrad (April 1915). He also reviewed Dunsany's *Book of Wonder* in *Town Topics* (24 September 1914) and Dreiser's *The Titan* in *Town Topics* (18 June 1914). HLM did not review Bennett's *The Old Wives' Tale* (1908).

8. *Pollyanna* (1913) is a best-selling children's novel by Eleanor H. Porter (1868–1920) about a relentlessly cheerful orphan girl. For *Bambi* see chapter 4: Marjorie Benton Cooke.

9. HLM refers to his initial brief notice of James Truslow Adams's *The Founding of New England* (1921) in *SS*, September 1921, and his more exhaustive review in *SS*, December 1921.

10. Charles Frohman (1860–1915) and his brother Daniel Frohman (1851–1940) were leading theatrical producers of their day.

11. Richard Mansfield (1854–1907) was an American actor. Alla Nazimova (1879–1945) was a Russian-born actress who came to the United States in 1905 and starred in many Ibsen plays. David Belasco (1853–1931) was a popular American playwright. Joseph Jefferson (1829–1905) was the most popular American comedian of the nineteenth century.

12. HLM refers to the *Literary Review*, a weekly book review supplement in the *New York Evening Post* published from 1920 to 1927.

13. Dreiser's *Sister Carrie* (1900) sold poorly upon publication by Doubleday (fewer than nine hundred copies in the first two years). Dreiser maintained that Frank Doubleday's wife was so shocked by the novel's daring sexual content that she urged her husband to withdraw from the contract, but that when Dreiser held Doubleday to the terms of the contract, he grudgingly published the book but made no effort to market it.

14. Moses Coit Tyler, *History of American Literature during the Colonial Time, 1607–1765* (1897); Fred Lewis Pattee, *A History of American Literature since 1870* (1915), reviewed by HLM in *SS*, October 1916.

15. HLM reviewed *The Cambridge History of American Literature* (4 vols., 1917–21) in *SS*, February 1918, July 1919, and June 1921.

Chapter 2
Establishing the Canon

1. HLM alludes specifically to Howells's memoir, *My Mark Twain* (1910), which he reviewed in *SS*, January 1911.

2. William Lyon Phelps praised Twain in *Essays on Modern Novelists* (1910), a book HLM reviewed favorably in SS, June 1910.

3. "3,000 Years among the Microbes," written in 1905, is a satirical autobiography of a microbe living on the person of a tramp. A brief excerpt was published as Appendix V of Albert Bigelow Paine's biography; the full text was first published in Twain's *Which Was the Dream? and Other Symbolic Writings of the Later Years* (1967).

4. *Héliogabalisme* is a term derived from Heliogabalus (more properly Elagabalus, r. 218–222 C.E.), known in antiquity as a decadent voluptuary.

5. Friedrich Schönemann, "Mark Twain and Adolph Willebrandt [sic]," *Modern Language Notes* 34 (June 1919): 372–74. Other scholars have acknowledged the probable influence of Wilbrandt's verse play of 1889 on Twain's work. See Colman O. Parsons, "The Background of *The Mysterious Stranger*," *American Literature* 32 (March 1960): 55–74.

6. John Wooster Robertson, *Edgar A. Poe: A Study* (1921), revised as *Edgar A. Poe: A Psychopathic Study* (1922). HLM reviewed it in SS, September 1921.

7. Peruna was a patent medicine devised by Dr. Samuel B. Hartman in 1879; by 1900 it was one of the most popular medicines in the country. HLM frequently used the word peruna to refer to a bogus remedy or panacea.

8. A reference to the followers of British religious leader Lodowicke Muggleton (1609–1698), who believed that he had received revelations from God and that God himself has a real body and descended from heaven in human form to die on the cross.

9. *Ein Heldenleben* is a tone poem (1897–98) by Richard Strauss.

10. HLM refers to a succession of best-sellers over the past century of American literature: *Rob of the Bowl* (1838) by John Pendleton Kennedy; *The Gates Ajar* (1868) by Elizabeth Stuart Phelps Ward; *Ben-Hur* (1880) by Lew Wallace; *David Harum* (1898) by Edward Noyes Westcott; *Lewis Rand* (1908) by Mary Johnston (reviewed by HLM in SS, January 1909); *Richard Carvel* (1899) by Winston Churchill.

11. Black Friday was a panic that occurred on 24 September 1869 as a result of the attempt by Jay Gould and others to corner the gold market.

12. Etienne Lantier is the central character in Zola's *Germinal* (1885). He is a laborer who becomes an ardent Marxist and strives to organize the workers of the mine where he is employed.

13. A reference to James M. Munyon (1848–1918), a hugely popular and successful manufacturer of homeopathic patent medicines. Although not an actual physician, he always referred to himself as "Dr. Munyon." His pet phrase, circulated widely through advertisements, was "There is hope."

14. Marguerite Gautier is the protagonist of Alexandre Dumas's novel (later play), *La Dame aux Camélias* (1852), about a prostitute. It was the basis for Verdi's opera *La Traviata*.

15. *The Prisoner of Zenda* (1894) was a best-selling adventure novel by British writer Anthony Hope (pseudonym of Anthony Hope Hawkins [1863–1933]).

16. Ouida was the pseudonym of Marie Louise de la Ramée (1839–1908), popular British writer of melodramas. "The Duchess" is possibly a reference to the Baroness

Orczy (1865–1947), Hungarian-born novelist and author of *The Scarlet Pimpernel* (1905) and other tales of adventure.

17. The expression "trims her boobs" means "fleeces her customers."

18. "Eternal recurrence"—Nietzsche's notion that, given a cosmos infinite in time and space and a finite amount of matter in it, all objects and events in the universe are bound to recur over enormously long intervals.

19. F. C. Prescott, *Poetry and Dreams* (1916).

20. Reviewed by HLM in *SS*, February 1914.

21. Paul Dresser (1857–1906), Dreiser's brother (he changed the spelling of his surname) and a prolific and popular songwriter, best known for "On the Banks of the Wabash, Far Away" (1899). Max Schneckenburger (1810–1849) wrote the lyrics to the popular German song "Die Wacht am Rhein."

22. Charles Francis Richardson, *American Literature, 1607–1885* (2 vols., 1886–88).

23. HLM did not review Cather's *O Pioneers!* (1913).

24. Carol Kennicott is one of the protagonists of Sinclair Lewis's *Main Street* (1920). See HLM's discussion of the novel later in this chapter.

25. *The Three-Cornered Hat* (*El sombrero de tres picos*, 1874) is a long short story by Pedro Antonio de Alarcon.

26. George W. Crile (1864–1943) was an American surgeon and author. HLM is probably alluding to his *A Mechanistic View of War and Peace* (1915), a biological and physiological analysis of some of the soldiers serving in World War I.

27. From Kipling's ballad, "McAndrew's Hymn" (1893), line 168.

28. HLM did not review Anderson's book of poems, *Mid-American Chants* (1918).

29. Dreiser's *Twelve Men* (1919), a series of biographical sketches, was reviewed by HLM in the *New York Sun* (13 April 1919) and in *SS*, August 1919.

30. The reference is to Carl Sandburg's prediction (cited and ridiculed by HLM in *SS*, September 1920) that "the next fifty years will see a magnificent flowering of literature in America—in fact, in all the arts." HLM saw this as an echo of similar (and, to his mind, unfulfilled) predictions made by Emerson and Whitman nearly a century earlier.

31. The Doukobors were a nonconformist Christian sect originating in Russia in the eighteenth century. They migrated to Canada in the 1890s.

32. The Chandala are the lowest ("untouchable") caste of Hindu society.

33. From HLM's review of Cabell's *Cords of Vanity* in *SS*, June 1909.

34. Ben Jonson, "To the Memory of My Beloved, the Author, Mr. William Shakespeare" (1623), line 30.

35. Julia Marlowe (1866–1950) was an English-born American stage actress highly popular in Shakespearean and other roles in the 1880s and 1890s.

36. Nine of Fitzgerald's stories and sketches and two short plays appeared in *SS* from September 1919 to June 1922.

37. Samuel Ward McAllister (1827–1895) was a lawyer and a leader of New York society for a quarter-century following the Civil War.

38. See n. 29 above.

39. I.W.W. refers to the Industrial Workers of the World, a radical labor organization.

40. Jane Addams (1860–1935) was an American social reformer. Nan Patterson was a New York actress who was involved in a sensational murder case in 1904; after several trials she was ultimately freed, even though she was widely believed to be guilty. Jack Dempsey (1895–1983) was an American boxer who held the heavyweight title from 1919 to 1926. Charles Schwab (1862–1939) was an industrialist who served as president of U.S. Steel (1901–03) and then founded a rival company, the Bethlehem Steel Company.

41. HLM reviewed Lippmann's *Public Opinion* (1922) acerbically in SS, June 1922, remarking: "What Mr. Lippmann says about public opinion under democracy, in his volume of 418 pages, is simply that it is ignorant, credulous, superstitious, timid and degraded—which might have been said just as well in a hundred words. . . . His *coda* . . . reminds me strongly of the mystical gurgle at the end of James Bryce's *Modern Democracies*. What he says, in brief, is that we must keep on hoping that the mob will one day grow intelligent, despite the colossal improbability of it."

42. Rudolf (Carl) Virchow (1821–1902) was a German pathologist who did pioneering work in the aetiology of diseases. John William Strutt, 3d Baron Rayleigh (1842–1919), was a British physicist whose chief work was in acoustics and optics. He received the Nobel Prize for physics in 1904.

43. Johannes Müller (1801–1858) was a German physiologist and anatomist and author of the landmark treatise *Handbuch der Physiologie des Menschen* (1833–40). Karl Ludwig (1816–1895) was a German physiologist whose studies chiefly concerned digestion and urine secretion.

44. HLM alludes to Robert Millikan (1868–1953), of Morrison, Illinois, who won the Nobel Prize for physics in 1923, and Theodore Richards (1868–1928), of Germantown, Pennsylvania, who won the Nobel Prize for chemistry in 1914.

45. Paul De Kruif (1890–1971) worked for two years with Lewis on researching the medical background for *Arrowsmith*; Lewis acknowledged De Kruif's assistance in the preface. De Kruif had been a close friend of HLM's since at least the 1920s. His most famous work, *Microbe Hunters* (1926), was reviewed by HLM in the *Nation*, 3 March 1926.

46. Reviewed by HLM in AM, August 1926.

47. Jerry Simpson (1842–1905), farmer and politician, was U.S. representative from Kansas (1891–95 and 1897–99). He advocated a Populist doctrine and supported the single tax. His nickname was derived from a biased reporter's suggestion, during the campaign of 1888, that Simpson wore no socks whereas his opponent, a wealthy banker, wore silk socks.

48. George Creel (1876–1953) was a progressive politician whom President Woodrow Wilson named chairman of the Committee on Public Information in April 1917 to drum up support for the war. Hog Island Shipyard on the Delaware River was

involved, during the war, in the construction of merchant ships that could outrun German U-boats.

49. A reference to the Kiralfy brothers, Imre (1845–1932), Bolossy (1848–1932), and Arnold (d. 1908), Hungarian-born dancers and impresarios who staged lavish theatrico-musical spectacles in Europe, Great Britain, and the United States in the late nineteenth and early twentieth centuries.

50. W.C.T.U. refers to the Woman's Christian Temperance Union, founded in 1874.

Chapter 3
Some Worthy Second-Raters

1. The references are to the stories "A Horseman in the Sky" and "Killed at Resaca."

2. The others—all published in 1929—were Walter Neale's *Life of Ambrose Bierce*, Adolphe (Danziger) de Castro's *Portrait of Ambrose Bierce*, and C. Hartley Grattan's *Bitter Bierce: A Mystery of American Letters*.

3. Walter Hines Page (1855–1918), journalist and diplomat, served as U.S. ambassador to Great Britain (1913–17) and lobbied vigorously for early U.S. involvement in World War I. Franklin K. Lane (1864–1921), Canadian-born lawyer, served on the Interstate Commerce Commission (1906–13) and as secretary of the interior (1913–20) in the Wilson administration.

4. These are leading characters, respectively, in Ibsen's *Little Eyolf* (1894) and *The Wild Duck* (1884).

5. HLM refers to several works he had reviewed in previous columns: Will Levington Comfort, *Fate Knocks at the Door* (1912) (*SS*, November 1912; see chapter 4); John Masefield, *Multitude and Solitude* (1912) (*SS*, November 1912); A. E. W. Mason, *The Turnstile* (1912) (*SS*, November 1912); H. G. Wells, *Marriage* (1912) (*SS*, January 1913); Sir Arthur Conan Doyle, *The Lost World* (1912) (*SS*, January 1913); Edith Wharton, *The Reef* (1912) (*SS*, February 1913; see the preceding section of this chapter); Gerhart Hauptmann, *Atlantis* (1912) (*SS*, March 1913); Alfred Ollivant, *The Royal Road* (1912) (*SS*, March 1913); George Moore, *Salve* (1912) (*SS*, February 1913); Elizabeth Robins, *My Little Sister* (1913) (*SS*, May 1913).

6. The review of *The Leatherwood God* in the *New York Times Book Review* (29 October 1916, pp. 453, 460) was unsigned.

7. The phrase was coined by German naturalist Ernst Haeckel (1834–1919; see chapter 4, note 7) to indicate the paradoxical and contradictory qualities of God as found in traditional Christian teaching.

8. Joseph Smith (1805–1844) was the author of the *Book of Mormon* (1830) and founder of the Mormon church. Michael Schlatter (1716–1790) was a Swiss-born religious leader who was significant in the establishment of German Reformed churches in the United States. John Alexander Dowie (1847–1907) was the founder in 1896 of the Christian Catholic Church in Zion City, Michigan.

9. Thomas Chandler Haliburton (1796–1865), *Sam Slick*, edited, with a critical estimate and a bibliography, by R. P. Baker (New York: George H. Doran Co., 1923). The Sam Slick sketches are humorous tales about an itinerant Yankee clockmaker written by the Canadian writer Haliburton for the *Novascotian*, beginning in 1835. They were immensely popular in Canada, the United States, and England.

10. Blanche Colton Williams edited the annual *O. Henry Memorial Award Prize Stories* from 1919 to 1932.

11. Frank McKinney ("Kin") Hubbard (1868–1930) was a humorist, caricaturist, and creator of the character Abe Martin, widely published in newspapers from 1904 onward. Arthur ("Bugs") Baer (1886–1969) was a sportswriter, cartoonist, and columnist known for his zany humor.

12. Clifton Fadiman, "Ring Lardner and the Triangle of Hate," *Nation*, 22 March 1933, pp. 315–17. The article was a landmark in Lardner's critical recognition.

13. Byron Patton ("Pat") Harrison (1881–1941) was a Democratic politician and U.S. representative (1910–19) and senator (1919–41) from Mississippi.

14. James Cannon (1864–1944), Methodist clergyman, was elected bishop in 1918. He was a vigorous advocate of temperance and was a leading lobbyist for the Anti-Saloon League.

15. Frank Hague (1876–1956) was a political boss and Democratic mayor of Jersey City, New Jersey (1917–47). Coleman Livingston Blease (1868–1942) was governor of South Carolina (1911–17) and U.S. senator (1925–31), known for his reactionary social and economic stances. Mabel Walker Willebrandt (1889–1963) was assistant U.S. attorney general (1921–29), charged with prosecutions arising out of the National Prohibition Act. Wayne Bidwell Wheeler (1869–1927) was superintendent of the Anti-Saloon League of Ohio (1904–15) and general counsel for the Anti-Saloon League of America (1915–27).

16. Ellen Glasgow, "What I Believe," *Nation*, 12 April 1933, pp. 404–6.

Chapter 4
Trade Goods

1. HLM refers to a succession of best-sellers of a former day: *The Rosary* (1909) by Florence L. Barclay; *Soldiers of Fortune* (1897) by Richard Harding Davis; *Laddie* (1892) by Evelyn Whitaker (or possibly *Laddie* [1913] by Gene Stratton Porter); *The Helmet of Navarre* (1901) by Bertha Runkle; *Little Lord Fauntleroy* (1886) by Frances Hodgson Burnett; *Freckles* by Gene Stratton Porter (1904); *Eben Holden: A Tale of the North Country* (1900) by Irving Bacheller; *V.V.'s Eyes* (1913) by Henry Sydnor Harrison (reviewed by HLM in SS, August 1913).

2. Owen Johnson, *The Salamander* (1914). HLM reviewed it in *Town Topics*, 18 June 1914, and in SS, August 1914. In the latter review he wrote that the book "seems to be making a stir, but as for me, I can find nothing in it to raise the pulse. That there is a variety of prostitute who retains her physical virtue cannot be news to any man who

has faced the hazards of life in a large city. The breed is familiar, in fact, on the musical comedy stage, and the name of 'salamander' is commonly applied there to a chorus girl who has sense enough to know that the sort of satyr who pursues her kind is always an arrant sentimentalist at bottom, with a superstitious reverence for what he calls the 'good' woman."

3. Robert H. Davis (1869–1942) actually was a longtime editor of *Munsey's Magazine*.

4. See chapter 2, n. 7.

5. For Munyon, see chapter 2, note 11. Lydia Pinkham (1819–1883) achieved tremendous success in marketing a patent medicine, Lydia Pinkham's Vegetable Compound, made up of ground herbs and alcohol and designed to cure any "feminine complaint." It continued to be sold well into the 1920s.

6. HLM refers to four politicians (all Republicans), two of whom exhibited hostility to social reform and the other two of whom advocated progressive measures of various kinds. Eugene Hale (1836–1918) was U.S. representative (1869–79) and senator (1881–1911) from Maine. Nelson Wilmarth Aldrich (1841–1915), U.S. senator from Rhode Island (1881–1911), was one of the most powerful Republican politicians of his day. Hubert Work (1860–1942) was postmaster general (1922–23) and secretary of the interior (1923–28) in the Harding and Coolidge administrations. William Squire Kenyon (1869–1933) was U.S. senator from Iowa (1911–22).

7. HLM refers to Marie Bashkirtseff (1860–1884), a Russian emigré who shocked readers with the frankness of her autobiographical work, *Journal de Marie Bashkirtseff* (1887).

8. Francis Xavier Bushman (1883–1966), one of the first great romantic leads in the movies, starred in numerous popular films of the 1910s. Enrico Caruso (1873–1921) was the world-renowned Italian tenor. William Vincent Astor (1891–1959) was a financier and public benefactor.

9. Madison Grant (1865–1937) wrote a vicious racist tract, *The Passing of the Great Race* (1916), that became a best-seller. It proposed a tripartite racial division of Europe—the Nordics, the Mediterraneans, and the Alpines.

10. Brander Matthews reviewed Lewisohn's autobiography, *Up Stream* (1922), unfavorably in the *New York Times Book Review*, 9 April 1922, p. 8.

11. Leonard Doughty wrote an attack on modern American literature in *Alcalde*, a monthly magazine of the ex-students of the University of Texas. Several months after writing this review column, HLM attacked Doughty more vigorously in "The American Tradition," *Literary Review (New York Evening Post)* 4, no. 13 (24 November 1923): 277–78. Doughty responded with an indignant letter, published as "Doughty vs. Mencken," *Literary Review (New York Evening Post)* 4, no. 21 (19 January 1924): 466.

12. Bert Williams (1876–1923) was a pioneering African American comedian and songwriter, and the leading comedian in the Ziegfeld Follies from 1909 onward.

13. HLM refers to some of the leading journalists, wits, and commentators of the day: Christopher Morley (1890–1957), who wrote extensively for the *Ladies' Home*

Journal, Philadelphia Public Ledger, and *New York Evening Post*; Heywood Broun (1888–1939), who wrote for the *New York Morning Telegraph* and *New York Tribune*; Franklin P. Adams (1881–1960), who wrote for the *Chicago Tribune, New York Evening Mail,* and *New York Tribune* (see HLM's favorable review of his poetry in SS, April 1913); John V. A. Weaver (1893–1938), a newspaperman in Chicago and Brooklyn who, on HLM's advice, took to writing in slang and gained a wide following; Charles Hanson Towne (1877–1949), chiefly an editor for such magazines as the *Designer, Smart Set* (1904–8), *McClure's Magazine,* and *Harper's Bazaar*; Frank Crowninshield (1872–1947), who worked for many years at *Vanity Fair*; and Nicholas Murray Butler (1862–1947), longtime president of Columbia University and author of many books on education, politics, and other subjects.

Chapter 5

Some Thoughts on Literary Criticism

1. Old Cap Collier was a character in a series of dime novels written by W. I. James in the 1870s and 1880s. *Only a Boy* (1899?) is a mildly pornographic tale attributed to Eugene Field (1850–1895).

2. Scott Nearing (1883–1983) was a Socialist and prolific author on politics and society. In 1915 he was dismissed as professor of economics at the University of Pennsylvania for speaking out against child labor. Although he subsequently served for two years (1915–17) as professor of social sciences at the University of Toledo, he then found it impossible to secure a teaching position. In 1932 he and his wife Helen retired to a farm in Vermont. HLM later reviewed his *Where Is Civilization Going?* (1927; rev. in AM, January 1929).

3. *The Yoke* (1904) by Elizabeth Jane Miller; *The History of Sir Richard Calmady* (1901) by Lucas Malet; *The Awakening* (1904) by Kate Chopin.

4. *Studies in the Psychology of Sex* (1897–1910), a landmark study by British writer Havelock Ellis (1859–1939). *The Secret Agent* (1907) by Joseph Conrad.

5. *Die geflügelte Erde* (1910) by German poet Max Dauthenday (1867–1918) is indeed influenced by Whitman. Johannes Schlaf (1862–1941), a prominent German dramatist and novelist of the period, translated *Leaves of Grass* into German in 1907 and became Whitman's chief advocate in Germany. See Walter Grünzweig, *Constructing the German Walt Whitman* (Iowa City: University of Iowa Press, 1995), ch. 3. Paul Remer (1867–1943) was a poet and journalist. No writing by him on Whitman has been located. British poet Algernon Charles Swinburne first read Whitman around 1860 and later wrote a poem, "To Walt Whitman in America" (1871); but then he turned against Whitman in a harsh article, "Whitmania" (*Fortnightly Review,* August 1887). They never met.

6. French novelist Henri Barbusse (1873–1935) wrote several distinguished novels about the war, notably *Le Feu* (1916) and *Clarté* (1919). Friedrich von Bernhardi (1849–1930) was a Prussian general who held commands in the German army during

World War I. He wrote numerous militaristic treatises before the war and several after it, including *Vom Kriege der Zukunft* (1920; translated as *The War of the Future in the Light of the Lessons of the World War*, 1920) and *Deutschlands Heldenkampf, 1914–1918* (1922). Adolf Andreas Latzko (1876–1943) was a German novelist and essayist, and the author of the treatise *Menschen in Krieg* (1918; translated as *Men in War*, 1918) and a novel, *Friedensgericht* (1918; translated as *The Judgment of Peace*, 1919).

7. In fact, Beethoven's Symphony no. 5 in C minor, op. 67, was dedicated to the Duc de Raudnitz and the Comte de Rasumoffsky. Beethoven had initially dedicated his Symphony no. 3 in E-flat major ("Eroica"), op. 55, to Napoleon, but then tore up the dedication (and almost tore up the symphony itself) when Napoleon declared himself emperor.

8. Robert Andrews Millikan (1868–1953), son of a Congregational preacher, became one of the leading physicists of his day, known chiefly for his work on cosmic rays. He won the Nobel Prize in 1923. In the 1920s he devoted his efforts to reconciling science and religion in such works as *Science and Life* (1924) and *Evolution in Science and Religion* (1927).

9. The *Little Review* began a serialization of *Ulysses* in the issue of March 1918, publishing monthly installments for more than two years. The July–August 1920 issue was seized and burned by the New York Society for the Suppression of Vice, led by John S. Sumner (1876–1971). New York lawyer John Quinn defended Anderson and her colleague Jane Heap in a trial that began in February 1921, but they lost the case. Anderson and Heap had to pay a fine of $50 and cease publication of *Ulysses*.

10. Mary Garden (1874–1967) was a renowned American soprano of Scottish birth.

11. Otto H. Kahn (1867–1934) was a prominent banker.

✒ Glossary of Names

All names are of Americans save where otherwise indicated.

Ade, George (1866–1944), fabulist and journalist who achieved tremendous celebrity with *Fables in Slang* (1900) and its numerous sequels. HLM consistently regarded him as one of the leading wits and satirists of his time. *In Babel* (1903) is a collection of short stories about Chicago. See "George Ade" (P1).

Akins, Zoe (1886–1958), poet, dramatist, and novelist. HLM thought highly of her play *Papa* (1913; rev. in SS, February 1915). He later became acquainted with her.

Allen, James Lane (1849–1925), Kentucky novelist who enjoyed great popularity from the 1890s to the 1920s. HLM tended to dismiss him as a second-rater. See his reviews of *The Doctor's Christmas Eve* (1910; rev. in SS, March 1911) and *The Heroine in Bronze* (1912; rev. in SS, February 1913).

Anderson, Margaret (1886–1973), journalist and editor best known for coediting (with Jane Heap) the avant-garde journal *Little Review* (1914–29). HLM reviewed her first autobiography, *My Thirty Years' War* (1930; rev. in AM, July 1930). Anderson subsequently wrote two more autobiographies, *The Fiery Foundations* (1951) and *The Strange Necessity* (1969).

Anderson, Sherwood (1876–1941), novelist and poet whom HLM regarded as one of the leading writers of the day. His most celebrated works—all reviewed by HLM—are *Windy McPherson's Son* (1916), *Marching Men* (1917), *Winesburg, Ohio* (1919), *Poor White* (1920), *The Triumph of the Egg* (1921), *Many Marriages* (1922–23), *Horses and Men* (1923), and *Dark Laughter* (1925). See also his autobiography, *A Story Teller's Story* (1924).

Andreyev, Leonid (1871–1919), Russian novelist and playwright whose grim, horrific works inspired critics to compare him to Poe. HLM considered him superior to Poe. His most famous tales are *The Red Laugh* (1905) and

The Seven Who Were Hanged (1909; rev. in SS, July 1909). HLM also took note of the plays *Anathema* (1910; rev. in SS, February 1911) and *Savva and The Life of Man* (1914; rev. in SS, September 1914).

Atherton, Gertrude (1857–1948), California novelist who enjoyed a great vogue in her day, outselling Edith Wharton and Willa Cather. HLM reviewed her novels *Tower of Ivory* (1910; rev. in SS, June 1910), *Julia France and Her Times* (1912; rev. in SS, September 1912), *Mrs. Balfame* (1916; rev. in SS, July 1916), her best-selling *Black Oxen* (1923; rev. in SS, May 1923), and *The Crystal Cup* (1925; rev. in AM, October 1925). In general he found her fluent and entertaining but insubstantial.

Babbitt, Irving (1865–1933), literary critic and proponent of the New Humanism. His most celebrated work is *Rousseau and Romanticism* (1919), a condemnation of romanticism and a championing of classicism. HLM reviewed his *Democracy and Leadership* (1924; rev. in AM, September 1924), finding that it is "based upon questionable premises and it comes to no forthright conclusion."

Babson, Roger W. (1875–1967), statistician and prolific writer on politics, economics, and religion, with such volumes as *New Tasks for Old Churches* (1922) and *A Business Man's Creed* (1928).

Beach, Rex (1877–1949), popular novelist and longtime president of the Authors' League. HLM regarded him as the prototype of the best-selling author.

Becque, Henry (1837–1899), pioneering French naturalist playwright best known for the plays *Les Corbeaux* (1882) and *La Parisienne* (1885).

Beecher, Henry Ward (1813–1887), clergyman and prolific author and editor who was one of the most popular lecturers in the nineteenth century. He wrote numerous tracts on religion, personal conduct, and other subjects.

Benét, William Rose (1886–1950), poet, playwright, and journalist, and brother of Stephen Vincent Benét (1898–1943). He initially established his reputation as a poet with several volumes of verse in the 1910s and 1920s, some of which HLM reviewed, including *Merchants from Cathay* (1913; rev. in SS, May 1914). He later wrote the column "The Phoenix Nest" for the *Saturday Review of Literature*.

Bennett, Arnold (1867–1931), British novelist and critic best known for *The Old Wives' Tale* (1908). HLM regarded him as one of the leading novelists of his day and consistently reviewed his books as they appeared: *Hilda Lessways* (1911; rev. in SS, January 1912), *Paris Nights* (1913; rev. in SS, February 1914), *The Lion's Share* (1916; rev. in SS, Dec. 1918), *The Pretty Lady* (1918; rev. in SS, August 1918), *The Roll-Call* (1918; rev. in SS, June 1919), etc. HLM devoted nearly the entirety of his SS column in September 1919 to Bennett (rpt. as "Arnold Bennett," *P1*).

Bergson, Henri (1859–1941), French philosopher who invented the concept of "creative evolution." His rather opaque mysticism enjoyed a vogue during the early decades of the twentieth century.

Beyle, Henri. *See* Stendhal.

Bierce, Ambrose (1842–1914?), short-story writer and satirist. Although HLM did not think highly of Bierce's tales — even the Civil War tales gathered in *Tales of Soldiers and Civilians* (1891; later titled *In the Midst of Life*) — he considered Bierce to be the premier (and perhaps only) wit in American literature and greatly relished *The Devil's Dictionary* (1906). Bierce's *Collected Works* (edited by himself) appeared in twelve volumes in 1909–12. HLM corresponded briefly with Bierce in 1913. His most exhaustive analysis occurred in an article in *CST*, 1 March 1925, reprinted. as "Ambrose Bierce" (*P6*).

Bindloss, Harold (1866–1945), prolific author of adventure novels, usually set in the Northwest. HLM reviewed *Sydney Carteret, Rancher* (1910; rev. in *SS*, April 1911), remarking of his work generally: "Mr. Bindloss writes these tales with considerable fluency and skill. They are suave, they have movement and color, and their characters are interesting and plausible. But the thought will not down that they would be even better done if the author gave a bit more time to the doing of them."

Bok, Edward W. (1863–1930), longtime editor of the *Ladies' Home Journal* (1889–1919). HLM charitably reviewed his autobiography, *The Americanization of Edward Bok* (1920; rev. in *SS*, January 1921), but found less interest in Bok's biography of the publisher Cyrus H. K. Curtis, *A Man from Maine* (1923; rev. in *BES*, 26 May 1923, and *SS*, August 1923).

Bourget, Paul (1852–1935), French novelist and essayist who expressed an increasing conservatism in religion and politics in his later novels.

Bourne, Randolph (1886–1918), critic and essayist who wrote extensively for the *New Republic*. His *History of a Literary Radical* (1920; rev. in *SS*, March 1921) appeared posthumously.

Boyd, Ernest A. (1887–1946), critic who became one of HLM's best friends. HLM thought highly of *Ireland's Literary Renaissance* (1916; rev. in *SS*, March 1917), *Appreciations and Depreciations* (1918; rev. in *SS*, February 1918), *Studies in Ten Literatures* (1925; rev. in *AM*, June 1925), and *Literary Blasphemies* (1927; rev. in *AM*, February 1928). He also wrote a monograph, *H. L. Mencken* (1925).

Boynton, Percy H. (1875–1946), literary critic and professor long associated with the University of Chicago. HLM tended to find his criticism unadventurous and academic.

Braithwaite, William Stanley (1878–1962), African American poet and editor whose annual *Anthology of Magazine Verse* (1913–29) established him as a leading arbiter of American poetry.

Braun, Otto (1897–1918), German soldier who died in World War I. His diary was translated as *The Diary of Otto Braun* (1924).

Brisbane, Arthur (1864–1936), prolific journalist and editor who worked initially for the *New York Sun* (1883–90), became managing editor of the *New York World* (1890–97), then worked for the Hearst newspapers.

Brooke, Rupert (1887–1915), British poet whose death in World War I caused his work to enjoy a transient popularity. HLM reviewed his *Collected Poems* (1915) in *SS*, May 1916.

Brooks, Van Wyck (1886–1963), critic and biographer whose *Letters and Leadership* (1918; rev. in *SS*, February 1919) and *The Ordeal of Mark Twain* (1920; rev. in *SS*, October 1920) were favorably reviewed by HLM. He is best known for *The Flowering of New England* (1936) and *New England: Indian Summer* (1940).

Broun, Heywood (1888–1939), journalist and novelist who wrote voluminously for a variety of New York newspapers (the *Morning Telegram*, the *Tribune*, and the *World*). HLM took notice of his biography, *Anthony Comstock* (1927; rev. in *New York Herald Tribune Books*, 6 March 1927) and his study of Christian anti-Semitism, *Christians Only* (1931; rev. in *AM*, May 1931).

Brown, Alice (1857–1948), novelist, poet, and playwright who wrote chiefly of New England life.

Brownell, William Crary (1851–1928), editor and critic whose *The Genius of Style* (1924; rev. in *AM*, March 1925) was reviewed harshly by HLM, who regarded him as an exemplar of the moralizing school of criticism. HLM also took note of the volume *Standards* (1917).

Bruno, Guido (1884–1942), eccentric editor who produced numerous avant-garde little magazines in New York in the 1910s and 1920s.

Butcher, Fanny (1888–1987), journalist who wrote articles on books and authors in the *Chicago Tribune* for fifty years (1913–63) and also became friends with leading Modernist writers of the 1920s, including Gertrude Stein and Ernest Hemingway. See her autobiography, *Many Lives—One Love* (1972).

Butler, Ellis Parker (1869–1937), humorist and editor chiefly known for the comic story "Pigs Is Pigs" (1905).

Butler, Samuel (1835–1902), British novelist and philosopher best known for the utopian fantasy *Erewhon* (1872) and the posthumously published *The Way of All Flesh* (1903). HLM favorably reviewed an edition of his collected works in *AM*, June 1928.

Cabell, James Branch (1879–1958), Virginia novelist whom HLM regarded as one of the leading authors of his day. HLM reviewed almost every one of his works from 1909 to the late 1920s; he also helped defend Cabell when his novel *Jurgen* (1919) came under attack from the New York Society for the Suppression of Vice. See HLM's brief monograph, *James Branch Cabell* (1927).

Cahan, Abraham (1860–1951), Jewish journalist and novelist born in Russia who settled in the United States in 1882. Cahan worked on a number of Yiddish journals in New York, notably the Socialist daily *Vorwaerts* ("Forward"), which he established as a major Jewish-American paper. He wrote several novels and story collections aside from his best-known work, *The Rise of David Levinsky* (1917; rev. in *SS*, May 1918).

Caine, Hall (1853–1931), British popular novelist whose work HLM regularly ridiculed. See his reviews of *The White Prophet* (1909; rev. in *SS*, December 1909), *The Woman Thou Gavest Me* (1913; rev. in *SS*, November 1913), and Caine's autobiography, *My Story* (1908; rev. in *SS*, September 1909).

Canby, Henry Seidel (1878–1961), literary critic and editor whose *American Estimates* (1929) was reviewed by HLM in the magazine that Canby founded, the *Saturday Review of Literature*, 6 April 1929.

Cather, Willa (1876–1947), novelist and poet whom HLM considered the best American woman writer of her age. She won the Pulitzer Prize for *One of Ours* (1922). Aside from numerous reviews of her novels, HLM also wrote a brief essay, "Willa Cather" (in *The Borzoi 1920* [1920]).

Chambers, Robert W. (1865–1933), novelist whose shopgirl romances enjoyed a tremendous vogue in the 1910s and 1920s. HLM heaped abuse upon him in his reviews of *Ailsa Page* (1910; rev. in *SS*, January 1911), *The Adventures of a Modest Man* (1911; rev. in *SS*, May 1911), *The Gay Rebellion* (1913; rev. in *SS*, July 1913), and *The Business of Life* (1913; rev. in *SS*, December 1913).

Chekhov, Anton (1860–1904), Russian dramatist and short-story writer. HLM reviewed his *Nine Humorous Tales* (1918) in *SS*, July 1918.

Chesterton, G. K. (1874–1936), British novelist and critic best known today for his Father Brown detective stories. Although HLM initially found Chesterton's wit stimulating, he later came to weary of Chesterton's religiosity and overuse of paradox. See his reviews of *Orthodoxy* (1908; rev. in *SS*, February 1909), *The Ball and the Cross* (1909; rev. in *SS*, March 1910), and *The Flying Inn* (1914; rev. in *SS*, April 1914).

Churchill, Winston (1871–1947), prolific and popular novelist of his day. He achieved best-seller status with *Richard Carvel* (1899) and other historical novels and melodramas. HLM regarded him as, at best, a second-rater; see his reviews of *A Modern Chronicle* (1910; rev. in *SS*, July 1910), *The Inside of the Cup* (1913; rev. in *SS*, September 1913), and *A Far Country* (1915; rev. in *SS*, August 1915).

Comfort, Will Levington (1878–1932), novelist and journalist whose mystical and melodramatic novels were reviewed with relentless hostility by HLM: *Routledge Rides Alone* (1910; rev. in *SS*, July 1910), *She Buildeth Her House* (1911; rev. in *SS*, October 1911), *Fate Knocks at the Door* (1912; rev. in *SS*, November 1912), *Down among Men* (1913; rev. in *SS*, January 1914). HLM also took note of his autobiography, *Midstream* (1914; rev. in *Town Topics*, 25 June 1914, and *SS*, August 1914), finding it interesting as a revelation of a "chronic emotionalist."

Comstock, Anthony (1844–1915), founder of the New York Society for the Suppression of Vice in 1873. Attaining tremendous power and influence, Comstock and his allies carried on numerous campaigns to prevent the distribution of "obscene" books and other matter. He was one of HLM's *bêtes noires*. See his review of Charles Gallaudet Turnbull's *Anthony Comstock, Fighter* (1913; rev. in *SS*, April 1914).

Conrad, Joseph (1857–1924), Polish-born British novelist. HLM regarded him as perhaps the leading writer of his time and became his most vigorous American advocate. He wrote extensively on Conrad in *A Book of Prefaces* (1917) as well as in many reviews of his novels and tales, including *The Point of Honor* (1908; rev. in *SS*, December 1908), *Under Western Eyes* (1911; rev. in *SS*, January 1912), *Chance* (1913; rev. in *SS*, March 1914), *Victory* (1915; rev. in *SS*, April 1915), *The Arrow of Gold* (1919; rev. in *SS*, August 1919), and *The Rescue* (1920; rev. in *SS*, August 1920). See also his review of several works by and about Conrad in *AM*, April 1924.

Coogler, J. Gordon (1865–1901), Southern poetaster who self-published several books of his own poetry in the 1890s, including *Purely Original Verse* (1897).

Cook, Frederick Albert (1865–1940), explorer who achieved momentary notoriety by claiming (apparently falsely) that he had reached the North Pole in 1908.

Cooke, Marjorie Benton (1876–1920), novelist and playwright whose *Bambi*

(1914; rev. in *Town Topics*, 29 October 1914, and SS, December 1914) became a best-seller, much to HLM's chagrin.

Corelli, Marie (pseud. of Mary Mackay, 1855–1924), British novelist whose mix of spiritualism and melodrama made many of her novels best-sellers, beginning with *The Sorrows of Satan* (1895). HLM reviewed *Holy Orders* (1908; rev. in SS, November 1908) and *Innocent, Her Fancy and His Fact* (1914; rev. in SS, February 1915), remarking of the latter: "Sadness . . . stalks through it like some great murrain through the countryside; it is a sure cure for joy in every form. I myself, a mocker at all sweet and lovely things, a professional snickerer, a saucy fellow by trade, have moaned and blubbered over it like a fat woman at *La Dame aux Camélias*."

Crane, Frank (1861–1928), clergyman and journalist who was one of the most widely syndicated columnists of his day. HLM regarded his work as trite and naively optimistic.

Crawford, F. Marion (1854–1909), novelist whose historical novels enjoyed tremendous popularity in the later nineteenth century. HLM took brief note of a few of his very late works, some of which appeared posthumously.

Croce, Benedetto (1866–1952), Italian critic and philosopher who exercised great influence on the development of literary theory in the early twentieth century.

Curwood, James Oliver (1878–1897), novelist whose tales of adventure and the outdoors were popular in their day. HLM wrote a lukewarm review of his *The Danger Trail* (1910; rev. in SS, April 1910).

D'Annunzio, Gabriele (1863–1938), Italian poet, novelist, and playwright who enjoyed a vogue in the English-speaking world at the turn of the century.

Davis, Richard Harding (1864–1916), journalist and novelist whose novels and tales of adventure and romance enjoyed a great vogue in his time. HLM took note of only one of them: the story collection *The Man Who Could Not Lose* (1911; rev. in SS, December 1911), most of whose contents HLM found "silly beyond description."

Dawson, Coningsby (1883–1959), journalist and novelist born in England but domiciled in the United States since 1905. His novels achieved a transient popularity in the early twentieth century.

Dawson, Francis Warrington (1878–1962), novelist active in the 1910s and 1920s and a disciple of Joseph Conrad.

Day, Holman Francis (1865–1935), Maine poet and novelist. He published two popular books of versified tales about Maine life, *Up in Maine* (1900) and *Pine Tree Ballads* (1902).

De Casseres, Benjamin (1873–1945), eccentric journalist and critic known for the flamboyance of his style and the extravagance of his critical judgments.

Dell, Floyd (1887–1969), journalist and novelist associated with the "Chicago School." HLM favorably reviewed his novel, *Moon-Calf* (1920; rev. in SS, March 1921), but thought less well of its sequel, *The Briary-Bush* (1921; rev. in SS, January 1922).

Dixon, Thomas, Jr. (1864–1946), Southern writer who achieved notoriety with the novel *The Clansman* (1905), a sympathetic portrait of the original Ku Klux Klan (the basis for D. W. Griffith's film *The Birth of a Nation*). HLM heaped abuse on *Comrades* (1909; rev. in SS, April 1909), *The Root of Evil* (1911; rev. in SS, April 1911), and, most witheringly, *The Love Complex* (1925; rev. in *AM*, September 1925).

Dos Passos, John (1896–1970), novelist and playwright whose early novel, *Three Soldiers* (1921), HLM considered one of the best novels about World War I. HLM also took note of *Streets of Night* (1923) and *Manhattan Transfer* (1925; rev. in SS, April 1926), but did not review the *U.SA.* trilogy (1930–36), for which Dos Passos is now best known.

Doyle, Sir Arthur Conan (1859–1930), prolific novelist and short-story writer now best known for his many novels and tales about Sherlock Holmes. HLM found a late Sherlock Holmes novel, *The Valley of Fear* (1915; rev. in SS, June 1915) mildly entertaining, as well as his adventure novel *The Lost World* (1912; rev. in SS, January 1913); but he ridiculed Doyle's descent into naive spiritualism in *The New Revelation* (1918; rev. in SS, August 1918).

Dreiser, Theodore (1871–1945), pioneering novelist; HLM became his chief advocate. For their tortured personal relationship see *Dreiser-Mencken Letters* (1977; 2 vols.) as well as HLM's *My Life as Author and Editor*.

Dunsany, Lord (Edward John Moreton Drax Plunkett, 1878–1957), Anglo-Irish novelist, short-story writer, and playwright whose tales and plays of fantasy enjoyed a tremendous vogue in America in the 1910s and 1920s and remain central works in modern fantastic literature. HLM reviewed them enthusiastically in SS, July 1917, and published much of Dunsany's work in SS.

Eddy, Mary Baker (1821–1910), founder of Christian Science with the volume *Science and Health* (1875).

Eliot, Charles W. (1834–1926), longtime president of Harvard (1869–1909) and one of the most influential educators of his era.

Eliot, T. S. (1888–1865), Modernist poet whose poetry and criticism HLM regarded with reservations. He briefly reviewed *Prufrock and Other Observa-*

tions (1917; rev. in *SS*, June 1918), took no notice of *The Waste Land* (1922), and wrote a mixed review of Eliot's volume of criticism, *For Lancelot Andrewes* (1929; rev. in *AM*, September 1929).

Emerson, Ralph Waldo (1803–1882), a leading poet and essayist of the nineteenth century. For HLM's early evaluation of him, see "An Unheeded Law-Giver" (*P1*).

Eucken, Rudolf (1846–1926), German philosopher who was awarded the Nobel Prize for literature in 1908.

Farrar, John (1896–1974), poet and longtime editor of the *Bookman*; subsequently an editor with several prestigious New York publishing houses.

Finger, Charles J. (1869–1941), editor of the little magazine *All's Well* (1920–35) and author of several juvenile novels.

Firkins, Oscar W. (1864–1932), playwright and critic. He published studies of Emerson (1915) and Howells (1924), as well as several volumes of plays. See his *Memoirs and Letters* (1934).

Fiske, John (1842–1901), philosopher and historian whose works of popular science and history—including *Myths and Myth-Makers* (1872) and *The Beginnings of New England* (1889)—were highly popular and influential in their day.

Fitch, Clyde (1865–1909), playwright whose plays of social realism represented an advance in American drama. HLM reviewed the posthumous volume, *Clyde Fitch and His Letters* (1924; rev. in *AM*, January 1925).

Fitzgerald, F. Scott (1896–1940), novelist and short-story writer whose early work HLM published in *SS* and whose novels HLM held in high esteem. His complex involvement with Scott and Zelda Fitzgerald is chronicled in *My Life as Author and Editor*.

Follett, Wilson (1887–1963), critic and editor. HLM reviewed his *Joseph Conrad* (1915; rev. in *SS*, January 1916) and *The Modern Novel* (1918; rev. in *SS*, February 1919), calling the former the "best study of Joseph Conrad that has yet appeared." With his wife, Helen (Thomas) Follett (1884?–1970), Follett wrote *Some Modern Novelists* (1918; rev. in *SS*, September 1918).

France, Anatole (1844–1920) French novelist and man of letters who won the Nobel Prize for literature in 1921. HLM regarded him as one of the towering literary figures of his day and especially appreciated the wit and anticlericalism found in such works as *The Revolt of the Angels* (1914; rev. in *SS*, January 1915). HLM also reviewed the first volume of France's *On Life and Letters* (1910; rev. in *SS*, January 1910) and *The Opinions of Anatole France*, recorded by Paul Gsell (1922; rev. in *SS*, August 1922).

Freeman, Mary E. Wilkins (1852–1930), short-story writer and novelist known for her homely tales of New England life, including *A Humble Romance and Other Stories* (1887) and *A New England Nun and Other Stories* (1891).

Freytag-Loringhoven, Baroness Elsa von (1874-1927), German artist and poet whose work (in English) appeared in several little magazines in the 1920s, chiefly the *Little Review* but also the *Transatlantic Review* and *transition*.

Fuller, Henry Blake (1857–1929), pioneering writer of naturalist fiction. He wrote novels prolifically from 1890 to 1908, then chiefly devoted himself to literary criticism for Chicago newspapers.

Gale, Zona (1874–1938), Wisconsin novelist. HLM thought little of her early work, but felt that she came into her own with the best-selling *Miss Lulu Bett* (1920; rev. in *SS*, October 1920).

Galsworthy, John (1867–1933), British novelist and playwright best known for the multivolume Forsyte Saga, beginning with *The Man of Property* (1906). HLM regarded him as a leading author of his time but dogged by inconsistency. Among the books by Galsworthy reviewed by HLM are the novels *Fraternity* (1909; rev. in *SS*, June 1909), *The Dark Flower* (1913; rev. in *SS*, July 1914), and *In Chancery* (1920; rev. in *SS*, February 1921), and a volume of *Plays* (1909; rev. in *SS*, September 1909).

Garland, Hamlin (1860–1940), novelist and essayist. HLM poked fun at his study of spiritualism, *The Shadow World* (1908; rev. in *SS*, February 1909), but was more charitable toward Garland's autobiography, *A Son of the Middle Border* (1917; rev. in the *New York Evening Mail*, 29 September 1917).

Gerould, Katharine Fullerton (1879–1944), novelist and essayist. HLM reviewed her *Modes and Morals* (1919; rev. in *SS*, May 1920), finding it "hollow stuff—kittenish but correct."

Gilman, Lawrence (1878–1939), journalist and critic chiefly known for his music criticism. HLM found interest in his *Aspects of Modern Opera* (1909; rev. in *SS*, March 1909).

Gissing, George (1857–1903), prolific British novelist best known for a succession of novels about working-class people in London, including *New Grub Street* (1891) and *Born in Exile* (1892).

Glasgow, Ellen (1873–1945), Virginia novelist. HLM did not care for her earlier work—see his review of *The Romance of a Plain Man* (1909; rev. in *SS*, August 1909)—but felt that her novels of the 1920s revealed an incisive dissection of Southern society.

Glass, Montague (1877–1934), short-story writer whose tales of American Jewish life in New York, many featuring the recurring characters Abe Potash and Morris ("Mawruss") Perlmutter, enjoyed a great vogue in the 1910s. HLM regarded them with great favor, enthusiastically reviewing such volumes as *Abe and Mawruss* (1911; rev. in SS, December 1911), *Elkan Lubliner: American* (1912; rev. in SS, February 1913), and *The Competitive Nephew* (1915; rev. in SS, July 1915). Glass achieved further renown with a succession of Broadway plays involving these and other Jewish characters.

Glyn, Elinor (1864–1943), British novelist and playwright who created a sensation with the novel *Three Weeks* (1907), which featured more explicit sexuality than was customary for its time.

Gorky, Maxim (1868–1936), Russian playwright and short-story writer. HLM reviewed his *The Spy* (1908; rev. in SS, March 1909), *Tales of Two Countries* (1914; rev. in SS, February 1915), the autobiographical *My Childhood* (1915; rev. in SS, December 1915), and *Fragments from My Diary* (1924; rev. in AM, January 1925).

Grant, Robert (1852–1940), jurist and popular novelist. HLM found some merit in *The Chippendales* (1909; rev. in SS, July 1909), but on the whole considered Grant a second-rater.

Grey, Zane (1875–1939), novelist who achieved tremendous popularity with a succession of westerns.

Griswold, Rufus W. (1815–1857), editor and journalist who achieved permanent infamy by writing a harsh biographical sketch of Poe after the latter's death, adversely affecting Poe's reputation for decades.

Hackett, Francis (1883–1962), critic, historian, and novelist. HLM thought well of the essay collections *Horizons* (1918; rev. in SS, September 1918) and *The Invisible Censor* (1921; rev. in SS, June 1921), the novel *That Nice Young Couple* (1925; rev. in AM, August 1925), and the biography *Henry the Eighth* (1929; rev. in AM, August 1929).

Hamilton, Clayton (1881–1946), prolific and popular drama critic whose work HLM held in low esteem.

Hansen, Harry (1884–1977), journalist, critic, and historian best known for *Midwest Portraits* (1923) and other works on literary life in Chicago.

Harris, Joel Chandler (1848–1908), journalist and short-story writer who achieved celebrity and critical renown for his tales of Uncle Remus, with their faithful recreations of African American dialect and folk myth.

Harrison, Mrs. Burton (Constance Cary Harrison) (1843–1920), Southern novelist, short-story writer, and playwright who wrote prolifically and popularly from the 1890s to the 1910s.

Harrison, Henry Sydnor (1880–1930), journalist and novelist whose sentimental romances were scorned by HLM. See his reviews of *Queed* (1911; rev.

in *SS*, July 1911), *V.V.'s Eyes* (1913; rev. in *SS*, August 1913), and *Andrew Bride of Paris* (1925; rev. in *AM*, April 1926).

Harte, Bret (1836–1902), poet, short-story writer, and novelist who became the first California author to achieve national and international fame. His first collection of tales, *The Luck of Roaring Camp* (1868), remained his most popular. HLM felt, however, that his work had already been consigned to the dustbin of literary history.

Hauptmann, Gerhart (1862–1946), German dramatist whom HLM regarded as a leading playwright of the period. See his successive reviews of the multivolume *Dramatic Works of Gerhart Hauptmann*, translated by Ludwig Lewisohn (1912–24; rev. in *SS*, March 1913, December 1913, September 1914, and April 1915); also his reviews of *The Weavers* (1899, 1911; rev. in *SS*, August 1911), *The Fool in Christ* (1911; rev. in *SS*, February 1912), *The Sunken Bell* (1899, 1914; rev. in *SS*, September 1914), and the novel *Atlantis* (1912; rev. in *SS*, March 1913).

Hawthorne, Julian (1846–1934), novelist, historian, and son of Nathaniel Hawthorne.

Hearn, Lafcadio (1850–1904), journalist and novelist who moved permanently to Japan in 1890 and wrote numerous works expounding Chinese and Japanese myth and legend. HLM took brief note of his *Fantastics and Other Fancies* (1919; rev. in *SS*, January 1920) and a reprint of his *Creole Sketches* (1924; rev. in *AM*, June 1924).

Hearst, William Randolph (1863–1951), one of the most influential newspaper and magazine publishers of his day, whose career began at the age of twenty-three when his father gave him the *San Francisco Examiner* to edit in 1887.

Hecht, Ben (1894–1964), prolific Chicago journalist, novelist, and playwright. His novel *Erik Dorn* (1921) was both hailed and condemned as a representative of iconoclastic Modernism. *Fantazius Mallare* (1922), a sexually explicit fantasy novel, was banned for obscenity. Hecht later achieved celebrity for the stage play *The Front Page* (1928; with Charles McArthur) and for numerous Hollywood screenplays.

Henry, O. (pseud. of William Sydney Porter, 1862–1910), short-story writer who attained tremendous popularity in the first decade of the twentieth century. HLM generally considered his work facile and hackneyed. See his reviews of *Cabbages and Kings* (1904; rev. in the *Baltimore Sunday Herald*, 18 December 1904), *Roads of Destiny* (1909; rev. in *SS*, July 1909), and *Strictly Business* (1910; rev. in *SS*, May 1910). See also "O. Henry" (*CST*, 25 October 1925).

Herford, Oliver (1863–1935), poet and playwright whose volumes of humorous poetry were frequently illustrated by himself.

Hergesheimer, Joseph (1880–1954), novelist whose work enjoyed both critical and popular esteem in his day. HLM regularly reviewed his novels as they appeared and considered him a leading writer of his day; see his reviews of *The Lay Anthony* (1914; rev. in *Town Topics*, 22 October 1914, and SS, December 1914), *The Three Black Pennys* (1917; rev. in SS, December 1917), *Java Head* (1919; rev. in SS, March 1919), and *Cytherea* (1922; rev. in SS, April 1922). Hergesheimer became a close friend of HLM in the 1920s.

Herrick, Robert (1868–1938), novelist and short-story writer whose novels of middle-class society enjoyed considerable popularity in the first two decades of the twentieth century. HLM did not regard his work highly. See his reviews of *One Woman's Life* (1913; rev. in SS, June 1913) and *His Great Adventure* (1913; rev. in SS, January 1914).

Holst, Eduard (1843–1899), Danish composer of songs, pieces for a military band, and one opera. He is not to be confused with the well-known British composer Gustav Holst (1874–1934).

Holt, Henry (1840–1926), founder, in 1873, of the publishing company that bears his name. HLM poked fun at his ventures into spiritualism, as in the volume *On the Cosmic Relations* (1914).

Howard, Blanche Willis (1847–1898), novelist who wrote prolifically from the 1870s to the 1890s, including the best-sellers *One Summer* (1875) and *Guenn: A Wave on the Breton Coast* (1884).

Howe, E. W. (1853–1937), novelist and journalist whose novels—especially *The Story of a Country Town* (1883)—HLM regarded highly. HLM favorably reviewed his treatises *Success Easier Than Failure* (1917; rev. in SS, January 1918) and *The Blessing of Business* (1918; rev. in SS, April 1918), remarking cynically that they perfectly reflected the American ideal of money-making over aesthetic appreciation. HLM also reviewed his autobiography, *Plain People* (1929; rev. in AM, June 1929). HLM arranged for the publication of Howe's *Ventures into Common Sense* (1919) in his "Free Lance" series of books edited for Alfred A. Knopf.

Howells, William Dean (1837–1920), fiction writer, editor, and critic who was perhaps the most highly regarded American writer of the later nineteenth century, chiefly on the strength of *The Rise of Silas Lapham* (1885) and other novels of social realism. HLM, however, considered him only a second-rater. By the time HLM began reviewing, Howells's best days were over, and HLM's reviews of *New Leaf Mills* (1913; rev. in SS, June 1913) and *The Leatherwood God* (1916; rev. in SS, January 1917) are condescending at best. HLM did not think much of the memoir *My Mark Twain* (1910; rev. in SS, January 1911).

Hubbard, Elbert (1856–1915), editor and essayist who frequently printed his own work in fancy limited editions under his imprint, the Roycroft Press, inspired by William Morris's Kelmscott Press.

Hull, Edith Maude (?–?), British popular novelist who achieved best-seller status with *The Sheik* (1919; rev. in SS, October 1921), which was followed up by several other novels set in the Sahara, including *The Shadow of the East* (1921) and *The Sons of the Sheik* (1925).

Huneker, James Gibbons (1860–1921), critic, novelist, and memoirist who befriended HLM in the 1910s and exercised a considerable influence on his critical manner. HLM considered Huneker a pioneering American critic, especially in the realm of music criticism, and admired the vigor and iconoclasm of his writing. He regularly reviewed Huneker's works as they appeared: *Egoists* (1909; rev. in the *Baltimore Sun*, 11 April 1909, and SS, June 1909); *The Pathos of Distance* (1913; rev. in SS, October 1913); *Old Fogy* (1913; rev. in SS, July 1914); *New Cosmopolis* (1915; rev. in SS, July 1915); *Ivory, Apes and Peacocks* (1915; rev. in SS, December 1915); *Unicorns* (1917; rev. in SS, December 1917); the autobiography *Steeplejack* (1920; rev. in the *Literary Review [New York Evening Post]*, 2 September 1920, and SS, December 1920); etc. He devoted an extensive chapter to Huneker in *A Book of Prefaces* (1917). See also "James Huneker" (*Century Magazine*, June 1921); reprinted with revisions as "Huneker" (*P3*). HLM also edited a selection of Huneker's *Essays* (1929).

Huxley, Thomas Henry (1825–1895), pioneering naturalist and enthusiastic supporter of Darwin whose "plain English" and fearless challenging of religious orthodoxy were much appreciated by HLM. See HLM's "Huxley" (*CST*, 2 August 1895).

Huysmans, Joris-Karl (1848–1907), French novelist best known for the Decadent novels *A rebours* (1884; usually translated as *Against the Grain*) and *Là-bas* (1891).

Ibsen, Henrik (1828–1906), Norwegian dramatist. See HLM's extensive introductions to new translations of *A Doll's House* (1909), *Little Eyolf* (1909), and *The Master Builder, Pillars of Society, and Hedda Gabler* (1918).

Ingersoll, Robert G. (1833–1899), lawyer and essayist who became one of the most prominent freethinkers, agnostics, and lecturers in the later nineteenth century. See his *Some Mistakes of Moses* (1879) and other tracts attacking religion. See HLM's "Editorial" (AM, November 1924), speaking of the need for a new Ingersoll to challenge religious orthodoxy. (HLM himself filled such a role in his reporting on the Scopes trial in 1925 and in numerous other writings on religion.)

James, Henry (1843–1916), novelist and short-story writer. By the time HLM began reviewing, James had written most of his major works, and HLM managed to review only such minor volumes as *Julia Bride* (1909; rev. in SS, January 1910), *The Finer Grain* (1910; rev. in SS, March 1911), and *The Outcry* (1911; rev. in SS, January 1912). It becomes evident that HLM had little patience with James's mincing style or the excessively detailed psychological analyses of his characters, although he speaks frequently with praise of *What Maisie Knew* (1897).

James, William (1842–1910), philosopher and psychologist who attained celebrity with *The Varieties of Religious Experience* (1902) and *Pragmatism* (1907), which launched the American school of pragmatism. For HLM's cynical evaluation of James's fading popularity, see SS, May 1919.

Jesup, Morris K. (1830–1908), a wealthy banker who became a leading philanthropist, giving large amounts of money to a variety of organizations, notably the American Museum of Natural History.

Johns, Orrick (1887–1946), poet whose work was influenced by Whitman and A. E. Housman. HLM thought well of his early volume of poetry, *Asphalt and Other Poems* (1917; rev. in SS, November 1917).

Johnson, Owen (1878–1952), novelist and boys' writer. HLM thought *The Eternal Boy* (1909; rev. in SS, April 1909) "the best book about boys that I have ever read, saving only *Huckleberry Finn*," but did not think much of the daring *The Salamander* (1914; rev. in *Town Topics*, 18 June 1914, and in SS, August 1914), a novel about a prostitute. See also HLM's reviews of *The Woman Gives* (1916; rev. in SS, November 1916) and *Virtuous Wives* (1918; rev. in SS, November 1918), both of which he considered marred by conventionality.

Kellner, Leon (1859–1928), Polish literary historian whose *American Literature* (1915; rev. in SS, October 1915) HLM regarded with approbation. It is a translation of *Geschichte der nordamerikanischen Literatur* (1913). Among other works by Kellner translated into English are *Historical Outlines of English Syntax* (1892) and *Restoring Shakespeare* (1925).

Key, Ellen (1849–1926), Swedish feminist whose works, translated into English, French, German, and other languages, exercised a considerable influence in the first two decades of the twentieth century. They include *The Century of the Child* (1909), *The Education of the Child* (1910), *Love and Marriage* (1911; rev. in SS, September 1911), and *The Renaissance of Motherhood* (1914), and proposed various radical solutions to problems of women's status, motherhood, and the raising of children. Of *Love and Marriage* HLM wrote: "Let it suffice to praise Miss Key for an honest and in the main successful attempt to throw the light of reason into a subject long obscured by sentimentalists, special pleaders and muddle-headed theologians."

King, Charles (1844–1933), soldier and author of numerous popular novels about war and the conquest of the West, including *The Colonel's Daughter* (1883) and *Between the Lines* (1889).

Kipling, Rudyard (1865–1936), prolific British poet, novelist, and short-story writer. HLM was profoundly influenced by Kipling's ballads and tales in his own apprentice work, but he later came to despise Kipling for the latter's pro-British propaganda during World War I. See his reviews of the story collections *With the Night Mail* (1909; rev. in SS, June 1909) and *Abaft the Funnel* (1909) and *Actions and Reactions* (1909; rev. in SS, January 1910).

Krafft-Ebing, Richard, Freiherr von (1840–1902), German psychiatrist and author of the pioneering volume on sexual aberrations, *Psychopathia Sexualis* (1886).

Lagerlöf, Selma (1858–1940), Swedish novelist and the first woman to win the Nobel Prize for literature, in 1909. HLM reviewed only the short-story collection *The Girl from the Marsh Croft* (1910; rev. in SS, August 1910), noting that "the short stories here printed are, in the main, of an exceedingly commonplace sort."

Lardner, Ring (1885–1933), journalist, humorist, and author of numerous collections of stories and sketches, many of them written in a racy slang that accurately and vibrantly reflected American proletarian speech of the day. HLM reviewed several of Lardner's later volumes, including *You Know Me, Al* (1916; discussed in CST, 31 May 1925), *How to Write Short Stories* (1924; rev. in AM, July 1924), and others. Lardner's *Collected Short Stories* appeared in 1941.

Leblanc, Georgette (1869–1941), French memoirist and the wife of Maurice Maeterlinck. She wrote several volumes about her husband, including *Maeterlinck and I* (1932).

Lee, Vernon (pseud. of Violet Paget, 1856–1935), British novelist and essayist who lived largely in Italy and wrote a succession of critically acclaimed novels, tales, and travel volumes.

Lewis, Sinclair (1885–1951), novelist who, after several poorly received early works, achieved celebrity and critical renown with a succession of novels that HLM considered landmarks in social, political, and religious satire:

Main Street (1920; rev. in *SS*, January 1921), *Babbitt* (1922; rev. in *SS*, October 1922), *Arrowsmith* (1925; rev. in *CST*, 8 March 1925, and *AM*, April 1925), *Mantrap* (1926; rev. in *AM*, August 1926), *Elmer Gantry* (1927; rev. in *AM*, April 1927), *The Man Who Knew Coolidge* (1928; rev. in *AM*, June 1928), *Dodsworth* (1929; rev. in *AM*, April 1929), *Ann Vickers* (1933; rev. in *AM*, March 1933), and *It Can't Happen Here* (1936). Lewis received the Nobel Prize for literature in 1930.

Lewis, Wyndham (1882–1957), British novelist and critic associated with a variety of avant-garde literary movements in the 1910s and 1920s; best known for his editing (with Ezra Pound) of the magazine *Blast* (1914–15) and for the novels *Tarr* (1918) and *The Apes of God* (1930).

Lewisohn, Ludwig (1883–1955), editor, critic, and translator whose work HLM held in high regard. HLM reviewed several of his books, including his two autobiographies, *Up Stream* (1922; rev. in the *Nation*, 12 April 1922) and *Mid-Channel* (1929; rev. in *AM*, July 1929), his novel *The Case of Mr. Crump* (1926; rev. in *AM*, March 1927), and his treatise *The Modern Drama* (1915; rev. in *SS*, July 1915).

Lippmann, Walter (1889–1974), journalist and essayist whose volumes on politics and ethics were highly influential in their time. HLM wrote with wry amusement of his backhanded defenses of democracy in *Drift and Mastery* (1914; rev. in *SS*, April 1915), *Public Opinion* (1922; rev. in *SS*, June 1922), and *The Phantom Public* (1925; rev. in *AM*, January 1926). He also reviewed *A Preface to Morals* (1929; rev. in *AM*, July 1929): "His book is the work of a man of unusually eager and independent mind. It does not solve any of the problems it raises, but it gives every one of them a new clarity of statement, and so helps toward their solution later on."

London, Jack (1876–1916), prolific short-story writer and novelist. HLM regarded him as a highly skilled technician in the craft of writing but felt that much of his later work was crippled by overt didacticism in promoting Socialism. HLM reviewed many of his later works as they appeared. See also "Jack London" (P1).

Long, John Luther (1861–1927), short-story writer and playwright best known today for writing the story (later a play) upon which Puccini's opera *Madame Butterfly* was based. HLM passed a mixed verdict on his historical novel, *War* (1913; rev. in *SS*, June 1913).

Lowell, Amy (1874–1925), poet, critic, and leader of the Imagist movement in the 1910s and 1920s. HLM regarded her work with considerable skepticism. See his review of *Sword Blades and Poppy Seed* (1914; rev. in *SS*, May 1915).

Mabie, Hamilton Wright (1845–1916), editor and critic whose work HLM always regarded as prototypical of conventional, moralizing, unimaginative criticism.

MacGrath, Harold (1871–1932), journalist whose best-selling novels enjoyed a brief vogue. HLM tartly reviewed several of them: *The Goose Girl* (1909; rev. in SS, October 1909), *A Splendid Hazard* (1910; rev. in SS, July 1910), *The Carpet from Bagdad* (1911; rev. in SS, October 1911), and *Parrot & Company* (1913; rev. in SS, July 1913).

Machen, Arthur (1863–1947), Welsh mystic and short-story writer whose tales of horror and the supernatural enjoyed a vogue in the 1920s in the United States when they were republished by Alfred A. Knopf. HLM delivered a harsh verdict on them in SS, August 1923.

Mackaye, Percy (1875–1956), playwright, some of whose work was esteemed by HLM. See his reviews of *A Garland to Sylvia* (1910; rev. in SS, September 1910), in which he concluded that Mackaye was "the best dramatic poet that the United States has yet produced"; *Anti-Matrimony* (1910; rev. in SS, February 1911); and *To-morrow* (1912) and *Yankee Fantasies* (1912; rev. in SS, June 1912). HLM thought very little, however, of his treatise *The Playhouse and the Play* (1909; rev. in SS, August 1909).

MacLane, Mary (1881–1929), memoirist who wrote a scandalous autobiography, *The Story of Mary MacLane* (1902), which candidly discussed her frequent sexual escapades. HLM took note of its revision, *I, Mary MacLane* (1917). In 1918 she starred in a silent film adaptation of this work, playing herself.

Macy, John (1877–1932), critic whose treatise, *The Spirit of American Literature* (1913; rev. in SS, June 1917), was much appreciated by HLM for its iconoclastic treatment of hallowed American writers of the nineteenth century. HLM thought less well of his *The Critical Game* (1922; rev. in SS, March 1923).

Maeterlinck, Maurice (1862–1949), Belgian playwright and essayist whose work—notably the play *Pelléas et Mélisande* (1889) and *The Blue Bird* (1908)—enjoyed great popularity at the turn of the century. HLM expressed irritation at his vague mysticism and melancholy.

Manning, William Thomas (1866–1949), Episcopal clergyman most prominently associated with Trinity Parish in New York City. He was consecrated bishop of the Diocese of New York in 1921.

Mansfield, Katherine (pseud. of Kathleen Mansfield Beauchamp, 1888–1923), New Zealand–born British short-story writer whose experimental tales were highly regarded by the advanced intelligentsia. In his review of *The*

Dove's Nest and Other Stories (1923; rev. in *SS*, November 1923) HLM considered her overrated.

Masefield, John (1878–1967), a leading British poet, dramatist, and novelist who became poet laureate in 1930. HLM had a generally high opinion of his poetry, and also favorably reviewed the plays *The Tragedy of Nan* (1909; rev. in *SS*, February 1911) and *The Tragedy of Pompey the Great* (1913; rev. in *SS*, July 1914), but was less appreciative of the novel *Multitude and Solitude* (1909; rev. in *SS*, November 1912).

Mason, A. E. W. (1865–1948), British novelist and short-story writer best known today for his detective stories, notably *At the Villa Rose* (1910) and *The House of the Arrow* (1924). HLM took note of his mainstream novel, *The Turnstile* (1912; rev. in *SS*, November 1912).

Masters, Edgar Lee (1868–1950), poet whose *Spoon River Anthology* (1915) was a pioneering volume in its use of free verse and in its grim psychological realism. HLM appreciated it even before it appeared in book form, but had less regard for its sequel, *The New Spoon River* (1924; reviewed in *AM*, October 1925), as well as for other such poetry collections as *The Great Valley* (1916; rev. in *SS*, November 1917) and *Toward the Gulf* (1918; rev. in *SS*, June 1918) and for the novel *Mitch Miller* (1920). He had still less regard for the novel *Mirage* (1924; rev. in *AM*, June 1924), but he spoke glowingly of Masters's controversial biography, *Lincoln, the Man* (1931; rev. in *New York Herald Tribune Books*, 8 February 1931).

Matthews, Brander (1852–1929), well-known literary critic whose work HLM considered pedantic and hackneyed; but he praised *A Study of the Drama* (1910; rev. in *SS*, August 1910) as "book showing keen observation, wide knowledge, profitable reflection and good sense."

Merrick, Leonard (1864–1939), British novelist and short-story writer who enjoyed a vogue in the 1910s and 1920s. HLM reviewed *The Actor-Manager* (1898, 1912; rev. in *SS*, November 1912), *Conrad in Quest of His Youth* (1903, 1911; rev. in *SS*, August 1911), and *The Position of Peggy Harper* (1911; rev. in *SS*, July 1912), finding them entertaining but insubstantial.

Miller, Joaquin (1837–1913), California poet whose *Songs of the Sierras* (1871) created a great sensation in England and was the forerunner of a multitude of poetry collections, chiefly evoking the spirit of the frontier.

Mitchell, S. Weir (1829–1914), physician whose historical and other novels enjoyed popularity in their day. HLM reviewed *The Red City* (1907; rev. in *SS*, January 1909) and *Westways* (1913; rev. in *SS*, December 1913), which HLM found "second rate but workmanlike."

Monroe, Harriet (1860–1936), editor and poet who founded *Poetry* magazine in 1912 and made it the chief organ of avant-garde poetry in its day.

Montessori, Maria (1870–1952), Italian educator who designed the Montessori method, an educational system that sought to enhance the child's creative potential by the use of simple material objects in an unstructured classroom setting. It enjoyed a great vogue at the turn of the century, but HLM regarded it with considerable skepticism.

Moore, George (1862–1933), Anglo-Irish novelist and memoirist whom HLM regarded as one of the leading writers of his age. He sympathetically reviewed the three volumes of Moore's autobiography, *Hail and Farewell: Ave* (1911; rev. in *SS*, March 1912), *Salve* (1912; rev. in *SS*, February 1913), and *Vale* (1914; rev. in *SS*, October 1914). He also reviewed *A Story-Teller's Holiday* (1918; rev. in *SS*, December 1918) and *An Anthology of Pure Poetry* (1924; rev. in *AM*, October 1925).

More, Paul Elmer (1864–1937), prominent literary critic who achieved critical esteem with his eleven-volume series, *Shelburne Essays* (1904–21). HLM considered him a proponent of an attenuated and timorous classicism. HLM reviewed the last two volumes of the *Shelburne Essays: With the Wits* (1919; rev. in *SS*, February 1920) and *A New England Group* (1921; rev. in *SS*, June 1921), as well as *The Catholic Faith* (1931; rev. in *AM*, April 1932).

Morley, John, Viscount (1838–1923), British journalist and biographer best known for his lives of Edmund Burke (1867), Voltaire (1872), Richard Cobden (1881), Oliver Cromwell (1900), and William Ewart Gladstone (1903).

Morris, Gouverneur (1876–1953), short-story writer whose tales enjoyed great popularity in the first two decades of the twentieth century. They were collected in several volumes, including *The Footprint and Other Stories* (1908), *It and Other Stories* (1912), and *The Incandescent Lily and Other Stories* (1914).

Nathan, George Jean (1882–1958), editor and theater critic who became one of HLM's closest friends and colleagues. He assisted HLM in editing *SS* (1914–23) and for a time was a coeditor of *AM* (1924–25). His pungent theater reviews (beginning in *SS* in 1909) provoked much controversy. He collaborated with HLM on *Europe after 8.15* (1914), the play *Heliogabalus* (1920), and other works. He continued writing reviews for the next forty years, attaining celebrity with the annual *Theatre Book of the Year* (1943–51).

Nietzsche, Friedrich (1844–1900), revolutionary German philosopher whose anticlericalism and theories of the superman significantly influenced

HLM. See HLM's *The Philosophy of Friedrich Nietzsche* (1908); his slim selection, *The Gist of Nietzsche* (1910); and his translation of *The Antichrist* (1920). HLM wrote frequently of Nietzsche in *SS* (see the issues of November 1909, March 1910, March 1912, August 1913, and August 1915). See also "Nietzsche" (*CST*, 23 August 1925).

Norris, Frank (1870–1902), novelist whose early novels, *McTeague* (1899), *The Octopus* (1901), and *The Pit* (1903) were pioneering works of naturalism. HLM appreciatively reviewed the posthumous novel *Vandover and the Brute* (1914; rev. in *Town Topics*, 18 June 1914, and in *SS*, August 1914).

Norris, Kathleen (1880–1966), novelist and short-story writer whose many sentimental novels made her one of the most popular writers of the 1920s and 1930s.

Noyes, Alfred (1880–1959), popular British poet, playwright, and novelist who enjoyed great popularity in his day but for whom HLM had little esteem. He reviewed the poetry collections *The Enchanted Island and Other Poems* (1909; rev. in *SS*, August 1910) and *The Book of Earth* (1925; rev. in *AM*, October 1925) and the play *Sherwood, or Robin Hood and the Three Kings* (1911; rev. in *AM*, June 1912).

Ochs, Adolph (1858–1935), publisher who purchased the *New York Times* in 1896 and transformed it into one of the most distinguished and influential papers in the nation. HLM, however, considered the *Times* stodgy and its book reviews unadventurous.

Ollivant, Alfred (1874–1927), British popular novelist and author of *Bob, Son of Battle* (1898) and other works.

O'Neill, Eugene (1888–1953), leading dramatist whose early one-act plays HLM published in *SS*. HLM did not, however, formally review any of his volumes of plays.

Oppenheim, E. Phillips (1866–1946), prolific British author of novels of adventure and suspense. HLM reviewed several of them—*The Illustrious Prince* (1910; rev. in *SS*, September 1910), *The Moving Finger* (1910; rev. in *SS*, July 1911), *The Mischief-Maker* (1912; rev. in *SS*, May 1913), *A People's Man* (1914; rev. in *SS*, March 1914), and others—remarking of the first: "There is something going on every second."

Page, Thomas Nelson (1853–1922), Southern novelist and essayist who wrote numerous nostalgic and sentimental novels about the antebellum South. HLM found his story collection *The Land of the Spirit* (1913; rev. in *SS*, July 1913) full of "pifflish sentimentality."

Paul, Elliot H. (1891–1958), journalist and novelist whose novels *Indelible* (1922;

rev. in *SS*, August 1922) and *Impromptu* (1923) were highly regarded by the intelligentsia. With Eugene Jolas, he founded the avant-garde journal *transition* (1927), and still later he turned to the writing of detective novels.

Perry, Bliss (1860–1954), critic and editor who edited the *Atlantic Monthly* (1899–1909) and wrote numerous treatises on American literature. HLM reviewed his *The American Spirit in Literature* (1918; rev. in *SS*, July 1919), finding it "suave in manner" but with a "paucity of ideas."

Phelps, William Lyon (1865–1943), longtime professor at Yale University (1891–1933) and a prominent literary critic of his day. Although praising Phelps's early championing of Mark Twain, HLM condemned him for the superficiality of his critical judgments and his neglect of important modern poets, novelists, and dramatists. See HLM's reviews of *Essays on Modern Novelists* (1910; rev. in *SS*, June 1910), *Essays on Russian Novelists* (1911; rev. in *SS*, June 1911), *The Advance of the English Novel* (1916; rev. in *SS*, June 1917), *The Advance of English Poetry* (1918; rev. in *SS*, January 1919), *Essays on Modern Dramatists* (1921; rev. in *BES*, 23 April 1921), and other works.

Phillips, David Graham (1867–1911), novelist and journalist who wrote more than twenty novels in just over a decade (1901–11). Although HLM felt that some of his work was marred by appeals to popular taste, he felt that the novels *The Hungry Heart* (1909; rev. in *SS*, December 1909) and *The Husband's Story* (1911; rev. in *SS*, January 1911) were among the best novels of their time; at this time he even pronounced Phillips the leading American novelist. HLM also reviewed *The Grain of Dust* (1911; rev. in *SS*, July 1911). Phillips's life was cut short when he was killed in Gramercy Park in New York.

Phillpotts, Eden (1862–1960), prolific British novelist whose tales of adventure and romance, chiefly set in Dartmoor, enjoyed great popularity in their day. HLM, however, professed an inability to read him.

Pinero, Arthur Wing (1855–1934), British playwright whose numerous "well-made" plays enjoyed great popularity on both the British and the American stage in the 1880s and 1890s until they were superseded by the work of Ibsen and Shaw.

Poe, Edgar Allan (1809–1849), poet, short-story writer, and critic about whom HLM had mixed feelings. Scorning his poetry as sing-song and his tales as shilling shockers, HLM nonetheless felt that Poe—chiefly on the strength of his trenchant and often vituperative essays and reviews—was one of the leading American writers of the nineteenth century, with Twain and Whitman.

Pollard, Percival (1869–1911), critic and journalist whose review columns in *Town Topics* (1897–1911) and his several volumes of criticism—*Their Day in Court* (1909; rev. in *SS*, February 1910), *Masks and Minstrels of New Germany* (1911; rev. in *BES*, 29 April 1911, and *SS*, August 1911), and others—influenced HLM in their outspoken challenging of literary orthodoxy.

Poole, Ernest (1880–1950), journalist and novelist whose proletarian novels—notably his first, *The Harbor* (1915; rev. in *SS*, June 1915)—were well received in their day. HLM found this novel disappointing, and called *His Second Wife* (1918; rev. in *SS*, August 1918) "a piece of mush."

Porter, Gene Stratton (1863–1924), popular novelist whose sentimental novels of Indiana life were leavened by a love of nature. HLM reviewed one of her best-known novels, *Laddie* (1913; rev. in *SS*, November 1913), remarking that she wrote deftly but that her story was "commonplace and tedious."

Pound, Ezra (1885–1972), poet and critic whose revolutionary work was early appreciated by HLM; see his reviews of *Provença* (1910; rev. in *SS*, April 1911) and *Lustra* (1917; rev. in *SS*, June 1918) and of the essay collection *The Instigations of Ezra Pound* (1920; rev. in *SS*, August 1920). HLM also found his *Antheil and the Treatise on Harmony* (1924, 1927; rev. in *AM*, August 1928) entertaining.

Rascoe, Burton (1892–1957), journalist and critic who was the literary and drama editor of the *Chicago Tribune* (1912–20) and then worked for several newspapers in New York. He wrote such treatises as *Theodore Dreiser* (1925) and *Titans of Literature* (1932).

Rideout, Henry Milner (1877–1927), novelist whom HLM found to be promising, but who he felt ruined his talents by catering to the popular magazines. See HLM's reviews of *Dragon's Blood* (1909; rev. in *SS*, July 1909) and *The Twisted Foot* (1910; rev. in *SS*, July 1910).

Riley, James Whitcomb (1849–1916), Indiana poet whose voluminous poetry—much of it written in Hoosier dialect—won him great popularity but also much ridicule from fastidious critics like Ambrose Bierce and HLM.

Rinehart, Mary Roberts (1876–1958), novelist who won instant popularity with *The Circular Staircase* (1908; rev. in *SS*, November 1908) and many other detective novels. HLM reviewed several of the earlier ones—*The Man in Lower Ten* (1909; rev. in *SS*, June 1909); *When a Man Marries* (1909; rev. in *SS*, February 1910); *The Window at the White Cat* (1910; rev. in *SS*, November 1910); *The Case of Jennie Brice* (1913; rev. in *SS*, May 1913), finding them competent works of their kind. Rinehart also wrote humorous stories about a vigorous spinster, Letitia Carberry, the first of which—*The Amazing Adventures of Letitia Carberry* (1911; rev. in SS, February 1912)—HLM thought was "in Mrs. Rinehart's very best manner."

Robins, Elizabeth (1862–1952), actress and novelist who was the first woman to play *Hedda Gabler* in London. She published novels under the pseudonym C. E. Raimond. Under her own name she wrote a sentimental novel about white slavery, *My Little Sister* (1913; rev. in SS, May 1913), which HLM ridiculed.

Roe, E. P. (1838–1888), clergyman and author of numerous best-selling novels in the 1870s and 1880s.

Rose, Edward E. (1862–1939), playwright. He was one of the most prolific adapters of popular novels for the stage in his time; among his adaptations are *The Prisoner of Zenda* (1895), *David Harum* (1900), and *Penrod* (1918).

Sandburg, Carl (1878–1967), poet and biographer. HLM found much merit in his *Chicago Poems* (1916; rev. in SS, February 1917) as well as in his collection of updated fairy tales, *Rootabaga Stories* (1922; rev. in SS, March 1923) and his collection of folksongs, *The American Songbag* (1927; rev. in AM, March 1928). Of the first installment of Sandburg's biography of Lincoln, *Abraham Lincoln: The Prairie Years* (1926; rev. in AM, July 1926), HLM remarked: "No man has ever written of the young Lincoln with a finer insight, or with greater eloquence."

Sanger, Margaret (1879–1966), founder of the birth control movement in the U.S. She founded and edited the *Birth Control Review*, for which HLM wrote a brief article on Havelock Ellis, "Man of Science, Artist and Gentleman" (February 1926). HLM wrote an extensive review of one of her tracts on birth control, *The Pivot of Civilization* (1922; rev. in SS, February 1923), saying that it was "lyrical and sometimes almost hysterical."

Schnitzler, Arthur (1862–1931), German playwright and novelist whose sexually daring psychological novels and plays created controversy. HLM reviewed the play *Professor Bernhardi* (1913; rev. in SS, December 1913), but found it "pretty dull stuff."

Scott, Leroy (1875–1929), author of numerous popular novels in the 1910s and 1920s.

Serao, Mathilde (1856–1927), Italian novelist and journalist who wrote numerous novels and tales (mostly focusing on women's issues) in the 1880s and 1890s. At the turn of the century she was one of the most widely translated authors of her time.

Service, Robert W. (1874–1958), English-born poet who migrated to Canada in 1902, served in World War I, and settled in France after the war. Of his numerous novels and poetry volumes, which attained great popularity in the 1920s, HLM reviewed only the novel *The Trail of '98* (1911; rev. in *SS*, June 1911), finding both flaws and merits in this tale of the Klondike gold rush.

Shaw, George Bernard (1856–1950), Anglo-Irish playwright. HLM's first treatise was *George Bernard Shaw: His Plays* (1905). He consistently reviewed Shaw's new plays as they appeared in book form—*Man and* Superman (1903; rev. in the *Baltimore Sunday Herald*, 30 October 1904); *The Doctor's Dilemma* (1907), *Getting Married* (1910), and other works (rev. in *SS*, August 1911); *Misalliance* (1911) and other works (rev. in *Town Topics*, 16 July 1914); *Androcles and the Lion* (1912; rev. in *SS*, August 1916); etc. HLM generally concluded that Shaw, with his immense technical skill in dramaturgy, had a penchant for uttering the obvious in a scandalous manner and thereby provoking controversy.

Sherman, Stuart P. (1881–1926), critic and editor who earned HLM's scorn for the superficiality and parochialism of his judgments, especially in his championing of a narrowly "American" ideal of literature. HLM savaged his *Americans* (1922; rev. in *SS*, March 1923) and also heaped abuse on a small pamphlet issued at the end of World War I, *American and Allied Ideals* (1918), which he felt embodied the worst of Sherman's thought. Later he reviewed Sherman's *Life and Letters*, edited by Jacob Zeitlin and Homer Woodbridge (1929; rev. in *AM*, December 1929).

Sinclair, Upton (1878–1968), novelist, journalist, and political activist whose numerous and multifarious attempts at social and economic reform (chiefly of a Socialist variety) earned HLM's continual scorn and amusement. He attained celebrity with the novel *The Jungle* (1906), exposing the appalling conditions of the Chicago stockyards. HLM took note of many of his subsequent works, including the novel *The Moneychangers* (1908; rev. in *SS*, November 1908), *The Brass Check: A Study of American Journalism* (1919; rev. in *SS*, April 1920), *The Book of Life, Mind and Body* (1921; rev. in *SS*, July 1922), *The Goose-Step: A Study of American Education* (1923; rev. in *SS*, May 1923), *Money Writes!* (1927; rev. in *AM*, February 1928), and *The Wet Parade* (1931; rev. in the *Nation*, 23 September 1931). HLM actually agreed with many of Sinclair's criticisms of American journalism, education, and politics, but his congenital distaste for anything smacking of "uplift" prevented him from envisaging that any of Sinclair's reforms would have any effect.

Smith, F. Hopkinson (1838–1915), short-story writer and novelist whose novels and tales were popular from the 1890s to the 1910s. HLM took note of some of his later works: *Peter* (1908; rev. in *SS*, November 1908), *Forty*

Minutes Late (1909; rev. in SS, January 1910), and *Kennedy Square* (1911; rev. in SS, November 1911), finding them saccharine and lacking in ingenuity and wit.

Spingarn, Joel E. (1875–1939), literary critic whose *Creative Criticism* (1917; rev. in SS, August 1917) was lauded by HLM for its scorn of didacticism and its emphasis on the critic's aesthetic sensitivity.

Stearns, Harold (1891–1943), journalist and essayist. HLM reviewed his *Liberalism in America* (1919; rev. in SS, May 1920), finding it "a capital piece of work—temperate, well-informed, well-reasoned, extremely well-written." HLM also read (but did not review) *America and the Young Intellectual* (1921) and contributed a chapter on "Politics" to Stearns's compilation *Civilization in the United States* (1922). Stearns was one of the first of the American expatriates, living in Paris for most of the 1920s. See his autobiography, *The Street I Know* (1935).

Stedman, Edmund Clarence (1833–1908), poet, critic, and editor best known for such anthologies as *Poets of America* (1885) and *An American Anthology* (1900). Although an early champion of Walt Whitman, he nonetheless symbolized for HLM an attitude of Victorian rectitude still prevailing in the literary criticism of the early twentieth century.

Stendhal (pseud. of Henri Beyle, 1783–1842), French novelist, essayist, and journalist best known for the novels *Le Rouge et le noir* (1830; *The Red and the Black*) and *La Chartreuse de Parme* (1839; *The Charterhouse of Parma*).

Sterling, George (1869–1926), California poet who attained local renown with *The Testimony of the Suns* (1903), *A Wine of Wizardry* (1909), and other volumes of lushly evocative verse, but whose hostility to the Modernists spelled his doom as a voice in contemporary American poetry. A longtime correspondent of HLM (see *From Baltimore to Bohemia: The Letters of H. L. Mencken and George Sterling*, ed. S. T. Joshi [Rutherford, N.J.: Fairleigh Dickinson University Press, 2001]), he was disappointed that HLM never reviewed any of his volumes of verse or drama, including *Selected Poems* (1923).

Stirner, Max (1806–1856), German philosopher whose chief treatise, *Der Einzige und sein Eigenthum* (1844; trans. as *The Ego and His Own*, 1907) aroused controversy by its rejection of conventional moral and religious values.

Street, Julian (1879–1947), Chicago journalist and novelist who later became an authority on gastronomy and wines. In this context HLM glowingly reviewed his *Wines: Their Selection, Care and Service* (1933; rev. in the *Nation*, 14 February 1934).

Sunday, Billy (1862?-1935), itinerant evangelist who became immensely popular in the first two decades of the twentieth century for his histrionic outdoor sermons. HLM accompanied him on one of these lecture circuits for a few days in 1916, reporting pungently about Sunday and his antics (see *BES*, 17 February, 14 and 27 March, 2 May 1916), and also reviewed William T. Ellis's *Billy Sunday: The Man and His Message* (1914; rev. in *SS*, July 1916).

Synge, J. M. (1871–1909), Irish playwright whose plays were enthusiastically welcomed by HLM. See his review of *Riders to the Sea* (1905) and *The Tinker's Wedding* (1908; rev. in *SS*, August 1911) and of a collected edition of Synge (*SS*, October 1912).

Taine, Hippolyte (1828–1893), French critic and literary historian whom HLM regarded as a prototype of the academic literary critic.

Tarkington, Booth (1869–1946), Indiana novelist and playwright who attained tremendous popularity with such novels as *The Gentleman from Indiana* (1899), *Penrod* (1914; rev. in *Town Topics*, 25 June 1914, and in *SS*, August 1914), and *The Magnificent Ambersons* (1918). HLM also reviewed *Ramsey Milholland* (1919; rev. in *SS*, October 1919) and *Alice Adams* (1921; rev. in *SS*, October 1921). HLM thought *Penrod* "an amazingly accurate and amusing picture of a small boy," but felt that *Alice Adams* was "a bit too well-made, too direct and flashy, too slick and logical." Both *The Magnificent Ambersons* and *Alice Adams* won the Pulitzer Prize.

Teasdale, Sara (1884–1933), poet whose delicate lyrics HLM found some of the more effective verse of their time. He reviewed *Helen of Troy and Other Poems* (1911; rev. in *SS*, May 1912), *Rivers to the Sea* (1915; rev. in *SS*, May 1916), and *Love Songs* (1917; rev. in *SS*, June 1918).

Thanet, Octave (pseud. of Alice French, 1850–1934), novelist and short-story writer whose tales focused on local color and economic issues. Of her *By Inheritance* (1910; rev. in *SS*, June 1910) HLM commented that it was "far from a masterpiece, but it is written earnestly and with skill, and it shows a sound knowledge of Southern problems and the Southern people."

Thayer, Scofield (1889–1982), editor of the cutting-edge Chicago literary journal, the *Dial*, from 1919 to 1926.

Thomas, Augustus (1857–1934), actor and playwright whose plays—notably *The Witching Hour* (1907) and *As a Man Thinks* (1911; rev. in *SS*, October 1911)—were popular in their day. HLM thought the latter play "piffle."

Timrod, Henry (1828–1867), South Carolina poet who was regarded as the leading Southern poet of his era.

Townsend, Edward W. (1855–1942), novelist and short-story writer best known for a volume of dialect stories, *"Chimmie Fadden"; Major Max; and Other Stories* (1895). HLM reviewed the comic novel *The Climbing Courvatels* (1909; rev. in *SS*, May 1909), calling it "an excellent story maimed in the telling."

Trites, W. B. (1872–?), British novelist who enjoyed brief critical esteem in the 1910s when he was hailed by William Dean Howells. Of the novel *John Cave* (1909; rev. in *SS*, August 1913) HLM remarked that "there is nothing very profound in it, and certainly nothing very artistic."

Twain, Mark (pseud. of Samuel Langhorne Clemens, 1835–1910), novelist, short-story writer, and essayist. HLM vaunted *Adventures of Huckleberry Finn* (1885) as one of the great works of American literature, and had much praise for *Life on the Mississippi* (1883), *A Connecticut Yankee in King Arthur's Court* (1889), *Extract from Captain Stormfield's Visit to Heaven* (1909), *The Mysterious Stranger* (posthumously published in 1916), and the philosophical dialogue *What Is Man?* (1905). Other books discussed by HLM are *The Adventures of Tom Sawyer* (1876), the travel books *The Innocents Abroad* (1869) and *A Tramp Abroad* (1880), and *Personal Recollections of Joan of Arc* (1896).

Untermeyer, Louis (1885–1977), poet, critic, and anthologist whose early verse—included in such volumes as *First Love* (1911; rev. in *SS*, April 1913), *Challenge* (1914; rev. in *Town Topics*, 30 July 1914), and *"—And Other Poets"* (1917; rev. in *SS*, November 1917)—HLM admired for its wit and technical brilliance. But HLM thought Untermeyer even better as a critic than as a poet, and he found his *The New Era in American Poetry* (1919; rev. in *SS*, July 1919) to be "the first cogent and exhaustive statement of the case for the new poetry by one who has helped to give it form and direction."

Van Doren, Carl (1885–1950), editor and critic who taught at Columbia University (1911–30) and was the managing editor of *The Cambridge History of American Literature* (1917–21; see HLM's reviews in *SS*, February 1918, July 1919, and June 1921, although Van Doren is not mentioned in these reviews). HLM had much admiration for Van Doren's volumes of criticism and biography, including *The American Novel* (1921; rev. in *SS*, September 1921), *Swift: A Biography* (1930; rev. in *New York Herald Tribune Books*, 19 October 1930), and his autobiography, *Three Worlds* (1936; rev. in the *Nation*, 19 September 1936).

van Dyke, Henry (1852–1933), clergyman and essayist who achieved tremendous popularity with a succession of volumes on religion, nature, and personal conduct. HLM felt that his work was a byword for unoriginality and superficiality of thought. HLM excoriated him in his reviews of the story collection *The Unknown Quantity* (1912; rev. in *SS*, February 1913) and *Six Days of the Week: A Book of Thoughts about Life and Religion* (1924; rev. in *SS*, March 1925). The latter review consists of nothing but quotations of banal utterances from the volume.

Van Loon, Hendrik Willem (1882–1944), Dutch historian and journalist who settled in the United States in the early twentieth century. He became well known for two celebrated historical works, *The Fall of the Dutch Republic* (1913) and *The Rise of the Dutch Kingdom* (1915), but achieved greater popular acclaim for *The Story of Mankind* (1921). In 1921 he became HLM's colleague when he was hired as assistant editor of the *Baltimore Sun*.

Verhaeren, Emile (1855–1916), Belgian poet and playwright who was frequently deemed "the Belgian Walt Whitman" for his use of symbolism and free verse forms. He died in France while fleeing the German occupation of Belgium in World War I.

Wallace, Lew (1827–1905), lawyer and soldier who achieved spectacular fame as the best-selling author of *Ben-Hur: A Tale of the Christ* (1880) and *The Prince of India* (1893).

Walpole, Hugh (1884–1941), British novelist whose work HLM regarded as solid but not first-rate. He reviewed numerous works by Walpole: *The Gods and Mr. Perrin* (1911; rev. in *SS*, February 1912), *The Duchess of Wrexe* (1914; rev. in *SS*, December 1914), *The Green Mirror* (1917; rev. in *SS*, March 1918), and *The Cathedral* (1922; rev. in *SS*, March 1923), and also spoke highly of the treatise *Joseph Conrad* (1916; rev. in *SS*, October 1916).

Watts, Mary Stanbery (1868–1958), novelist whose realistic novels HLM considered some of the better work of their day. See his reviews of *Van Cleve* (1913; rev. in *SS*, January 1914) and *The Rise of Jennie Cushing* (1914; rev. in *SS*, January 1915).

Wells, H. G. (1866–1946), prolific British novelist and historian. HLM dismissed his early science-fiction novels, but regarded his later novels of social realism—*Tono-Bungay* (1909; rev. in *SS*, April 1909), *Ann Veronica* (1909; rev. in *SS*, February 1910), *The History of Mr. Polly* (1910; rev. in *SS*, July 1910), *The New Machiavelli* (1911; rev. in *SS*, April 1911), *Marriage* (1912; rev. in *SS*, January 1913)—as some of the best novels of the period. HLM felt that Wells's subsequent novels revealed a disastrous falling off, an opinion recorded in the essay "The Late Mr. Wells" (*SS*, August 1918; reprinted in *P1*). But HLM felt that Wells made a striking comeback with the treatises *The Outline of History* (1920; rev. in *BES*, 10 January 1921, and in *SS*, March 1921), *The Science of Life* (1931; rev. in *AM*, March 1931), and *The Work, Wealth and Happiness of Mankind* (1931; rev. in *AM*, April 1932). He also reviewed Wells's *Experiment in Autobiography* (1934; rev. in the *Nation*, 14 November 1934).

Wharton, Edith (1862–1937), novelist of New York society whose many novels — including *The House of Mirth* (1905) and *The Age of Innocence* (1920; rev. in *SS*, February 1921) — have given her high rank among American writers of her time. HLM, however, had praise only for the grim New England tale *Ethan Frome* (1911; rev. in *SS*, December 1911), and had little regard for her subsequent work.

Whitman, Stephen French (1880–?), novelist and short-story writer active in the 1910s to 1930s. HLM reviewed *Predestined* (1910; rev. in *SS*, June 1910) and *The Isle of Life* (1913; rev. in *SS*, June 1913), finding much merit in the first but being extremely disappointed with the second: "I know of no more lamentable collapse of a talent clearly pledged to serious and dignified things."

Whitman, Walt (1819–1892), poet and journalist and one of the leading writers of the nineteenth century, chiefly on the strength of *Leaves of Grass* (1855). HLM had high regard for him; his most exhaustive comments on his place in American literature occur sporadically through the long essay "The National Letters" (*P2*). HLM also took note of the posthumous compilation *Uncollected Poetry and Prose*, edited by Emory Holloway (1921; rev. in *SS*, January 1922).

Williams, William Carlos (1883–1963), poet, novelist, and playwright who helped to usher in a new era in American poetry with such works as *Paterson* (1946–51) and the prose work *In the American Grain* (1925). HLM did not think much of the poetry volume *Al Que Quiere!* (1917; rev. in *SS*, June 1918).

Wilson, Harry Leon (1867–1939), novelist, short-story writer, and playwright whose humorous tales HLM found stimulating: *Bunker Bean* (1912; rev. in *SS*, May 1913), *Ruggles of Red Gap* (1915; rev. in *SS*, June 1915), and *Somewhere in Red Gap* (1916; rev. in *SS*, December 1916).

Winter, William (1836–1917), prolific drama critic for the *New York Tribune*, *Harper's Weekly*, and other papers. HLM had little respect for his work.

Wise, Stephen S. (1874–1949), rabbi, Zionist leader, and one of the most prominent and distinguished Jewish Americans of his time. He founded the Free Synagogue in New York in 1907 and served there for the rest of his life. Devoted to a succession of liberal causes, he helped to found the

NAACP (1909) and the ACLU (1920). He was a longtime president of the American Jewish Congress (1925–49).

Wister, Owen (1860–1938), novelist, essayist, and biographer who attained best-seller status with *The Virginian* (1902), a western.

Woodberry, George E. (1855–1930), critic, poet, and editor best known for his biographies of Hawthorne (1902), Emerson (1907), and Poe (1909). HLM regarded his poetry as academic and lifeless.

Worcester, Elwood (1862–1940), clergyman and voluminous writer on religion, including such works as *The Book of Genesis in the Light of Modern Knowledge* (1901). See his autobiography, *Life's Adventure* (1932).

Wright, Harold Bell (1872–1944), clergyman and author of a succession of novels that made him one of the most popular writers of the first three decades of the twentieth century. HLM had nothing but scorn for his work; he formally reviewed only *The Calling of Dan Matthews* (1909; rev. in SS, November 1909), saying of it: "The author's style wanders far from the canons of good English, but his story shows no little earnestness and plausibility. It is, in brief, not half so bad as the publisher's encomiums lead you to expect."

Ziegfeld, Florenz (1869–1932), Broadway producer and founder in 1907 of the Ziegfeld Follies.

Index

Adam Bede (Eliot), 7
Adams, James Trunslow, 236 n. 9
Addams, Jane, 118
Ade, George, 6, 176, 210
Adventures of Huckleberry Finn (Twain), xii, 8, 24, 25, 27, 30, 32–33, 39, 155, 217
Adventures of Tom Sawyer, The (Twain), 30, 33
Age of Innocence, The (Wharton), 149–50
Akins, Zoë, 95
Aldrich, Nelson Wilmarth, 188
Alexander's Bridge (Cather), xiv, 73–74, 75
"Alibi Ike" (Lardner), 164
Alice Adams (Tarkington), 92
Alice in Wonderland (Carroll), 7
Allen, James Lane, xii, 40, 218
All's Well, 194
Almayer's Folly (Conrad), 4
"Alpine School of Fiction, The" (Atherton), 198
Ambrose Bierce: A Biography (McWilliams), 144–47
American and Allied Ideals (Sherman), 225
American Language, The (Mencken), viii, xviii
American Literature (Kellner), 214–19
American Literature, 1607–1885 (Richardson), 68
American Mercury, vii, xiv, xvii, xviii, 94
American Tragedy, An (Dreiser), 68–73
Americans (Sherman), 225–27
Anderson, Margaret, 194, 229–33
Anderson, Sherwood, xiv–xv, 81, 83–94
Andrewes, Lancelot, 228
Ann Vickers (Lewis), 133–36, 169
Anna Karenina (Tolstoi), 40
Aristophanes, 166

Aristotle, 63
Arnold, Matthew, 8
Arrowsmith (Lewis), 121–24, 131, 136
Atherton, Gertrude, xiv, 191, 198–204, 208
Atlantic Monthly, 155
Aucassin et Nicolette, 102
Authors' League of America, 1

Babbitt (Lewis), xvi, 17, 118–21, 124, 127, 128, 131, 132, 133, 136
Babbitt, Irving, 140, 227–28, 229
Bach, Johann Sebastian, 151–52
Baer, Bugs, 165
Balfour, Arthur James, 195
Baltimore Evening Sun, vii, viii, xviii
Baltimore Herald, vii, viii
Balzac, Honoré de, 217
Bambi (Cooke), xiii, 180–83
Bashkirtseff, Marie, 190, 242 n. 7
Beach, Rex, 101
Beautiful and Damned, The (Fitzgerald), 110–11, 114
Beethoven, Ludwig van, 23, 74, 221, 244 n. 7
Belasco, David, 12, 13
Benét, William Rose, 194
Bennett, Arnold, 222
Bergson, Henri, 48
Berkeley, George, 62
Beyond Life (Cabell), 98–100, 102
Bhagavad Gita, 178
Bierce, Ambrose, x, xii, xiv, 143–47, 212, 217
Bitter Bierce (Grattan), 145
Black Oxen (Atherton), 198–204
Boccaccio, Giovanni, 212
Bonheur, Rosa, 180
Book of Prefaces, A (Mencken), vii
Bookman, 14, 18, 198, 202

Booth, Franklin, 65
Bourget, Paul, 150
Boyer, Norman, viii, 13
Brahms, Johannes, 85, 103–4, 184
Brisbane, Arthur, 36
Brooks, Van Wyck, 194
Brothers Karamazov, The (Dostoevsky), 7, 48
Broun, Heywood, 194
Brown, Alice, 85
Brownell, W. C., 211
Browning, Robert, 8
Bruno, Guido, 229
Bryan, William Jennings, 188, 193
Bryant, William Cullen, 218
Bryce, James, 239 n. 41
Bulwer-Lytton, Edward, 5
Bunker Bean (Wilson), 7
Butcher, Fanny, 194
Butler, Ellis Parker, 32
Butler, Samuel, 5
Byron, George Gordon, Lord, 5, 8, 34, 43

Cabell, James Branch, xi, xiii, xiv, xv, xvi, 81, 85, 94, 95–109, 115, 162, 170, 199
Cahan, Abraham, 75, 159–62, 225
Caine, Hall, 5
Cambridge History of American Literature, The, 20
Canby, Henry Seidel, 194
Cannon, James, 170, 227
Captain Stormfield's Visit to Heaven (Twain), 25, 32
Carlyle, Thomas, 7–8
Carnegie, Andrew, 225
Cather, Willa, x, xiii, xiv, 14, 17, 73–83, 85, 92, 115, 164, 204
"Celebrated Jumping Frog of Calaveras County, The"(Twain), 32
Century Magazine, 77
Cervantes, Miguel de, 217
Chambers, Robert W., xii, 68, 193, 203, 213
Chaminade, Cécile, 85
Chesterton, G. K., 191
Chicago Daily News, 230
Chicago Evening Post, 230
Chicago Sunday Tribune, xviii
Chopin, Frédéric, 151, 223
Christian Science, 54–55, 65, 228, 230
Christianity, 125–28, 155–57, 225, 227–29
Christiansen, Carrie, 145

Churchill, Winston, xiv, xvi, 17, 183–90
Cicero, M. Tullius, 118
Clemens, Samuel Langhorne. *See* Twain, Mark
Clemm, Virginia, 34
Collier, Old Cap, 209
Comfort, Will Levington, 150, 176–79
"Coming, Aphrodite!" (Cather), 77
Comstock, Anthony, xiii, 4, 11, 16, 69, 92, 104, 157, 194
Congreve, William, 213
Connecticut Yankee in King Arthur's Court, A (Twain), 25, 27, 32
Conrad, Joseph, viii, 3–4, 8, 40, 48, 49–50, 54, 61–63, 97, 147, 159, 212, 222, 223
Coogler, J. Gordon, 194
Cooke, Marjorie Benton, xiii, xiv, 180–83
Coolidge, Calvin, 106, 128, 131
Cooper, James Fenimore, 8, 28, 40, 215, 226
Corelli, Marie, 73
Corot, Jean-Baptiste-Camille, 180
Cosmopolitan, xiii, 115
Crabbe, George, 209
Crane, Frank, 21
Crawford, F. Marion, 68
Cream of the Jest, The (Cabell), 97, 98
Creel, George, 137, 225, 226
Crile, George W., 84
Crime de Sylvestre Bonnard, Le (France), 8
Croce, Benedetto, 194
Cytherea (Hergesheimer), 15

Daily Mail (London), 190
"Danse de Nymphes" (Corot), 180
Danziger, Gustav Adolphe. *See* de Castro, Adolphe (Danziger)
Dark Laughter (Anderson), 93–94
Dauthendey, Max, 215
Davis, Richard Harding, 68, 214
Davis, Robert H., 183, 242 n. 3
Day, Holman F., 68
Death Comes for the Archbishop (Cather), 82–83
Death in the Afternoon (Hemingway), xiv, xviii, 140–42
"Death in the Desert, A" (Cather), 77
"Death in the Woods" (Anderson), 94
Debs, Eugene V., 180
De Casseres, Benjamin, 194
de Castro, Adolphe (Danziger), 145
De Kruif, Paul H., 124

Delineator, 115
Dell, Floyd, 17
Dempsey, Jack, 118
Devil's Dictionary, The (Bierce), x, 144
Dial, 14, 68, 194, 218, 232
Díaz, Porfirio, 3
Dickens, Charles, 5
"Discounters of Money, The" (O. Henry), 176
Divine Comedy, The (Dante), 8
Dixon, Thomas, Jr., xiv, 101, 204–8
Dodsworth (Lewis), 129–33
Doll's House, A (Ibsen), 12, 15
Dos Passos, John, 79, 80, 136–39
Dostoevsky, Feodor, 7, 150, 154
Double-Dealer, 194
Doughty, Leonard, 199, 202, 242 n. 11
Doyle, Sir Arthur Conan, 150
Dragon's Blood (Rideout), 212
Dreiser, Theodore, viii, x, xi, xii, xiii, 4–5, 6, 14, 15–16, 17, 39–73, 76, 81, 83, 86, 91–92, 111, 115, 117, 157, 183–84, 199, 216, 222, 223, 235 n. 5, 236 n. 13
Dresser, Paul, 67, 238 n. 21
Dunsany, Lord, xv, xvi

Eagle's Shadow, The (Cabell), 96
Eddy, Mary Baker, 90, 228, 230
Edgar Allan Poe: A Study in Genius (Krutch), 33–35
Edwards, Jonathan, 224, 226
Einstein, Albert, 228
Eliot, Charles W., 17
Eliot, George, 7
Eliot, T. S., xvii, 227–29
Elmer Gantry (Lewis), xvi, 124–29, 131, 133, 135, 136, 168
Emerson, Ralph Waldo, 8, 15, 21, 25, 27–28, 29, 30, 35–37, 115, 209, 215, 226, 238 n. 30
English Traits (Emerson), 215
Enraptured Yankee, The (Michaud), 35–37
Erewhon (Butler), 5
Essay on Man, An (Pope), 8
Ethan Frome (Wharton), 6, 148
Euripides, 62

Fables in Slang (Ade), 6
Fadiman, Clifton, 167
Far Country, A (Churchill), xvi, 183–90
Farewell to Arms, A (Hemingway), xviii, 139–40

Farrar, John, 202
Fate Knocks at the Door (Comfort), 176–79
Fergusson, Harvey, 82
Fichte, Johann Gottlieb, 62
Figures of Earth (Cabell), 104–5
Financier, The (Dreiser), 44–48, 51, 52, 57
Finer Grain, The (James), 38–39
Finger, Charles J., 194
Firkins, Oscar W., 194
Fiske, John, 218
Fitzgerald, F. Scott, xv, xviii, 109–14, 164
Fitzpatrick, Vincent, xvi
Flappers and Philosophers (Fitzgerald), 111
Flaubert, Gustave, 50
Floradora, 2, 235 n. 2
Follett, Helen, xii, 219–22
Follett, Wilson, xii, 219–22
For Lancelot Andrewes (Eliot), 227–29
Founding of New England, The (Adams), 236 n. 9
France, Anatole, 8, 98, 101, 102, 108
Franklin, Sidney, 142
Frederick the Great (Carlyle), 7
Freeman, 194
Freud, Sigmund, 72, 73, 91, 93, 169, 225, 227
Freytag-Loringhoven, Elsa von, 232
"Friends in San Rosario" (O. Henry), 175
Frohman, Charles, 12, 183
Fuller, Henry Blake, 17

Gale, Zona, 115
Galsworthy, John, 149, 184
Garden, Mary, 231
Garland, Hamlin, 14
Geflügelte Erde, Die (Dauthendey), 215
"Genius," The (Dreiser), xiii, 4, 6, 54–61, 68, 70, 71, 73, 235 n. 5
George V (King of England), 140
George Bernard Shaw: His Plays (Mencken), vii
Germinal (Zola), 40, 48, 237 n. 12
Gerould, Katharine Fullerton, 85
Gilman, Lawrence, 194
Glasgow, Ellen, xvi, 169–74
Glass, Montague, 161, 210
Glyn, Elinor, 193
Godey's Lady's Book, 232
"Golden Honeymoon, The" (Lardner), 164
Goldman, Emma, 230
Good Housekeeping, 230
Gounod, Charles François, 67

Grant, Madison, 199
Grant, Robert, 6
Grattan, C. Hartley, 145
Great Gatsby, The (Fitzgerald), xviii, 111–14
Grisham, John, xiv
Griswold, Rufus W., 28

Hackett, Francis, 194
Haeckel, Ernst, 240 n. 7
"Haircut" (Lardner), 165
Hale, Eugene, 188
Haliburton, Thomas Chandler, 162–63,
    241 n. 9
Hamilton, Clayton, 95
Hansen, Harry, 194
Harding, Warren G., 35
Hardy, Thomas, 40, 43, 222, 223
Harper's Magazine, 115
Harris, Frank, 172
Harris, Joel Chandler, 218
Harrison, Byron Patton ("Pat"), 169
Harte, Bret, 175, 199
Hartman, Samuel B., 237 n. 7
Hauptmann, Gerhart, 48, 150
Hawthorne, Julian, 68
Hawthorne, Nathaniel, 15, 25, 28, 29, 218
Heap, Jane, 230–32, 244 n. 9
Hearst, William Randolph, xiii, 115
Heaven and Hell (Swedenborg), 151
Hecht, Ben, 230
Heldenleben, Ein (Strauss), 39
Hemans, Felicia Dorothea, 115
Hemingway, Ernest, xiv, xviii, 139–42
Henry Esmond (Thackeray), 7
Hergesheimer, Joseph, xiii, xv, 14, 15, 17, 80,
    81, 94, 101–2, 162
Hermit and the Wild Woman, The (Wharton), 147
Herrick, Robert, 6
High Place, The (Cabell), 105–6, 109
History of American Literature since 1870, A
    (Pattee), 68
Holloway, Emory, 21
Holmes, Oliver Wendell, 24
Holst, Eduard, 8
Holt, Henry, 224
Hoosier Holiday, A (Dreiser), 61–68
"Horse Fair, The" (Bonheur), 180
Horses and Men (Anderson), 91–93
How to Write Short Stories (Lardner),
    162–65
Howard, Blanche Willis, 68

Howe, E. W., 115, 154, 157
Howells, William Dean, xii, xvi, 8, 24, 25,
    87, 150–57, 218
Hubbard, Elbert, 36, 235 n. 3
Hubbard, Frank McKinney ("Kin"), 165
Huckleberry Finn (Twain). See *Adventures
    of Huckleberry Finn*
Hull, E. M., xiv, 194–98, 235 n. 3
Huneker, James Gibbons, x, 95, 115, 211
Huxley, Thomas Henry, 22–23, 144, 179
Huysmans, Joris-Karl, 98, 149–50

"I Am a Fool" (Anderson), 89, 92
I, Mary MacLane (MacLane), 190–94
"I Want to Know Why" (Anderson), 89
Ibsen, Henrik, 6, 15, 220, 223
Impromptu (Paul), 92
In Babel (Ade), 176, 212
In Chancery (Galsworthy), 149
In Defense of Women (Mencken), viii
In the Midst of Life (Bierce), 147–48
Indian Summer of a Forsyte (Galsworthy),
    149
Ingersoll, Robert G., 32, 132
Innocents Abroad, The (Twain), 25, 32, 217
Inside of the Cup, The (Churchill), 185
Irving, Washington, 8, 25, 28, 226
Isgrigg, Helen, 145

Jackson, Andrew, 20
Jackson, Stonewall, 74
James, Henry, xii, 8, 37–39, 43, 87, 162, 164,
    222
Java Head (Hergesheimer), 80
Jeffers, Robinson, xvi
Jefferson, Joseph, 12
Jennie Gerhardt (Dreiser), 14, 16, 39–43, 44,
    49, 51, 60, 71
Joan of Arc (Twain). See *Personal Recollec-
    tions of Joan of Arc*
John Barleycorn (London), 157–58
Johns, Orrick, 95
Johnson, Owen, 241 n. 2
Joseph Conrad (Walpole), 61
Joyce, James, 229
Judge, 194
Julia Bride (James), 37–38
Jurgen (Cabell), xiii, 100–104, 105

Kahn, Otto H., 231
Kant, Immanuel, 90
Keats, John, 191

Kellner, Leon, 214–19
Kenyon, William Squire, 188
King, Charles, 68
King, Stephen, xiv
Kipling, Rudyard, 51, 84, 147, 238 n. 27
Kiralfy brothers, 139, 240 n. 49
Krafft-Ebing, Richard, Freiherr von, 192
Krutch, Joseph Wood, 33–35
Ku Klux Klan, 137, 208, 225, 226

Ladies' Home Journal, 78, 155, 192, 212, 230
Lane, Franklin K., 146
Lardner, Ring, 162–69
Laughlin, Clara E., 230
Lawrence, D. H., 106
Lay Anthony, The (Hergesheimer), 14
Leatherwood God, The (Howells), xvi, 154–57
Leblanc, Georgette, 233
Lee, Vernon, 149–50
Leibnitz, Gottfried Wilhelm, 126
Lewis, Sinclair, xi, xiii, xv, xvi, 115–36, 139, 167, 168, 226
Lewis, Wyndham, 232
Lewisohn, Ludwig, 199, 226
Life of Ambrose Bierce (Neale), 145
Life of Gladstone (Morley), 7
Life on the Mississippi (Twain), 25, 27
Lippmann, Walter, 120, 239 n. 41
Little Review, 194, 229–33, 244 n. 9
Lohengrin (Wagner), 217
London, Jack, 157–59
Longfellow, Henry Wadsworth, 218
Lord Jim (Conrad), 40, 48, 49
Lose with a Smile (Lardner), 167–69
Lost Lady, A (Cather), 80
Love Complex, The (Dixon), 204–8
Love Nest and Other Stories, The (Lardner), 165–67
Lowell, Amy, 11, 14, 115, 223
Lowell, James Russell, 8, 226
Ludwig, Karl, 123
Lustra (Pound), xvii

Mabie, Hamilton Wright, xi, 8, 14, 212
Macaulay, Thomas Babington, 144
Macchiavelli, Niccolò, 213
Machen, Arthur, 92
MacLane, Mary, 190–94
Maeterlinck, Maurice, 6, 90, 117
Main Street (Lewis), xiii, xv, 115–17, 121, 124, 127, 128, 132, 133, 136

Man of Property, The (Galsworthy), 149
"Man's Story, The" (Anderson), 92–93
Mansfield, Katherine, 92
Mansfield, Richard, 12, 13, 136
Mantrap (Lewis), 131
Many Marriages (Anderson), 89–91, 92, 93
Marching Men (Anderson), 84, 85, 86, 87, 88, 89, 93
Mark Twain: A Biography (Paine), 22–27
Marlowe, Christopher, 100
Marlowe, Julia, 100, 238 n. 35
Marthe (Huysmans), 150
Marx, Karl, 132
Masefield, John, 150
Mason, A. E. W., 150
Masters, Edgar Lee, 17, 75
Matthews, Brander, 199
McAllister, Samuel Ward, 114, 238 n. 37
McClure, John, xvi
McClure's Magazine, 115
McTeague (Norris), 39, 50
McWilliams, Carey, xii, 144–47
Meister von Palmyra, Der (Wilbrandt), 32
Mellon, Andrew, 180
Melville, Herman, xii
Men without Women (Hemingway), xviii
Meredith, George, 7, 43, 54
Metropolitan, 115
Michaud, Régis, 35–37
Mid-American Chants (Anderson), 85
Millikan, Robert A., 228, 229, 239 n. 44, 244 n. 8
Miss Lulu Bett (Gale), 115
Mitchell, S. Weir, 40
Molière (Jean-Baptiste Poquelin), 217
Monroe, Harriet, 14
Moore, George, 40, 43, 105, 150, 223
More, Hannah, 209
More, Paul Elmer, xi, 14, 194, 222–25, 226, 227
Morley, John, 7
Morris, Gouverneur, 85
Moszkowski, Moritz, 184
Mozart, Wolfgang Amadeus, 220–21
Müller, Johannes, 123
Munsey's Magazine, 183, 242 n. 3
Munyon, James M., 48, 115, 187, 237 n. 13
Musical Courier, 115
My Antonia (Cather), xi, 75–77, 78, 80, 81, 92, 204
My Life as Author and Editor (Mencken), viii, x–xi, xv

My Thirty Years' War (Anderson), 229–33
Mysterious Stranger, The (Twain), 32

Napoleon Bonaparte, 221, 244 n. 7
Nathan, George Jean, viii, xv, xvii, 13, 183
Nation, xviii, 5, 14, 59, 68, 194, 218
Nazimova, Alla, 12, 13
Neale, Walter, 145
Nearing, Scott, 210, 243 n. 2
"Next to Reading Matter" (O. Henry), 175
New England Group and Others, A
   (More), 222–25
New Leaf Mills (Howells), 150–54
New Republic, 2, 133, 155, 194
New York Evening Journal, 165, 180
New York Evening Post, 180
New York Society for the Suppression of
   Vice, xiii, 235 n. 5, 244 n. 9
New York Times, 14, 101, 155, 180, 195, 199,
   214, 218
New York Tribune, 79, 194
New Yorker, 133
Nietzsche, Friedrich, 23, 62, 178, 223–24,
   238 n. 18
Nigger of the Narcissus, The (Conrad), 4
Nilsson, Christine, 149
Norris, Frank, 15, 49, 50, 88, 110, 212
Notes on Democracy (Mencken), viii, xvi

O. Henry, 175–76
O Pioneers! (Cather), 75, 76
Ochs, Adolph, 199
Octopus, The (Norris), 50, 88
Offenbach, Jacques, 175
"Ohio Pagan, An" (Anderson), 92
Ollivant, Alfred, 150
"On the Banks of the Wabash" (Dresser),
   67
One of Ours (Cather), 78–80
O'Neill, Eugene, 15
Only a Boy (Field), 209
Oppenheim, E. Phillips, 73
Ouida, 53
Outcry, The (James), 39

Page, Thomas Nelson, 194
Page, Walter Hines, 146
Paine, Albert Bigelow, 22–27, 30
Paine, Thomas, 132
Paradise Lost (Milton), 209
Parkhurst, Charles H., 157

Pasteur, Louis, 74
Pater, Walter, 179, 190
Pattee, Fred Lewis, 20, 68
Patterson, Nan, 118
Paul, Elliot H., 92
"Paul's Case" (Cather), 77
Penrod (Tarkington), 6
Perry, Bliss, 101
Personal Recollections of Joan of Arc
   (Twain), 25, 30, 32
Personal Record, A (Conrad), 61
Peruna, 237 n. 7
Phelps, William Lyon, xi, 15, 24, 167, 194
Phillips, David Graham, xii–xiii, 49
Philosophy of Friedrich Nietzsche, The
   (Mencken), vii
Pilgrim's Progress, The (Bunyan), 7
Pinkham, Lydia, 187, 242 n. 5
Pit, The (Norris), 39
Poe, Edgar Allan, xii, 8, 20–21, 25, 28,
   33–35, 144, 151, 154, 209, 210, 219, 221
Poetry and Dreams (Prescott), 63
Poetry Society, 1
Police Gazette, 2, 180
Pollak, Gustav, 214
Pollard, Percival, x, 212–14
Pollyanna (Porter), 236 n. 8
Poor White (Anderson), 86–88, 89
Pope, Alexander, 8
Porter, Eleanor H., 236 n. 8
Porter, Gene Stratton, 214
Portrait of Ambrose Bierce (de Castro), 145
Pound, Ezra, xvii, 230, 232
Prejudices (Mencken), viii, xvi
Prescott, F. C., 63
Prescott, William H., 8
Prisoner of Zenda, The (Hope), 51
Professor's House, The (Cather), 81–82
Profiteers' Review, 194
Prufrock and Other Observations (Eliot),
   xvii
Public Opinion (Lippmann), 120, 239 n. 41

Quinn, John, 229, 244 n. 9

Rabelais, François, 26, 101, 102, 104, 213
Rayleigh, John William Strutt, baron, 122
Reef, The (Wharton), 148–49
Reese, Lizette Woodworth, xvi
Remer, Paul, 216
Reviewer, 194

"Rhythm" (Lardner), 165
Richards, Theodore, 239 n. 44
Richardson, Charles Francis, 68
Riley, James Whitcomb, 212
Rinehart, Mary Roberts, 3, 15
Rise of David Levinsky, The (Cahan), 75, 159–62
Rise of Silas Lapham, The (Howells), 39, 154
Rivet in Grandfather's Neck, The (Cabell), 97
Roads of Destiny (O. Henry), 175–76
Robertson, John W., 33
Robins, Elizabeth, 150
Roe, E. P., 68
Romantic Comedians, The (Glasgow), 174
Roosevelt, Theodore, 2, 3, 7, 191
Rose, Edward E., 15
Rousseau, Jean-Jacques, 37
Ruggles of Red Gap (Wilson), 7

"Sad Horn Blows, The" (Anderson), 92
"Sahara of the Bozart, The" (Mencken), xvi
Salamander, The (Johnson), 181, 241 n. 2
Sam Slick (Haliburton), 162–63, 241 n. 9
Sandburg, Carl, 87, 115, 199, 238 n. 30
Sartor Resartus (Carlyle), 7
Saturday Evening Post, xiii, xv, 6, 17, 78, 102, 115, 167
"Scandal" (Cather), 77
Scarlet Letter, The (Hawthorne), 24, 39
Schlaf, Johannes, 216
Schubert, Franz, 221–22
Schwab, Charles, 118
"Sculptor's Funeral, The" (Cather), 77
Second Funeral of Napoleon, The (Thackeray), 4
Secret Agent, The (Conrad), 213
Shakespeare, William, 22, 74, 209
Shaw, George Bernard, 6, 74, 223
Sheik, The (Hull), 194–98
Sheldon, Sidney, xiv
Sherman, Stuart P., 14, 194, 199, 225–27
Simpson, Jerry, 132
Sinclair, Upton, 3, 17
Sister Carrie (Dreiser), x, xii, 4, 15, 17, 18, 40–41, 44, 49, 50, 51, 60, 63, 66, 72, 92, 216, 236 n. 13
Smart Set, vii, viii, ix, xiv, xv, xvi, xvii, 3, 11, 13, 109

Socrates, 227–28
"Some Like Them Cold" (Lardner), 164
Some Modern Novelists (Follett/Follett), xii, 219–22
Some Reminiscences (Conrad), 4
Something about Eve (Cabell), 108–9
Song of the Lark, The (Cather), 74–75, 76
Spingarn, Joel E., 211
Splint, Fred, viii, 13
Spoon River Anthology (Masters), 75, 85
Stall, Sylvanus, 236 n. 6
Standards (Brownell), 211
Star Rover, The (London), 159
Stearns, Harold, 138
Steel, Danielle, xiv
Sterling, George, xvi, 95
Stevenson, Robert Louis, 144, 175
Story of a Country Town, The (Howe), 154, 157
Story of Mary MacLane, The (MacLane), 190
Straws and Prayer-Books (Cabell), 106–8
Street, Julian, 85
Streets of Night (Dos Passos), 138–39
Strength of the Strong, The (London), 158–59
Strife (Galsworthy), 184
Studies in the Psychology of Sex (Ellis), 213
Sumner, John S., xiii, 229, 244 n. 9
Sunday, Billy, 2, 5, 137, 156, 157, 193, 226
Swedenborg, Emanuel, 150–53
Swift, Jonathan, xiv, 102, 165
Swinburne, Algernon Charles, 216
Synge, J. M., 6

Taft, William Howard, 228
Taine, Hippolyte, 194
Tamburlaine the Great (Marlowe), 209
Tar: A Midwest Childhood (Anderson), 94
Tarkington, Booth, 6–7, 17, 92
Tarr (Lewis), 232
Teasdale, Sara, xvi, 95
Thackeray, William Makepeace, 4, 144, 150
Thanet, Octave, 68
Thayer, Scofield, 194
Their Day in Court (Pollard), 212–14
They Stooped to Folly (Glasgow), 169–72
This Side of Paradise (Fitzgerald), xv, 109–10, 111, 112, 113, 114
Thompson, Mame, 94
Thoreau, Henry David, 36

Three-Cornered Hat, The (Alarcon), 83
Three Soldiers (Dos Passos), 17, 79, 136–38, 139
"3,000 Years among the Microbes" (Twain), 26, 237 n. 3
Three Weeks (Glyn), 212, 220
Timrod, Henry, 194
Titan, The (Dreiser), 48–54, 57, 60, 66, 67, 73, 83, 183–84, 216
Titian, 217
Tolstoi, Leo, 8
Tom Sawyer (Twain). *See Adventures of Tom Sawyer, The*
Tramp Abroad, A (Twain), 25, 30, 32, 33, 217
Traveller at Forty, A (Dreiser), 65
Treatise on the Gods (Mencken), viii
Triumph of the Egg, The (Anderson), 88–89
Troll Garden, The (Cather), 77
True Confessions, 70
Turgenev, Ivan, 8, 50, 154
Twain, Mark, xii, xiii, 8, 15, 22–33, 62, 110, 132, 146, 154, 163, 167, 210, 217–18, 221
Twelve Men (Dreiser), 86
Tyler, Moses Coit, 20

Ulysses (Joyce), 229, 232, 244 n. 9
"Unused" (Anderson), 92

Van Doren, Carl, 194
van Dyke, Henry, 211, 214
"Velvet Glove, The" (James), 38–39
Virchow, Rudolf (Carl), 122

Wagner, Richard, 223
Walpole, Hugh, 61, 63
Waste Land, The (Eliot), xvii, 228
Watts, Mary Stanbery, 162

Wells, H. G., 131, 150, 159, 212
Wharton, Edith, 6, 14, 40, 73, 75, 147–50, 164
"What I Believe" (Glasgow), 172
What Is Man? (Twain), 26, 30–31
What Maisie Knew (James), 37, 39
Wheeler, Wayne B., 227
Whitman, Walt, xii, 21, 25, 28, 29, 36, 115, 167, 178, 199, 210, 215–16, 221, 238 n. 30
Whittier, John Greenleaf, 210–11
Wilbrandt, Adolf, 32
Williams, Bert, 200
Williams, Blanche Colton, 164
Williams, William Carlos, xvii, 232–33
Willis, N. P., 28
Wilson, Harry Leon, 6–7
Wilson, Woodrow, 2, 137, 180
Windy McPherson's Son (Anderson), xv, 83–84, 85, 86, 88, 89
Winesburg, Ohio (Anderson), 84–86, 87, 88
Winter, William, 95
Wise, Stephen S., 232
Wister, Owen, 68
Wolf Song (Fergusson), 82
Woodberry, George E., 115, 211
Worcester, Elwood, 213
Work, Hubert, 188
Works of Ellen Glasgow (Glasgow), 172–74
Wright, Harold Bell, xii, 195, 203, 214

You Know Me, Al (Lardner), 163
Youth and the Bright Medusa (Cather), 77

Zeno of Elea, 62
Ziegfeld, Florenz, 232, 242 n. 12
Zola, Emile, 43, 50, 63, 237 n. 12
"Zone of Quiet" (Lardner), 165